ClarisWorks® Office Fo...

MW00564414

Tool Buttons and Their Environments

General Buttons

- New word-processing document
- New paint document
- New draw document
- New spreadsheet document
- New database document
- New communications document
- Undo/Redo
- Cut
- Copy
- Paste
- Open document
- Save document
- Insert file
- Print
- Tile windows
- Show/hide styles

Text Buttons

- Bold text
- Italic text
- Underline text
- Align left
- Align center
- Align right
- Justify
- Larger font size
- Smaller font size
- Show/hide invisibles
- Spell check document
- Copy ruler
- Apply ruler
- Tabbed text to table
- Mail merge

Paint & Draw Buttons

- Rotate 90 degrees
- Opaque mode
- Transparent mode
- Tint mode
- Lighter
- Darker
- Tint
- Fill
- Blend
- Invert
- Pickup
- Irregular text wrap
- Move forward
- Move backward

Spreadsheet Buttons

- Auto Sum
- Currency format
- Percent format
- Commas format
- Align wrap
- Show/hide formulas
- Insert cells
- Delete cells
- Sort ascending
- Sort descending

Internet Buttons

- Launch browser
- Open URL
- Preview in browser
- Launch email
- Claris tech support site
- Live links on/off
- New bookmark
- New document link
- New URL link

Database Buttons

- Match equal
- Match unequal
- Match less
- Match greater
- Sort ascending
- Sort descending
- Sort again
- New record
- Show all records
- Hide selected

...For Dummies: #1 Computer Book Series for Beginners

ClarisWorks® Office For Dummies®

COMPUTER BOOK SERIES FROM IDG

Cheat Sheet

Text Ruler Guide

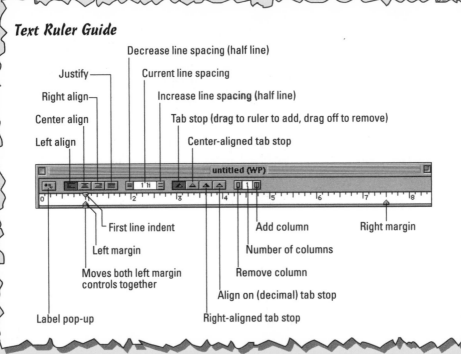

Decrease line spacing (half line)

Justify

Current line spacing

Right align

Increase line spacing (half line)

Center align

Tab stop (drag to ruler to add, drag off to remove)

Left align

Center-aligned tab stop

untitled (WP)

First line indent

Add column

Right margin

Left margin

Number of columns

Moves both left margin controls together

Remove column

Align on (decimal) tab stop

Label pop-up

Right-aligned tab stop

Keyboard Shortcuts of the Rich and Famous

Command	Mac	Windows
New	⌘-N	Ctrl+N
Open	⌘-O	Ctrl+O
Save	⌘-S	Ctrl+S
Undo	⌘-U	Ctrl+U
Cut	⌘-X	Ctrl+X
Copy	⌘-C	Ctrl+C
Paste	⌘-V	Ctrl+V
Select All	⌘-A	Ctrl+A
Delete Selection	Delete	Delete
Print	⌘-P	Ctrl+P
Spell check document	⌘-=	Ctrl+=
Spell check selection	Shift-⌘-Y	Shift+Ctrl+Y
Page view	Shift-⌘-P	Shift+Ctrl+P
Show/hide buttons	Shift-⌘-X	Shift+Ctrl+X
Help	⌘-?	F1

Tool Panel Guide

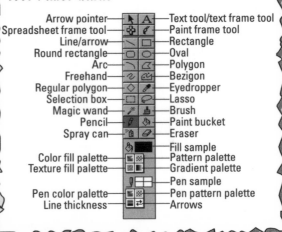

Arrow pointer — Text tool/text frame tool

Spreadsheet frame tool — Paint frame tool

Line/arrow — Rectangle

Round rectangle — Oval

Arc — Polygon

Freehand — Bezigon

Regular polygon — Eyedropper

Selection box — Lasso

Magic wand — Brush

Pencil — Paint bucket

Spray can — Eraser

Fill sample

Color fill palette — Pattern palette

Texture fill palette — Gradient palette

Pen sample

Pen color palette — Pen pattern palette

Line thickness — Arrows

IDG BOOKS WORLDWIDE

...For Dummies: #1 Computer Book Series for Beginners

®

COMPUTER BOOK SERIES FROM IDG

References for the Rest of Us!®

Are you intimidated and confused by computers? Do you find that traditional manuals are overloaded with technical details you'll never use? Do your friends and family always call you to fix simple problems on their PCs? Then the *...For Dummies*® computer book series from IDG Books Worldwide is for you.

...For Dummies books are written for those frustrated computer users who know they aren't really dumb but find that PC hardware, software, and indeed the unique vocabulary of computing make them feel helpless. *...For Dummies* books use a lighthearted approach, a down-to-earth style, and even cartoons and humorous icons to diffuse computer novices' fears and build their confidence. Lighthearted but not lightweight, these books are a perfect survival guide for anyone forced to use a computer.

> *"I like my copy so much I told friends; now they bought copies."*
>
> **Irene C., Orwell, Ohio**

> *"Quick, concise, nontechnical, and humorous."*
>
> **Jay A., Elburn, Illinois**

> *"Thanks, I needed this book. Now I can sleep at night."*
>
> **Robin F., British Columbia, Canada**

Already, millions of satisfied readers agree. They have made *...For Dummies* books the #1 introductory level computer book series and have written asking for more. So, if you're looking for the most fun and easy way to learn about computers, look to *...For Dummies* books to give you a helping hand.

5/97

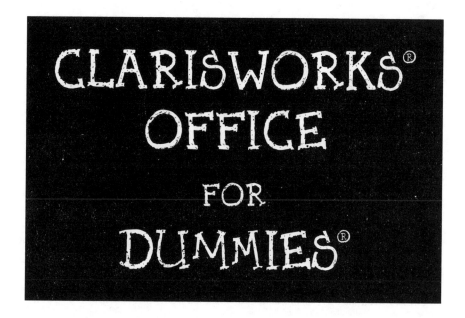

CLARISWORKS® OFFICE FOR DUMMIES®

by Bob LeVitus, Frank Higgins, and Deborah Shadovitz

IDG Books Worldwide, Inc.
An International Data Group Company

Foster City, CA ♦ Chicago, IL ♦ Indianapolis, IN ♦ Southlake, TX

ClarisWorks® Office For Dummies®

Published by
IDG Books Worldwide, Inc.
An International Data Group Company
919 E. Hillsdale Blvd.
Suite 400
Foster City, CA 94404
www.idgbooks.com (IDG Books Worldwide Web site)
www.dummies.com (Dummies Press Web site)

Library of Congress Catalog Card No.: 97-80750

ISBN: 0-7645-0113-5

Printed in the United States of America

10 9 8 7 6 5 4 3 2

1B/RT/QS/ZY/IN

Distributed in the United States by IDG Books Worldwide, Inc.

Distributed by Macmillan Canada for Canada; by Transworld Publishers Limited in the United Kingdom; by IDG Norge Books for Norway; by IDG Sweden Books for Sweden; by Woodslane Pty. Ltd. for Australia; by Woodslane Enterprises Ltd. for New Zealand; by Longman Singapore Publishers Ltd. for Singapore, Malaysia, Thailand, and Indonesia; by Simron Pty. Ltd. for South Africa; by Toppan Company Ltd. for Japan; by Distribuidora Cuspide for Argentina; by Livraria Cultura for Brazil; by Ediciencia S.A. for Ecuador; by Addison-Wesley Publishing Company for Korea; by Ediciones ZETA S.C.R. Ltda. for Peru; by WS Computer Publishing Corporation, Inc., for the Philippines; by Unalis Corporation for Taiwan; by Contemporanea de Ediciones for Venezuela; by Computer Book & Magazine Store for Puerto Rico; by Express Computer Distributors for the Caribbean and West Indies. Authorized Sales Agent: Anthony Rudkin Associates for the Middle East and North Africa.

For general information on IDG Books Worldwide's books in the U.S., please call our Consumer Customer Service department at 800-762-2974. For reseller information, including discounts and premium sales, please call our Reseller Customer Service department at 800-434-3422.

For information on where to purchase IDG Books Worldwide's books outside the U.S., please contact our International Sales department at 650-655-3200 or fax 650-655-3295.

For information on foreign language translations, please contact our Foreign & Subsidiary Rights department at 650-655-3021 or fax 650-655-3281.

For sales inquiries and special prices for bulk quantities, please contact our Sales department at 650-655-3200 or write to the address above.

For information on using IDG Books Worldwide's books in the classroom or for ordering examination copies, please contact our Educational Sales department at 800-434-2086 or fax 817-251-8174.

For press review copies, author interviews, or other publicity information, please contact our Public Relations department at 650-655-3000 or fax 650-655-3299.

For authorization to photocopy items for corporate, personal, or educational use, please contact Copyright Clearance Center, 222 Rosewood Drive, Danvers, MA 01923, or fax 978-750-4470.

is a trademark under exclusive license to IDG Books Worldwide, Inc., from International Data Group, Inc.

About the Authors

Bob LeVitus: (pronounced Love-eye-tis) was the editor-in-chief of the wildly popular MACazine until its untimely demise in 1988. Since 1989, he has been a contributing editor/columnist for MacUser magazine, writing the "Help Folder," "Beating the System," "Personal Best," and "Game Room" columns at various times in his illustrious career. In his spare time, Bob has written 25 popular computer books, including *WebMaster Macintosh,* Second Edition, the "everything you need to build your own web site on a Mac" book and CD-ROM; and his latest book/CD before this one, *WebCaster Macintosh*, the "everything you need to create a cool webcast on a Mac" book.

Always a popular speaker at Macintosh user groups and trade shows, Bob has spoken at more than 100 international seminars, has presented keynote addresses in several countries, and serves on the Macworld Expo Advisory Board. He was also the host of Mac Today, a half-hour television show syndicated in over 100 markets, which aired in late 1992.

Bob has forgotten more about the Macintosh than most people know. He won the Macworld Expo MacJeopardy World Championship an unbelievable four times before retiring his crown. But most of all, Bob is known for his clear, understandable writing, his humorous style, and his ability to translate "techie" jargon into usable and fun advice for the rest of us.

He lives in Austin, Texas, with his wife, two children, and dogs.

Frank Higgins: A computer user since the tender age of 11, Frank first used a Mac in 1985. He is the coauthor of the best-selling and award winning *Upgrading and Fixing Macs For Dummies*. Frank is also the owner and president of Yoyodyne Systems, a San Francisco Bay Area Macintosh consulting firm that is dedicated to helping people get the most out of their Macs. When not writing about the Mac or helping clients, Frank enjoys cycling, surfing, and reading medieval German literature.

Deborah Shadovitz: Deborah started playing with computers in high school, where a terminal called into a mainframe at a local university. Throughout her years in video and audio/visual production, computers kept coming back into her life. And then came the Mac. . . . She got into the Mac for its creative abilities, did some art and desktop publishing, and then found herself being called a computer "expert."

Deborah has been on the Los Angeles Macintosh Group's (LAMG) Board of Directors since 1993. She's also a member of the Association of Database Developers and the Association of Macintosh Trainers. You can find her teaching classes or leading Special Interest Groups at the LAMG, speaking at MacFair and at Macworld Expo, or teaching computers and computer software all over L.A.

ABOUT IDG BOOKS WORLDWIDE

Welcome to the world of IDG Books Worldwide.

IDG Books Worldwide, Inc., is a subsidiary of International Data Group, the world's largest publisher of computer-related information and the leading global provider of information services on information technology. IDG was founded more than 25 years ago and now employs more than 8,500 people worldwide. IDG publishes more than 275 computer publications in over 75 countries (see listing below). More than 60 million people read one or more IDG publications each month.

Launched in 1990, IDG Books Worldwide is today the #1 publisher of best-selling computer books in the United States. We are proud to have received eight awards from the Computer Press Association in recognition of editorial excellence and three from *Computer Currents'* First Annual Readers' Choice Awards. Our best-selling *...For Dummies®* series has more than 30 million copies in print with translations in 30 languages. IDG Books Worldwide, through a joint venture with IDG's Hi-Tech Beijing, became the first U.S. publisher to publish a computer book in the People's Republic of China. In record time, IDG Books Worldwide has become the first choice for millions of readers around the world who want to learn how to better manage their businesses.

Our mission is simple: Every one of our books is designed to bring extra value and skill-building instructions to the reader. Our books are written by experts who understand and care about our readers. The knowledge base of our editorial staff comes from years of experience in publishing, education, and journalism — experience we use to produce books for the '90s. In short, we care about books, so we attract the best people. We devote special attention to details such as audience, interior design, use of icons, and illustrations. And because we use an efficient process of authoring, editing, and desktop publishing our books electronically, we can spend more time ensuring superior content and spend less time on the technicalities of making books.

You can count on our commitment to deliver high-quality books at competitive prices on topics you want to read about. At IDG Books Worldwide, we continue in the IDG tradition of delivering quality for more than 25 years. You'll find no better book on a subject than one from IDG Books Worldwide.

IDG BOOKS
WORLDWIDE

John Kilcullen
CEO
IDG Books Worldwide, Inc.

Steven Berkowitz
President and Publisher
IDG Books Worldwide, Inc.

**Eighth Annual
Computer Press
Awards ≥1992**

**Ninth Annual
Computer Press
Awards ≥1993**

**Tenth Annual
Computer Press
Awards ≥1994**

**Eleventh Annual
Computer Press
Awards ≥1995**

IDG Books Worldwide, Inc., is a subsidiary of International Data Group, the world's largest publisher of computer-related information and the leading global provider of information services on information technology. International Data Group publishes over 275 computer publications in over 75 countries. Sixty million people read one or more International Data Group publications each month. International Data Group's publications include: **ARGENTINA:** Buyer's Guide, Computerworld Argentina, PC World Argentina; **AUSTRALIA:** Australian Macworld, Australian PC World, Australian Reseller News, Computerworld, IT Casebook, Network World, Publish, Webmaster; **AUSTRIA:** Computerwelt Osterreich, Networks Austria, PC Tip Austria; **BANGLADESH:** PC World Bangladesh; **BELARUS:** PC World Belarus; **BELGIUM:** Data News; **BRAZIL:** Annuário de Informática, Computerworld, Connections, Macworld, PC Player, PC World, Publish, Reseller News, Supergamepower; **BULGARIA:** Computerworld Bulgaria, Network World Bulgaria, PC & MacWorld Bulgaria; **CANADA:** CIO Canada, Client/Server World, ComputerWorld Canada, InfoWorld Canada, NetworkWorld Canada, WebWorld; **CHILE:** Computerworld Chile, PC World Chile; **COLOMBIA:** Computerworld Colombia, PC World Colombia; **COSTA RICA:** PC World Centro America; **THE CZECH AND SLOVAK REPUBLICS:** Computerworld Czechoslovakia, Macworld Czech Republic, PC World Czechoslovakia; **DENMARK:** Communications World Danmark, Computerworld Danmark, Macworld Danmark, PC World Danmark, Techworld Denmark; **DOMINICAN REPUBLIC:** PC World Republica Dominicana; **ECUADOR:** PC World Ecuador; **EGYPT:** Computerworld Middle East, PC World Middle East; **EL SALVADOR:** PC World Centro America; **FINLAND:** MikroPC, Tietoverkko, Tietoviikko; **FRANCE:** Distributique, Hebdo, Info PC, Le Monde Informatique, Macworld, Reseaux & Telecoms, WebMaster France; **GERMANY:** Computer Partner, Computerwoche, Computerwoche Extra, Computerwoche FOCUS, Global Online, Macwelt, PC Welt; **GREECE:** Amiga Computing, GamePro Greece, Multimedia World; **GUATEMALA:** PC World Centro America; **HONDURAS:** PC World Centro America; **HONG KONG:** Computerworld Hong Kong, PC World Hong Kong, Publish in Asia; **HUNGARY:** ABCD CD-ROM, Computerworld Szamitastechnika, Internetto online Magazine, PC World Hungary, PC-X Magazin Hungary; **ICELAND:** Tolvuheimur PC World Island; **INDIA:** Information Communications World, Information Systems Computerworld, PC World India, Publish in Asia; **INDONESIA:** InfoKomputer PC World, Komputek Computerworld, Publish in Asia; **IRELAND:** ComputerScope, PC Live!; **ISRAEL:** Macworld Israel, People & Computers/Computerworld; **ITALY:** Computerworld Italia, Macworld Italia, Networking Italia, PC World Italia; **JAPAN:** DTP World, Macworld Japan, Nikkei Personal Computing, OS/2 World Japan, SunWorld Japan, Windows NT World, Windows World Japan; **KENYA:** PC World East African; **KOREA:** Hi-Tech Information, Macworld Korea, PC World Korea; **MACEDONIA:** PC World Macedonia; **MALAYSIA:** Computerworld Malaysia, PC World Malaysia, Publish in Asia; **MALTA:** PC World Malta; **MEXICO:** Computerworld Mexico, PC World Mexico; **MYANMAR:** PC World Myanmar; **NETHERLANDS:** Computer! Totaal, LAN Internetworking Magazine, LAN World Buyers Guide, Macworld Netherlands, Net, WebWereld; **NEW ZEALAND:** Absolute Beginners Guide and Plain & Simple Series, Computer Buyer, Computer Industry Directory, Computerworld New Zealand, MTB, Network World, PC World New Zealand; **NICARAGUA:** PC World Centro America; **NORWAY:** Computerworld Norge, CW Rapport, Datamagasinet, Financial Rapport, Kursguide Norge, Macworld Norge, Multimediaworld Norge, PC World Ekspress Norge, PC World Nettverk, PC World Norge, PC World ProduktGuide Norge; **PAKISTAN:** Computerworld Pakistan; **PANAMA:** PC World Panama; **PEOPLE'S REPUBLIC OF CHINA:** China Computer Users, China Computerworld, China InfoWorld, China Telecom World Weekly, Computer & Communication, Electronic Design China, Electronics Today, Electronics Weekly, Game Software, PC World China, Popular Computer Week, Software Weekly, Software World, Telecom World; **PERU:** Computerworld Peru, PC World Profesional Peru, PC World SoHo Peru; **PHILIPPINES:** Click!, Computerworld Philippines, PC World Philippines, Publish in Asia; **POLAND:** Computerworld Poland, Cyber, Macworld Poland, Networld Poland, PC World Komputer; **PORTUGAL:** Cerebro/PC World, Computerworld/Correio Informático, Dealer World Portugal, Mac*In/PC*In Portugal, Multimedia World; **PUERTO RICO:** PC World Puerto Rico; **ROMANIA:** Computerworld Romania, PC World Romania, Telecom Romania; **RUSSIA:** Computerworld Russia, Mir PK, Publish, Seti; **SINGAPORE:** Computerworld Singapore, PC World Singapore, Publish in Asia; **SLOVENIA:** Monitor; **SOUTH AFRICA:** Computing SA, Network World SA, Software World SA; **SPAIN:** Communicaciones World España, Computerworld España, Dealer World España, Macworld España, PC World España, PC World Taiwan, Windows World Taiwan; **SWEDEN:** CAP&Design, Computer Sweden, Corporate Computing Sweden, Internetworld Sweden, it.branschen, Macworld Sweden, MaxiData Sweden, MikroDatorn, Natverk & Kommunikation, PC World Sweden, PCaktiv, Windows World Sweden; **SWITZERLAND:** Computerworld Schweiz, Macworld Schweiz, PCup; **TAIWAN:** Computerworld Taiwan, Macworld Taiwan, NEW ViSiON/Publish, PC World Taiwan, Windows World Taiwan; **THAILAND:** Publish in Asia, Thai Computerworld; **TURKEY:** Computerworld Turkiye, Macworld Turkiye, Network World Turkiye, PC World Turkiye; **UKRAINE:** Computerworld Kiev, Multimedia World Ukraine, PC World Ukraine; **UNITED KINGDOM:** Acorn User UK, Amiga Action UK, Amiga Computing UK, Apple Talk UK, Computing, Macworld, Parents and Computers UK, PC Advisor, PC Home, PSX Pro, The WEB; **UNITED STATES:** Cable in the Classroom, CIO Magazine, Computerworld, DOS World, Federal Computer Week, GamePro Magazine, InfoWorld, I-Way, Macworld, Network World, PC Games, PC World, Publish, Video Event, THE WEB Magazine, and WebMaster; online webzines: JavaWorld, NetscapeWorld, and SunWorld Online; **URUGUAY:** InfoWorld Uruguay; **VENEZUELA:** Computerworld Venezuela, PC World Venezuela; and **VIETNAM:** PC World Vietnam.   3/24/97

Dedication

For my wife Lisa: L.Y.A.T.M.A.T.S.

Authors' Acknowledgments

Special thanks to our friends at Claris, who were there for us every step of the way: Alexei Folger, Karri Chamberlain and Alisa Winkel of the ClarisWorks Tech Support team; Tom D'Arezzo, ClarisWorks Product Manager; and Debbie Hutchings, a constant contact within Claris. Thank you all. We couldn't have done it without your help.

Thanks also to superagent Carole "Swifty" McClendon of Waterside Productions, for deal making beyond the call of duty. You're a piece of work!

Big-time thanks also to the gang at IDG Books: Mike Kelly, Diane Steele, Mary Bednarek, Ellen Camm, and the big guy himself, John Kilcullen. Nobody does it better. . . .

Extra special thanks to our editor, Kyle "Whipcracker 2.0" Looper, who has been better than great and more than patient. Thanks also to the editorial team of Ryan Rader, Gwenette Gaddis, Bill McManus, and Paul "the Warbler" Kuzmic, without whom this book would not have been wrapped up on schedule.

Thanks to our families and friends for putting up with our all-too-lengthy absences during this book's gestation.

Thanks to Sean Figueroa, Christopher Shaw, and Chris Swinney at EarthLink tech support for their knowledge and verification.

Thanks to Lani Spear for her Windows wisdom and the loan of her laptop to Deborah.

Thanks to Jim Cadenhead for getting Deb hooked on ClarisWorks so many years ago.

Bob: And finally, huge thanks to Deborah, who did all the hard work. I couldn't have done it without you.

Deb: Thanks to my sister, Donna Shadovitz, for hearing out all my ideas and for the late-night proofreading sessions. And, of course, thanks to Bob for remembering how much I love ClarisWorks and inviting me onto his team.

Last but not least, thanks to you for buying it.

Publisher's Acknowledgments

We're proud of this book; please register your comments through our IDG Books Worldwide
Online Registration Form located at http://my2cents.dummies.com.

Some of the people who helped bring this book to market include the following:

Acquisitions, Development, and Editorial

Project Editors: Kyle Looper, Ryan Rader

Acquisitions Editor: Ellen Camm

Associate Permissions Editor:
Heather Heath Dismore

Copy Editors: Gwenette Gaddis,
William McManus

Technical Editor: Gene Steinberg

Editorial Manager: Colleen Rainsberger

Editorial Assistant: Paul Kuzmic

Production

Project Coordinator: Valery Bourke

Layout and Graphics: Angela F. Hunckler,
Brent Savage, Cameron Booker,
Linda M. Boyer, Maridee V. Ennis

Proofreaders: Nancy L. Reinhardt, Kelli Botta,
Michelle Croninger, Rebecca Senninger,
Janet M. Withers

Indexer: Sherry Massey

General and Administrative

IDG Books Worldwide, Inc.: John Kilcullen, CEO; Steven Berkowitz, President and Publisher

IDG Books Technology Publishing: Brenda McLaughlin, Senior Vice President and
Group Publisher

Dummies Technology Press and Dummies Editorial: Diane Graves Steele, Vice President and
Associate Publisher; Mary Bednarek, Acquisitions and Product Development Director;
Kristin A. Cocks, Editorial Director

Dummies Trade Press: Kathleen A. Welton, Vice President and Publisher; Kevin Thornton,
Acquisitions Manager

IDG Books Production for Dummies Press: Beth Jenkins Roberts, Production Director; Cindy L.
Phipps, Manager of Project Coordination, Production Proofreading, and Indexing;
Kathie S. Schutte, Supervisor of Page Layout; Shelley Lea, Supervisor of Graphics and
Design; Debbie J. Gates, Production Systems Specialist; Robert Springer, Supervisor of
Proofreading; Debbie Stailey, Special Projects Coordinator; Tony Augsburger, Supervisor of
Reprints and Bluelines; Leslie Popplewell, Media Archive Coordinator

Dummies Packaging and Book Design: Patti Crane, Packaging Specialist; Kavish + Kavish,
Cover Design

◆

The publisher would like to give special thanks to Patrick J. McGovern,
without whom this book would not have been possible.

◆

Contents at Glance

Introduction 1

Part I: What ClarisWorks Does 7

Chapter 1: A Quick Overview of ClarisWorks Office 9
Chapter 2: How ClarisWorks Works 17
Chapter 3: Help: It's Not Just a Beatles Movie Anymore 37

Part II: Working with Text: The Keys to Success 47

Chapter 4: The Word Processor: It's Not Your Father's Smith Corona 49
Chapter 5: Fun with Text Formatting 63
Chapter 6: The Text Tools — Editor in a Drum 93
Chapter 7: Adding Tables, Charts, and Pictures 103
Chapter 8: Outlining — You Gotta Start Somewhere 119

Part III: Working with Graphics: Get the Picture? 127

Chapter 9: Drawing versus Painting 129
Chapter 10: Painting — by the Numbers 135
Chapter 11: Special Effects with Paint 155
Chapter 12: Draw, Pardner! 163
Chapter 13: The Lowdown on Page Layout 185
Chapter 14: Presenting Presentations 199

Part IV: Working with Numbers: It All Adds Up! 207

Chapter 15: Spreadsheets 101 209
Chapter 16: Formatting Spreadsheets 217
Chapter 17: Charting — Pictures from Numbers 231
Chapter 18: Making It All Add Up with Formulas and Functions 239

Part V: Working with Files: Smoothing Out the Rough Edges 247

Chapter 19: Your Rolodex Revisited — Database Basics 249
Chapter 20: Designing a Database 265
Chapter 21: Printing a Database 281
Chapter 22: Mail Merge — It's One Cool Trick 289

Part VI: Working with the World: Reaching Out and Touching Someone 295

Chapter 23: Connecting to the World the ClarisWorks Way 297
Chapter 24: Publishing for the World Wide Web 309

Part VII: The Part of Tens **327**

Chapter 25: Ten Real-Life Uses for ClarisWorks 329
Chapter 26: Ten Ways ClarisWorks Tries to Drive You Crazy, and
How to Stay Sane 333

Appendix: Buttoning Up **337**

Index **340**

Book Registration Information .... **Back of Book**

Cartoons at a Glance

By Rich Tennant

page 295

page 327

page 247

page 207

page 127

page 7

page 47

Fax: 978-546-7747 • E-mail: the5wave@tiac.net

Table of Contents

Introduction 1

    About This Book 2
    Conventions Used in This Book 2
    What You're Not to Read 3
    Foolish Assumptions 3
    How This Book Is Organized 4
        Part I: What ClarisWorks Does 4
        Part II: Working with Text: The Keys to Success 4
        Part III: Working with Graphics: Get the Picture? 5
        Part IV: Working with Numbers: It All Adds Up! 5
        Part V: Working with Files: Smoothing Out the Rough Edges 5
        Part VI: Working with the World: Reaching Out
          and Touching Someone 5
        Part VII: The Part of Tens 6
    Icons Used in This Book 6
    Where to Go from Here 6

Part I: What ClarisWorks Does 7

Chapter 1: A Quick Overview of ClarisWorks Office 9

    Basic ClarisWorks Functions 9
        Word processing (Typing) 10
        Drawing 11
        Painting 11
        Spreadsheets (Calculating and more) 12
        Databases (Data filing and maintenance) 12
        Communication 13
        Bringing these things together (Integration) 13
    Other ClarisWorks Features (Neat Helpful Stuff) 15
        Assistants 15
        Stationery 15
        Document passwords — security for all 15
        The Equation Editor 16
        Buttons 16
    ClarisWorks Bundle Additions 16
        Internet connectivity 16
        Claris Home Page Lite 16

Chapter 2: How ClarisWorks Works **17**

Starting ClarisWorks 17

Creating a New Document 18

　Choosing your primary environment 19

Opening Existing Documents 20

　Launching while you open 20

　Opening a document from within ClarisWorks 21

Getting to Know the ClarisWorks Interface 22

　View controls 23

　Other window controls 24

　Button, button, we've got the button 25

Tools 26

　Frame tools 27

　　Arrow pointer — the left-pointing arrow 27

　　Text tool — the letter A 28

　　Spreadsheet tool — fat plus sign 28

　　Paint tool — the thin paint brush 29

　Draw tools 29

　Paint tools 29

　Pen and fill palettes 29

Menu Tricks 30

　Magical morphing menus 30

　Menu constants 30

　　The File menu 30

　　The Edit menu 31

　　The Window menu 31

Page Setup or Print Setup 31

Saving Your Work 32

　Where to save? 32

　Save versus Save As 33

　Saving in other file formats 33

　Saving as stationery 33

Printing Documents 34

　Select your target printer 35

　How many, please? 35

Document Passwords — Security for All 36

Closing the Program 36

Chapter 3: Help: It's Not Just a Beatles Movie Anymore **37**

Helping You Use ClarisWorks 37

　Using ClarisWorks help 38

　　Mac help 38

　　Windows help 41

　　Help tips for all 41

　　Help, help on the Web 42

Doing It for You 42
    Using ClarisWorks stationery 42
    JIAN Business*Basics* 43
    Using ClarisWorks Assistants 44
    Using Help menu Assistants 45

Part II: Working with Text: The Keys to Success *47*

Chapter 4: The Word Processor: It's Not Your Father's Smith Corona **49**

When to Use Word-Processing Documents 49
Entering Text 50
    The insertion point 50
    The keyboard 50
    Text wrap 51
Navigating the Seas of Text 51
    For the mousy type 51
    Keyboard kicks 52
Selecting, Deleting, and Replacing Text 53
    Selecting 53
        Mouse selection 54
        Keyboard selection riffs 54
    Deleting 55
Undoing, Cutting, Copying, and Pasting 56
    Undo 56
    Cut 57
    Copy 57
    Paste 58
Staying Out of Word Processor Hell (Spaces, Tabs, and Returns) 59
    Don't get spacey 59
    The rule of tabs 59
    The rule of returns 60
Higher Math — the Equation Editor 60

Chapter 5: Fun with Text Formatting **63**

Text Preferences 63
Formatting Letters and Words 65
    Bold, italic, and underline 65
    Text size 66
    Changing fonts 67
    Changing font colors 67
    Using styles 68

Formatting Sentences and Paragraphs 70
    Using the text ruler 70
    Aligning text 70
    Indenting 72
        To indent the first line 73
        To indent the whole paragraph right or left 73
    Tab stops 74
        The four types of tab stops 74
        Setting tab stops 75
        Filled tabs 76
    Hanging indents 77
    Invisible men and other characters 79
    Line spacing 79
    Space between paragraphs 80
    Applying a ruler 81
    Paragraph styles 82
Formatting Pages and Documents 84
    Page breaks 84
    Page numbers and other placeholders 84
    Headers and footers 85
    Sections 86
    Facing pages 87
    Footnotes 88
    Margins 89
    Columns 90
        To change columns with the mouse 91
        To change columns with the Columns dialog box 91
    Paper size and orientation 92

Chapter 6: The Text Tools — Editor in a Drum 93

The Spell Checker — One Reason To Use a Word Processor 93
Find and Go Change 96
    Finding text 96
    Changing text 97
Counting Your Words 99
Finding Synonyms 99
Hyphenating 101

Chapter 7: Adding Tables, Charts, and Pictures 103

Adding Images (Charts and Graphs, too) 103
    Popping in a picture 104
    Aligning with the baseline 105
    Wrapping text 106
    Changing behaviors (of the graphic, not yourself) 107

Creating Tables 108
    Tables with a click or an Assistant 109
        The Make Table button 109
        The Make Table Assistant 109
    Tables from scratch 111
Entering Data into Your Table 111
Formatting a Table 112
    Changing column width and row height 114
    Hiding and showing column and row headings 115
    Positioning your table 116
Quick and Dirty Chartmaking 117

Chapter 8: Outlining — You Gotta Start Somewhere 119

Setting Up an Outline 120
Rearranging Outline Topics 121
Collapsing and Expanding Outlines 122
Outline Formats and Custom Outline Styles 123
    Built-in formats and labels 123
    Custom labels 124
    Custom outline styles 124

Part III: Working with Graphics: Get the Picture? **127**

Chapter 9: Drawing versus Painting 129

When to Draw 130
When to Paint 130
Advantages and Disadvantages 131
The Best of Both Worlds 132

Chapter 10: Painting — by the Numbers 135

Painting Pointers 135
Shaping Your World 136
Borders, Lines, and Fills 138
    Patterns 140
    Textures 141
    Gradients 141
    Line options 142
    Editing patterns, gradients, and textures 142
    Changing colors and filling in empty spaces 146
Paint Mode 147
Painting Freehand 148
Selecting Areas 149
Erasing and Deleting 150

Hot Rod Your Tools 151
    Modifier keys 151
        Shift 151
        Option(Mac)/Alt (Windows) 151
        Command (⌘)/Ctrl 152
    Dialog boxes 152

Chapter 11: Special Effects with Paint 155

Warping Your Graphics 155
    Distorting 155
    Putting it in perspective 156
    Shearing 157
Resizing 157
Rotating and Flipping 158
    Flipping 159
    Rotating via a dialog box 159
    Free rotating 160
Color Tricks and More 161
    The commands 161
    One last word about paint effects. 162

Chapter 12: Draw, Pardner! 163

Setting Up Your Draw Document 164
Drawing Tools 165
Selecting and Deleting 166
Copying 167
Setting Up Lines and Fills 168
Styles for Draw Objects 168
Resizing, Reshaping, and Rotating 169
    Resizing 169
        Dragging 169
        Scaling 170
        Resizing with a palette 171
    Reshaping 171
        Reshaping freehand objects 171
        Reshaping round rectangles and arcs 173
    Rotating 173
Setting Drawing Preferences 175
Using Text Boxes and Other Frames 176
Moving, Aligning, and Grouping 177
    Moving 177
    Aligning 179
    Grouping 179
    Joining 180
    Locking 181
Inserting Graphics 181
    Pasting and Inserting 182
    Using ClarisWorks Libraries 183

Chapter 13: The Lowdown on Page Layout 185

Page Layout Basics: The Envelope Template 185
Adding Pages to Your Draw Document 189
Text and Graphics Rulers 190
Linked Frames 191
Linking text frames 191
Wrapping text in a draw document 194
Linking spreadsheet and paint frames 194
Opening frames 196
Headers, Footers, and Page Numbers 197

Chapter 14: Presenting Presentations 199

Laying Out a Presentation 199
Editing Master Pages 200
Adding Movies 202
Controlling the Show 203
Using the Slide Show dialog box................................... 203
Order and visibility 204
Slide options 204
QuickTime options 205
Moving through the slide show 205

Part IV: Working with Numbers: It All Adds Up! 207

Chapter 15: Spreadsheets 101 209

Deciding When to Use a Spreadsheet 209
Working with Cells, Rows, and Columns 210
Selecting a single cell 210
Selecting a range of cells 211
Selecting columns and rows 212
Selecting the whole spreadsheet 212
Entering Data... 212
Setting Preferences 213
Editing 214
Moving Data 214
Filling Cells 215
Fill Down and Fill Right 215
Fill Special 215

Chapter 16: Formatting Spreadsheets 217

Formatting Numbers 217
Number formats 217
Date formats 219
Time formats 219

Formatting Cells 219
   Text styles 220
   Default font 220
   Text wrap 220
   Cell color 221
   Spreadsheet styles 222
Sorting 222
Inserting and Resizing Rows and Columns 224
   Inserting 224
   Resizing 225
      Resizing with the mouse 225
      Resizing with buttons 225
      Resizing with the dialog box 226
Adding Borders, Gridlines, and Headings 226
   Borders 226
   Gridlines 226
   Headings and other display settings 227
Using Titles, Page Breaks, and Print Ranges 228
   Locking titles 228
   Page breaks and new pages 229
   Print range 229

Chapter 17: Charting — Pictures from Numbers **231**

Getting to Know the Types of Charts 231
Making a Chart 233
Modifying a Chart 234
   Chart type and variations 234
   Other chart options 235
   Changing colors and line width 236
   Updating the chart with new numbers 236
   Adding your own picture to a pictogram chart 237
Resizing, Moving, and Deleting Charts 238
Making Charts in Other Document Types 238

Chapter 18: Making It All Add Up with Formulas and Functions **239**

The AutoSum Shortcut — First and Finest 239
Entering Formulas 241
   Math operations 241
   Entering cell references 242
   Naming your cells 242
   Editing cell names 243
Using Functions 244
Relative versus Absolute References 245

Part V: Working with Files: Smoothing Out the Rough Edges 247

Chapter 19: Your Rolodex Revisited — Database Basics 249

Deciding When to Use a Database 249
Database Records 250
Database Fields 251
Browse, Find, and Layout Modes 251
Entering Data 252
    Adding a new record 252
    Deleting records 253
    Filling in text fields 253
    Using multimedia fields 253
    Navigating through a database 255
    Importing data from other databases 255
Sorting 257
    Button sorts 257
    Saved sorts 257
    Old sorts 259
Finding 259
    Find mode 260
        Narrow your search 260
        Broaden your search with multiple requests 261
        Save your search 261
    Match records 262
Searching Shortcuts 263

Chapter 20: Designing a Database 265

Planning It Out 265
Defining Fields 266
Mastering Basic Field Types 268
    Text fields 268
    Number fields 268
    Date fields 268
    Time fields 269
    Name fields 269
    Serial number fields 269
    Record info fields 270
    Multimedia fields 270
Setting Options for Fields 270
Mastering Special Field Types 272
    Pop-up menu and radio button fields 272
    Value list fields 273
    Check box fields 273
Laying Out the Database 273

Adding Summary Reports for Printing 277
    Adding a grand summary part 277
    Adding a sub-summary part 278
    Understanding header and footer parts 279

Chapter 21: Printing a Database **281**
Adding Layouts for Printing 281
Printing Labels 283
    Using standard Avery label layouts 284
    Customizing label layouts 285
Closing Up Space When You Print 286
Using Reports 287

Chapter 22: Mail Merge — It's One Cool Trick **289**
What Is a Mail Merge and What Can It Do for Me? 289
Creating a Merge Document 290
Selecting Records to Print 290
Merging the Data 291
Printing Merged Documents 293

Part VI: Working with the World: Reaching Out and Touching Someone *295*

Chapter 23: Connecting to the World the ClarisWorks Way **297**
First Things First — Getting Internet Access 297
One-Click Web 298
    Launching your browser 299
    Visiting a Web site 299
Launching Your E-Mail Application 302
Customizing Your Button Bar for the Web 302
Netscape Navigator 305
    Getting to your first site 305
    Where do you go from here? 305
    Returning to a site 306
    Bookmarks 307
Unearthing the Communications Package 308

Chapter 24: Publishing for the World Wide Web **309**
The Secret Life of a Web Page 309
Creating Web Pages with ClarisWorks 310
    Adding elements 310
    Font attributes 311
    Tables 311
    Bulleted or numbered lists 312
    Images 312

QuickTime videos — movies 312
Other page elements 312
Adding a background 313
Creating links 314
Linking to a URL 314
Using the links palette to create links 317
Testing a link 318
Editing a link 318
Saving your document as a Web page 319
Creating Web Pages with Claris Home Page Lite 319
Telling your story with text 321
Paragraph styles 321
Saying it with pictures 322
Editing graphics 323
Alternate labels 323
Interlacing and transparency 323
Graphics as links 324
Alignment and borders 324
Resizing 324
Background colors and images 324
Tables 325
Linking 325
Previewing 325
Saving your Claris Home Page Web page 326

Part VII: The Part of Tens 327

Chapter 25: Ten Real-Life Uses for ClarisWorks 329

Make Magic 329
Write Screenplays 330
Run a Raffle 330
Printmaking 330
Manage a Project 331
Run Sports Teams 331
Run a Graphics Design Business 331
Create Fundraising Calendars and Materials 332
Do Public Relations 332
Publish a Book 332

Chapter 26: Ten Ways ClarisWorks Tries to Drive You Crazy, and How to Stay Sane 333

Arrgh! What Happened to the Menus? 333
Where Did My Button Go!? 334
Some Other Darned Program Won't Leave Me Alone! 334

What Are All These *&%#$! Symbols in My Text? 334
My Whole Line's Formatting Changed 335
My Printer Keeps Printing a Blank Page 335
My Text Won't Line Up 335
My Letters Are All Squished Together 336
My Two-Page Spreadsheet Prints on 20 Pages 336
My Fields Won't Slide on Mailing Labels 336

Appendix: Buttoning Up *337*
Editing Button Bars 337
Creating New Buttons 338
Creating an Icon 339

Index *340*

Book Registration information .... *Back of Book*

Introduction

● ●

*A*fter you invest in a computer, printer, and other such hardware, the last thing you want to do is lay out more money for several boxes of software. Worse, you hate to get the software home and try to run it, only to discover that it takes up too much space on your hard drive. So you get a different program, only it needs so much memory to run that you've got to go out to buy extra RAM.

But you've got a business to run and need a *lot* of software functionality:

- ✔ Maybe you've got a small business and need software that will do everything: correspondence, expense tracking, a client database, a slew of PR materials . . . and a Web site.

- ✔ Or maybe you run a large office full of staff on Windows machines, NT machines, and Macs, so you need your documents to move between platforms — and you need for users to pick up and be productive on any machine without having to rethink a software's operation.

- ✔ Or maybe your life is education-based: You're in school and you've got math projects, presentations, charts and graphs — or you're a teacher and you've got seating charts, grade books, projects, reports, and lesson plans to create.

- ✔ And you all need easy access to the Web, not wanting to waste time launching browsers and entering addresses.

Writing, spreadsheets, databases, charts and graphs, newsletters, floor plans, Web pages . . . wow! That's a tall order. You got your computer to make your life easier — not to spend the rest of your life figuring out heaps of complicated software.

Luckily for you, you're either looking at this book and checking out ClarisWorks as a solution or, even luckier, you already bought ClarisWorks or ClarisWorks Office and have found *ClarisWorks Office For Dummies*. You found an excellent solution — a simple, powerful software program and a book that gives it to you straight and keeps it simple. Never mind all the hype about computers being hard to master. You found a team that defies that trend.

About This Book

Whether you have the full ClarisWorks Office bundle or "just" ClarisWorks 5.0, this book works for you. ClarisWorks 5.0 provides most of the power and is the main focus of the book.

ClarisWorks 5.0 has so many features, chances are pretty good that you won't even use all of them . . . until that fateful day when you need to do something you've never done — and need to do it fast.

This book was written with this type of real-life need in mind. Take it out, get the lowdown on a feature, and then put it away again. Maybe you need to use just one function, such as word processing or spreadsheets. Just go over that chapter. Of course, you can read the book cover to cover. We made it easy to do either way.

Each section is set up so that you can find the answers you need without reading more than is absolutely necessary. There are plenty of cross-references if you need more information. Technical information and computer terms are set aside in little boxes that you don't have to deal with. Tips are clearly marked so you can just skim them. The idea is for you to get in, get the information you need to solve the problem at hand, and get back to work as quickly as possible.

Conventions Used in This Book

This book is for both Macintosh and Windows users. Claris has done an excellent job of making ClarisWorks cross platform. Of course, there are inherent differences between the operating systems. Claris fully respects each system, playing by its rules. For example, help is accessed in the title bar in Windows and via a Help icon on a Mac — but the contents and accessibility of the help are identical.

When we tell you how to do something, we tell you which menu to look in and which command to use. When a process involves several steps, we put them in a numbered list so they're easier to follow. When there's more than one way to get something done, we go over each, pointing out the fastest, easiest way.

By the way, ClarisWorks really adheres to the "keep it simple" rule. Everything you need is clearly found in a menu, rather than buried somewhere, forcing you to memorize yucky key combinations to get something done.

Menu commands are listed like this:

Edit⇨Copy

This means you pull down the Edit menu with your mouse and choose the Copy command. Windows users will be familiar with the lines under one letter of each menu or command name. This letter is a Windows shortcut that lets you issue that command by pressing the Alt key, and then the underlined letter. These underlines don't mean anything to a Mac user. They are there as a courtesy to our Windows-using friends.

Rather than pulling down menus, there are times you may be more comfortable using a keyboard shortcut, so we point them out to you. Keyboard shortcuts are different between Windows and the Mac.

Keyboard shortcuts are listed like this:

⌘-C (Mac) and Ctrl+C (Windows)

This translates to pressing and holding the ⌘ key (if on Mac) or the Control key (if in Windows), pressing the letter C, and then releasing them at the same time. Notice we use a hyphen between Mac commands and a plus sign between Windows commands. These keys aren't part of the combination. Don't press them. We use the symbols familiar to each platform to make it a bit easier for you to identify the ones you need.

By the way, you may notice that pretty much the ⌘ key on the Mac and the Ctrl in Windows are equivalent, as are the Option (Mac) and Alt (Windows) keys. Remembering that will help you when the day comes that you have to work on *that other* machine.

What You're Not to Read

Scattered throughout this book are short notes, definitions, and discussions of a more technical nature. They are here only for the curious. Do not read them. Well, okay, you can read them if you really want to. We've been careful to put all of these items in isolated gray boxes. These gray boxes are a great source of ClarisWorks trivia. Repeating anything you read in a gray box is the quickest way we know of to kill a conversation at a dinner party.

Foolish Assumptions

The first thing that we assume about you is that you're no dummy. Otherwise, you wouldn't have bought this book. The term *Dummies* is a written form of a nod and a grin to let you know that we understand how daunting all this computer stuff can be sometimes. We've been there. It's that feeling when you sit in front of your computer, mouse in hand, knowing that somehow you can use all this technology to do something wonderful, but having no idea how to do it.

We realize that you may be new to computing, so we make it as easy as possible for you. We tell you when to use the mouse, when to hold down the mouse button, and when to release it. However, we expect that you have the basics down — getting around your screen, clicking, dragging, and selecting a command from a menu.

(For help mastering the general behavior of your computer's operation, we recommend that you check out Bob LeVitus's *Mac OS 8 For Dummies,* or Andy Rathbone's *Windows 95 For Dummies,* 2nd Edition, both published by IDG Books Worldwide, Inc.)

We also assume that you are currently using ClarisWorks, either on a Mac or on a PC running Windows 95 or Windows NT. If you're not, then run out and buy ClarisWorks Office right now; you'll be glad you did.

How This Book Is Organized

This book is divided into seven major parts. Each covers a different area of ClarisWorks Office. Each part is divided into chapters, and the chapters are broken into bite-sized bits. You can quickly wolf down the morsels of information you need without getting mental heartburn.

Here's what you can find in each part:

Part I: What ClarisWorks Does

This part provides an overview of ClarisWorks Office: its features the methods and practices common to all areas of the application, and the on-screen help systems. This part points out the main *environments* or functions of ClarisWorks 5, as well as what the other bundled software has to offer. You can find out about how to open and save documents, the parts of a window, the tools, the menus, and the buttons. It's a good place to start if you're a beginner.

Part II: Working with Text: The Keys to Success

At some point, we all need to work with text, whether to write a letter or to add captions to a spreadsheet or illustration. Text handling, whether in a word-processing document or in a text frame within another environment, is the focus here.

Part III: Working with Graphics: Get the Picture?

Graphics can be created by *drawing* or *painting*. These methods are compared here, followed by chapters focusing on each. When you want to create a company logo or add a diagram to your document, this is the place to go. It's also the place to find out about page layout — something that comes in handy for everyone because you can add text, spreadsheets, charts, and data from databases to a draw document to do full-fledged page composition. Clip art and the ClarisWorks Libraries are covered here too. And then there are presentations. Presentations are actually in a class by themselves 'cause they can incorporate database information and such. But we had to put them somewhere, so they're here.

Part IV: Working with Numbers: It All Adds Up!

Spreadsheets are the focus here from formulas to formatting. It's easy to create a chart (even one with custom icons) from your spreadsheet data, so come here to find out how. Spreadsheets are the basis of tables, so if you use a table, come here for more details on formatting it.

Part V: Working with Files: Smoothing Out the Rough Edges

Databases are great places to keep customer or student records. Discover how to create and use them here.

Part VI: Working with the World: Reaching Out and Touching Someone

ClarisWorks offers basic communications software and Internet connectivity. The basics are all introduced here. ClarisWorks also has the ability to create Web pages. Claris Home Page Lite, part of the Office bundle, offers even more Web page creation ability, as well as the ability to upload your pages to your Web server. That's all covered here.

Part VII: The Part of Tens

These days everyone seems to love top ten lists, so we've got our own lists of things relating to ClarisWorks Office.

Icons Used in This Book

Icons in this book form a kind of a road map you can use to navigate the text. Scan the margins for the following types of information:

Points out a useful hint, trick, or shortcut.

Reminds you to do something, or points out a concept to file in your memory bank.

Reminds you not to do something you may regret later (or sooner!).

Points out geeky, technical stuff you can feel free to skip.

Alerts you to Macintosh- or Windows-specific ClarisWorks information, or differences between the two platforms.

Where to Go from Here

For your reading pleasure, may we suggest . . .

✔ If you're totally new to ClarisWorks, begin with Part I for the basics, and then jump to the part that covers what you need to do first.

✔ If you have a specific project in mind and already have the basics, turn directly to the part that covers what you need.

✔ If you haven't got any specific project to do, but just wanted this book handy for when you need it, put it away and have some fun (of course, get back to work if you have to). We'll wait till you need us.

Part I

What
ClarisWorks Does

The 5th Wave

By Rich Tennant

WE'VE TRIED EVERYTHING, BUT SHE STILL GETS THIS SHARP JABBING PAIN IN THE BACK OF HER NECK FROM WORKING AT THE COMPUTER ALL DAY.

In this part . . .

ClarisWorks isn't flashy and it isn't overkill. It's simple to use: It doesn't bury commands tons of levels deep. In fact, it doesn't bury them at all. It doesn't cost a bunch of money, but don't let that fool you. It doesn't come in a huge box with inches of manuals. Don't let that fool you, either.

Like we said, it's powerful. Simple and powerful — *simply* powerful.

This part gives you an overview of what ClarisWorks can do. It covers the basics you need to start working with the application. If you're just beginning with ClarisWorks, take a quick look here. Part I introduces you to the things ClarisWorks does. There's some good stuff in this part even for old hats to discover.

Chapter 1

A Quick Overview of ClarisWorks Office

In This Chapter

▶ What is ClarisWorks?

▶ Word processing

▶ Drawing

▶ Painting

▶ Spreadsheets

▶ Databases

▶ Communication

▶ Things that ClarisWorks provides to help you

▶ Internet stuff in the bundle

*T*here are two parts to ClarisWorks Office. There's ClarisWorks 5.0, the application, and there's the additional software in the ClarisWorks Office bundle. We begin by showing you what ClarisWorks does. Then we show you what the rest of the bundle has to offer.

Basic ClarisWorks Functions

The first question most people have about ClarisWorks is: What is it? A word processor? A drawing program? A spreadsheet program? The answer is "Yes." It's all that and more. ClarisWorks is the software equivalent of a Swiss Army knife — a whole tool chest rolled into one application.

Computer software tends to fall — or be placed by us — into categories: word processing, drawing, painting, spreadsheets, and communications. *Works* is a generic term for a program that provides the basics of all these types of programs. Originally works programs gave you a miniversion of each software type. ClarisWorks goes way beyond that, incorporating full-fledged versions of each, not just samplers. So, the *Works* in ClarisWorks refers to getting it all.

But ClarisWorks is more than just six separate applications integrated in one package. It's *seamlessly integrated,* as the Claris people say. If it were only six separate applications, you would have to do your typing, then your drawing, and *then* try to paste your illustration into your text.

Seamlessly integrated means you can use its different functions together in one document without switching programs. Not impressed yet? Wait till you get into this seamless stuff! You don't have to start a separate drawing document to create a picture — you can draw right there in the middle of your letter to Aunt Barbara or right on top of your sales spreadsheet.

Word processing (Typing)

Perhaps the most used function of ClarisWorks is word processing. That's not just writing simple letters. The word processing function pops up all over the place: when you're creating a spreadsheet and need to enter an introduction, or when you're doing a drawing and want to title it.

Are you wondering why it's called *word processing* and not just *typing?* If you're used to a typewriter and this is your first introduction to word processing, you're in for a treat. A word processor lets you do far more than just enter text. You now have the full ability to *manipulate* the text you enter. For example, you can type your text, move it anywhere you like, style it in many ways, check your spelling, find synonyms in a thesaurus, count your words, use footnotes, and much more. ClarisWorks includes a full-featured word processor that gives you all these abilities.

For those of you who are students, those who have found out (the hard way) that your teachers were right and work is easier with a plan, and those of you who still haven't figured this out (but will someday), ClarisWorks also offers outlining, an easy way to list the main points of your document and then organize and build upon them.

Word-processing documents can do one more thing that may surprise you. They can become Web pages. All you have to do is create your regular document and then save it, selecting HTML as the save format. ClarisWorks has built-in translators that convert your document for you, and pack it up, graphics and all, into a neat folder ready to place on the Web. You don't have to learn a thing about HTML if you don't want to. But, in case you do, or in case you want more control over your HTML output, you can access and customize these translators. Access to them is just a click away.

Drawing

Like word processing, drawing can pop up almost anywhere. The drawing functions provide line tools and shape tools to help you create graphics. Additionally, ClarisWorks gives you palettes full of colors, editable patterns, gradients, and textures to complete your image.

You can create a drawing document on which you do page layout or an entire work of art. Or you can take advantage of the drawing functions within other documents to create a letterhead or fliers in a word processing document, make maps and diagrams, add graphics to a database, and much more.

You can also create presentations using drawing functions. The Presentation feature lets you display information on-screen or for printing onto overhead slides or hard copy (handouts).

In drawing mode, lines and shapes are composed of points and invisible, behind-the-scenes mathematical formulas. When you resize drawings, move your objects on top of one another, and so on, they still look good on the screen and print with crisp lines and smooth curves. You also can easily change your drawing anytime.

Painting

Before you get your hopes up, we have to tell you that this painting is limited to what you do on-screen. Even a great program like ClarisWorks can't make your computer paint your house (although it can help you hire a painter, chart the progress, and send out fliers announcing the paint job).

The Paint feature gives you electronic pencils to create your works of art and colors to fill your shapes and color your lines.

Like real paint, this paint can't be rearranged after it's been applied. Instead of formula-driven lines, you are working on a pixel-by-pixel basis. Imagine that you are coloring a sheet of graph paper and each square on the graph paper is a pixel on your computer's screen. To create your painting, you either color in a square or leave it empty. If you make a shape and then need to make it larger, you uncolor some squares and color in new ones. Text can also be added to your painting. Doing so *paints* the text in — the text turns it into dots that are part of the painting instead of individual characters you can edit. You can use the paint functions to design logos, manipulate clip art, or edit scanned images. Better than real paint, you can select any part of your painting and move, rotate, stretch, or distort it — creating interesting effects.

Spreadsheets (Calculating and more)

You may be thinking, "Spreadsheets — sheesh, I'll never use those. They're just for accountants!" After you're comfortable with ClarisWorks, however, you may be surprised at the uses you find for a spreadsheet. Okay, you may not be into things like creating business invoices, maintaining financial statements, tracking stocks, and balancing your checkbook, but one day you may need to make that recipe for 100 into a recipe for 9 and you may just find yourself saying "Hey, I can do that with a spreadsheet!" (Honest, it could happen. But only if you cook to begin with.)

ClarisWorks uses spreadsheet mode to create tables in text documents. As a matter of fact, anything set up in rows and columns is spreadsheet fodder. How about your daily schedule or a monthly calendar?

Do you like visualizing trends with graphs and charts? Just enter the data into a spreadsheet, and ClarisWorks does the rest. You can choose from many types of charts. You may need to graph data from a chemistry experiment, for example, or you may need to chart profits.

Databases (Data filing and maintenance)

Putting your address book or client list into your computer is the number one way to use the ClarisWorks database functions. You can use a database document as your electronic Rolodex.

A database can be used anytime you want to store, search, or sort information such as addresses, the contents of a baseball card collection, a business inventory, or any other collection of information.

ClarisWorks lets you customize databases to work with information in any way you like. Because of the integration features of ClarisWorks, you can use the graphics tools to add color and pictures to your database. After you have your information organized and sorted, you can easily print it on standard labels.

One of the most useful database features is the ability to merge information from your database into any text area or spreadsheet. This feature makes printing personalized forms or letters a cinch. Ed McMahon's notices saying you may have already won a prize pale in comparison to what you can do.

Communication

There are actually two communications options within ClarisWorks Office: the original flavor — the communications environment within ClarisWorks — and now . . . hot and spicy — integration with the World Wide Web.

The plain vanilla form of communication is the part in the official communications environment of ClarisWorks. It allows you to connect with another computer for text-only communication. With it, you have to type special text commands to tell the computer on the other end of the line what to do. You can use it to connect to your friend's or associate's computer, online services, or electronic bulletin board systems. Because the world has gone the way of the graphical Web browser, however, you'll probably have to use the ClarisWorks communications environment only in a pinch.

The hot and spicy form of communication, which is much more fun, lets you cruise the Internet in graphical splendor. You can place links or buttons into any ClarisWorks document that, when clicked, launch your Internet browser and connect you to the Web. If you're not in a document that has a link, just click one of the convenient buttons at the top of your screen: One button launches your browser, another button takes you directly to any Web address you highlight within your document, or you (or an associate) can create a custom button that takes you directly to a specific Web site.

Bringing these things together (Integration)

ClarisWorks is cool because of how it mixes its parts together — easily. How? By using the concept of frames. A *frame* is sort of a window from one kind of ClarisWorks function into another.

Claris uses the term *environment* to refer to each of its main functions or application types. By choosing a document type, you indicate which environment you predominately want to work in. You access the others by creating frames within your document. When you're in a frame, you are fully within that frame's environment or function.

The best way to explain is with an example. Say you're preparing a report. Reports are mostly words, so you begin with a word-processing document. Then you want to include a table to display data. You can use the Tab key to make the numbers line up in columns, but if you later edit that data in any way, it becomes quite a mess. (Besides, you can't create a chart from numbers lined up with tabs.) Wouldn't it be easier to put your data in neat columns that can be maintained, even when you edit them? You can — in a spreadsheet.

"But wait," you say, "I'm in a word-processing document, right?" Yup, you are, but ClarisWorks allows you to use all the functions of a spreadsheet right there, smack-dab in the middle of your word-processing document. By simply selecting the spreadsheet tool and dragging it, you create a spreadsheet frame where you want your table to appear. Within that spreadsheet frame, you're in spreadsheet mode, with full access to the commands and functions you use for spreadsheets.

The same concept applies when you add text to a draw document. To add words to your graphics, you drag the text tool, creating a text frame. Within that area, you can access all the text tools that you have in a word processing document, including text styles and spell check.

You can add as many frames to a document as you like. Of course, you can add different kinds of frames within a document. For example, use a draw document as your main environment to lay out your invoice; add your company logo in a paint frame, your address in a text frame, and a tally for the charges in a spreadsheet frame. The spreadsheet actively calculates your costs and fees, so you can truly prepare your invoices within one document!

Frames are not linked with any particular line of text or spreadsheet cell. Instead, they are floating objects that can be moved around anywhere in the document. You can see what we mean when you edit the data in the main document and find your frame overlapping. That's when you click the frame and move it into place in relation to your recent edits. Of course, you can embed a frame into a line of text if you prefer. That way, the frame moves as you edit your text. We show you more about embedding frames and graphics into a line of text in Chapter 7.

Actually, frames only apply to text, spreadsheets, and painting. The other environments don't need frames. The draw tools are available at all times (except in a communications document), so you don't need a separate frame. Database data gets inserted into documents by a technique called *merging,* which inserts database data into special placeholders you set up in your documents. This may sound difficult, but it's really simple. We explain it all in Chapter 22. The ClarisWorks communications documents don't use frames because they're for sending and receiving data via modem, not creating documents.

Other ClarisWorks Features (Neat Helpful Stuff)

In the preceding sections, we show you the major things ClarisWorks does. The following sections show you some ClarisWorks bells and whistles.

Assistants

Sometimes it seems you spend a lot of time re-creating the same types of documents, except with different content or formatting. Respecting your valuable time, Claris gives you Assistants — short interviews that ask you a few focused questions and then present you with a preformatted document ready to use.

Stationery

Stationery can be another great time-saver. Stationery refers to the good, solid, premade starting points for specific types of documents. ClarisWorks comes with many stationery documents to cover your needs or give you ideas. Among the stationery is JIAN Business*Basics* — an entire bundle of business-productivity stationery.

Document passwords — security for all

At any point in a document's life, you may decide you're more comfortable assigning a password so prying or curious eyes can't see what they shouldn't. Any ClarisWorks document can be assigned a password at any time. You can also change the password as needed — as long as you know the current word.

The Equation Editor

The Equation Editor is not for everyone, but if you're doing math, it's the greatest thing since sliced bread. This great little mini-app makes it very easy to build intricate math statements with barely more than a few clicks and pop them right into your document with one last window-closing click.

Buttons

Buttons are shortcuts to common tasks. They not only provide one-click access to commands, but they also give you visual clues as to what you can do from where you are. You have nine buttons waiting to make your travel on the Internet superhighway smooth driving. Another dozen build a chart for you in a jiffy. The rest mostly help you with document formatting. And then there are the buttons you set up yourself to launch another program, open another document, take you to a specific Web site, or perform other tasks. The more creative you are with buttons, the more time you save.

ClarisWorks Bundle Additions

Internet connectivity

These days, it's hard to succeed in business without access to the Internet for communications, research, marketing, and such. ClarisWorks has an excellent bunch of conveniences with their buttons and links. In order to help unravel your path to the Web, they also provide a choice of two Internet Service Providers for you to hook up with. Each provides a full complement of Internet and Web software ready for your use the moment you sign up. Whether you use these providers or find your own, ClarisWorks is wired to help you connect.

Claris Home Page Lite

Any ClarisWorks word-processing document can become a Web page by simply saving the document in an HTML format. But savvy computer users always want more. And Claris has more — so they bundled Claris Home Page Lite in ClarisWorks Office to give you more options for creating Web pages.

Chapter 2

How ClarisWorks Works

In This Chapter

▶ Launching ClarisWorks

▶ Creating and opening documents

▶ Getting familiar with the ClarisWorks window controls

▶ Using button bars

▶ Using tools and menus

▶ Working with Page Setup

▶ Saving

▶ Printing

▶ Adding or changing a password

▶ Closing the program

*I*f ClarisWorks were a car, this is where you would take it out for a little spin and try to figure out how to work the gearshift. This chapter gives you the information you need to handle the basic stuff common to all ClarisWorks document types — things like opening a new document, saving, and printing. So dig in and don't forget to fasten your seat belt!

Starting ClarisWorks

First things first. Before you can use ClarisWorks, you need to start it up, or launch it. How you do that depends on how you have your system set up.

On the Mac, whether viewing by icon or as a list, open the ClarisWorks 5 folder, locate the ClarisWorks icon, and double-click it to start. You can also use the Mac's launcher, or if you've got a ClarisWorks alias on your desktop, double-click it. For maximum efficiency add an alias of ClarisWorks to your menu, and launch it by selecting it from there.

In Windows from the Start menu, choose Programs⇨ClarisWorks⇨ ClarisWorks. If you added a shortcut in your Start menu, use that. If you've got a shortcut on your desktop, double-click it.

If you can't find ClarisWorks, try these tips (your setup may be different):

✔ In Windows, start ClarisWorks by double-clicking the My Computer icon; then double-click your hard drive (called the (C:) drive), the Programs folder, the Claris Corp folder, and finally the ClarisWorks 5.0 folder. The actual application is called ClarisWorks.exe.

✔ On the Mac, ClarisWorks is inside your hard drive, which is in the top-right corner of your desktop (called Macintosh HD by default). You can find it in the ClarisWorks 5.0 folder, which may be in a folder called Applications. The application is called ClarisWorks.

If you still can't find ClarisWorks, use your system's Find feature to locate it. After that, if you *still* can't find it, pick up a copy of Andy Rathbone's *Windows 95 For Dummies,* 2nd Edition, or Bob LeVitus's *Mac OS 8 For Dummies* — both published by IDG Books Worldwide, Inc.

Creating a New Document

Each time you turn on your computer and open ClarisWorks, you are *launching* it. When you launch, ClarisWorks presents you with a New Document selection window such as the one in Figure 2-1. You see a list of the six document types on the left. Double-click the document type. This opens a new document for you.

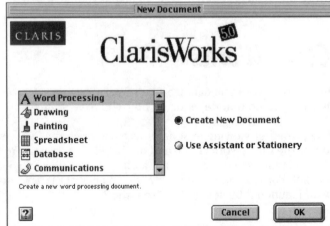

Figure 2-1:
The New
Document
dialog box.

After ClarisWorks is running, it no longer displays the New Document window, even if you switch to another program and then switch back. You then have two options to create another new document:

✔ **Click the button in the button bar for the type of document you want to create.**

✔ **Select File⇨New to get the New Document window.**

The only difference between these options is that the New Document window has the option to use Assistants or Stationery, which we cover in Chapter 3. (Although Assistants can be opened from the button bar, too — when you select the Assistants button bar.)

If ClarisWorks is already running and you switch to another application and back again, ClarisWorks gives you a clue that you're back. In Windows, you can tell that you're back in ClarisWorks because the *title bar* of your window (that's the strip at the top of each window) reads ClarisWorks 5.0. On the Mac, the clue is the Application menu at the top-right corner of your screen, where you can see the ClarisWorks icon. Additionally, on both platforms, you can see the button bar, unless you turned it off.

After a while, you don't always want to start from a new blank document; you develop your own stationery templates to launch instead. After you develop a document you like, you can save time by making it into a stationery document. When you want to use that style document, you can just open it, rather than formatting a whole new document. You also have the option of using an Assistant to help you create a custom template. Find out about Assistants in Chapter 3.

Choosing your primary environment

Which type of document you want to open depends on the kind of work you primarily plan to do. As we go into detail about each document type, throughout this book, you get a better idea of when to use each one. Meanwhile, here's a quick reference guide:

✔ Use a **word-processing document** for jobs that are mostly text — for example, a letter, a school report, or an outline.

✔ Use a **draw document** to create graphics like maps, diagrams, and plans. You can also use draw documents for laying out pages that combine graphics with blocks of text and/or spreadsheets, such as newsletters or manuals, or for creating presentations.

✔ Use a **paint document** for creating logos, freehand pictures, and special effects with graphics and text.

- ✔ Use a **spreadsheet document** to display information in columns and rows — schedules, financial reports, or calendars, for example.

- ✔ Use a **database** to store information. Addresses, product inventory, and such are good candidates for a database.

- ✔ Use **communications documents** for connecting to other computers, or some text-based electronic bulletin boards or online services.

- ✔ Use **Top Secret documents** for obtaining covert mission information. Burn or eat them after reading.

The document type you choose is your primary environment, but you are not limited to that type of function. Remember, you can use one kind of function within another by creating a frame.

Opening Existing Documents

While we're talking about opening a document, opening existing documents can be done in a couple of different ways. We give the basics here. For more information on creative ways to open documents, check out one of these *...For Dummies* books: *Macs For Dummies,* 5th Edition, by David Pogue, or *Windows 95 For Dummies,* 2nd Edition, by Andy Rathbone, both published by IDG Books Worldwide.

Launching while you open

A common way to launch a file is to open the folder the document is in and double-click the document's icon. If ClarisWorks isn't running yet, this method launches it while opening your document. If your computer's icon is covered — preventing access to your folders — Mac users, simply reduce the size of your document, and Windows users, reduce the size of the ClarisWorks window.

Another more efficient way to get to documents is the same for users of both platforms. Windows users can create a shortcut to any project they work on and drop it on the Start button. Mac users can create an alias of any project they work on often and place it in the menu. Users can now go to the Start or menu, move into the project folder, and select a document to open it.

Opening a document from within ClarisWorks

Most people prefer the visual method of opening documents that we explain in the previous section. The other way to open a document is to use the Open/Save dialog box (Mac) or the Open dialog box (Windows).

A special benefit to this method is that you can use it to open a document that was created in another application. The dialog box method translates the document as it opens it.

Here's how it works:

1. Choose File⇨Open.

This brings you to what Windows users call the Open dialog box and Mac users call the Open/Save dialog box.

2. Navigate to the document you want to open.

3. Double-click the document's name.

The Open and Open/Save dialog boxes are shown in Figures 2-2 and 2-3. Take a few minutes to play around with finding and opening files to get the hang of it. These dialog boxes, with minor variations, are used by almost every application. A little time invested now to figure out how it works pays off in big dividends later.

The contents of the letters folder

Look here to find out where you are

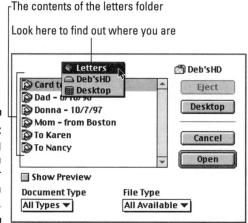

Figure 2-2: Navigating through your Macintosh hard drive.

The contents of the My Briefcase folder

Look here to find out where you are

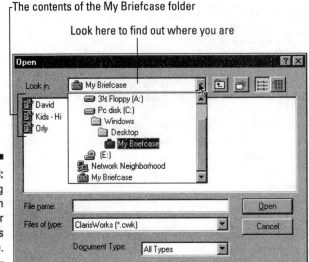

Figure 2-3:
Navigating
through
your
Windows
hard drive.

You can look for just a specific type of ClarisWorks document by choosing that type from the Document Type pop-up menu in the Open (or Open/Save) dialog box. You can also narrow your selections to a specific file format by choosing that format from the File Type or Files of Type pop-up menu in the same dialog box. If the folder you are looking in contains tons of files, you can use these menus to locate a specific document more quickly.

If you are using a Mac and have QuickTime installed, you can see a preview of a document before you open it by selecting Show Preview at the bottom of the Open/Save dialog box. If you don't see a preview, try clicking the Create button in the dialog box.

Getting to Know the ClarisWorks Interface

Interface . . . such a designer's term. *Interface* is the technical term for the look, feel, and controls of something. Your dashboard or the buttons on your microwave are interfaces. In ClarisWorks, it's the windows, buttons, menus, and tools. For the most part, both platforms have the same interface. Figure 2-4 shows the Macintosh interface. The only differences between it and the Windows version are the system-based controls.

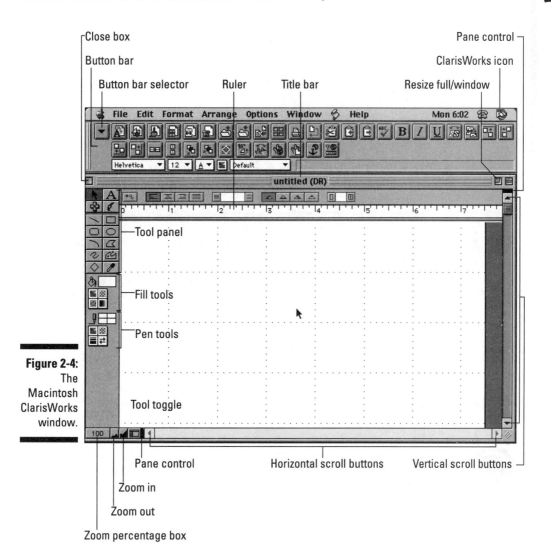

Figure 2-4:
The
Macintosh
ClarisWorks
window.

Close box
Button bar
Button bar selector
Ruler
Title bar
Pane control
ClarisWorks icon
Resize full/window
Tool panel
Fill tools
Pen tools
Tool toggle
Pane control
Horizontal scroll buttons
Vertical scroll buttons
Zoom in
Zoom out
Zoom percentage box

View controls

We assume that as a computer user, you have some experience with the general window controls for your system. In addition to those, Claris Corp has a few of its own that make working in ClarisWorks more pleasant.

> ✓ **Zoom Controls:** At the bottom of your window are three zoom controls. Zoom in, which looks like big mountains, magnifies your document by 100 percent each time you click it. Zoom out (little mountains) does

the opposite. The percentage box next to them tells you at what size your document is currently displayed. It is also a pop-up menu. Click, hold, and drag to choose from a list of commonly used percentages. "Other" brings up a dialog box allowing you to enter any percentage you like.

These zoom controls should not be confused with the Zoom or Restore buttons at the top-right corner of the window. Those change the size of the window. These change the magnification.

✔ **Tool Panel toggle:** This button, located next to the zoom controls, shows/hides the Tool Panel. By default this button is deselected in word-processing documents and selected in the other environments. (Except in Communications where tools don't apply.) The tools are incredibly handy, but you may want to hide them to gain a bit more room to work in your document. More about the tools later in this chapter.

✔ **Page indicator:** You can tell which page(s) you are working on by looking at the page indicator. Double-clicking it calls up the Go to Page dialog box. Type a page number in the box and click OK to instantly transport to that page.

✔ **Pane controls:** These are the thick strips above the vertical scroll bar and to the left of the horizontal scroll bar. You can split the window into multiple "panes" by positioning your pointer in the strip, clicking, and dragging either down or right (depending on the pane). You can divide the window into as many as nine smaller sections, each of which can display different parts of the document.

Pane controls are handy if you want to look at the start of a report as you compose a summary at the end. Or maybe you have a large diagram and want to keep an eye on the left edge as you finish the right. To resize any split, click the split line and drag. To unsplit, double-click the split line. On the Mac, these strips are black. In Windows, they are blue.

Other window controls

While we're on the subject of windows, here are some commands that also help you view your documents:

✔ To view several documents at once, click the Tile Windows button on the default button bar or use Window⇨Tile (Tile Windows on the Mac). Tiling resizes all open ClarisWorks documents to fit on-screen all at once.

✔ You can also use Window⇨Cascade (Stack Windows on the Mac) to reposition all open windows so you see all title bars at once. Click any title bar to bring that document forward and work with it.

✔ To work in the normal full-screen mode, but switch between documents, use the Window menu to bring a document forward. All open ClarisWorks documents are listed in the Window menu.

Button, button, we've got the button

Granted, it's really simple to move your mouse to a menu and select a command. But buttons are even easier. They provide immediate access to frequently used menu commands. One of the best things is that the ClarisWorks buttons are dynamic — these function-specific buttons change, depending on which environment you are working in. For example, text commands are only appropriate when you are word processing, so they only show at that time.

The button bar normally attaches to the top of your ClarisWorks window, but you can use the Button Bar Setup feature (located in the pop-up menu at the left of the button bar) to move the button bar to the top, bottom, or either side of your screen or to have it float freely as a resizable palette.

Buttons can really save you time. For example, our favorite, Show/Hide Invisibles, toggles the invisible formatting characters (spaces, tabs, and returns) on and off so you can see what you're doing, then get the Invisibles out of the way. To do this manually, you have to open the Preferences dialog box and click the option each time you want to hide or show the formatting characters.

There are actually serveral button bars to choose from. The most common is the *Default,* which contains the buttons you'll probably use most often. From the arrow on the button bar you can select any other bar instead. We have a few to show you in Figure 2-5. Don't let them fool you — these are just the bars for unopened documents. When you open a document, you get the document's function buttons, too.

Figure 2-5:
The default
button bar
to open a
document
(top), the
Assistants
button bar
(center),
and the
Internet
button bar
(bottom).

What do all those buttons do? Move your mouse over any one and a description appears to tell you. Windows users see the description in the standard status bar the Start menu and have the Windows pop-up balloons (called *ToolTips*) too. On the Mac, there's an Info line on the button bar. (On the button bar set up, Mac users can also choose to show button balloons.)

ClarisWorks allows you to edit any button bar, removing the ones you don't use often and add new buttons. We show you all about editing buttons and button bars in the Appendix.

You may not always see all the buttons on your current button bar. Some may be hiding. To check or remedy this, move your mouse to the bottom of the button bar until your pointer becomes a double-headed arrow. Click and drag downward to expand the number of rows on your bar. (If the bar is at the side of your screen, the double-headed arrow appears at the inside edge and you drag inward.) Once you adjust a specific button bar, you don't have to do so again, unless you add more buttons to form another row.

One of the best things you can do is create your own task bar to launch your frequently used documents or connect to Web sites you access often. Refer to the Appendix — when you're ready for this.

Tools

Tools do exactly what their name implies — get things done. You can access the standard Tool Panel anytime in the word processor, spreadsheet, draw, and paint environments. When using a database document, the standard Tool Panel is available only when you are designing a layout — and special database tools are available at other times. None of these tools apply to communications documents, so showing tools in the communications environment brings up other, communications-oriented stuff instead.

If the tools are hidden, just click the Tool Toggle button in the lower-left corner of the window to show them or select Window⇨Show Tools.

When you use the paint environment, an extra set of painting tools is added to the standard Tool Panel. Both versions of the Tool Panel are shown in Figure 2-6. Notice the eight extra painting tools. We go over each tool in detail in Part III as each comes up.

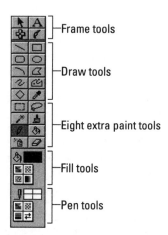

Frame tools

Draw tools

Eight extra paint tools

Fill tools

Pen tools

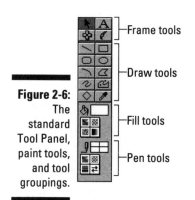

Frame tools

Draw tools

Figure 2-6:
The
standard
Tool Panel,
paint tools,
and tool
groupings.

Fill tools

Pen tools

Frame tools

The frame tools are the four tools at the very top of the standard Tool Panel. You use these tools to create or edit a frame within a document. Frames are the secret to the ClarisWorks magic. You hear a lot more about them as we cover each function of ClarisWorks. For now, here are some quick descriptions and a few tips and pointers.

Arrow pointer — the left-pointing arrow

 This is the left-pointing arrow that looks like your standard mouse pointer. Use this tool to select, move, and resize frames or graphics you made with the draw tools. (Are you thinking you've caught us in an error because the pointer looks different on the Windows and Mac platforms? Uh uh. Claris made their arrow pointers look right for each platform.)

The arrow pointer is the secret key to the power of ClarisWorks. When you use the arrow pointer to click a frame or a drawn object, you are selecting it as an object. Keep the mouse held down and you can drag the frame, as an object, within your document. But when you double-click a frame or drawn object, it enters the environment within the frame. Each time you change environments, the pointer changes. For example, if you want to edit a spreadsheet frame and you are using the selection pointer, click twice in the spreadsheet frame to edit the data in the cells. The first click selects the frame, and the second changes the pointer to the spreadsheet tool.

 You know any object (or frame) is selected because four (or eight) small, black boxes appear at its corners. They are called *handles*. Clicking a handle and dragging it resizes the object or frame. Be careful with resizing: It can distort graphics and add or delete rows and columns to spreadsheets. For proportional graphic resizing, press Shift before you click the handle and hold as you resize.

Text tool — the letter A

 Clicking the text tool changes your pointer to an I-beam. Use the I-beam to position the text insertion cursor, which, in a word-processing environment, allows you to enter new text or select text. The I-beam is also used to place a text frame within a drawing or spreadsheet document. All you do is click it, move your mouse (don't drag) onto your document, and then click and drag within the document to define your text area.

The text insertion cursor, or *the cursor* as its friends call it, is the flashing vertical line that tells you where the each character you type will appear in your document. Characters you type always appear to the left of the cursor and push that cursor to the right.

 Text frames can be handy even when you're already in a word-processing document. They allow you to add a caption to a graphic or a spreadsheet frame that is independent of the body of text, enabling you to move it along with the graphic or spreadsheet frame. To add a text frame to a word-processing document, choose the text tool and press the Option key (Mac) or Alt key (Windows) as you drag to create the frame.

Text frames act differently in a painting environment. As soon as text is entered, it turns into paint-type pixels, and cursor-type editing is no longer available.

Spreadsheet tool — fat plus sign

 The spreadsheet tool enables you to create or edit spreadsheet frames. Spreadsheets are most commonly added into word-processing or drawing documents to create tables, reflect calculations, or create charts or graphs. To add a spreadsheet frame to a document, click the tool, move your mouse (don't drag) onto your document; then click and drag within the document to define your spreadsheet.

Spreadsheets act differently in a painting environment. You can enter data into cells initially, but clicking outside of the spreadsheet turns that spreadsheet into paint-type pixels; editing is no longer available. Instead, create spreadsheets in their native environment; then paste them into the paint environment.

 If you are working in a spreadsheet document, holding down the Option key (Mac) or Alt key (Windows) while dragging the spreadsheet tool creates a spreadsheet frame. The frame can be placed anywhere on the document because it's not tied to a specific cell. See Part IV of this book for more information on spreadsheets.

Paint tool — the thin paint brush

 As you've probably figured out by now, the paint tool is for creating a paint environment within your document (unless you're already in a paint document, of course). All you do is click it, move your mouse (don't drag) onto your document, and then click and drag within the document to define your painting area. After the area is defined, special paint tools appear in your Tool Panel. From there, you select your specific paint tool and create to your heart's content.

Draw tools

The ten draw tools are elite because they are almost always available. Unlike the word-processing, paint, and spreadsheet tools, the draw tools don't need a frame to make them active. Whenever you select a draw tool, you automatically switch to the draw environment. You can simply create objects wherever you want them. Look back at Figure 2-6 to see the draw tools. We look at them in detail in Chapters 10 and 12.

Paint tools

The paint tools appear only when you use the paint environment. If you're an artist, you'll become very familiar with them. If you're a business user, you may never even see them. In Chapters 9–11, we talk more about them.

Pen and fill palettes

The pen and fill palettes are used when working in the draw and paint environments. These palettes are tear-off menus, which means that you can use them like pop-up menus on the Tool Panel or you can tear off the palette and move it around the screen.

The fill palettes let you change the fill color and/or pattern of a draw or paint object. You can also use one of the fill palettes to fill an object with a *gradient,* where one color fades into another inside the object, or a texture. The pattern and texture palettes are editable. The pen palettes let you control the thickness, color, and pattern of lines and borders around shapes or lines. You can also make an arrowhead appear at one or both ends of a straight line. More on this in Chapter 10.

Menu Tricks

The menus in ClarisWorks work pretty much like they do in any other program. They just do tricks from time to time, changing to suit what you're working on. We want to make sure you're comfortable with this.

Magical morphing menus

Probably the most confusing thing for new ClarisWorks users is that the menu bar changes when you change environments. Which menus appear in the menu bar depends on what you are doing. Because of this, you may find yourself thinking, "Hey, just a minute ago, I had Font, Size, and Style menus, and now they're gone!" In that case, you've changed from the word-processing environment to one of the others. Font options are still available, but they aren't a priority, so they are submenus under the Format menu.

We promise you'll get used to these ever-changing menus. They're a good thing and really cool after you're used to them. For more information on the specific menu options in each environment, skip to the chapters that describe each ClarisWorks environment.

Your pointer is the key to knowing which environment you're in.

Menu constants

No matter which environment you work in, three menus are always in the menu bar: the File, Edit, and Window menus. We don't want to go off on long, boring descriptions of what every command under every menu does — and you probably don't want us to. Instead, we just do a quick overview of the sorts of things you can expect to find in these menus. The rest of the book explains how to use the commands in the menus, presented in the context of trying to get something done rather than in the abstract.

The File menu

This menu's commands don't put all your papers in the filing cabinet for you, but they do help you handle your ClarisWorks documents. The File menu is where you work with your document in a very general way — opening it, saving changes, printing it, or closing ClarisWorks down. In case you mess up, it also has the Revert command, which puts your document back to how it was the last time you saved it. The File menu also has commands for inserting other documents into yours and merging database information into your document. Don't worry if you're not familiar with some of these things; we cover each as it is called for throughout the book.

The Edit menu

The Edit menu contains everything you need to edit your documents. You may not think this is a big deal, but some applications scatter edit-type commands like spell checking all over the place in arcane menus so you never know where to find them.

The queen of the Edit menu is the Undo command. This miracle command can undo the very last thing you did in ClarisWorks. If you accidentally click somewhere and screw up your document, use Undo to fix it. There's a catch, though. It only undoes the very last action you took, so if it took you ten steps to muck up your document, you still have to deal with the first nine on your own (unless you can use File⇨Revert).

In addition to the standards such as Cut, Copy, and Paste, the Edit menu is home to the spell checker and replacement feature. Look for them in the Writing Tools submenu.

The Window menu

We prefer a view of the Matterhorn. Alas, this menu doesn't let you choose what you see out of your room's window, but it does help you work with ClarisWorks windows. It lets you arrange windows on-screen, bring open documents to the front, and show or hide the tools, panels, button bar, and ruler. The Window menu is also where you access the Slide Show command, to display your document as an on-screen slide show or presentation. Read more about Slide Shows in Chapter 14.

Page Setup or Print Setup

Whether it's called Page Setup or Print Setup, this command not only tells the computer how to print your document, it also sets up your page. If, when you open your new document, you like the page's orientation, never mind. Otherwise, use this command.

In Page Setup lingo, portrait is vertical (tall) and landscape is horizontal (wide). Most of the time, you want portrait. For a spreadsheet with many columns or a draw document with a wide picture, choose landscape.

By the way, A-4 is the British parallel to 8 ½ x 11 and B-4 is similar to legal-size paper.

From here, you also choose paper size and paper source. On the Mac, you can also enlarge or reduce your image. In Windows, this box leads to several other printer-related options. Anytime you change printers, come back here, make sure it all looks right, and then click OK. This tells ClarisWorks about your new printer.

Saving Your Work

We're putting save immediately after Page Setup for a reason: As soon as you begin your document and enter something worth keeping, save it! Simply select File⊅Save. This brings up the Save dialog box shown in Figure 2-7. Type a name for your document, but don't be so quick to click Save! First take a good look at where you're saving to. In this case, the Letters folder, wherever that is.

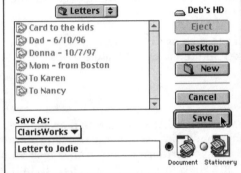

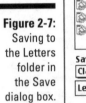

Figure 2-7:
Saving to
the Letters
folder in
the Save
dialog box.

The keyboard shortcut for Save is ⌘-S (Mac) or Ctrl+S (Windows). Make this a reflex! You'll hear tons of advice on when to save. We say, whenever you do something you like, save it! Not only will you be grateful in the event of a power outage or a computer freeze . . . the best part is that when you are totally mucked up, you can simply use File⊅Revert to revert to your last saved version.

Where to save?

When it's time to save your work, a dialog box allows you to specify where you want to save your document. Paying attention to where the document gets saved is *really* important. The first time you save a particular document and whenever you choose the Save As command, the Save dialog box appears. Never mind where *ClarisWorks* wants to save your work. Before you click Save, navigate to where *you* want it to go.

To avoid a nightmare when you reinstall or update any program, *never* store documents in the folder that contains a program. Instead, create a logical filing system that helps you find your work. Create new folders by project to store your documents. Mac users should make sure not to store anything in the System folder. Windows users should make subfolders in the My Documents folder for all documents.

Save versus Save As

After you save your document initially, use the Save command to include any changes you have made since your last save. The Save dialog box is not displayed because you are just updating the same document. Use Save As when you want to create a new document to work on and safely put away the version you have so far. Give the new version a different name so it doesn't replace the first version.

For example, perhaps on Monday you create a new document and save it with the name "Frank's Doc." You work on that file on Tuesday and Wednesday and save your changes as you go each day. If you save your document using the Save command, come Thursday you have one file named Frank's Doc that includes all of the changes you've made so far. But if you save your work once a day, using the Save As command and name each document with a version number, you'd have three files: Frank's Doc1, Frank's Doc2, and Frank's Doc3. In this way, Save As lets you keep a history of changes you made to a document or use a previously saved document as a starting point for creating a new document without changing the original.

Don't use Save As unless you specifically want to have separate documents. If you create several documents with the same material and same name, especially if you don't pay attention to where you save them, you are bound to have a hard time knowing which is the one you were working on last.

Saving in other file formats

Another option in the Save dialog box is saving your document in another format. For example, you can save a word-processing document as a WordPerfect document to give to a friend. When you conjure up the Save dialog box, you see a pop-up menu offering several file types. The default is ClarisWorks (as shown back in Figure 2-7). To choose another file type, just select it from the pop-up of choices, then name your new document, and Save as usual.

Saving as stationery

If you find yourself setting up the same document formats over and over or retyping the same information again and again, try saving a document as Stationery. A document saved as stationery always remains intact. Instead of opening that document, ClarisWorks actually opens a new, untitled copy — the original is never changed. It's like designing a form for a tear-off pad: Each time you open a stationery document, you tear off a form from the pad to fill out with new information. Some people — and programs — call this document a *template*. Same thing.

To create stationery, set up the elements that should always appear in future documents. Constant elements may include headers and footers, a logo and company information at the top of the first page, return address information, and "boilerplate" text such as a standard greeting and closing. Set your font and font size as desired. Be sure to position your cursor exactly where you want it to be when the new document opens.

After all common elements are in place, choose File⇨Save As. Type a name for your template. Then set the document type to Stationery. In Windows, it's a pop-up choice like all the other type options. On the Mac, click the radio button next to the icon labeled Stationery.

After you decide where to save your new template, give it a name, set the document type to Stationery, and click Save.

 If you want your template to appear in the stationery list in the New Document dialog box, save it in the folder named ClarisWorks Stationery. On the Mac, ClarisWorks saves there automatically. Some people prefer to save stationery into a separate folder and open the stationery from that folder whenever they need it. Better yet, place that folder under the Start menu (in Windows) or under the menu (on the Mac).

 One piece of stationery that's very powerful is a default document you can create that opens whenever you open a new document of that type. For example, to set up a new drawing document, turn off the Grid and Autogrid. Turn on Page View and Rulers. Set the rules to text for handy text editing. Then — this is the key — call it **ClarisWorks DR Options** and save it as stationery to the stationery folder. Every new draw document comes up with those settings. Don't like them? Change the settings and save the document as a new Stationery or replace the old template. You can have one template (or stationery) for each environment. Just substitute the DR with WP for the word-processing default, PT for the paint document default, SS for spreadsheet, DB for database, or CM for communication.

Printing Documents

Computers are supposed to create a paperless world, but we often need to present our work on paper. To print, you basically just go to File⇨Print or use ⌘-P (Mac) or Ctrl+P (Windows). However, that assumes your target printer is already selected. In case it isn't already selected as your default printer, read the following sections.

Select your target printer

You can print to any printer that's hooked up to your computer or network. In order to select it, though, it has to be turned on and ready to print.

Choosing a printer on a Mac is pretty simple. If there are icons of your printers on your desktop and your target printer has a black outline, it is already selected. If the icon is on your desktop but not selected, click the target printer once, and select Set Default Printer (⌘-L) in the Printing menu that appears. (If you want one full copy printed, without opening your document, drag the icon for your document onto the icon of your printer. If you don't have a desktop printer icon, choose ⌘⇨Chooser; then select the printer and close the Chooser window.)

Here's how to select your target printer in Windows:

1. **From the Print dialog box, click Setup.**

2. **From the Print Setup dialog box that appears next, select the printer from the pop-up Name list.**

   You can check your page setup from there, too.

3. **Click OK.**

How many, please?

If you want to print one copy of the entire document, just call up the Print dialog box and click Print on the Mac or OK in Windows. To print multiple copies, enter the number in the Copies box.

To print just one page, type the same page number in the From and To boxes. For example, for page three, From: 3 To: 3 should be displayed. To print from a certain page through the end of the document, type the starting page in the From box and leave the To box empty. To print up to a certain page number, enter that number in the To box and leave From empty.

In each printer's print dialog box you also find the option to print only the left or right pages. An example of when this is handy is when creating a presentation. See Chapter 14 to get the idea.

Document Passwords — Security for All

At any point in a document's life, you may decide you're more comfortable assigning a password so prying, or curious, eyes won't see what they shouldn't. Any ClarisWorks document can be assigned a password at any time. You can also change the password as needed — as long as you know the current word.

To add a password, select File⇨Document Summary. Click the Set Password button. A dialog box comes up, asking you to enter the password to use. Type it in and click OK. The same dialog box comes up again. ClarisWorks isn't being dense — just careful. Enter your password a second time to ensure you typed it correctly.

The next time anyone tries to open that document, ClarisWorks requires the password.

If you want to change your password, follow these steps:

1. **Choose File⇨Document Summary.**

2. **Enter your current password in the first dialog box; then click OK.**

3. **Enter your new password in the second dialog box, and then click OK.**

   Each dialog box looks exactly the same, which may be confusing.

4. **Enter your current password again in the third dialog box; then click OK.**

5. **Click OK to leave the Document Summary dialog box.**

Closing the Program

When you're ready to call it a day and put ClarisWorks to bed, just choose File⇨Quit or ⌘-Q on the Mac, or File⇨Exit or Ctrl+Q in Windows. That's it. Don't worry about closing up all the windows you have open — ClarisWorks asks if you want to save changes to any open documents before closing them.

Chapter 3

Help: It's Not Just a Beatles Movie Anymore

In This Chapter

▶ Using help for Macs

▶ Using help for Windows

▶ Getting moving with stationery

▶ Letting Business*Basics* give you the business

▶ Getting "Assistants" from ClarisWorks

*I*sn't there a famous saying about help coming in all shapes and sizes? If not, there should be. Within ClarisWorks, you can use several different types of help. The traditional help tells you how to use ClarisWorks, and a different type of help starts your documents or even custom-creates documents for you. Thus, we begin our magical mystery ClarisWorks Help tour.

Helping You Use ClarisWorks

As you use ClarisWorks, you'll undoubtedly have questions — that's why you bought this book. You have a few options for finding answers to your questions. The first is to look here. We like that and we wanna help. The second is to check the Claris online help (on-screen, not on the Web, in this case). The third is to use the other Claris online help — the Web kind. Claris keeps their paper manual short, building their help directly into the program instead. So here's how to use this on-screen help.

At the right end of the ClarisWorks menus is the Help menu. Not surprisingly, you find the built-in help there.

Using ClarisWorks help

The ClarisWorks Help menu actually hosts more than the help you usually expect in a manual. The Help menu also provides an overall introduction to ClarisWorks and to ClarisWorks Assistants. (And, in Windows, help tells you about your version of ClarisWorks. Mac users can find this information under the menu instead.)

Claris does a fabulous job of making ClarisWorks behave similarly on the Mac and in Windows. Because help systems are more a reflection of the platform, help looks and acts differently between platforms. Don't let this throw you. This entire book is not going to be Mac this and Windows that. We promise.

ClarisWorks help is actually a separate application, opened whenever you select the Help command. It remains open until you close it, so if you plan to use it a lot, keep it running.

Mac help

The Mac Help menu has several elements. Figure 3-1 shows you examples of each. Here's what they do:

- ✔ **About help:** Believe it or not, this is a help file about getting help. Honest. If we don't make everything clear enough, check this out.

- ✔ **Show Balloons:** Balloons? Yep. One of the Mac programmers must've had a fondness for comic books. With balloon help on, you point to an item on-screen and a cartoon-style text balloon appears with a brief explanation of what that item is or does. Help⇨Show Balloons turns them on. The menu then toggles to Hide. Help⇨Hide Balloons turns them off.

- ✔ **Frequently Asked Questions:** Frequently Asked Questions provides answers to frequently asked How-do-I?, Why-Can't-I?, and other Why-type questions. It not only answers questions — it also shows you how to do things! Simply double-click a question, answer any questions posed, and do as it says. This stuff is smart! (That's because it uses the Mac's interactive AppleGuide interface.)

- ✔ **ClarisWorks Help Contents:** This menu item takes you to the main Help menu by topic. (You can also use the Help key to arrive here.) Clicking a blue, underlined topic jumps you to related information. Clicking a dotted, underlined word brings up a definition of the underlined word to help you understand the sentence better. You can also enter a keyword to search for, or jump to the index.

- ✔ **ClarisWorks Help Index:** This menu item brings you directly to the Help index, an alphabetical listing of all Help topics, keywords, and terms. Type the first couple of letters in the index window to jump to entries starting with those letters. When you see your topic, double-click it to jump to its details.

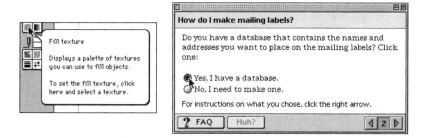

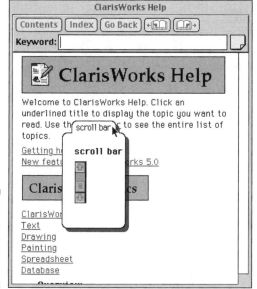

Figure 3-1:
Balloons,
an Apple-
Guide, and
QuickHelp.

✔ **Introduction to ClarisWorks:** This menu item launches the "Introduction to ClarisWorks" — an overview of what ClarisWorks can do.

✔ **ClarisWorks Assistants:** Assistants are a whole other kind of help. They don't teach you; they do things for you. See "Using Help menu Assistants" later in this chapter.

From any dialog box, you can access the exact help you need by clicking the question mark icon in that window. This takes you directly to help that is specific to that dialog box's topic.

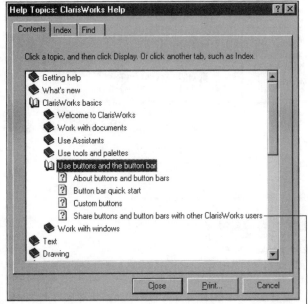

Figure 3-2a:
ClarisWorks
Windows
help.

Double-clicking this...

opens the help topic.

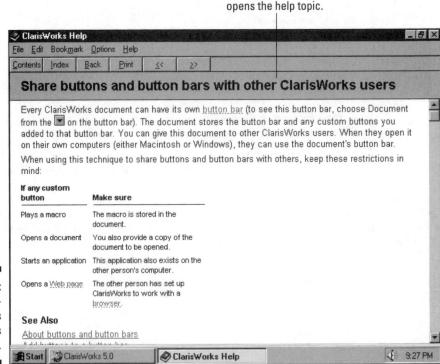

Figure 3-2b:
A Claris-
Works
Windows
help topic.

Windows help

The Windows Help menu has several elements. Here's what they do:

- ✓ **ClarisWorks Help Contents:** This menu item takes you to the list of help contents. The various topics look like folders. Double-clicking any folder reveals all related subtopics, as shown in Figures 3-2a and 3-2b. Double-clicking one of them brings you to further details. You are then presented with links (underlined green topics) to related topics. Click any link to explore further. Or click a tab at the top to return to Contents, explore the Index, go forward or backward through topics, or print the topic.

- ✓ **ClarisWorks Help Index:** This menu item takes you to the Index tab of the help topics. In the top box, type the first letters of what you seek. When you see what you want in the box below, double-click it. If there are further options, a window presents them. Double-click the one you want or press Cancel.

- ✓ **Introduction to ClarisWorks:** This menu item launches the "Introduction to ClarisWorks" — an overview of what ClarisWorks can do.

- ✓ **ClarisWorks Assistants:** These are a whole other kind of help. They don't teach you; they do things for you. See "Using Help Menu Assistants" later in this chapter.

- ✓ **About ClarisWorks:** This menu item brings up the ClarisWorks splash screen, providing information about the version you are using, some of your computer information, and software creation credits.

In Windows, ClarisWorks Help Contents and ClarisWorks Help Index actually take you to the same Help application. This application presents you with three tabs that, in turn, take you to the best type of help. Regardless of which one you select from the Help menu, you can click any of the three tabs at the top to search by Contents or Index, or do a more specific Find.

Help tips for all

Check out these tips for using either Help system:

- ✓ Add an electronic bookmark for a topic, using the commands in the Bookmark menu. A bookmark puts that topic into the Bookmark menu for fast access. For even faster access, Windows users can use the underlined number assigned as a shortcut. Mac users can also assign ten bookmarks as shortcuts, using the Bookmarks⇨Edit Bookmarks menu items.

- ✓ Use the Find commands to search for a specific word or phrase in the Help system. Windows users click a tab to get to Find. Mac users have QuickHelp's Find menu.

- ✓ Print the text of a topic with File⇨Print.

> ✔ Mac users can also do note-taking. Just click the sticky note and drag it onto the Help window. Type any notes you like, move the sticky anywhere on the page, and it stays where you put it for future reference. Use the Return key to break up your note into short lines.

Help, help on the Web

For the most up-to-the-minute help, you can also access Claris technical support on the Web via a button on your default button bar. This button connects you to the Web (if you have an Internet connection available) and takes you directly to the Claris Tech Support Home Page. From there, you have access to any update information, some update downloads, and responses to timely questions. Most importantly, you have access to the fully searchable TechInfo Database — the same database that the Claris technical support team uses to help when you phone them.

Doing It for You

ClarisWorks help is great for showing you how things work and how to do it yourself. But there are times when it's just plain silly to do something yourself — especially when it has already been done for you. And with stationery, it *has* been done for you.

Using ClarisWorks stationery

ClarisWorks *stationery* are premade documents. When you open a stationery document, you actually open an automatically generated copy, so the original remains intact. The copy you create may be saved or discarded independent of the original. The stationery documents that come with ClarisWorks include business letters, address lists, and presentations. You can use stationary right away by filling in your own information, or customize the stationary to suit your needs.

To select a stationary account, follow these steps:

1. **Select File⇨New.**

   This takes you to the New Document dialog box.

2. **Click the Use Assistant or Stationery radio button.**

   This brings up the list box as shown to the left in Figure 3-3. Notice that it says All Assistants when it comes up.

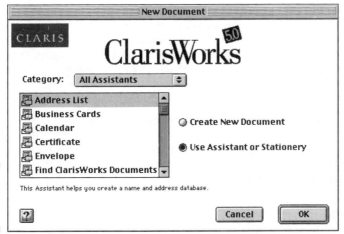

Figure 3-3:
Picking
stationery.

3. **Click in the Category pop-up menu and select All Stationery.**

   All stationery documents now appear in the scrolling window. The icon at the left of each item tells you what type of document it is. Scroll to the one you want.

4. **Click once on your stationery choice and then click OK. (Better yet, double-click directly on the stationery's name.)**

   Your new document opens, ready for you to work with it. Directions are incorporated into each document.

JIAN BusinessBasics

In addition to the stationery Claris has for everyone, Claris called in the big guns to meet your business needs. JIAN Business*Basics,* Claris Edition stationery is a collection of stationery documents designed specifically to help you with the most commonly needed areas of business. Business*Basics* includes templates for creating letters, documents, checklist forms, and so on. To make it easier to find what you need, JIAN's stationery falls into one of the following three categories, which is how you find them in the pop-up menu in the New Document window. To see the entire list of Business*Basics* stationery, select All Stationery and then JIAN Business*Basics* Index. This brings up a document that describes each stationery and provides links to it.

With each document you open in JIAN Business*Basics,* you find notes and sample data to guide you. All sample data is in blue so you know which data to replace with your own. Alerts are in red. To give you an idea of what you can find in each category, the following list describes some of the most important samples:

✔ **Finance and accounting:** Samples devoted to finance and accounting include the 3 Year Financial Comparison spreadsheet for computing liabilities, assets, income, and revenues for a three-year period. The Company Operating Budget spreadsheet helps you prepare annual budgets. The Promissory Note letter forms a loan agreement. The Cash Receipts Procedure and Check Acceptance Procedure help you to establish a company policy for handling cash and checks.

✔ **Management and operations:** Samples devoted to management and operations include a Trademark Tracking Worksheet, which helps you record the ways you use your trademarks or servicemarks. Action Planning Guidelines is a word-processing document that aids you in company planning. The Commercial Lease is a lease agreement that you can customize for your business leasing needs.

✔ **Sales and marketing:** Samples devoted to sales and marketing include the Direct Mail Analysis form, which computes your costs for a direct-mail campaign. The Competitive Checklist is designed as a comprehensive plan for competitive analysis and tactical response. The Retail Merchandising Budget spreadsheet helps you prepare merchandising budgets.

Remember one thing, though: These forms are designed for U.S. use and are not state-specific. Use them as guidelines, starting points, and samples, not as legal agreements.

Using ClarisWorks Assistants

Two types of Assistants are standing by to serve you. The Assistants that you access from the New Document dialog box create brand new documents for you. The Assistants that you access from the Help menu perform specific tasks to help you with a document you are already working on. Here, we talk about the new document creators.

These ClarisWorks Assistants are like "smart stationery." As you use an Assistant, you create a new document by providing information about how you want the document to look and what you want it to say. The Assistant, after asking, one or more "pages" of questions, creates a new custom template tailored to your needs. Assistants are available for creating several types of documents. You can select an Assistant via the New Document dialog box, or select one from the Assistant button bar. (To get to the Assistant buttons, you can switch button bars by clicking the arrow at the left of the button bar and selecting Assistant from the list of buttons.)

An Assistant may have a page or more of questions. At the end of the questioning, the Next button changes to a Create button. For example, look at the Envelope Assistant shown in Figure 3-4 asking for the name and address of the envelope's addressee. The Envelope Assistant has three pages of questions: You provide the addressee, the return address, and the printer setup selection. When you click the Create button, the Assistant presents you with your document, as shown in Figure 3-5. (We discuss the Envelope Assistant further in Chapter 13.)

To see a list of all stationery available to you, viewed by topic, select All Stationery; then select any one that says . . . Index. This brings up a document that describes each stationery, each with a link to a fresh new piece of that stationery.

Using Help menu Assistants

Help menu Assistants actively aid you with tasks that apply to the document you are working in, rather than with the task of creating a new document. When you choose ClarisWorks Assistants from the Help menu, you have a choice of one or more of these:

- ✔ **Address Envelope:** Available in the text environment. It's best to use the regular Envelope Assistant first. Otherwise, it just takes the address you select within your document and places it in the middle of a new, non-envelope-sized document.

- ✔ **Insert Footnote:** This most powerful and useful Assistant works from within the main body of a text document to add a footnote to the bottom of the document you are in. You can select from a variety of footnote styles, including a custom format.

- ✔ **Make Table:** Automates the process of making a table. Available within the word-processing and draw environments. The table can be placed with your line of text, or as an object.

- ✔ **Paragraph Sorter:** This quickie works within any text environment. Select the paragraphs to sort, choose this Assistant, select a sort method, and then let it work its magic.

- ✔ **Create Labels:** Available within a database. After your database is up and running, select this Assistant to help you create labels from your data.

Now you've got all types of help whenever you need it. You've got us. You've got Claris. What more could you ask for? Umm . . . never mind.

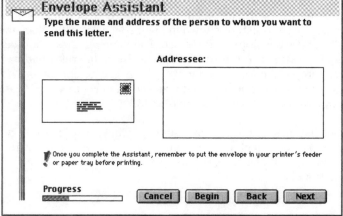

Figure 3-4:
The Create
Envelope
Assistant
working
its way
toward a
personalized
envelope
template.

Figure 3-4:
The Create
Envelope
Assistant
working
its way
toward a
personalized
envelope
template.

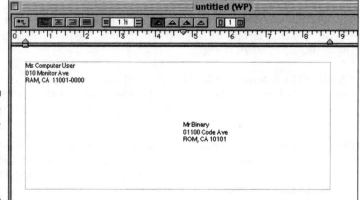

Figure 3-5:
Your
envelope,
ready to
print, stuff,
and stamp.

Part II
Working with Text: The Keys to Success

The new desktop publishing software not only lets Rags produce a professional looking greeting card quickly and inexpensively, but it also allows him to say it his way.

©RICHTENNANT

ARF!!
Whooof arf!

Arf, arf, arf

In this part . . .

Whether you're new to word processing or have been doing it a while, there's stuff for you to discover here. ClarisWorks is a powerful word processor. This part not only shows you the basics of working with text, but how to do some fun stuff as well.

Would you like some graphics to jazz up your pages? How about free-rotated graphics — and free-rotated text! Need to add a table or chart to your document? No problem. How about an outline? That's a great place to have your presentations and such grow from. It's all easy in ClarisWorks — and all right here in this part.

Chapter 4

The Word Processor: It's Not Your Father's Smith Corona

In This Chapter

▶ Deciding when to use a word-processing document

▶ Typing text

▶ Moving through your document

▶ Selecting, deleting, and replacing chunks of text

▶ Cutting, copying, pasting, and undoing

▶ Using spaces, tabs, and returns correctly

▶ Figuring out the Equation Editor

*T*he word-processing environment of ClarisWorks is probably the most used of all the environments. In this chapter, we cover the basic word-processor functions — the baby steps of text entry on a computer. If you are accustomed to a typewriter, you have to start over and unlearn some habits that don't translate very well to the computer world. If you never learned to type, this chapter helps you figure out how to put words where you want them on the screen. After all, you have to crawl before you can walk!

When to Use Word-Processing Documents

When should you use a word-processing document as opposed to another kind? As a rule of thumb, choose word processing as your main environment when the bulk of your document is text — for example, a letter or report. Sometimes your master environment is obvious; at other times you can go with one of two or more environments. A case in point would be a newsletter, which is an obvious candidate for the word-processing environment but is much cooler within the drawing environment.

When you sit down to write to mom or create the great American novel, go for a new word-processing document. And when you're not totally sure, go for word processing. It's a cinch to copy the text and paste it into any other document later on, so you can't go wrong.

Entering Text

Before you can process words, you have to get the words into your computer. So that's the natural place to start.

The insertion point

When you begin a new word-processing document, you are presented with a page containing only a thin blinking line. Your creation is waiting to happen. To put your pen to paper (metaphorically speaking), simply begin typing.

The job of the blinking line is to let you know where your text will appear. You may hear this called the *insertion point*. We prefer its friendlier name — *the cursor*.

Every time you type a character, you push the cursor farther toward the end of the document. In other words, whatever you type appears to the left of the cursor.

The keyboard

Unless you have a fancy speech-to-text dictation program, you use a keyboard to enter text into your computer. You don't need to know how to type to use a computer, but knowing how to type makes things a lot easier. If your typing skills are nil, treat yourself to a typing instruction program.

For the most part, all keyboards are the same. However, PC users use the Ctrl and Alt keys near the space bar, while Macs use the ⌘ (Command) and Option keys. We make your key commands clear throughout this book so that you won't be confused. The key you press to go to a new line or paragraph is called Enter by PC users and Return by Mac people. Because its function is to create a new line, like the Return key on a typewriter, we use Return. When doing data entry, another key comes into play: the Enter key on the number pad. Luckily, this is marked Enter for everyone. (On some laptops, this is squeezed next to the space bar.) We call that the Enter key. Just get to know the keyboard you use most, and you'll be fine.

Text wrap

No, text wrap isn't a new, more intellectual style of gangsta music. Text wrap is what happens when you reach the end of a line when entering text. If you learned to type on a manual Underwood, you may remember smacking the carriage return when your line approached the right side of the paper. In more modern times, you may have used an electric typewriter with a Return key. Entire days of typing class were spent hitting Return at the end of a line. Now you get to unlearn that. In a word-processing document, the computer magically transports any word that doesn't fit to the next line. Pressing Return at the end of every line is not only unnecessary, it is bad and can cause you problems later.

Do not press the Return key at the end of a line. The only appropriate time for Return is when you want to end one paragraph and begin a new one. In word processing, returns are for paragraphs, not lines.

Navigating the Seas of Text

The best thing about using a computer, instead of a typewriter or paper, is that you can get all your thoughts out while they're hot in your head. Then, after you let them all flow out, you can go back, organize, edit, and rethink to your heart's content. This is the true power of word processing. So get ready for a brave new world. Break those habits. And have fun!

For the mousy type

Before the mouse was invented, the only way to move around in your document was to use the arrow or page scroll keys, pressing and pressing until you finally got where you needed to be. The mouse makes it easy to jump anywhere, anytime. It takes a bit of getting used to, but hang in there. In a short time, you'll be hooked.

Have you done a bit of mousing on-screen? Start a word-processing document and notice that when you move the pointer into the text area of the document, the pointer changes to what's known as the I-beam pointer, shown in Figure 4-1. We call this cursor the *I-beam* because it looks like a cross section of a steel I-beam used in construction.

The I-beam is a type of pointer that places the cursor at a different location on the screen. To move the cursor, move the I-beam to where you want the cursor to be, and then click the mouse button to place the cursor. For maximum speed, use the up and down scrollbar to move between pages, and then click the I-beam to place the cursor on that page.

Figure 4-1:
The Pointer
and I-beam
cursors on
the left are
from a PC;
the cursors
on the right
are from
the Mac.

Pointers

I-beams

The I-beam is a guideline, not the actual cursor. You have to click to place the cursor in your document. If you just position the I-beam and start typing, your text appears where the cursor really is, which is not necessarily where your I-beam is! Remember: Click to place the cursor.

Keyboard kicks

If you feel more efficient keeping your fingers on the keyboard, you can use the keyboard shortcuts instead of mousing. You can move the cursor with the keyboard using the four arrow keys. You can also use the modifier keys to affect how the arrow keys work. (See Table 4-1 for a list of modifications.)

Table 4-1	Moving the Cursor with the Keyboard	
To Do This	*Press This on a Mac*	*Press This in Windows*
Move right one character	→	→
Move left one character	←	←
Move up one line	↑	↑
Move down one line	↓	↓
Move right one word	Option-→	Ctrl+→
Move left one word	Option-←	Ctrl+←
Move to beginning of paragraph	Option-↑	Ctrl+↑
Move to end of paragraph	Option-↓	Ctrl+↓
Move to end of line	⌘-→	End

To Do This	Press This on a Mac	Press This in Windows
Move to beginning of line	⌘-←	Home
Move to beginning of document	⌘-↑	Ctrl+Home
Move to end of document	⌘-↓	Ctrl+End

You may also have four more keys to move you through a document. These keys work a little differently than the arrow keys:

- ✔ The **Home key** takes you to the beginning of your document if you're on a Mac and if you're using Windows.

- ✔ The **End key** takes you to the end of your document if you're on a Mac and if you're using Windows.

- ✔ The **Page Up** and **Page Down keys** move you up and down, a page at a time, through your document.

The Home, End, Page Up, and Page Down keys do *not* move the cursor. They only move your *view* to a different location in the document. If you push the End key and start typing, your text will *not* be added to the end of your document. Whatever you type will be inserted wherever you left the cursor — which is probably not where you want it. If you use these keys, remember to place the cursor before you start typing.

Selecting, Deleting, and Replacing Text

Selecting, deleting, and replacing text are very important to the editing process. So are chocolate, highlighters, and cola. We can help you with selecting, deleting, and replacing, but for the others . . . our publisher said no food was allowed in the bookstores. . . .

Selecting

Did your mom tell you that it pays to be selective? And then later, that you're too selective? Well, this is one of those cases where it does pay to be selective. You can't make a change to anything until you tell the computer what it is you want to change. In other words, if you want to make a change to your text, select it.

After you're used to positioning your cursor, you're halfway to selecting text. You can use the mouse or the keyboard, depending on your preference. When you select something, the background of the selection changes color to let you know what you have selected. This change of color is called highlighting.

Mouse selection

Here, now, for your computing pleasure, are some mighty mousing selection techniques:

- **Clicking:** One way to select things with the mouse is to click something — a lot:

  - *To select a word:* Double-click the word.

  - *To select a line:* Triple-click anywhere in the line.

  - *To select a paragraph:* Quadruple-click anywhere in the paragraph.

- **Dragging:** The most common way to select a chunk of text is to drag over it. To do this, position the I-beam cursor at one end of the chunk, click to kinda position the cursor, and then, holding the mouse button down, move (or *drag*) the I-beam to the opposite end. When the text is selected exactly to your liking, release the button. Don't release the mouse button until it's right. Until you release the button, you can always change it. Remember to begin at one end or the other. You can't begin in the center and go in two directions at once.

A faster way to select a long chunk is to position the I-beam at one end of what you want to select. Then release the mouse button and move the I-beam to the opposite end of your desired selection, press Shift and then click where you want the selection to end. All text between the two clicks is highlighted. You can make the first click, then scroll anywhere before positioning that last click. It's way faster than dragging over a long bunch of pages to select all that text. It even works from character to character, not just in whole word or whole line chunks. Pretty slick click trick, eh?

Keyboard selection riffs

The Shift key is also the secret, for both platforms, when you want to make a selection with the keyboard. Uh-oh, we feel a table coming on. It's Table 4-2, and it lists nifty key selections. You can also use the mouse and keyboard in combination to really gang up on your text. If you drag over a block of text and find that you forgot a word or picked up an extra space at the end, you can add or subtract from your selection with the keyboard combinations.

Table 4-2	Selecting Stuff with the Keyboard	
To Select	**Press This on a Mac**	**Press This in Windows**
Right, one letter at a time	Shift-→	Shift+→
Left, one letter at a time	Shift-←	Shift+←
Up, one line at a time	Shift-↑	Shift+↑
Down, one line at a time	Shift-↓	Shift+↓
Right, one word at a time	Shift-Option-→	Shift+Ctrl+→
Left, one word at a time	Shift-Option-←	Shift+Ctrl+←
From cursor to beginning of paragraph	Shift-Option-↑	Shift+Ctrl+↑
From cursor to end of paragraph	Shift-Option-↓	Shift+Ctrl+↓
From cursor to end of line	Shift-⌘-→	Shift+End
From cursor to beginning of line	Shift-⌘-←	Shift+Home
From cursor to beginning of document	Shift-⌘-↑	Shift+Ctrl+Home
From cursor to end of document	Shift-⌘-↓	Shift+Ctrl+End
Every bit of text in your document	⌘-A or Edit⇨Select All	Ctrl+A or Edit⇨Select All

Deleting

To completely erase your text, leaving not a trace, use the Delete key, located in the upper-right corner of the letter keys. On some keyboards, it is labeled Backspace and has an arrow pointing backwards. Don't be fooled by the word *Backspace*. It's not just going to move your cursor back. Its job is to remove all text it backs over.

The Delete key on the Mac is equivalent to the Backspace key on a PC. PCs also have a Delete key, however, and it deletes text to the right of the cursor. This is equivalent to the Mac key that has an X over a right-pointing arrow. Most people call this the *forward delete key*.

For greater efficiency, select the block you want to remove; then press Delete. The entire selection is removed from existence with one press of a button. Carried to the extreme, you can select all your text and clean out your entire document at once!

It's easy to select text, scroll to another part of the document, see something you want to delete, and press Delete without repositioning the cursor. This wipes out the block of text you previously selected, even though you don't see it on-screen. At least you'll have a clue, though — the section containing the cursor jumps into view — momentarily. Needless to say, that's a bad thing. Always make sure that you know where your cursor is before you delete. But, if you do accidentally delete something, use the Undo command *right away* to get it back. That's the Undo button on the default button bar or Edit⇨Undo, and we talk more about it in the next section.

Replacing is way cooler and faster than deleting. It's sort of an auto-delete. To replace a block of text with something new, don't waste a key action deleting the selected text. Just select the text you want to delete and start typing your new stuff. That's it. The selected text disappears and whatever you type appears in its place. You can do this with one character or an entire page.

Undoing, Cutting, Copying, and Pasting

These commands live happily together in the Edit menu ready to help you shuffle your text around.

Undo

If you happen to delete the wrong text, fear not! Don't press anything for a moment. Take a few deep breaths. Then click Undo on the default button bar or choose Edit⇨Undo. Your text returns as if nothing happened.

As its name implies, Undo undoes the last action you did. Don't get too comfortable, though. *Last* is the operative word. You get only one shot with Undo — right after you make a mistake. If you accidentally delete the wrong chunk of text, you can undo it right away. But, if you delete that text, type a few lines, and then realize you want the deleted text back, you're out of luck.

There are some things not even the magic Undo can help you with, though. For example, you cannot unsave a document. When you can't undo your last action, Undo is grayed out in the menu.

The Clipboard

When you cut something, whether it's text or graphics, it doesn't disappear into nothingness as when you delete. Instead, it is transferred to an invisible storage container called the Clipboard. The Clipboard lets you move and copy by combining the Cut or Copy command with the Paste command. By first cutting text out of your document and into the Clipboard, you can paste it back into a different spot. Or you can copy something, then paste it into several locations — not just one — to save typing or graphic creation. You can only have one thing on the Clipboard at a time, so whatever you've cut or copied to the Clipboard stays there until you replace it by cutting or copying something else. The really cool thing is that the contents of the Clipboard carry over to other applications, so you can copy and paste between documents running in two different programs!

Cut

If you took out your trusty shears and cut out a word from a printed document, it would be gone and you'd have the word waiting to be pasted elsewhere. That's the way Cut works on-screen, too — except you don't need the shears, which is good because they'd just scratch the screen anyway.

As with the Delete key, you first have to select what you want to cut. But that's where the similarity ends. When you delete, the text is removed from your document. Unlike deleting, cut text gets moved to a safe haven — the Clipboard.

To cut, select Edit⇨Cut or use ⌘-X (Mac) or Ctrl+X (Windows). The text you selected disappears.

Copy

Copy leaves your selected text where it is but makes a copy of it to paste into another location. Copy makes it easy to duplicate frequently used or difficult-to-type text. If only it worked with twenty-dollar bills!

To copy text, select it and choose Edit⇨Copy or use ⌘-C (Mac) or Ctrl+C (Windows). It doesn't look as if anything happens, but a copy of the selected text goes to the Clipboard to await a Paste command. (See the nearby sidebar for more information about the Clipboard.)

Paste

Paste takes whatever is in your Clipboard and places it into your document. Usually, you want to paste something in a different location from where you picked it up. After cutting or copying the desired text, just position the cursor where you want the text to appear and choose Edit⇨Paste. That's ⌘-V (Mac) or Ctrl+V (Windows).

You can also replace text using the Paste command. First, select the text you want to replace, and then choose Paste. Your selected text disappears and is replaced by whatever you previously cut or copied.

There's one more command, called Clear. Like Cut, it removes your text. But unlike Cut, it doesn't place it on the Clipboard. It's just gone . . . forever. Why use Clear? You use it only when you want to delete text but leave the contents of the Clipboard intact. Basically, it's just like using the Delete key. It isn't used very often.

This Cut, Copy, Paste, and Undo stuff is pretty universal. After you master it, you can use it almost anywhere.

Keyboard shortcuts

Have you noticed some of the menu commands have symbols and letter combinations to their right? These are called keyboard shortcuts. They are another way to choose a command. Keyboard shortcuts are quicker to use than choosing a command from a menu. We explain the shortcuts for Undo, Cut, Copy, and Paste in this sidebar. ClarisWorks has plenty more.

You don't have to memorize these shortcuts. They are listed in the menu every time you select a command. You can pick them up one at a time at your own pace.

Sometimes the shortcut key is the first letter of the command and sometimes it isn't. Basically, sometimes logical keys were available and sometimes they were already taken. Use these mnemonics to help you:

✔ **Z for Undo.** Zee what you did! Undo that right now! Also remember Z is the last letter of the alphabet and Undo only undoes the last thing you did.

✔ **X for Cut.** Think of it like x-ing out something, or the visual of an open pair of scissors.

✔ **C for Copy.** C is the first letter of the command, easy and logical!

✔ **V for Paste.** Well, you've got us on this one. Suffice it to say that this one is right next to all the rest.

You can drag and drop text (or graphics) between most documents and even between programs. This bypasses the Clipboard. Remember this when you want to copy a second object but leave the contents of the Clipboard untouched for further pasting.

Staying Out of Word Processor Hell (Spaces, Tabs, and Returns)

If you aren't into reading about formatting, we want at least to impress these major rules on you. These rules should be etched onto the front of every computer monitor.

Don't get spacey

Never, ever, use the spacebar to position text on the page. Using the spacebar to align text is one of the most common mistakes people make when they start using a word processor (almost as common as improperly using the Return key at the end of a line). While this worked on a typewriter, it fails on a computer. On the typewriter, the spacebar moves the carriage a set space. A computer has no need for physical carriage movement. Computer fonts use variable-width letters. For example, an *i* is narrower than a *w*. Therefore, no matter how many spaces you add to a column of text, unless the text in both lines is identical, you can't make the text line up. It may look right on-screen, due to the limitations of the screen, but on a printer, the funkiness shows up.

The rule of tabs

Tabs solve the problem of how to align text. A tab is always measured by how far it is from the margin. They are an exact measurement and therefore always line up, on-screen and in print. That brings us to another common mistake: pressing Tab several times in a row to indent text. The correct rule is one tab per indent or jump on a line. We go into more detail on this in Chapter 5.

The rule of returns

No, we're not talking about taking your computer back to the store when you get frustrated — although there are times when that option is tempting. Earlier in the chapter, we said not to press the Return key at the end of a line. That's what *text wrap* is for. It also keeps your text fresher longer. The only time to press the Return key is at the end of a paragraph. Think of the Return key as the "new paragraph key." Use it to create a new paragraph, and for that reason only.

Higher Math — the Equation Editor

We had a hard time deciding where to put this section on the Equation Editor. It's cool, powerful, and important — but it's not just for any one environment. Anyway, it landed here.

For those of you who work with high-end mathematical formulas, ClarisWorks licenses Equation Editor from Design Science and includes it right in the menus. The most common places to access it from are text areas, which place equations inline or as objects, as with any other inserted item, and drawing documents, where equations come in as objects. You can also access Equation Editor when creating a database layout. It appears as a part of the layout, not as data. It can't be used to enter data into a database field.

To insert an equation into a text area, follow these steps:

1. **Place your cursor where you want the equation to appear.**

2. **Choose Edit⇨Insert Equation.**

   A small window opens that contains several pop-up menus. The window offers any equation component you need, as well as a composition area which displays the cursor encased in a dotted rectangle. (That's the *field* or spaceholder where you enter your equation.)

3. **Click a pop-up menu and select a function, if one applies right away. If not, begin typing your equation.**

   As you check out the various equation components, notice that some components have dotted lines depicted. Those lines represent more fields to hold your numbers or letters.

   The formula you select pops into place in the main field.

4. **If your function has fields in it, enter the numbers or letters to complete that component.**

   To move from field to field, either use the mouse to position the cursor or press Tab.

5. **Continue to select equation elements or type your own data as needed.**

6. **Format your text.**

   Select any part of your formula to be formatted; then use the program's own menu commands. You should be able to find what you need. Look at the Format, Style, and Size menus.

7. **When you are done, close the Equation Editor window as you close any window — with the close box or X in the corner.**

8. **(Optional) After the formula is placed, adjust its baseline alignment.**

   Use the Format⇨Descent command to move the formula up or down on the line of text. (See "Aligning with the baseline" in Chapter 7 for more on this.)

   Your equation inserts itself into your document where your cursor was flashing when you opened the Equation Editor. The equation comes in selected. If you want to continue typing, click anywhere in your text document. Regardless of where you click, your cursor positions itself at the end of the text in that document. If you want to actually use that equation in another environment, because it came in preselected, use the Copy command to copy it, and then switch to your destination and issue the Paste command.

To insert an equation into a drawing document:

1. **Choose Edit⇨Insert Equation.**

2. **Follow Steps 2 through 7 in the previous list.**

   If the Editor window doesn't cover up your document, you may notice that, as the window opens, ClarisWorks creates a special object area in your document. That's where your equation drops into your document. Here's a trick: The object area places itself in the position that you last clicked with the arrow pointer.

   When you close the Equation Editor window, your equation places itself in your document preselected as an object, ready for placement.

Here are some additional tips about the Equation Editor:

- ✔ Equations can be copied and pasted into a painting.

- ✔ Equations can be edited. Double-click the equation to bring up the editor. (If you paste your equation into a paint document, it can't be edited.)

✔ Equations that are inline within text can be aligned with regard to the baseline, as can any object. See "Aligning with the baseline" in Chapter 7 for more on this.

✔ There is a *lot* to this program. Detailed online help can be found, when in the editor, under the Help menu. You can also find the information on MathType there.

Chapter 5

Fun with Text Formatting

● ●

In This Chapter

▶ Text preferences

▶ Formatting letters and words

▶ Shaping up sentences and paragraphs

▶ Stylizing pages and documents

● ●

*T*he combination of a good computer and good word-processing software makes it easy to format your text to look sharp. A variety of fonts, the use of boldface and italics, and all the other ways you can format text give you quite a bit of creative power. Do be careful, though; with so many formatting options, you may find yourself producing documents that look more like ransom notes. This chapter shows you how to format your text. We leave it to you to find your own level of grace and style.

Text Preferences

Preferences are more important here than anywhere else. In other places, they're convenient. Here, they're downright necessary — at least if you ever quote someone or use contractions. In word-processing documents, Preferences are your first line of formatting. They control how your quotation marks look, how the date appears when it's automatically entered, and more. Edit⇨Preferences is the magic door into the Preferences dialog box. If you open it now, you can follow along.

When you open Preferences from the word-processing environment, the Text preferences come up automatically. As shown in Figure 5-1, a pop-up menu allows you to select a category of preference settings to work with. If you're following along, but opened Preferences from another environment or without any document open, just click the Topic pop-up menu to get to the text preferences to see what we're talking about.

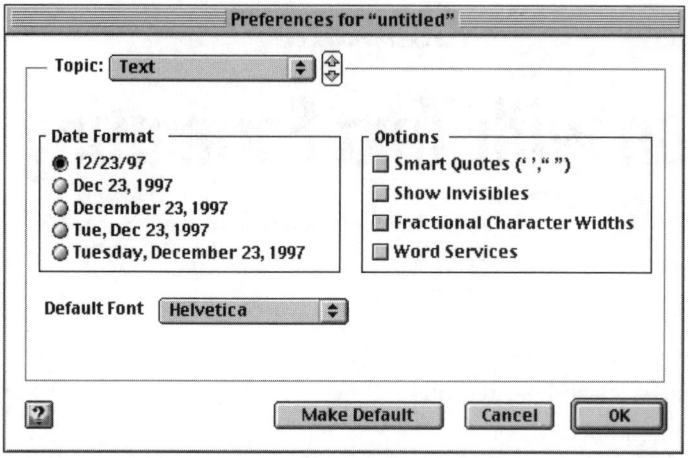

Preferences for "untitled"

Topic: Text

Date Format
- ● 12/23/97
- ○ Dec 23, 1997
- ○ December 23, 1997
- ○ Tue, Dec 23, 1997
- ○ Tuesday, December 23, 1997

Options
- ☐ Smart Quotes (' ' " ")
- ☐ Show Invisibles
- ☐ Fractional Character Widths
- ☐ Word Services

Default Font Helvetica

[?]   Make Default   Cancel   OK

Figure 5-1:
The Preferences dialog box: It works magic.

And now . . . the grand text preference tour:

✔ **Date Format:** Choose how you want the date to appear in your document when ClarisWorks automatically inserts the current date (see "Page numbers and other placeholders" later in this chapter). There are five choices. To pick one, click on the radio button next to it. You can come back to change it anytime.

✔ **Smart Quotes:** Types printers' curly quotes and apostrophes (" " ' ') instead of the dumb "tick" marks the computer normally types. We recommend you keep this box checked because curly quotes look much better than inch marks do — unless you really mean to show inch and foot marks (' "), in which case you should uncheck this box temporarily.

✔ **Show Invisibles:** Displays the invisible formatting characters hiding in your document, which makes it easier for you to see your tabs and other formatting. (We discuss them later in this chapter.) And it's great to notice that you have two spaces between words before you print your page! It's normally unchecked, but some people (us!) like to see invisible characters all the time.

✔ **Fractional Character Widths:** Fine-tunes the space between letters, which is good for printing on a laser printer when using Adobe Type Manager (ATM), but bad for seeing your text on-screen because it scrunches it all up (due to the resolution limitations of your monitor). Most people keep this box unchecked.

✔ **Word Services:** (This option is available only on the Mac.) Word Services is a utility that allows you to link to third party dictionaries. This preference simply adds a submenu to the Edit⇨Writing Tools menu.

✔ **Default Font:** The font you select here is the one all your text will be typed in when you select New Document for word processing or any text — unless you create an entire default document as shown in "Saving as stationery" in Chapter 2.

Formatting Letters and Words

It's time to give your document some finesse. This is easy and fun, because you can try anything, see the effect immediately, and keep experimenting until you love what you see.

Bold, italic, and underline

When words are spoken, inflection adds to their meaning and interpretation. Left alone, the printed word is rather unemotional. By adding a bit of texture to your words, you can help your reader see your inflections.

Here are a couple of quick tips on when to use each attribute:

✔ **Bold text stands out,** it demands attention and looks important. In typewriter days, our closest option was typing in all caps. With word processing, that's definitely out now. In fact, with the advent of electronic mail *(e-mail),* caps are considered very rude because they are the equivalent of yelling. For extra emphasis, you can also italicize bold text.

✔ *Italic text emphasizes without being overly obtrusive.* It also replaces all the times you used to underline with a typewriter. Although hard to read on-screen, it prints nicely. For extra emphasis, you can also bold italicized text.

✔ <u>Underlining is *out* as a way of emphasizing text</u>. For one thing, it is hard to read text when underlines distract you from the words. (That's why highlighters have replaced the ancient method of underlining text to mark it.) Also, the World Wide Web has changed the way we interpret underlines. These days, an underline indicates a <u>hypertext link</u>, which means clicking the text will jump you to another, related place.

You can apply these text attributes as you go (as you enter the actual text) or after the fact (by going back to a word or phrase after it has been entered).

Typing your text first and going back to it later offers you the benefit of making sure that your formatting is consistent. It also allows you to get all your thoughts on track, without getting hung up on the look.

You have four ways to choose bold, italic, or underline:

- ✔ Choose the attribute you want from the Style menu.
- ✔ Press the keyboard shortcut for the Menu command.
- ✔ Select it from the drop-down Style menu located in the button bar strip.
- ✔ Click the attribute's button.

Here's how to apply formatting attributes:

- ✔ **Apply as you go:** Turn on the attribute, type your text, and then turn off the attribute.

  Style commands are controlled in a *toggle* fashion — like a light switch. If the command is off when you choose it, you turn it on. If it is on, selecting it turns it off.

- ✔ **Format later:** Type, type, type. Get all your thoughts out. When you're finished, select the text you want to format and apply an attribute. Jump to the next chunk, select, format, and move on. This is faster because you don't have to turn the attribute on and then off again.

You can mix and match styles to make your word both bold and italic, or bold, italic, and underlined if you really want to induce eyestrain. Just activate one style after the other. If you check the Style menu, you can see that the styles currently in use have check marks next to them.

Choose Style⇨Plain Text style to turn off all special styles at once.

Text size

Sometimes you want to write LARGE. Or sometimes very small. (You never know when you'll need to create legal contract fine print. Just don't ask us to sign anything.) The standard size for text is 12 point, or sometimes 10, depending on the font and how much text you need to cram on a page. (Publishers even sneak down to 9 point.)

We don't mean *point* as in "What's your point?" Nope, this point is a special measurement used by printers and typesetters. One point equals $1/72$ of an inch. A bit of an awkward number, but it goes way, way back to before inches. And inches aren't very logical anyway. You apply a font size like any other formatting — either as you go or later.

Here's how you tell ClarisWorks that you want a different font size:

✔ **Menu bar:** Choose your size from the Size menu. It offers common sizes from 9 to 72 points and Other so you can type in any size from 4 to 255 points. It also includes a command for smaller and larger which increments selected text one point at a time.

✔ **Button bar:** Choose the size you want from the Size pop-up menu located below the buttons. This menu contains the same options as the Size menu. The main benefit of this pop-up menu is that it tells you what size you're already at, without having to click anywhere.

✔ **Button:** Click the Increase Font Size and the Decrease Font Size buttons. These are the buttons with an up arrow for increasing size and a down arrow for decreasing size. Each time you click one, the font changes one point size.

The little-known keyboard shortcuts for increasing and decreasing font size by one point in either direction are Shift-⌘-> and Shift-⌘-< (Mac) and Shift+Ctrl+> and Shift+Ctrl+< (Windows). Select some text and try them!

Changing fonts

Changing the font is like applying a text attribute, except you use the Font menu or the Font pop-up menu located in the button bar strip. As with other formatting, you can apply it as you go or after your text is typed.

✔ To apply as you go, select the font you want to use from the Font menu and start typing.

✔ If you want to change the font of text you already typed, select the text, and then choose the font you want from the Font menu.

Nothing could be easier. A word of warning, though: Limit yourself to just a couple of fonts per document. Your document looks more classy that way. Also, the more fonts you use, the longer your document takes to print because the font information has to be transferred to the printer.

Changing font colors

Changing the color of any text is a breeze. As with any other changes, you select the text first. Then simply pick a color from the little color pop-up at the bottom of the button bar. It's the one with the colors on it — easy to recognize.

Using styles

Style is a commonly misused word. People use it to refer to bolding a word when bold is more accurately defined as an attribute. The ambiguity is compounded by the *Style* menu which is more accurately defined as an *Attribute* menu. A style is actually a *set* of formatting properties. After you choose the font, size, and formatting, you can group all of this information together, create a style to reflect it, and then apply that style to other parts of your text.

The ClarisWorks stylesheet palette is universal to all the environments except communications. The stylesheet palette is available under the Window menu. There are four types of styles: Basic, Paragraph, Outline, and Table. The first two styles are options for word processing, so we cover them in this chapter. The third style — Outline style — is for outlines, which are also a function of the word processor, so we cover this style in Chapter 8. Table styles apply to tables, so we tell you about them in Chapter 7. Here we talk about creating styles, but ClarisWorks provides a lot of nice-looking predefined styles, too.

The Basic style is the most general style. It lets you create a style that includes font, size, text style, and color. (It does not include paragraph indents or tab stops. We get to those attributes later in this chapter.) The most efficient way to create a Basic text style is to follow these steps:

1. **Apply formatting to one chunk of text until it's the way you want it. Then select it.**

2. **If the stylesheet palette is not already showing, choose <u>W</u>indow⇨ Show St<u>y</u>lesheets.**

   Or click the Stylesheet button, which features an S with a red arrow pointing to it.

   You should now see the stylesheet palette, shown in Figure 5-2.

Figure 5-2:
The
stylesheet
palette —
pretty
stylish,
huh?

3. Click the New button at the bottom of the palette.

Doing so brings up the New Style dialog box, shown in Figure 5-3.

4. Type a name for your new style.

ClarisWorks automatically fills in something like Style 1, but it's best to use a meaningful name, like **The Big Giant Heading.**

5. Use the following settings in the New Style dialog box:

- Click the Basic radio button.

- Check the Inherit Document Selection Format check box.

- Choose Default in the Based On list box or choose None. If you base it on None, it's your style, free and clear. If you base it on default, your new style builds upon the preset style and any changes you make to that style affect this new style. This can be a good thing if you want continuity in your document. If this is a standalone style, use None.

Check out your default style's properties: When you finish with this style, select default in the list of styles in the stylesheet palette and click Edit. Click Done after you've had your peek.

6. Click OK to create the style.

Your new style now appears in the stylesheet palette.

From now on, to apply that style to your existing text, choose from the following methods:

- *Stylesheet palette method:* Select the text, and then click the desired style from the Stylesheet palette.

- *Pop-Up Stylesheet Box method:* Select the text, and then choose the desired style from the pop-up Stylesheet box just below the buttons in the button bar.

- *Format As You Go method:* Just choose a style before you start typing. But remember to deselect that style when you don't want it anymore.

An alternative to creating a style from formatted text is to create a new style and then select its attributes from the menus. We cover that in this chapter in the "Paragraph styles" section.

You can copy styles between documents. Select Window⇨Show Stylesheet, and then in the stylesheet palette's menu select File⇨Export Styles. Click the box for each style you want to export, and then click OK. Save this export as you do any other document, saving it to the box it automatically jumps to — the ClarisWorks Styles folder. To import, reverse the steps and begin by using File⇨Import Styles. You have the option to replace styles that have the same name. If you don't replace a style and two have the same name, you get to rename the new one, skip it, or replace it.

Formatting Sentences and Paragraphs

After you've got some of the formatting basics down, you can move on to formatting lines, sentences, and paragraphs. Remember: You can either format as you go or apply formatting changes to text you have already typed. Go ahead — make my paragraph!

Using the text ruler

The text ruler in ClarisWorks is an on-screen ruler that shows you where your text appears across the page. The ruler also includes some handy formatting buttons. If you don't see the ruler at the top of your page, choose Window⇨Show Ruler.

Aligning text

If your text is out of alignment, you feel a lot of vibration when you drive on the freeway. No, wait, that's when your front end is out of alignment. Text alignment has to do with how your text lines up on the page.

You can align text in various ways:

- **On the left:** This is the standard alignment for Roman text-based languages such as English. Called flush left, left-justified, or ragged-right.
- **On the right:** This is the standard for some languages, but mostly decorative in English. Called flush right, right-justified, or ragged-left. Right alignment may be used for dates and other items in headers and footers. It may also be used to align numbers at times.

✔ **On both sides:** This is common in many American books and newspapers. It is called justified, force-justified, or right-and-left-justified. Justified text can look really good or really bad because the text is expanded or contracted to line up on each side. Justification is also accomplished by the addition of white space between words. The trick is to use it only for wide columns. In narrow columns, the gaps between words create rivers of white space that distract the reader and/or cause the need for too many hyphens. Beginners tend to overuse this alignment. It's probably best to stay away from this alignment unless you are doing a newsletter with columns of text.

✔ **From the center:** This is used decoratively or in headlines. This justification is simply called *centered*.

To align text, place your cursor in the paragraph you want to align, or, if you are aligning several contiguous paragraphs, select at least part of each of those paragraphs and then use one of these methods:

✔ **The text ruler:** In the ruler are buttons that depict each type of alignment. Click the button for the one you want to apply. (If the text ruler isn't visible, select Window⇨Show Ruler.)

✔ **The button bar:** Click the button that depicts the alignment you want to apply.

✔ **Keyboard shortcut:** Use one of the shortcuts in Table 5-1 to apply an alignment.

The buttons look the same in the ruler and in the button bar. Figure 5-4 shows you what they look like.

Table 5-1		Keyboard Shortcuts for Aligning Text	
To Do This	*Click This Button*	*Mac Keyboard Shortcut*	*Windows Keyboard Shortcut*
Align left	▤	⌘-[(left bracket)	Ctrl+[(left bracket)
Align right	▤	⌘-] (right bracket)	Ctrl+[(right bracket)
Center	▤	⌘-\ (backslash)	Ctrl+\ (backslash)
Justify	▤	Shift-⌘-\ (backslash)	Shift+Ctrl+\ (backslash)

Unlike applying an attribute such as bolding, coloring, or changing fonts, you don't have to select the text you are aligning. Why not? Because aligning applies to the entire paragraph your cursor is in.

Indenting

Denting is what you'd like to do to the side of your computer with a baseball bat when you get frustrated. *Indenting* is when you shove the first line of a paragraph over a bit so people know it's a new paragraph.

Of course, the simplest way to indent the first line of a paragraph is to press the Tab key. The problem is that, if you're typing a ten-page report, you probably have to press Tab about 40 or 50 times. Then, when you need to change the indent, you have to change it 40 or 50 times! Naturally, ClarisWorks has a way to save you from those 40 or 50 keystrokes: Just use the indent markers in the text ruler. Figure 5-4 shows you where the indent markers live.

On the ruler are two arrows, one hanging from the top and one resting on the bottom. The top controls the first line of any paragraph. The bottom affects all subsequent lines within that paragraph. Each time you begin a new paragraph by pressing Return, your cursor jumps to the point of the top arrow, called the first line indent. ClarisWorks continues laying text on that line until the cursor gets to the single arrow on the bottom right of the ruler. At that point, it automatically moves the next word to wherever the bottom arrow on the left is positioned. Text continues being placed between the two bottom arrows until you press Return to begin a new paragraph.

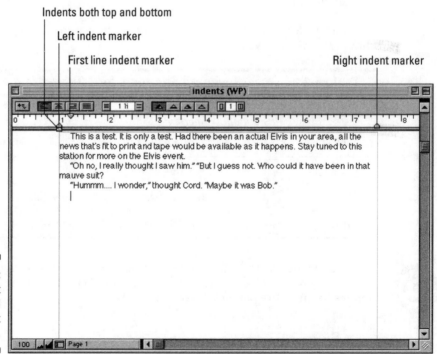

Indents both top and bottom

Left indent marker

First line indent marker

Right indent marker

Figure 5-4:
The text ruler and the indent markers.

Position the cursor in the paragraph that you want to indent before you slide the markers. Each paragraph has its own indent setting, so you need to tell ClarisWorks which paragraph you want to indent by positioning the cursor in that paragraph. To affect more than one paragraph, select at least a part of each paragraph.

When you click any of the ruler arrows, a dotted line appears up and down your page all the way to the ruler. This is a guideline to help you align your text. The guideline moves along as you move the arrow.

To indent the first line

To indent the first line, drag the top arrow (the first line indent marker) to the right as far as you want the first line to indent:

- ✔ If you set the first line indent for a new paragraph, just start typing; the first line starts at the indent point.
- ✔ If you set the first line indent in an existing paragraph, the first line moves over when you move the indent marker in the ruler.

Here's another typewriter habit to break. The half-inch indent we're used to is a holdover from typewriter days. Check out a few professionally printed books and you'll notice the proper spacing is smaller. An *em-space* to be precise — the width of a capital letter *M* in the font you are using. On the ClarisWorks text ruler, that's about a notch or two.

To indent the whole paragraph right or left

Notice that the bottom arrow has two parts: the point and a small rectangle that rides along the ruler's bar. Moving that rectangle moves both left arrows together. So, to indent the entire paragraph from the left, move the small rectangle under the bottom arrow along the ruler.

If you click and drag the bottom arrow, you move only the bottom arrow, leaving the first line of the paragraph unaffected. That creates a hanging indent, which we cover very soon.

Moving the right arrow causes all text in a paragraph to wrap at that point, rather than at the document's right margin.

To make a quotation or passage of text stand out — called *blocking text* — indent that text on both sides. Just slide both the right and left bottom arrows toward the center as far as you like.

You can indent every paragraph in your document by choosing Edit⇨Select All before you slide the indent marker.

Tab stops

If you really want to push your text around, use tab stops. Remember typewriters? You slid a doodad across the carriage to where you wanted the Tab key to take you. You then hit the Tab key and the carriage jumped to the tab stop to begin typing there. Word-processing tabs are similar.

You can have as many tab stops on a line as you want. In fact, although you don't see them, there are default stops every ¹/₂-inch. But maybe you already knew that. Have you ever lined up a column 1 ¹/₂ inches inward by pressing tab three times before typing? On each line, you did the same thing: Tab, Tab, Tab, type, Return, Tab, Tab, Tab, type, and so on.

That was the wrong way to align your text. The right way is to only press the Tab key one time for each jump along the ruler, and then to place a custom tab stop along the ruler at the point you want the column of text to begin. With that in mind, look at the possibilities.

It is much easier to format text, especially tabs, when you can see where you place the tabs in your document. To see tabs and other normally invisible characters on-screen, click the Show/Hide Invisibles button. The tab marker is the black arrow. The section called "Invisible men and other characters," later in this chapter, tells you more about this.

The four types of tab stops

ClarisWorks has four — count 'em, four — types of tab stops for you to choose from. Lots of power. Tabs work a lot like text alignment, except the text alignment begins at the tab, not the margin. Figure 5-5 gives you a quick breakdown of the different tab stops.

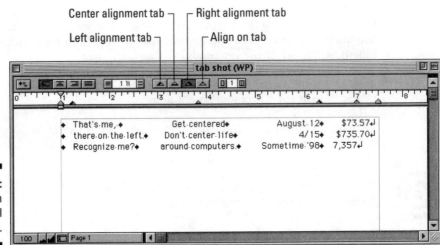

Figure 5-5:
Tab stops in their natural habitats.

Here's what each type of tab stop is good for (with Figure 5-5 to illustrate):

✔ **Left-aligned:** This is the "regular" tab stop. All text starting at one of these is aligned flush left.

✔ **Center-aligned:** Your text is centered at the point of the tab stop. It lets you do a little inline alignment, so you can center your text off-center. Use this tab when you to have a few short lines of text centered relative to each other, but not necessarily in the center of the page.

✔ **Right-aligned:** This pushes text out to the left so that the right edge of the text always lines up with the tab stop.

✔ **Align on:** This is the coolest and most flexible tab stop. By default, it awaits a decimal point and places that decimal point at the tab stop. (If there is no decimal it aligns the end of the text on the tab. This is perfect for invoicing or listing costs.)

If you choose the Align On tab option, use the Tab dialog box to change the symbol that the tab lines up on. Simply type a character into the field that appears next to the choice. Experiment and be creative.

Setting tab stops

There are two ways to set tab stops.

Here's the easy way — visually, from the ruler:

1. **Position your cursor in the paragraph you want to affect.**

2. **Click on the symbol for the type of tab you want and drag it to the spot on the ruler where you want the tab stop.**

   A guideline appears in order to help you place it perfectly.

   The tab stop snaps onto the bottom of the ruler. That's when you can let go of the mouse button.

3. **After the tab stop marker is in place on the ruler, you can slide it back and forth to fine-tune your tab stop.**

If you want to remove a tab stop, just drag it off the ruler. When you release the mouse button, the tab marker disappears.

Rather than dragging the tab stop to the ruler, you can just click the spot on the ruler where you want the tab to land. The type of tab that's selected above the ruler is the type that appears when you click. This is a time-saver when you're placing more than one of the same type.

Now the hard way — with the Tab dialog box:

1. **Position your cursor in the paragraph you want to affect.**

2. **Choose Format⇨Tab.**

   This brings up the dialog box shown in Figure 5-6.

Type the character on which to align here

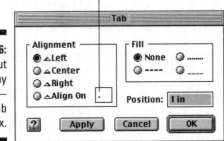

Figure 5-6:
Just put
it on my
tab —
the Tab
dialog box.

3. **Choose a type of tab from the Alignment selections on the left.**

4. **Type in the position where you want the tab to appear.**

   This position corresponds to the numbers on the ruler.

5. **Click the Apply button to place that tab stop.**

6. **To add another tab stop on that line, enter another position and click Apply again.**

7. **Click OK when you finish adding tabs for that line.**

If you want to copy your tab stops into other paragraphs you've already typed, see the section entitled "Applying a ruler," later in this chapter.

Filled tabs

One other Tab option is Fill. You have three fill characters to choose from — dash, dot, and understrike — and the one you choose fills the normally empty space of the tab (with dashes, dots, or understrike characters).

A filled tab is what you use to set up a table of contents or a theater program. Figure 5-7 shows you an example of formatting with filled tabs. Notice the tab stop in the ruler:

   ✔ Use the Tab dialog box to fill a tab with any of the four fillers.

   ✔ Programs usually look best with right-aligned tabs.

   ✔ Tables of contents look best with left-aligned tabs.

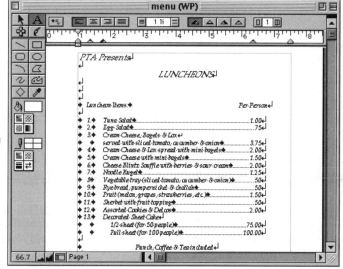

Figure 5-7:
Make this mouth-watering menu with tasty, filled tab stops!

To modify a tab stop that's already on the ruler, double-click it. The Tab dialog box appears. Select a new type of tab or select a fill. You can also use the dialog box to reposition the tab stop, but it's much easier to simply slide the tab stop along the ruler.

There are two parts to the formula. Make sure you have both parts in place. Be sure that you have placed the tab mark on the ruler and that you have pressed the Tab button to tell the text to jump into place at the next tab stop.

You can have several tabs in any line. Simply press the Tab key once for each tab stop you set in the ruler. The first tab symbol (from the Tab key) moves the text to the first tab stop. The second tab symbol moves the text to the next tab stop, and so on.

Hanging indents

A hanging indent makes the first line of your paragraph stick out to the left, as in Figure 5-8. They're easy to do — once you get the *hang* of it.

What's a hanging indent good for? Take a look at number four in Figure 5-8. You can use a hanging indent to create numbered steps, a bulleted list, several lines set off with check marks, or whatever. Here's how it works:

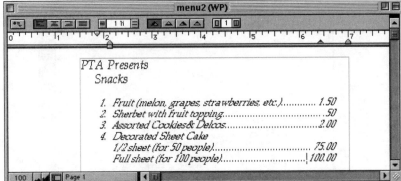

Figure 5-8:
An indent
hanging out
for cake.

1. **Click the small rectangle that moves both left arrows and drag it to the right to where you want the second line, and all subsequent lines, to start.**

   It isn't possible to bring text past the left margin.

2. **To bring the first line of text back out toward the margin, drag the top arrow to where you want it.**

3. **Type your bullet or number, press Tab, and then type your body text.**

   The position of the bottom margin marker is now the default tab stop, so pressing Tab takes you there.

   If you are applying this hanging indent to a paragraph you already typed, do Steps 1 and 2, and then insert the bullet or number and a tab at the beginning of the first line.

For a really sharp list, insert a right-aligned tab stop between the top line arrow and the bottom line arrow. Now type a tab, the number, and a right-aligned tab. This way, if your list goes into the double digits, you always have the same amount of space between the number and the body of the paragraph. Look back at the ruler in Figure 5-7 to see an example of how this is set up.

We'll let you in on a secret. ClarisWorks has a built-in style to do this for you. Select the text that you want to have this style and then Number from the pop-up Style menu in the bottom of your ruler. Actually, it differs in two ways. First, it does more because it auto-numbers your lines as long as you keep the style applied. Second, it doesn't really create a hanging indent. There is also a built-in Bullet style.

Invisible men and other characters

 Formatting is always easier when you can actually see what you're doing. Instead of leaving formatting characters invisible, let 'em show themselves. Just click the Show/Hide Invisibles button to show them. Click it again to hide them. You can also show the invisible characters with the Preferences dialog box: Select Edit⇨Preferences, click the Text pop-up, and check the box next to Show Invisibles. Figure 5-9 shows you the various formatting characters and what they do.

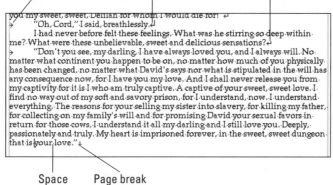

Figure 5-9:
Return of
the Son of
the Invisible
Formatting
Character!

Line spacing

Line spacing is what happens to an actor when he forgets his lines on stage. More important, in a text document, it's how much white space you place between lines of text. This is called leading in typographical terms because typesetters used to place a blank strip of plain lead between text lines to set them apart.

You can create as much line spacing as you like, simply by using the ruler. Experiment and you notice it has the effect of setting apart sections, thoughts, and so on. It also affects the feeling of the page — called *color* by typographers.

Figure 5-10 points out the line spacing controls. Notice that the current line spacing is displayed in the box between the text alignment and tabs. The spacing increment is half a line at a time; so, as you click the Increase Line Spacing button (right), the line spacing goes up from 1 line to 1.5 to 2, and so on. It can also be set to go up by points. The unit of measurement is stated in the box.

Figure 5-10:
Spacing
your
lines...uh,
what was
I going
to say?

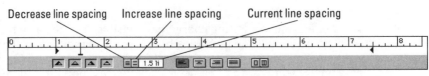

To change the line spacing, just position the cursor anywhere in the paragraph you want to affect and click the Increase or Decrease button. Your paragraph should expand or contract, depending on which button you click.

To change the unit of measurement to adjust line spacing by points, double-click the box that reports the current spacing. The paragraph dialog box that we show you in the next section pops up, allowing you to change from lines to points. It also lets you choose inches, millimeters, centimeters, and picas.

Space between paragraphs

To add an extra line or two before or after a paragraph, you are probably used to pressing Return an extra time or two or three. While that works decently in short documents such as one-page letters, it can become problematic in larger documents. Here's how to do it the professional way.

To adjust the space between paragraphs, with your cursor in a paragraph you want to affect, choose Format⇨Paragraph or double-click the box on the ruler that shows the current line spacing. You should see a Paragraph dialog box like the one in Figure 5-11.

Figure 5-11:
The
Paragraph
dialog box
lets you
change all
kinds of
nifty things!

Here's an example of how to use the dialog box to add space between paragraphs: Say you have a document currently all single-spaced and want to add an extra line between each paragraph. Just choose Edit⇨Select All, open the Paragraph dialog box, and enter **1** in the box next to Space After, making sure the measurement is by line. Click Apply to see the effect without leaving the dialog box. Click OK if you like it. All the paragraphs in your document are now separated by blank lines. It's nice and tidy and there is no need to press Return twice after each paragraph.

Here's another reason for using proper spacing technique. Remember the example of the single line between each paragraph? What if that document was too long? Because you used line spacing, you can select all your text again, open the Paragraph dialog box, and decrease the line spacing to make the text all fit on the already full pages. Switch to the points measurement. If your text is in 12-point type, the box now says 12. Type in **11** instead, click Apply, and check out your result. Not enough? Try **10**.

You can use the Paragraph dialog box to change the indents, the line spacing, or the paragraph spacing. If you prefer to set indents by typing in a number rather than dragging the triangle in the ruler, use this dialog box. Just so you know, the Paragraph dialog box is the only way to set the space between paragraphs.

Applying a ruler

No, we won't rap your knuckles for positioning text on the page with the spacebar. In ClarisWorks, applying a ruler means to copy the ruler settings from one paragraph and paste them into another. After you set up a paragraph the way you like it, you can copy the tab stops, the indents, the line spacing, and the space between paragraphs — all the settings in the Paragraph dialog box — and paste them into any other paragraph. Here's how:

1. **Start by formatting one paragraph the way you want it.**

   Remember, to have the cursor in the paragraph you are formatting. Include all tab stops, indents, and line spacing.

2. **With the cursor in that paragraph, choose Format⇨Copy Ruler or Shift-⌘-C (Mac) or Shift+Ctrl+C (Windows).**

3. **Move the cursor to the paragraph to which you want to add the settings. To apply the ruler to several paragraphs, select those paragraphs.**

4. **Choose Format⇨ Apply Ruler or press Shift-⌘-V (Mac) or Shift+Ctrl+V (Windows).**

The shortcuts are easy — the same as Copy and Paste, plus the Shift key. Copying and applying a ruler doesn't copy the text style. To copy and apply a set of formatting such as font, style, and size, use a custom style, mentioned in "Using styles" earlier in this chapter.

If you set up your tabs, indents, line spacing, and so on in a paragraph and then press the Enter key (in Windows) or Return key (on the Mac) at the end of that paragraph, in front of the invisible Enter character, the formatting will be carried into the next paragraph you create by pressing Enter.

Paragraph styles

Paragraph styles save a set of formatting that includes text and ruler settings. That means you can apply custom formatting, indents, tab stops, and line spacing in one step. It also means you can change the formatting on every paragraph in your document that uses that paragraph style simply by changing the style itself.

Think about it — you decide to change all the body text in your document from Helvetica to Times. Just change the paragraph style settings, and all the paragraphs (in that document) that use that style are updated automatically. For long documents with many different headings or other areas of specially formatted text that are used repeatedly, paragraph styles are the way to go.

To create a paragraph style, do this:

1. **If the stylesheet palette is not showing, choose Window⇨Show Stylesheet or Shift-⌘-W (Mac) or Shift+Ctrl+W (Windows).**

   You should now see the stylesheet palette. Refer back to Figure 5-2 for a picture of the stylesheet palette.

2. **Click the New button at the bottom of the palette.**

   This action brings up the New Style dialog box, as in Figure 5-3.

3. **Type a name for your new style.**

   ClarisWorks calls it Style 1, but it's best to use a meaningful name, like Chapter Heading or Caption.

4. **Click the Paragraph radio button, under Style type.**

5. **Choose a style to be the starting point for your new style from the Based On pop-up menu.**

   You can use any existing style for the basis of your new style. If you want to start completely from scratch, choose None. To start with the normal default formatting, choose Default.

If you use one style for the basis of another, any future modifications to the first style also apply to the second style. For example, if your first style includes Arial as the font, so will the second style. If you change Arial to Courier in the first style, the second style will also change to Courier.

6. Uncheck the box next to Inherit Document Selection Format.

7. Click OK.

Your new style now appears in the Edit Style window of the stylesheet palette.

Now the pointer changes to an outline S with an arrow in the upper-left corner.

8. Choose the settings for your new style from the menus, ruler, buttons, or button bar formatting controls.

Use the S pointer to choose the formatting options for your new style. The choices you make show up in the Properties box at the right of the Edit Style window, as shown in Figure 5-12.

You can see a miniature representation of how your style looks by choosing Show Sample on the Edit menu of the stylesheet palette. This menu is not the regular Edit menu on the menu bar, but the small Edit menu at the upper left of the stylesheet palette.

9. Click Done when finished.

Your new style appears in the stylesheet list.

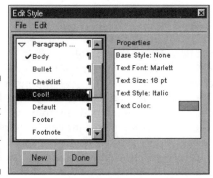

Figure 5-12: The Edit Style window — Cool, eh?!

To apply a style to an existing paragraph, position the cursor in that paragraph; then choose a style from the stylesheet. If you want to format as you go, just choose a style before you start typing.

You can also create a style based on a selected paragraph. First, select a paragraph and do Steps 1 through 4 in the previous list. Then skip to Step 6 and check the box labeled Inherit Document Selection Format. Click OK and then Done in the Edit Style window. Your new style now appears in the stylesheet palette.

Formatting Pages and Documents

Now that you've got your text and paragraphs whipped into shape, it's time to look at the big picture — the document as a whole.

Page breaks

Suppose you are typing along, and you get to the middle of the page and decide your next thought would look really good at the top of the next page, rather than there in the middle of this page. You can press Enter dozens of times to get you there (as the ghost of formatting past whispers "That would be bad"), or you can insert a page break (which would be good). To insert a page break, position your cursor where you want the break to occur, and then choose one of these options:

- Press Shift-Enter (Mac) or Ctrl+Enter (Windows). The Enter key is the one on your number pad. On a PowerBook, the Enter key is next to the spacebar. If your Enter key and Return key are one and the same, this may not work.

- Choose Format⇨Insert Break.

The problem with using returns to move to the top of a page is that, if you go back and insert a couple of lines of text on the previous page, you push all the following text down a couple of lines. When this happens, the text that used to be at the top of the page is now an inch or two down. If your document is opened on another machine, which is likely to have different margins and different fonts, your document's pages may fall differently. In short, your reader may see a mess of ugly returns at the tops and bottoms of pages. Page breaks don't do that to you. They give you proper breaks when and where you want them. (And they save you some typing.)

Page numbers and other placeholders

We can all use a little magic in our lives. How about a magic command that automatically numbers the pages in your document? No problem. ClarisWorks can take care of that for you, as well as time and date stamps that are automatically updated every time you open your document.

Where can you find these wonders? In the Edit menu, in the guise of three commands: Insert Date, Insert Time, and Insert Page #.

Actually, these commands don't insert the real date, time, or page number. Instead, each inserts a placeholder — a special invisible character that tells ClarisWorks it needs to look up some information. When one or more of these placeholders is in place at the time you open your document, ClarisWorks inserts the current time, date, or page number at the place-holder.

Just position the cursor and choose the command you want from the Edit menu. The time, date, or page number appears. The date and time are automatically updated the next time you open the document. The page number is updated when pages are added or removed.

Here are some handy tricks for working with placeholders:

- ✔ If you want a date or time stamp but don't want that information updated when the document is next opened, press Option (Mac) or Alt (Windows) as you choose the command from the Edit menu.

- ✔ If you want to have the page number, time, or date appear on every page, insert the placeholder in a header or footer (which we get to in a moment).

- ✔ You can start the page numbers at any number you want. This option may come in handy if you have broken up a long work into several smaller documents, like chapters. That way, you can have page numbering in your current chapter start where it left off in the last chapter. The starting page number option is in the Format⇨Document dialog box.

- ✔ Insert Page # also lets you insert the section number, section page count, and document page count. That way, you can have your page say "page 2 of 4" and always be correct. More on sections coming right up.

Headers and footers

Headers and footers are like hats and shoes for your document. You wouldn't want your document running around without matching accessories, would you? Okay, here's what headers and footers do.

A *header* is an area of text at the top of the page that repeats on every page of the document. A *footer* is an area of text at the bottom of the page that repeats on every page of the document. You can put the same stuff in a footer as in a header.

Typical header/footer contents are:

- ✔ Your name
- ✔ The date and time of creation
- ✔ The page number and page count
- ✔ The title of your work
- ✔ Ribbons, barrettes, and little pink beads

To add a header or footer to your document, choose Format➪Insert Header or Insert Footer. After you insert one, the Format menu changes from Insert to Remove, in case you want to remove it later. Here are some more things to keep in mind about headers and footers:

- ✔ Anything in the header or footer appears on every page.

- ✔ You can format header and footer text using all alignment and styling techniques that apply to any other text. Tabs are common here, so you can have the date at the left, a page number in the center, and your name right-aligned.

- ✔ Choose Format➪Section and check the box next to Title Page to keep the header and footer from showing up on the first page of your document — which you can use as a title page.

- ✔ If you are using a title page and don't want it to count in the total number of pages in your document, choose Format➪Document and type a zero in the Starting Page # or Start at Page box. That way, the second page of your document counts as page one.

Sections

Remember one-room schoolhouses? The whole room was a school, but a few rows were one grade, and the next few rows were another grade learning entirely different things. That's what sections are like in a word-processing document. Each section can have different formatting options than the others. Within a section, you can change the header and footer, the number of columns, and the page numbering. You can even start a section with its own title page. More about sections:

- ✔ Sections are a great way to break up chapters in a document or to have different numbers of columns on the same page.

- ✔ To start a new section, position the cursor where you want the new section to start and choose Format➪Insert Section Break or press Option-(Num)Enter (Mac) or Shift+Ctrl+(Num)Enter (Windows).

- ✔ To delete a section, show Invisibles, select the section break, and press Delete or choose Edit➪Clear.

✔ To change a section's formatting, position the cursor anywhere in that section and choose Format⇨Section. You should see the Section dialog box, as shown in Figure 5-13.

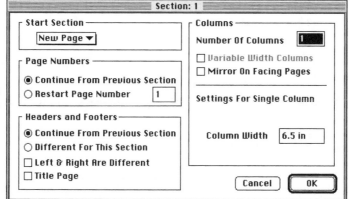

Figure 5-13:
Is this a
nonsmoking
section?
The Section
dialog box.

We cover column options soon. For now, just notice the left side of the dialog box. Most of the options are pretty straightforward, but a couple need a little bit of explaining:

✔ At the top is the Start Section pop-up menu. Your selection here tells ClarisWorks where the next section should start after the section break. If you choose New Page, the current section starts on the line below the previous section. If you choose New Left Page or New Right Page and you are using facing pages, you may wind up with a blank page between sections.

✔ In the Headers and Footers area, you can choose whether to use different headers and footers in this section and whether to use a title page. If you check the box next to Left & Right Are Different, you can use different headers and footers on facing pages.

Facing pages

There comes a time in everyone's life when you have to stand up and face the pages. I mean the music. Well, here we face pages, or talk about pages that face each other.

You want to use facing pages if you want your document to end up on double-sided pages. This way, you can set up headers and footers so that the page number — or other important information — always appears at the outside corner of the page.

You can also leave space at the inside edge of the page to accommodate a binding for your document. This space is known in page-layout circles as a *gutter.*

Here's how you set up facing pages:

1. **Choose Format⇨Document.**

2. **Check the Mirror Facing Pages box.**

   Notice that in the Margins area of the dialog box, the boxes labeled Left and Right have changed to Inside and Outside.

3. **(Optional) Increase the size of the inside margin to leave a gutter for binding.**

Here are a couple of tips for working with facing pages:

✔ To see two pages side by side on your screen, go to the Document dialog box's Page Display area and click the button next to the Facing Pages Side-By-Side option.

✔ To use different headers and footers on left and right pages, choose Format⇨Section and select the box labeled Left & Right Are Different in the Headers and Footers area. This selection lets you keep the page number at the outside corner of every page.

Footnotes

Footnotes are (a) letters you write with your toes or (b) comments that can appear at the bottom of the page and contain references, information sources, or other explanations.

To insert a footnote, position the cursor where you want the footnote marker to appear and choose Format⇨Insert Footnote, Shift-⌘-F (Mac) or Shift+Ctrl+F (Windows). Or select Help⇨ClarisWorks Assistants and select the Insert Footnote Assistant. The Assistant is a big help with detailed footnotes that cite reference sources. We recommend exploring it.

When you use the Insert Footnote command, ClarisWorks automatically inserts a footnote marker and takes you to the bottom of the page to type your footnote. Press Enter (on the number pad) to go back to your body text when you finish typing your footnote.

ClarisWorks is set up to automatically number your footnotes. So, when you insert a footnote marker, ClarisWorks puts in the correct number for the new footnote. If you want to use a symbol (like * or †) instead of a number, here's what you do:

1. **Choose Format⇨Document.**

2. **Uncheck the Automatic Numbering Start At box in the Footnotes area of the Document dialog box.**

   That's it. The next time you insert a footnote and automatic numbering is turned off, ClarisWorks displays a dialog box asking you to choose a symbol for the footnote. This symbol is automatically displayed superscript in your body text, just like numbered footnote markers.

You can also tell ClarisWorks to start the footnotes at a number other than one. This option comes in handy if you have broken up a long work into several smaller documents, like chapters. That way, you can have footnote numbering in one chapter start where it left off in the last chapter.

To go back to your body text, remember to press Enter (on the number pad) when you are finished typing your footnote.

If you happen to move a footnote marker during your editing, ClarisWorks automatically updates the number and order of that footnote, relative to the other footnotes in your document.

Margins

Margins are to your document what the shoulder is to a freeway. They're important, but nobody ever notices them. The clean, white space in the margins helps to offset the densely packed action of the body text.

By default, ClarisWorks sets the margins to one inch all around. This is a pretty good setting for most documents. In fact, it works well with most pre-printed business letterheads. But you may find that it's too much space.

To adjust the margins, choose Format⇨Document.

Just enter the margin you want in the appropriate boxes. Use decimals, not fractions, as shown in Figure 5-14 where we have a $1/2$-inch margin. You can use any unit of measure you want by simply entering the number and the unit. It will be converted to whatever unit you are currently using in the ruler. For example, if the ruler is using inches and you type **3 cm** for the top margin, the 3 cm will be converted to 1.18 inches.

Don't set your margins smaller than a half-inch to be safe. Most printers need a minimum of a $1/2$-inch margin or the edges of your document get cut off.

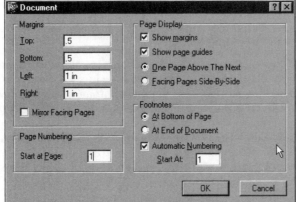

Figure 5-14:
The
Document
dialog box.

The gray lines at the edges of your document are the page guides. Page guides show you where the margins are. Anything inside the lines is your document; anything outside is margin. You can turn off the page guides if you want by choosing Format⇨Document and deselecting the Show Page Guides check box. To actually see the white margin space as you work, select the Show Margins check box. We recommend keeping both options checked. In Figure 5-14, you can see we always have them both checked.

While you've got the Document dialog box open, look at one more option you can set: how pages are displayed on-screen. Normally, the setting is one page above another, so you scroll down to see the next page. Alternatively, you can have two pages display side by side. This can be handy when you're designing a layout for your text. You still scroll down to see subsequent pages, but you see two at a time, side by side.

Columns

ClarisWorks really does columns right. All you need to do is click the Add Column button in the text ruler. One click and your document is divided into two columns on each page. Need another column? Just click the Add Column button again — now you have three columns. Keep going if you want. And to remove a column? The Remove Column button makes that just as easy.

You can see which button is which in Figure 5-15. You can have up to nine columns on a page. Of course, you'd better use very short words with nine columns, because with standard margins, each of the nine columns is only 0.57 inch across.

Figure 5-15:
Columns,
anyone?
Just click a
button.

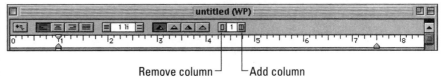

Remove column ── ──Add column

The Add column feature creates columns that are of equal width. If you want to change the column width or the space between the columns, you can use the mouse or type information in a dialog box. See the next two sections for more information.

To change columns with the mouse

After you have added columns, you can change them with your mouse. To do so, press Option (Mac) or Alt (Windows) and move the mouse over the column guide. The pointer changes to two arrows pointing in opposite directions. Move the pointer around a bit and notice that when the mouse is over the page guide lines at the edge of the column, the cursor has two lines between the arrows, but when the mouse is in the middle of the space between the columns, the cursor has a box between the arrows.

If you want to change the column width and leave the space between the columns the same, press Option/Alt and move the pointer between the two columns so the two arrows have a box between them. Then hold down the mouse button and drag the column guide lines to change the column width.

If you want to change the space between the columns, hold down the Option/Alt key and move the pointer over one of the column guide lines so that the arrows have two lines between them. Then hold down the mouse button and drag the column guide line to change the space between the columns.

To change columns with the Columns dialog box

For those of you who prefer to enter numbers in a dialog boxes: Choose Format⇨Section. Columns are controlled from the Columns area of the Section dialog box, as shown on the right of Figure 5-16.

If you have more than one column, you can select variable-sized columns. To change the size of a column, just select the column you want to change from the pop-up menu and type a width into the Column Width box. Do this for any columns you want to change. The space between columns depends on how much space is left when you have assigned all the column widths.

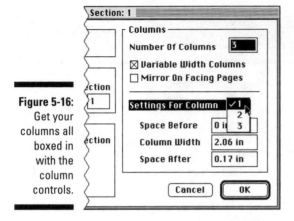

Figure 5-16:
Get your
columns all
boxed in
with the
column
controls.

When you're finished, click OK, and the changes are applied. If you don't like
the new widths, just undo the changes by clicking the Undo button on the
default button bar or with the Edit⇨Undo command.

Paper size and orientation

To set your document's paper size and orientation, use File⇨ Print Setup
(called Page Setup on the Mac). This controls whether the document prints
in the tall direction (portrait) or the wide direction (landscape) on the
paper. You can find this dialog box in the File menu. The actual dialog box
you see depends on the type of printer you are using, and which platform
you're on. (The Print/Page Setup dialog box is covered in Chapter 2.)

If you really want to get into the nitty-gritty of your printing options and find
out about extra features unique to your printer, you should bite the bullet
and take a look at your printer or operating system manual. Yes, it may be
gruesome. Skip over the icky parts and just look up the parts about the
Print/Page Setup dialog box.

Chapter 6

The Text Tools — Editor in a Drum

• •

In This Chapter

▶ Checking spelling

▶ Finding and changing text

▶ Looking up synonyms

▶ Counting words

▶ Hyphenating

• •

*Y*ou've typed all your text, moved it around, set up your tab stops, and applied styles; now comes the hard work: the editing. Luckily for you, ClarisWorks includes a whole slew of functions that help you hack your way through even the densest jungle of text.

The Spell Checker — One Reason To Use a Word Processor

The spell checker can save you a lot of embarrassment. A simple misspelling can make even the most polished report look like it was written by a monkey chained to a computer. If a former vice president had used a spell checker, he wouldn't have ended up looking like Mr. Potatoe (sic) head.

You can check your entire document at once or check a specific block of text.

To check your entire document, choose one of the following methods:

✔ Choose Edit⇨Writing Tools⇨Check Document Spelling. (If you're using Mac OS7, keep holding the mouse button down until you highlight the last selection; then release the button.)

✔ Use the keyboard shortcuts: ⌘-= (Mac) or Ctrl+= (Windows).

To check a block of text, first select the text you want to check, then choose one of the following methods:

✓ Choose Edit⇨Writing Tools⇨Check Selection Spelling. (If you're using Mac OS7, keep holding the mouse button down until you highlight the last selection; then release the button.)

✓ Use keyboard shortcuts: Shift-⌘-Y (Mac) or Shift+Ctrl+Y (Windows).

✓ Press the Spell Check button. It has the letters ABC and a red check mark as its icon.

Regardless of how you initiate your spell check, the next thing you should see is the Spelling dialog box shown in Figure 6-1.

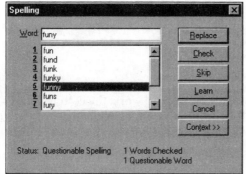

Figure 6-1:
Do you spell funny? The Spelling dialog box.

The spell checker starts at the beginning of the document or selection and checks each word in that document or selection. When it finds a word it doesn't recognize, it displays the word at the top of the dialog box and lists possible corrections below. You can replace the questionable word with one of the words in the scrolling list below in several ways:

✓ Double-click the word you want to use (in the scrolling list).

✓ Use the mouse to select a word in the list, and then click Replace (or press the Return or Enter key).

✓ Use the up- and down-arrow keys to select a word in the list, and then click Replace (or press the Return or Enter key).

✓ Press ⌘-1 through ⌘-6 (Mac) or Alt+1 to Alt+7 (Windows) to select the word that appears next to that number on-screen. For example, for the misspelled word in Figure 6-1, press ⌘-5 or Alt+5 to replace it with the word *funny*.

Sometimes the spell checker offers more than six suggestions for replacement words. You can scroll through the list with the scroll bar or use the up- and down-arrow keys. In case you're wondering, no matter where you scroll in the list, the number shortcut always selects the word currently next to that number on-screen.

If you don't see the correct spelling in the list, just type the word as it should be spelled and click Replace.

If the spell checker flags a word you know is spelled correctly, it means that the word in question is not listed in the built-in ClarisWorks dictionary. You have two choices:

- ✔ If this is a word you seldom use, click the Skip button. This leaves the word as is and moves on to the next misspelling.

- ✔ If you use this word often or it appears several times in your document, click Learn. This adds the word to a custom user dictionary. After the word is in the user dictionary, ClarisWorks knows it.

Here are some other useful hints about the spell checker:

- ✔ Handy things to add to the user dictionary are foreign words, proper nouns like street names, and frequently used e-mail addresses.

- ✔ If you want to check the spelling of a word that's not in your document, choose the Check Document Spelling command (in any method as above). When the Spelling dialog box appears, type in your word and click the Check button.

- ✔ To see the misspelled word in the context of your sentence, click the Context button or, if you're using a Mac, the triangle thingy at the lower-right corner of the dialog box. This expands the dialog box to include a line of text that shows the word in context. Click the same button again to get rid of the line of text.

- ✔ When the spell checker is finished checking your document, the Replace button changes to Done. In short documents with no misspellings, you may think that the dialog box starts out with the Done button because it changes from Replace to Done so fast. Click the Done button to dismiss the Spelling dialog box.

- ✔ If you're not into spell-checking at the moment and want to call it off, just click Cancel.

English is a tricky language. Many words have different spellings and meanings, although pronounced the same. Spell checkers don't know the context of your word usage, so they won't pick up on these errors. Sew, dew ewe no watt wee mean?

Find and Go Change

ClarisWorks loves to play hide-and-seek. It goes seeking anything you ask it to. And when it does, it can even do magic with it. Wanna see ClarisWorks turn fire into flowers?

Finding text

Where can you find the Find command? We find most people find the Find command in the Find/Change submenu of the Edit menu.

To bring up the Find/Change command dialog box shown in Figure 6-2, choose one of these options:

  ✔ Choose Find/Change from the Find/Change submenu of the Edit menu.
  ✔ Press ⌘-F (Mac) or Ctrl+F (Windows).

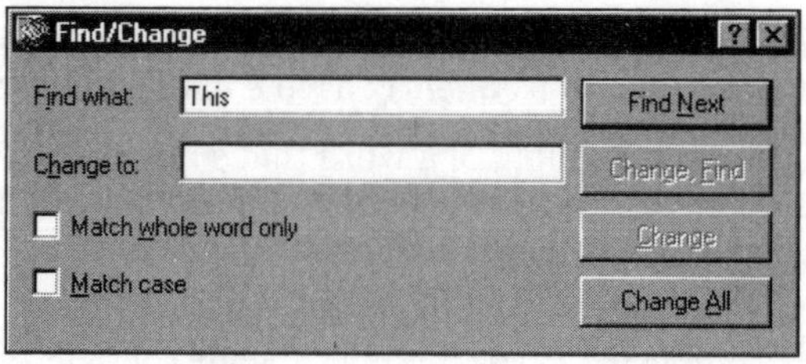

Figure 6-2:
Find that
which you
seek with
the Find/
Change
dialog box.

Find/Change

Find what: This   Find Next

Change to: Change, Find

☐ Match whole word only   Change

☐ Match case   Change All

You have three ways to find text:

  ✔ Bring up the dialog box, type in the text you seek, and click Find Next (or press Enter/Return).
  ✔ Select an example of the text you seek, and then bring up the Find dialog box. ClarisWorks automatically enters the text you seek into the Find What field.
  ✔ Select an example of the text you seek, and then choose Find Selection from the Find/Change submenu. ClarisWorks automatically looks for the next chunk of text in your document that matches what you selected.

ClarisWorks starts looking to the right of the current selection (or wherever the cursor is positioned) and continues to the end. If no match is found, ClarisWorks starts over at the beginning of the document. If it is unable to find a match anywhere in the document, a message appears to let you know.

If you decide you need to find the next match for the same text again but have already closed the Find/Change dialog box or deselected the text, use Find Again, located in the same submenu. (Of course, you can use ⌘-E or Ctrl+E, too.) If you're good at keyboard shortcuts, you may prefer using Find Selection and Find Again to find all matches for your text without ever seeing the Find/Change dialog box.

You have a couple of options to narrow your search a bit:

✔ Check the box labeled Whole Word to Match Text in the Find box only if the text is a separate word. For example, if you type **and** in the Find box without checking the Whole Word box, ClarisWorks finds the *and* in S*and*y, comm*and*, and b*and*. If the box is checked, only the word *and* is found.

✔ Check the box labeled Match Case to find only those words that match upper- and lowercase with the text in the Find box. If you type **AT** into the Find box and check the Match Case box, you get AT&T but not Attention because the case doesn't match.

✔ You can check both boxes at once to narrow your search even further.

Changing text

You may have noticed the Change to box in the Find/Change dialog box in Figure 6-2. After finding your text, ClarisWorks can turn it into anything you like. To turn fire into flowers, call up the Find/Change dialog box, type **fire** under Find and **flowers** under Change (see Figure 6-3), and click Change; voilà — flowers. Change can come in handy if you decide halfway through your latest love story that Cord is a much more romantic name than Bob. (Sorry, Bob.) Call on Find/Change, enter the name, and click Change All to give Bob an instant name change.

Figure 6-3:
Woh, ooh,
oh, it's
magic.

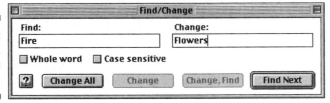

Find/Change

Find:
Fire

Change:
Flowers

☐ Whole word   ☐ Case sensitive

[?] [Change All] [Change] [Change, Find] [Find Next]

Here's another way to use Find/Change: If you are writing a report and don't have all the information at hand, you can put in an arbitrary placeholder like %%% or **XXXX** for a name or figure. Later, when you get the information, use Find/Change to locate your placeholders and change them to the real thing. Just make sure to keep track of which placeholder you use for each bit of information.

After you have typed what you want to find and what you want to change it to, you have several options for conducting your search-and-replace mission:

- ✔ To find the next occurrence of the text in the Find box, click Find Next (or press Return or Enter because that's the default choice).

- ✔ To change the text you see highlighted in the document to the text in the Change box, click Change.

- ✔ To change the highlighted text and find the next occurrence of the text in one very efficient, safe step, click Change, Find.

- ✔ To change every occurrence of the text in the Find box to the text in the Change box, click Change All.

Use the Change All button with caution. You cannot undo the changes made with it. ClarisWorks warns you about this. Most of the time, you want to check the Whole Word option before you click Change All. That way, you change Bob to Cord but not Bobbing to Cordbing or Shishkabob to Shishkacord. You may also want to check the Match Case option to be even more specific. Make sure you carefully consider how the Change All button will affect your document before you use it. (Or make a copy of your document using the Save As command before you attempt this trick at home.)

Now that you've had fair warning about Change All, here's a handy way to use it: Remember we told you not to use two spaces between sentences? We know, old habits are hard to break, and it's easy to forget now and then. You can use Change All to lose the extra space. Just type two spaces into the Find field, type one space in the Change field, and click Change All. ClarisWorks finds all instances of two consecutive spaces and replace them with one space. We do this all the time. Cool, huh?

At some point, you may need to find other invisible formatting characters. Table 6-1 shows you what to type in the Find field to find them.

Table 6-1	How to Find Invisible Formatting Characters	
To Find This	*Type This on Mac*	*Type This in Windows*
Space	Space	Space
Nonbreaking space	Option-space	Ctrl+space
Tab	\t or ⌘-Tab	\t or Ctrl+Tab
Return character	\p or ⌘-Return	\p or Ctrl+Enter
Line break	\n	\n
Column break	\c or ⌘-Enter (num)	\c
Page break	\b	\b

To Find This	Type This on Mac	Type This in Windows
Section break	\-Option-6	\+0167
Discretionary hyphen*	\– or ⌘+– (Command +dash)	Ctrl+– (Ctrl+dash)
Date placeholder	\d	\d
Time placeholder	\h	\h
Page number placeholder	\#	\#
Backslash**	\\	\\

* See the section on hyphenating for more on this.
** Because the backslash is used as part of the code to find formatting characters, you need to type in two backslashes to find just one.

Counting Your Words

You know those contests where you could win a year's supply of something by writing, in 50 words or less, why you like that product? If you like to enter contests like that, or need to write anything that has a limit on how many words you can use, you'll find the word count feature handy.

Use Word Count to get a complete report on how many characters, words, lines, paragraphs, and pages your document has. It's in the Writing Tools submenu of the Edit menu. To choose the Word Count command, pull down the Edit menu to Writing Tools. When the submenu appears on the right, carefully move the pointer over the Word Count command; then click. (Mac OS7 users, remember to keep the mouse button down and don't release until you arrive at the command.) A window appears with a complete accounting of how many of everything you have in your document. Click OK to dismiss the window when you're finished. You can also count any block of text by selecting the block before bringing up the Word Count window. Checking the Count Selection box changes the word count from a count of the total words in your document, to the total words in your selection.

Finding Synonyms

If you're ever at a loss for words, ClarisWorks has an online thesaurus — a very rare relative of the brontosaurus that lived in arboreal forests. No, no, no, everyone knows a thesaurus is a reference book used to look up synonyms.

You may be typing along without a care in the world when, suddenly, you want to say that something is "spiffy." Spiffy really isn't the word you are looking for, but that's all you can think of. Your train of thought gets completely derailed, flinging mental boxcars everywhere. To get back on track, select the word that caused the train wreck and choose Edit➪Writing Tools➪Thesaurus. That's Shift-⌘-Z (Mac) or Shift+Ctrl+Z (Windows) for you shortcutters out there. To your rescue comes the Word Finder Thesaurus dialog box shown in Figure 6-4.

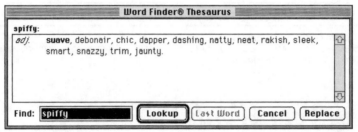

Figure 6-4:
The deadly,
synonym-
eating
thesaurus!

Here's how you use the thesaurus:

1. **(Optional) Select the word in question.**

2. **Bring up the Thesaurus by choosing Edit➪Writing Tools➪Thesaurus or other method.**

   Your word appears in the Find box at the lower left. (If you didn't select a word in your document, enter a word in the Find box yourself.)

3. **Click Lookup (or press Return or Enter since Lookup is the default).**

   You are rewarded with a scrolling list of synonyms to choose from to replace your original word.

4. **When you find a word you like, click it once to select it, and then click Replace. You may select any word from the list of synonyms.**

   The Thesaurus dialog box vanishes, and your original word is replaced with the synonym you selected.

   If you didn't select a word before you chose the Thesaurus command, clicking Replace inserts the new word in your document at the cursor.

If one of the words in the synonym list intrigues you and you want to delve into it, select it and click Lookup. Synonyms for that word will now appear. You can keep looking up words until you find one you like.

If you decide you liked one of the words you looked into, click the Last Word button for a list of the last few words you looked up since opening the Word Finder Thesaurus. Select the one you want and click Lookup again to bring this word back.

Hyphenating

Hyphenating comes in handy when you are working with columns of text. Hyphenating a column of justified text breaks the words up into smaller chunks and helps even out the spaces between words. The result can be a smoother-looking column of text — unless the column is too narrow and ends up with too many hyphenated words. You have three ways to hyphenate text:

- ✔ To add a hyphen that always appears in the word, no matter what, just type a regular dash or minus sign.

- ✔ To add a hyphen that only appears if the word moves to the end of a line, type ⌘- - (that's Command and a dash) or Ctrl+– (that's Control and a dash). This is known as a discretionary hyphen. (Discretionary hyphens don't appear when you show invisible formatting characters.)

- ✔ To automatically hyphenate an entire document or text frame, choose Edit⇨Writing Tools⇨Auto-Hyphenate. This is the easiest way to hyphenate columns of text.

Nit-picking hyphen stuff

Skip this sidebar unless where the hyphen appears in a word drives you crazy.

The Auto-Hyphenate command uses a special hyphenation dictionary to figure out where to put the hyphens in words — and may not always place the hyphen where you like it. You can give ClarisWorks specific instructions for placing your hyphens.

To call up the Hyphenation dictionary editing dialog box on the Mac, choose Edit⇨Writing Tools⇨Edit Hyphenation Dictionary.

To call up the Hyphenation dictionary editing dialog box in Windows, select Edit⇨Writing Tools⇨Select Dictionaries; then choose Hyphenation (*.chy) in the Files Of Type pop-up. Select the dictionary you want to edit from the list and click Edit.

When it appears, you can do the following:

- ✔ Add a word by typing the word in the Entry field, with hyphens where you want them, and then clicking Add.

- ✔ Edit a word you've added by clicking the word, changing the hyphenation, and clicking Replace.

- ✔ Remove a word you've added by clicking the word once, and then clicking Remove.

- ✔ Prevent a word from being hyphenated by typing the word in the Entry field without hyphens, and then clicking Add.

Chapter 7
Adding Tables, Charts, and Pictures

In This Chapter

▶ Spicing up your documents with images, charts, and graphs
▶ Creating tables with a button or with some assistance
▶ Making tables from scratch (like Grandma used to)
▶ Snapping out charts and graphs the quick way

*V*ariety is the spice of life, right? So this chapter shows you how to add variety — and, therefore, spice — to your text documents. Your documents will positively sparkle when you know how to place and position images, and how to create and position tables and charts. Why, with what you're about to learn in this very chapter, we daresay you may never create another bland, dull page again!

Adding Images (Charts and Graphs, too)

Whether you're adding a chart, graph, clip art, QuickTime video, drawing, or even a spreadsheet that's hanging out on your Clipboard doesn't make much difference to a ClarisWorks word-processing document or frame. The image can behave in two ways:

✔ **Images that act like text:** When the cursor is blinking, ClarisWorks expects text, so it attaches anything inserted *inline* as if it's a character. As you edit the text, the graphic moves along with the text. You can move the graphic to another line by pressing Return and then align it by using the text alignment options. You can select the graphic by dragging the cursor over it, as you would with text.

✔ **Images that act like objects:** When you see no cursor and the arrow pointer is the active tool, ClarisWorks expects graphics — which are object-based — so it puts the graphic in as an object. You can select objects with the arrow pointer and drag them anywhere in the document. You can *wrap* (flow) text around objects, overlap other objects, and so on. For more on working with objects, see Chapter 13.

To help you understand objects, think of transparent plastic sheets stacked on top of each other. Your text is on one layer, and each image or graph is on its own layer on top of the text.

The first step in inserting an image is to tell ClarisWorks where you want the image to be placed. You do this differently for inline and object-type images.

To tell ClarisWorks where you want to place an inline image, simply place the cursor where you want the graphic to appear, and click the mouse.

To insert an image as an object, you first need to select the arrow pointer tool. However, tools never show when you start a word-processing document. To place an image as an object, you must first make the tools visible by following these steps:

1. **Click the tool toggle icon at the bottom of the document's window (next to the page number).**

   The tools become visible.

2. **Click the arrow pointer tool.**

   The cursor changes to an arrow.

3. **Position the arrow pointer where you want the object, and click the mouse.**

   Your graphic is placed as an object at the point you clicked, even though you are still in the word-processing environment.

Popping in a picture

The previous section shows you how to control the placement and behavior of your graphic. This section shows you various ways to add images to your document:

✔ **Use copy and paste.** To copy a graphic from an existing document into your document, follow these steps:

1. **In the source document, select the graphic you want and choose Edit⇨Copy, or press ⌘-C (Mac) or Ctrl+C (Windows).**

   2. **Switch to the document to which you want to add the graphic
      and choose Edit⇨Paste, or press ⌘-V (Mac) or Ctrl+V (Windows).**

✔ **Use the Insert command.** To insert an existing graphic from your hard
   drive, follow these steps:

   1. **Choose File⇨Insert.**

      A modified open file dialog box appears. In Windows, this dialog
      box is called Insert. On the Mac, it has no name.

   2. **Navigate to the desired file, and click Insert.**

      To more easily find your image files, use the Show pop-up menu to
      choose the type of document you seek. This filters out all other
      types of document.

✔ **Use ClarisWorks Libraries.** These Libraries, located as submenus
   under File⇨Library, are floating palettes that let you browse and drag
   clip art into your document. See Chapter 12 for more on Libraries.

✔ **Draw a graphic.** Grab a draw tool and start drawing. Draw graphics are
   easy to make, and they look good when you print them. We cover them
   in Chapter 12.

✔ **Paint a graphic.** Click the paint frame tool to create a paint frame, and
   then paint away to your heart's content. Check out Chapters 10 and 11
   for more on painting.

Here's how to get rid of the rectangular border around a paint frame (or any
other frame): Select the frame (so that you see the handles at the corners).
Then click the pen thickness tool (at the bottom of the Tool Panel), and drag
to set the line thickness to none. No more border — on-screen or in print.

Aligning with the baseline

When a graphic is inline with text, it sits on the baseline of the text line. This
often doesn't look good, so you may want to move the graphic above or
below the baseline:

1. **Click the object once to select it.**

2. **Choose Format⇨Descent.**

   A simple dialog box, with only one entry option, appears.

3. **To move the graphic's base below the baseline of the text line, enter
   a positive number. To move it above the baseline of the text line,
   enter a negative number.**

   To help you select a number, the dialog box tells you the height and
   width of your graphic in points.

You can also resize a graphic, even when it is inline with text. First, select the graphic. Then drag the handle that appears on the lower right of the graphic, or choose Format➪Scale by Percent from the menu and enter the percentage you want to scale by. For more on resizing, see Chapter 12. (Don't be surprised later when Scale by Percent shows up under the Arrange menu instead. That's where it is for free-floating objects.)

Wrapping text

The main issue with graphics or frames floating around as objects within a word-processing document is that your text continues on its merry way, unaware that a table or image is on top of it. The graphic simply covers up any text that happens to be underneath it. The best way for you to remedy this is to have the text wrap around the object.

To tell the text to wrap around an object, follow these steps:

1. **Click once on your graphic to select it (with the arrow pointer).**

   The graphic is selected when you see black *handles* at the corners. If the graphic is a table or spreadsheet and you entered data in the spreadsheet environment, click once outside the table to switch environments and leave it selected. (You can do the same for a painting.)

2. **Choose Options➪Text Wrap.**

   This menu choice brings up the Text Wrap dialog box shown in Figure 7-1.

Figure 7-1:
Rapping
about how
your text
wraps.

3. **Pick a text wrap style and set the gutter:**

   • *None:* This selection is actually no text wrap. Select it to cancel previously added text wrap.

   • *Regular:* This selection wraps the text in a rectangular shape, as if an invisible rectangle is around the object.

- *Irregular:* This choice is the most fun. It wraps the text to fit the object's shape. Of course, if your object is a table, a spreadsheet, or a rectangular image, the outcome is the same as selecting Regular wrap. Remember one tricky thing, though: Sometimes your image is not rectangular, but the wrap thinks it is. Select your graphic and use Arrange⇨Ungroup to let the text flow around the individual components.

The *gutter* is the space between your text and your graphic. Enter a number, in points, to determine this space.

Now your text obediently flows around your graphic — whatever shape the graphic may be. As you edit the text or move your graphic, the text reflows. Remember that you can select the graphic as an object — regardless of what it is — and position it anywhere you like. Nudge the object around until the text flows nicely. Sometimes the tiniest nudge makes a huge difference.

Changing behaviors (Of the graphic, not yourself)

To bring a free-floating item inline with your text:

1. **Click once (with the arrow pointer) on your object to select it.**

   The object is selected when you see black handles at the corners. If you select a table, spreadsheet, or painting and you are still in that environment, click once outside of that object's borders to switch environments and select an object.

2. **Choose Edit⇨Cut.**

   Doing so removes your object and saves it in the Clipboard.

3. **Position the cursor in your text where you want the object to appear.**

   If your object is a table, chart, or something similar, putting it in its own paragraph provides the best results. That way, you can center the table with the text alignment buttons and leave the text around it aligned however you choose.

4. **Choose Edit⇨Paste to put your object into place.**

   After you paste the object into the line of text, you use the text-alignment buttons in the ruler or button bar to line up the object on the page.

To make an inline item free-floating:

1. **Click once on the object (table, spreadsheet, painting, or any object) to select it.**

   The object is selected when you see a dotted line around it, along with a black handle at the bottom right. If you're still in the object's environment, click once outside the object to switch environments and leave the object selected.

2. **Choose Edit⇨Cut.**

   Doing so saves your table to the Clipboard for safekeeping.

3. **Click the Arrow tool from the tool palette.**

   The cursor is gone.

4. **Choose Edit⇨Paste.**

   The item appears as an independent object somewhere in the center of your screen or page. Position it as you like.

Creating Tables

Before word processors had fancy table commands, you had to set up tables by using tab stops. Using tab stops is still a quick and dirty way to line up a few columns of text in your document, but not if any line needs to wrap to another line. In that case, you end up with a heck of a pain in your tab finger. The table in Figure 7-2 shows how much money the PTA has raised.

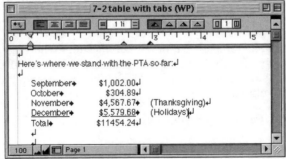

Figure 7-2:
We love the
PTA: A
sample
table made
with tabs.

Notice in Figure 7-2 that the line indent controls bring in the first column, and then the ruler has a tab stop for the next two columns. The first tab stop (on the left) is an *align on* or *decimal* tab, which is most appropriate for the column of numbers there. The next tab stop is an *align left* tab to place the comments text flush left. Chapter 5 gives you more information on the different kinds of tabs and on setting tab stops.

Tables with a click or an Assistant

Okay, you want a table with a little more flair — with more formatting options than you have with tab stops. No problem. ClarisWorks integration to the rescue! ClarisWorks tables are actually spreadsheets. But you don't have to deal with all the spreadsheet-like stuff. You see only a table that is ready to type information into.

The Make Table button and the Make Table Assistant share the same name, but they take different approaches to putting a table into your text document.

The Make Table button

The Make Table button is the economy-class way to put a table in your document. Although it offers no frills, the Make Table button acts in a single click — the nonstop, express route. The Make Table button (located on the default button bar) is the button that looks like — you guessed it — a table!

Just position the cursor where you want the table to appear, and click the table button once. We suggest putting the table on a line by itself and centering it with the Center Align button in the ruler. If you need to add or remove rows or columns, click once on the table (which selects it as an object) and drag the handle (the little black square) in the lower-right corner. If you need to do any more-complex formatting than that, use the Make Table Assistant or skip ahead to the section titled "Formatting a Table" for formatting tips.

If you've already begun a table using tabs, such as the one in Figure 7-2, the Make Table button converts it to a table in one click.

The Make Table Assistant

If the Make Table button is like flying economy class, the Make Table Assistant is like cruising on the QE II — not quite as fast, but someone is there to iron your newspaper. The Assistant asks you how you want the formatting before it makes the table. That way, you get a nifty-looking table without bothering with any scary spreadsheet-formatting stuff. If your table is a schedule and has days or months as headings, the Make Table Assistant automatically enters the headings for you. Basically, the only work you do is to answer a few simple questions. Figure 7-3 shows you a sample screen from the Make Table Assistant, as well as a sample of its table-making.

To summon the Make Table Assistant, choose ClarisWorks Assistants from the Help menu. When the Select Assistant dialog box appears, double-click Make Table.

When you get to the Table Assistant window, everything is pretty much self-explanatory. You just provide information on what kind of data you want in your table, how many rows and columns you want, which font you want, and so on. When you are satisfied with your choices, click the Next button. If you change your mind about a setting you made in a previous screen, click Back. To start all over, click Begin. Last, but not least, if you decide you don't want to make a table after all, click Cancel.

When the Table Assistant has all the information it needs, the Next button changes to a Create button, which you click to drop the table you've ordered into your document. If you need to change any of the formatting from there, see the "Formatting a Table" section, later in this chapter, for formatting tips.

Figure 7-3:
Your table
is ready, sir.
The Make
Table
Assistant
and a table
it created.

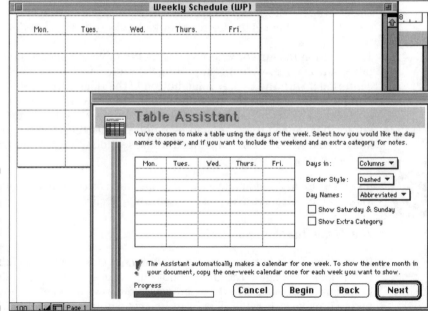

Tables from scratch

This section shows you how to create a table on your own. When you create a table, you are actually creating a spreadsheet frame in your text document:

1. **Bring up the Tool Panel by clicking the Tool toggle button in the lower-left corner of the document window, by choosing Window⇨ Show Tools, or by pressing Shift-⌘-T (Mac) or Shift+Ctrl+T (Windows).**

2. **Click once on the spreadsheet frame tool to select it.**

   It's the one that looks like a fat plus sign.

3. **Move your cursor (which now looks like a plus sign) to where you want to place the table. Hold down your mouse button while dragging to create a rectangle that is the size of the table you want. Then release the mouse button.**

   A spreadsheet now fills in the rectangle you just made.

Entering Data into Your Table

Entering data into a spreadsheet is a bit different from typing in a word-processing document. When you select a cell (by double-clicking it) and start typing, the text you enter does not go directly into the cell. Instead, it appears in the data entry bar at the top of the document window. The data entry bar appears above the text ruler whenever you switch to the spreadsheet environment. Figure 7-4 shows the data entry bar and the entry buttons. After you type the text that you want to appear in the cell, click the check mark to enter it or the X to delete it.

In addition to the check mark button, you can use several keys to enter text in the cell:

✔ Pressing the Return key enters the text and moves down one cell in the column.

✔ Pressing Tab enters the text and moves one cell to the right.

✔ Holding down Shift and pressing Tab enters text and moves left one cell.

✔ Pressing Option (Mac) or Ctrl (Windows), plus any arrow key, enters text and moves one cell in the direction of the arrow.

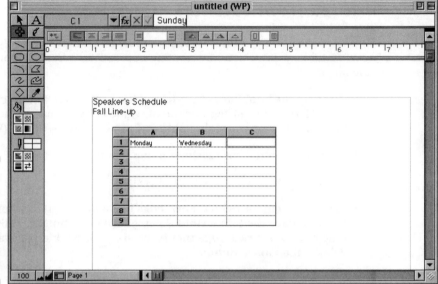

Figure 7-4:
Belly up to
the data
entry bar to
type text
into table
cells.

To enter text in adjacent columns or rows, select the entire block of cells you want to enter text into, and then use Return to enter text in columns or use Tab to enter text in rows.

When you use Tab to move around within the selection, you move to the end of a row and then skip back to the beginning of the next row. The same applies to Return: You first move down to the bottom of a column; then you skip back to the top of the column to the right. The cell that remains white in the selected block is where the text you type is entered.

A set of Spreadsheet Preferences is located under the Edit⇨Preferences menu. These preferences allow you to alter the way the arrows and the Return or Enter key behave. That's handy if you are used to these keys behaving differently. For more information on Spreadsheet Preferences, see Chapter 15.

Formatting a Table

You can use these formatting tips regardless of how you create the table. Because you are actually working in the spreadsheet environment when you format your table, you may notice that the menus change. Don't be alarmed. They change back to what you're used to when you go back to the text environment.

Quick tips for formatting tables

If you want the complete story on formatting spreadsheets, see Chapters 15 and 16. For now, here are some quick tips:

✔ You need to select the cells you want to format before you apply formatting commands.

✔ You can select one or more cells, columns, or rows, or select the whole table to format. (You can select blocks of cells in a rectangular shape only.)

✔ A selected cell has a heavy border around it.

✔ A group of selected cells is highlighted.

✔ The cell in the corner where you start your selection stays white, but it's still selected. The heavy border around the highlighted cells tells you which ones are selected.

Make sure that you're using the spreadsheet frame tool (the fat plus-sign pointer) before you try to select cells. If you try to drag a spreadsheet frame without the spreadsheet frame tool, you just end up moving the table. (If you move the table, select Edit➪Undo Move.) The fastest way to get the spreadsheet frame tool is to double-click the table.

Here's how you select cells in a spreadsheet frame:

✔ **To select a single cell,** click it. (Remember that you are actually double-clicking if this is the first time you are accessing the cells with a pointer cursor.)

✔ **To select a row,** click the number at the left side of that column. The numbers show only if you made the table from scratch or if you choose to have them show by using Options➪Display.

✔ **To select a column,** click the letter at the top of that column. The letters show only if you made the table from scratch or if you choose to have them show by using Options➪Display.

✔ **To select a row or column** if you used the button or Assistant and the letters and numbers are not visible along the top and side, just drag through an entire row or column.

✔ **To select a block of cells,** place the fat plus-sign pointer in one corner and drag to the diagonally opposite corner of the group of cells that you want to select.

After you select the cells, you can apply formatting commands by using menus, keyboard shortcuts, or buttons. Remember that the menus change to the spreadsheet environment menus when you are working on a table. All the text formatting commands are now located in submenus in the Format menu, including the commands for text size, style, alignment, font, and color. All keyboard shortcuts for the formatting commands remain the same, though. Speaking of buttons, they also change to be spreadsheet-specific.

Because you are working in the spreadsheet environment, all the number formatting and calculation abilities of a spreadsheet are available in your table. See Chapters 16 and 18 for more information on number formats and spreadsheet formulas.

You can use color to draw attention to all or part of your table. Just select the cells you want to color, and use the fill tool to pick a color. You can find out more about the fill tool in Chapter 12. The Stylesheet also provides predesigned table styles that you can use to create quite an eye-popping table.

Changing column width and row height

To change the width of your columns or the height of your rows, you can use the Column width or Row height dialog boxes or drag the column or row with the mouse.

To use the Column width or Row height dialog boxes:

1. **Select a column or row by clicking its heading.**

   For rows, the heading is the number on the left; for columns, the heading is the letter at the top. You can also select multiple columns or rows and change them all at once.

2. **Choose Format⇨Column Width or Format⇨Row Height.**

   The Column width or Row height dialog box appears. The Row height dialog box is shown in Figure 7-5, but the two dialog boxes look the same.

3. **Type the new value in the field, or check the box labeled Use Default.**

   The default is 72 for column width and 14 for row height. Click OK when you finish.

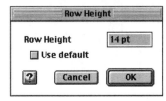

Figure 7-5:
The two
ways to
change row
height and
column
width.

To change the row height or column width manually with the mouse:

1. **Make sure that you are using the spreadsheet frame tool (the fat plus sign).**

   Select the spreadsheet frame tool from the Tool Panel if necessary.

2. **Move the pointer to the line between the rows or columns of the spreadsheet; click and drag that line to change the row height or column width.**

   The pointer changes to a double-headed arrow with a line in the middle. To see the pointer, refer back to Figure 7-5, in column A.

Hiding and showing column and row headings

After you format your table, you may want to get rid of the column and row headings — the numbers and letters at the top and left sides. Or perhaps you want to show the column and row headings to make formatting a premade table easier. Either way, here's what you do:

1. **Choose Options⇨Display.**

   If you don't see an Options menu, enter the spreadsheet environment first. Double-click the table with the arrow pointer tool to enter spreadsheet mode.

   You should now see the Display dialog box shown in Figure 7-6. You are interested in the top two check boxes on the right side — the ones labeled Column headings and Row headings.

Figure 7-6:
The Display
dialog box
lets you
turn off row
and column
headings.

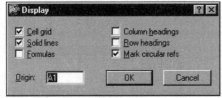

2. **Uncheck Column headings to make the letters disappear from the tops of the columns. Uncheck Row headings to make the numbers disappear from the left sides of the rows.**

3. **Click OK.**

One of the most useful buttons hides and shows the column and row headings with just one click. For some reason, it's not a default button on the spreadsheet button bar, so you have to add it. See Chapter 2.

While you're looking at the Display dialog box, notice that you can also turn the grid lines on or off and make them appear as solid black lines. Another button helps you with this.

Positioning your table

You can have your table in line with your text or as an object (on a transparent layer). Just be aware of the text cursor or lack thereof when you create your table. Regardless of how the table comes in, you can cut and paste it to behave as you like.

The Make Table button is available only in word-processing mode, so tables made with that button appear inline with your text. Tables made with the Make Table Assistant can be inline (if your cursor was flashing when you selected the Assistant) or free floating (if you clicked the arrow tool before you selected the Assistant). Tables from scratch are always free floating.

If you want your table to operate independently from your text, leave it as a floating frame.

To make a caption for your floating table that sticks to your table like bubble gum on a mustache, create a text frame in your text document. You can do this in two ways. One way is to select the text tool (the A) from the Tool Panel, and then press Option (Mac) or Alt (Windows) as you drag a box to create a text frame. Now type a caption for your table. The other way is to type your caption anywhere in your text environment, and then cut this text and paste it in as an object (by activating the arrow pointer instead of the cursor). Either way, after the caption is typed, click outside the frame to select it as an object and position it. To make life easier, select the two items as objects and select Arrange⇨Group. (You can find more about selecting multiple items and grouping in Chapter 12.)

Remember, here we're assuming that you are working in a word-processing document. In a drawing document, your tables, spreadsheets, and text blocks are all free-floating objects, so this stuff about text getting in the way won't happen. Of course, you could have a text frame on a drawing document and attach a spreadsheet inside the frame. Or you could make blocks of text wrap around the spreadsheet or table. You will come up with many ideas of your own as you explore the various chapters in this book and experiment with ClarisWorks yourself.

Quick and Dirty Chartmaking

You have two ways to put a chart in a document: Copy and paste a chart from a separate spreadsheet document, or create a chart from a spreadsheet frame right there in your document. This section shows you how to create a chart from a spreadsheet frame in your document because that method takes about the same effort as the other method — and it gives you more flexibility to update the chart if your numbers change.

1. **Start by creating a spreadsheet frame in your document.**

   If you already have a table or spreadsheet in your document, skip to Step 2 or 3. If you don't, select the spreadsheet frame tool and drag a box, which creates a new spreadsheet frame.

2. **Enter the data for your chart into the spreadsheet.**

   The number of columns of data determines what kind of chart works best for you. This example creates a pie chart, which needs only one column of numbers.

3. **Select the block of cells containing the data for your chart.**

4. **Click the button that represents the chart you want.**

Voilà, your chart is done. Is that cool, or what? Figure 7-7 shows you the spreadsheet, the pie chart, and the chart buttons.

The only thing left to do is tidy everything up so that your chart appears where you want it.

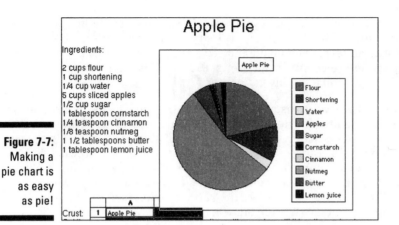

Charts, of course, can be either inline or floating. Flip back to the "Adding Images" section for more information on how to keep your chart inline or make it float. And to fine-tune the look or colors, see Chapter 17, which covers more than you ever thought you'd need to know about charts.

Chapter 8

Outlining — You Gotta Start Somewhere

In This Chapter

▶ Making outlines work for you

▶ Experimenting with your document structure using outlines

▶ Viewing and hiding the information in outlines

▶ Customizing outline formats and labels

*M*aking an outline lets you brainstorm the structure of your document before you fill in the details. The ClarisWorks outliner enables you to do cool stuff, such as rearrange the order of your topics, assign subtopics to other topics, and expand and collapse your outline to get the big picture. Believe it or not, people who don't have ClarisWorks shell out big bucks for special outlining applications to get the features you already have.

When you use an outline, paragraphs become *headings,* or *topics,* in your outline. Topics that are indented under another topic are *subtopics.*

Most people don't give outlining a chance because they take a quick look, get frustrated, and move on. Outlining is actually pretty simple to use, but unlike plain word processing, outlining has no real-world counterpart. Most people can see how word processing is like a typewriter, but they have never used a tool that lets them easily change the structure of their outline. Think of an outline as a bunch of sticky notes, with one topic on each note, that you put up on the wall and move around until you like the flow. Outlining goes beyond that analogy, though, because you also can collapse your outline down to see just the top-level structure and then expand it again to fill in or view the details.

Take a quick look through this chapter to get an idea of how ClarisWorks outlining works. Then, the next time you have to give a speech, do a presentation, write a report, or such, give it a try.

Setting Up an Outline

With ClarisWorks, you can add an outline anywhere in any text document or frame. All you have to do is use an outline style. You find these styles either in the Styles pop-up menu on the ruler or in the stylesheet palette. You can either select the text you want to use in an outline and apply a style or you can choose a style and start typing. The outline styles are grouped together at the bottom of the Styles pop-up menu. You can choose from three pre-defined outline styles, or you can create your own. The following examples use the diamond format.

Here are the basics for setting up an outline:

- ✔ To create a new topic at the same level as the present topic, press the Return key (the Enter key on most PCs).

- ✔ To create a subtopic under the current topic, choose Outline⇨New Topic Right or press ⌘-R (Mac) or Ctrl+R (Windows). Doing so indents the topic to the right.

- ✔ To create a new topic that is one level higher in the outline than the current topic, choose Outline ⇨New Topic Left, or press ⌘-L (Mac) or Ctrl+L (Windows). Doing so moves the topic to the left. (You can't create a new topic at a higher level than the main level. If you try, nothing happens, except maybe an error beep if you're on a Mac.)

- ✔ To change a topic you already created into a subtopic, choose Outline⇨ Move Right, or press Shift-⌘-R (Mac) or Shift+Ctrl+R (Windows). The topic becomes a subtopic, even if no higher-level topic is above it.

- ✔ To move an already-created topic one level higher, choose Outline⇨ Move Left, or press Shift-⌘-L (Mac) or Shift+Ctrl+L (Windows).

Figure 8-1 shows you a sample outline in the diamond format. Topics that don't have subtopics have empty diamonds, topics with subtopics under them have filled diamonds, and topics that have subtopics that are collapsed and not visible have shaded diamonds.

Figure 8-1:
Today's topic: Outlines and the traveling women who love them.

Rearranging Outline Topics

When you see your ideas for topics and subtopics on-screen, you'll undoubtedly want to rearrange them and move sections around. ClarisWorks outliner gives you the flexibility to restructure, which is why you use it instead of formatting your outline manually.

Moving text around works a little differently in an outline view. When you move a topic that has subtopics under it, the subtopics move with the main topic — unless you force ClarisWorks to leave the subtopics behind. You can move your topics up and down within your outline in several ways: with the mouse, with keyboard shortcuts, or with menu commands.

To use the mouse to move topics up and down, move the pointer to the left of the topic that you want to move, and press the mouse button. The pointer changes to a bar with up and down arrows. (You have to drag the mouse a tad before the moving pointer materializes.) Now drag the topic up or down. A black bar at the left edge of the document shows you where the topic ends up. Release the mouse when the topic's black bar is where you want it. Figure 8-2 shows you how it's done.

Figure 8-2:
Using a
mouse to
move a
topic.

Unfortunately, you can't move topics right or left by using the mouse or any special buttons. You need a menu command or a keyboard shortcut.

Keyboard or menu commands for shuffling your topics are listed in Table 8-1.

Table 8-1	Commands for Rearranging Your Outline Topics
To Make This Happen	**Do This**
Collapse a topic	Choose Outline⇨Collapse or double-click to the left of the topic.
Expand a topic	Choose Outline⇨Expand or double-click to the left of the topic.
Move a topic up in the outline	Choose Outline⇨Move Above or press Control-↑ (Mac). Windows has no shortcut.

(continued)

Table 8-1 *(continued)*

To Make This Happen	*Do This*
Move a topic down in the outline	Choose Outline⇨Move Below menu or press Control-↓ (Mac). Windows has no shortcut.
Move a topic right in the outline	Choose Outline⇨Move Right or press Shift-⌘-R or Control-→ (Mac) or Shift+Ctrl+R (Windows).
Move a topic left in the outline	Choose Outline⇨Move Left or press Shift-⌘-L or Control-← (Mac) or Shift+Ctrl+L (Windows).
Move a topic only, without its subtopics	Press Option (Mac)/ Alt (Windows) and choose a move command from the Outline menu, or, on a Mac, press Option-Control and an arrow key.
Select a topic and its subtopics	Click the topic's label (the number, letter, or symbol at its left). Drag to reposition.
Select a topic without its subtopics	Click anywhere in the topic's text.

Collapsing and Expanding Outlines

One of outlining's most powerful features is the capability to collapse subtopics and look at only the top-level headings. When you look at just top-level headings, you can get an overview of the structure of your document and make changes without the lower-level topics cluttering up the page. If you move a topic with collapsed subtopics under it, the subtopics follow along. Table 8-2 shows you how all this collapsing and expanding works.

Table 8-2   Expanding and Collapsing Subtopics

To Make This Happen	*Do This*
Collapse subtopics under a topic	Choose Outline⇨Collapse or double-click the topic's label.
Expand subtopics under a topic	Choose Outline⇨Expand or double-click the topic's label.
Expand or collapse the entire outline	Choose Outline⇨Expand To and type a level number in the Expand To dialog box.

If you need to expand your outline to show all subtopics, bring up the Expand To dialog box and type in **16**. That's the maximum number of levels ClarisWorks allows, and it expands your outline to the lowest level. To collapse the outline again, type in a smaller number, like 2 or 3.

Outline Formats and Custom Outline Styles

The diamond format is cool because it shows you which topics have subtopics under them, even when the subtopics are collapsed and not visible. However, you may be used to another outline format, or you may need to use another format because of the requirements for your document. ClarisWorks has three built-in outline styles, and you can create as many more as you like. The different formats use different kinds of labels for the different levels of topics.

Built-in formats and labels

The six built-in outline formats are Diamond, Numeric, Harvard, Legal, Bulleted list, and Check list. Diamond is the default; you've already seen examples of it.

Here's a quick breakdown of the formats and what each is good for:

- **Diamond format:** A straightforward format that easily helps to whip your outline structure into shape.

- **Harvard format:** The one to use if you are a student. It's what most of us think of when we hear the word *outline*.

- **Legal format:** The one to use if you're a lawyer. It's like the numeric format but more precise. Using the Legal format, topic 4, subtopic 2 is labeled 4.2. If three more subtopics fall under 4.2, you have 4.2.1 through 4.2.3. This format makes it easy to be precise — just what lawyers like.

- **Numeric format:** Simply numbers each topic and subtopic. It can be handy if you need to point out a specific subtopic. Refer to the topic and subtopic numbers like this: Topic 4, subtopic 2.

- **Bulleted list format:** Uses a bullet point as the label for each level of the outline. This format is very simple and looks good in presentations.

> ✔ **Check list format:** Like the Bulleted list format but uses a check box instead of a bullet. The check box is live — click it and a check mark appears or disappears. This format is great for presentations or check lists. A line appears under the check box in front of topics that have collapsed subtopics under them.

Custom labels

Apply one outline style or format to your whole outline — or change the label or style format for specific topics within an outline. This section shows you how to change the labels on isolated topics. (To change the label for all topics on a specific outline level, skip to the next section, "Custom outline styles.")

Suppose you have a Harvard outline but need a checklist somewhere within it. No problem. Or what if, within your diamond outline, you have a group of subheadings that need to show the order of steps in a set of instructions? Again, no problem.

To apply a different type of label to a topic or topics, follow these steps:

1. **Select one topic by clicking in the topic text. Select several topics by dragging through their text.**

2. **Choose the style you want from the Paragraph Styles pop-up menu or the stylesheet palette.**

Turning an ordered outline style into an unordered style such as bullets or a check list jumps that section back to the left margin. You can move it back. Just be sure to note where the sections are at the time you apply the new style.

You can make a topic into plain body text by selecting the topic and applying the body — or any other body text — style.

Custom outline styles

Because ClarisWorks has only three real outline styles built-in, you may feel a bit limited in your options. Fear not! You can create a custom outline style the same way you create a custom paragraph style. Here's how:

1. **If the stylesheet palette is not showing, choose Window⇨Show Stylesheet, or press Shift-⌘-W (Mac) or Shift+Ctrl+W (Windows).**

2. **Click the New button at the bottom of the palette.**

   The New Style dialog box appears.

3. Enter a name for your new style.

ClarisWorks automatically fills in something like Style 1, but it's best to use a meaningful name, such as *Chapter Heading* or *Caption*.

4. Click the radio button next to Outline, under Style Type.

5. Choose a style to be the starting point for your new style from the Based On pop-up menu.

You can use any existing style for the basis of your new outline style. If you want to start completely from scratch, choose None. To start with the normal default paragraph formatting, choose Default.

If you base your outline style on another paragraph style and later change the formatting of that paragraph style, your outline formatting changes, too.

6. Uncheck the box next to Inherit Document Selection Format.

Unless you want your outline style to use the formatting of some selected text, make sure that this box is not checked.

7. Click OK.

Your new outline style now appears in the Edit Style window of the stylesheet palette.

8. Click the triangle next to your new style to view and edit the different outline levels.

Choose an outline level to format.

9. Choose the settings for your new outline style from the menus, the ruler, or the button bar:

- *Selecting formatting:* While you are picking formatting for the style, the pointer changes to an outline S with an arrow in the upper-left corner. Use this pointer to choose the formatting options for your new style. The choices you make appear in the Properties dialog box at the right of the Edit Style window.

- *Easy selection:* You can select many formatting options with the Paragraph dialog box. To pull it up, choose Format⇨Paragraph.

- *Mixing outline types:* Choose topic labels from the Label pop-up menu at the lower-left corner of the Paragraph dialog box. You can mix different topic label types in the same outline style. For example, use the Harvard format, but make all level four topics into checklists.

- *Viewing a sample:* To see the result of your choices, choose Show Sample from the Edit menu of the stylesheet palette. (This is different from the Edit menu on the menu bar.)

- *Removing properties:* If you ever decide you don't like a property, select it in the Properties list and use Cut Properties from the Edit menu of the stylesheet palette. (Don't worry, it only cuts the one you select.)

- *Copying properties:* When you have set the look for one level, you can select the properties by clicking and dragging down the list or by pressing Option or Ctrl as you click each property you want. Then select Copy Properties from the Edit menu of the stylesheet palette and click the next style level and Paste Properties.

10. Click Done when you finish.

Your new style appears in the Stylesheet list.

For more information on styles and the Paragraph dialog box, see Chapter 5.

Part III
Working with Graphics: Get the Picture?

The 5th Wave   By Rich Tennant

Get the Huggies, hon— she's reaching for the Diaper icon

In this part . . .

Are you ready to flex your artistic muscle? Next to text, graphics is probably the most often used feature of ClarisWorks. Pictures liven up your text with clip art or a company logo. With the simple graphic tools in ClarisWorks, you can easily add artwork to your documents without figuring out a whole new application. And by using draw documents to set up pages of text and pictures, you can make documents that look like they were created with high-end page layout applications. Any way you slice it, graphics make you look good.

Chapter 9
Drawing versus Painting

• •

In This Chapter

▶ When to use a draw document

▶ When to use a paint document

▶ How drawing works

▶ How painting works

▶ How to combine draw and paint

• •

*1*f a picture is worth a thousand words, this chapter gives you a chance to save a hefty amount of typing. ClarisWorks is a natural for pictures and other *graphics,* as the designer folks call them.

The ClarisWorks paint environment and draw environment descend from the legendary early programs for the personal computer: MacPaint and MacDraw. You don't have to be able to draw a cartoon turtle to use these graphics tools, either. You can do wonders in the drawing environment by simply creating a few shapes and moving them together. Even a rectangle in the right place on your letterhead creates a nice accent. If you are artistic, you can create something as complex as a stylized logo with special effects in the paint environment. The graphic environments have their own special features and tricks. Don't worry — with this book, you can get through the dark alleys of graphic manipulation unscathed.

When it comes to graphics, the main question for most people is, "Do I draw or do I paint?" The answer depends on the kinds of graphics you want and how you want to manipulate them. In general, drawing lets you manipulate the big picture — for example, when you want to create a layout with both text and simple graphics — and it gives you sharp printouts. Painting works on a smaller scale — for example, when you want to apply special effects to your graphics and do more detailed editing — and its images may look somewhat coarse when printed out. The rest of this chapter goes into more detail about each of the graphic environments and helps you decide which is right for your work.

When to Draw

Draw documents are great when you need text and graphics on the same page. When printed, draw documents produce crisp graphics and razor-sharp text. These qualities make draw documents good for the following purposes:

- Diagrams
- Flowcharts
- Maps
- Line-drawing illustrations
- Envelopes
- Invitations
- Paper doll cutouts
- Pop-up paper geodesic domes that have your résumé on the inside
- Page layout

That's right; you read that last item correctly. One of the most popular uses for draw documents is for page layout — creating printed pages that contain some combination of graphics, text, charts, and spreadsheets on one page. Using a draw document gives you the most flexibility to position all those different types of information on a page.

When to Paint

Use a paint document for the following purposes:

- Create freehand art
- Make illustrations that you can edit down to the individual pixel
- Create logos
- Apply special effects like free rotate, distort, and perspective to text and graphics
- Edit scanned photos
- Forge copies of the world's art masterpieces

Painting gives you more flexibility to manipulate images. You edit paint images dot by dot (or pixel by pixel in computerese) to get the exact picture you want. This flexibility comes at a price. Graphics and text created in the paint environment may look coarse or jaggy when printed. The trick is to match the document's resolution, or the number of dots per inch, to your printer's resolution. When the printer and document resolutions match, your document prints as clearly as possible. For more information about resolution, see Chapter 10.

Advantages and Disadvantages

In order to help you decide which environment— draw or paint — is better for your graphic task, consider the advantages and disadvantages of each.

Advantages of the draw environment:

- You can always move, resize, or fill a draw shape with a different color.

- Each draw shape is an independent object and can be moved without disturbing other objects. Take a look at Figure 9-1 for an example.

- Draw graphics look great when you print them, even when they have been resized.

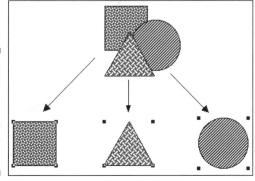

Figure 9-1:
Individual objects can be moved separately in the draw environment.

Advantages of the paint environment:

- ClarisWorks painting works like ink or watercolors. You can paint over an image or mix colors.

- You can make changes to every dot in a paint image.

- You can create more detailed artwork in the paint environment than in the draw environment.

✔ You can use a variety of special effects on a paint image that are not available in the draw environment.

✔ Paint lets you move chunks of your image, rather than individual shapes. See Figure 9-2 for an example.

Figure 9-2:
Moving a
selection in
the paint
environment.

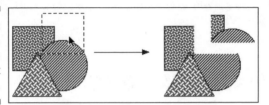

Here are some disadvantages to the draw and paint environments:

✔ After you put a shape on the page in the paint environment, it is no longer recognized as a specific shape, just as a pattern of color. That means you can't modify individual shapes like you can in the draw environment.

✔ Frames are draw objects that give you a window to another environment. As far as the draw environment is concerned, a frame is just another rectangle. Of course, when you start working inside the frame, that's another story. In that case, the frame is no longer an object to be moved, but it is a whole other tiny document all its own.

The Best of Both Worlds

Paint and draw environments have their unique advantages. Fortunately, you don't have to choose one over the other. Thanks to the ClarisWorks integration, you can paint and draw in the same document. Simply create one or more paint frames in a draw document. Using both environments in a single document gives you the flexibility to move objects and frames on the page and print high-quality text, while retaining the best features of the paint environment.

Are you wondering why we didn't say you can create a draw frame in a paint document? It's because you can't. Remember that the draw environment doesn't use a separate frame. Besides, all the graphics tools work in a paint-like way in the paint environment. You can select a draw tool and use it — but it turns "painted" when you click off of the object.

Actually, frames don't really exist in the paint environment. Everything you add is simply painted onto the page — even a spreadsheet. You can place a spreadsheet and even place information in it, but after you click outside of it, you can't go back to edit it with the spreadsheet tools.

When you use paint frames in a draw document, you typically use the draw tools for design elements, such as lines, solid shapes, diagrams, and maps. You use the paint frames for detailed graphics and graphics with special effects, such as company logos.

You can make some really awesome-looking graphics when you use each environment for what it does best. Look at Figure 9-3 for an example of what you can do when you combine the two graphics environments.

Figure 9-3:
Party time!
How
combining
paint and
draw
graphics
can make
you more
popular.

Chapter 10
Painting — by the Numbers

· ·

In This Chapter

▶ Things to remember when painting

▶ Painting with shapes

▶ Changing borders and fills

▶ Setting the paint mode

▶ Using freehand paint tools

▶ Selecting areas in paint

▶ Erasing and deleting mistakes

▶ Modifying how tools work

▶ Setting document size, resolution, and colors

▶ Editing patterns, gradients, and textures

· ·

*R*emember in preschool doing all those great works of art for your parents to hang proudly on the fridge? Working with the paint environment can bring back those fond memories.

Part of the fun of making graphics with the paint environment is simply playing around — trying all the tools, experimenting, and exploring new ways to make your pictures look cool. You can't get stains on your clothes, you never run out of paper, and the teacher won't scold you for eating the paint!

However, keep in mind that painting works much like real paint on a canvas: After something is on the page, you can't change its shape or size.

Painting Pointers

For the most part, tools in ClarisWorks work the same in every environment, so when you know what any tool does, you're set. Before you can work with a tool, you must select it by clicking the desired tool.

You don't bring a tool to your *paper* by dragging the tool. Instead, click the tool and release your mouse button. Then move your mouse to the page and click (holding the mouse button down) where you want to begin creating the shape. Bear this in mind as you work with any shape tool in any environment.

In the paint environment, double-clicking some tools not only selects the tool but also displays a dialog box that controls how the tool works. Bringing up a dialog box by accident is okay, but it creates an extra step when you have to close the dialog box. (The tool controls in those dialog boxes are explained later in this chapter.)

The frame tools, located at the top of the Tool Panel, work differently in the paint environment than in any other ClarisWorks environment. Here are the differences:

- The arrow pointer and the paintbrush don't have any frame-related functions in the paint environment. Instead, they provide a pencil that you can use to write all over your page.

- The text tool works within the text frame it creates, but after you click outside the text box, your text is painted onto the background, and you can't use text commands to edit it anymore. The only exception is when you add a header or footer to a paint document. Inside the header and footer, all the normal text features and editing capabilities are available at your command.

- The spreadsheet tool also works, but as with the text tool, after you click outside the spreadsheet frame, the spreadsheet is painted onto the background, and you no longer can change the numbers with the spreadsheet commands. You can't make a chart, either. (But you can paste in a chart from somewhere else.)

Although you can edit text and draw objects any time, after an object is placed in a painting, editing is trickier and can be tedious. Don't be afraid to try anything, but be aware that you should check your results right away in case you want to undo the last thing you did. If you realize that you want to undo something later, you still have the option of the File⇨Revert command, which reverts your entire document back to the way it was when you last saved it.

Shaping Your World

Do you like your pizza round or square? With the ClarisWorks paint environment, you can make your pizza any shape you like. Figure 10-1 shows the nine shape tools in the Tool Panel.

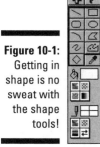

Figure 10-1:
Getting in
shape is no
sweat with
the shape
tools!

Each of the nine shape tools is described next, along with a display of its icon and a description of how you use the tool:

The line tool paints straight lines. Click the line tool icon to select it, and then click the location on your page where you want the line to begin. Without releasing the mouse button, drag the mouse to the point where you want the line to end. If you want to constrain the line to a horizontal, vertical, or 45-degree line, hold down the Shift key while you drag the mouse.

Rectangles and squares are easy to make with the rectangle tool. First select the rectangle tool by clicking once on its icon. Then click where you want a corner of the rectangle to appear. Keeping the left mouse button pressed, drag the mouse to the point where you want the opposite corner of the rectangle to be located. To draw a perfect square, press the Shift key while you drag the mouse.

The round rectangle tool works the same as the rectangle tool, except that it makes kinder and gentler rectangles, with rounded corners.

To create an oval or a perfect circle, use the oval tool. As with the other tools, click the tool, click the point where you want the oval to begin, and drag in any direction to expand it to the size you want. To constrain your shape to a circle, hold Shift as you draw.

Use the arc tool to make sections of round shapes. The default is a quarter of an oval. Click to select this tool. Then click the location where you want the arc to begin. While holding the mouse button down, drag in the direction that you want the arc to curve. Release the mouse button at the end of the arc. Later in this chapter, you find a description of the various adjustments you can make to your arc by using the Arc Tool dialog box.

Use the polygon tool to make odd shapes with straight edges. The polygon tool works differently from the other shape tools. Select the tool as usual. However, with this tool, you click at the starting point of your shape, but immediately release the mouse button. Now drag in the direction you want the line to go. As you drag, a line follows. Click the mouse button again to end that line segment. Repeat this process, dragging and clicking to create line segments. When you get to the place where you want the last segment to end, simply double-click.

The squiggle tool lets you paint a freehand line. Click the squiggle tool, and then click where you want to begin your line. Keep the mouse button pressed as you drag freehand-style in any direction you desire. Release the mouse button when you're done.

For freehand shapes with curved "sides," call on the bezigon tool. This tool works like the polygon tool but makes curves rather than straight lines. Think of the line as a piece of flexible wire; every time you click the mouse, you stake a *tack* that the wire curves around. As you bend the wire around a tack, the length behind it bows out as well. You really have to try this tool to see how it works. If you want a straight side, hold down the Option (Mac) or Alt (Windows) key.

The regular polygon tool draws multisided shapes, such as squares, pentagons, octagons, and so on, with all sides equal in length. After you select the polygon tool, click the location where you want one corner of your polygon to appear. While pressing the mouse button, drag away from your starting point to expand the shape. The direction you move in determines the direction of the shape. The shape pivots around the starting point. Your polygon can have anywhere from 3 to 40 sides. Double-click the polygon tool in the Tool Panel to bring up the Number of Sides dialog box, and enter the desired number.

You can modify how certain shape tools behave by pressing keys on the keyboard or by setting options in dialog boxes. Check out the section in this chapter called "Hot Rod Your Tools" for more information.

Borders, Lines, and Fills

Ladies and gentlemen, have your passports ready; we'll be crossing into Indonesia in three minutes. Actually, this border is the kind that outlines the shapes you create in the paint environment.

Any shape you create can have any color, fill, or border but, in the paint environment, choose these aspects before you make the shape. You can't always change them after the shape is placed on the page.

If all your shapes were solid black, life would be pretty boring. The fill palettes enable you to avoid such a tedious fate. You have several choices of fill types: solid colors, patterns, colors and patterns in tandem, gradient fills, and textures. Each fill type can be edited, except the solid colors — but you can change those, too. Figure 10-2 shows the fill palette icons.

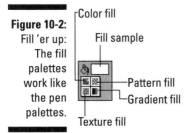

Figure 10-2:
Fill 'er up:
The fill
palettes
work like
the pen
palettes.

Color fill

Fill sample

Pattern fill

Gradient fill

Texture fill

The pen palettes control the borders and lines of the shape and lines you create. Borders are preset to a thin black line around a solid black shape, so you may not even know they are there. You can change borders and lines to any color, thickness, or pattern you want. Straight lines can also have arrowheads. Figure 10-3 shows the icons for the pen palettes and the palettes that pop up when you click the icons.

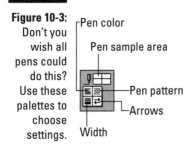

Figure 10-3:
Don't you
wish all
pens could
do this?
Use these
palettes to
choose
settings.

Pen color

Pen sample area

Pen pattern

Arrows

Width

To select the color of your new shape or line, click the icon for the palette you want to choose from. These icons are actually pop-up palettes. Hold down the mouse button and drag to the color, pattern, texture, or gradient you want. The color you select appears with a ring around it.

✔ To select fill for a shape, use the fill palettes beneath the paint bucket.

✔ To select a line color or pattern, use the palettes beneath the pen tool.

The color you select appears in the sample area next to the tool you selected it for. The sample area gives you an opportunity to preview your choices.

> **TIP**
>
> If you want to see all your fill or line choices more clearly or if you just don't like pop-up menus, you can *tear off* a part of the toolbar and position it anywhere on-screen. To tear off any pen or fill palette, click the icon for the palette. When the palette pops up, move your pointer to the edge of it, hold for a few seconds, and drag it away from the tool bar. After you tear off a pen palette, simply click to select your choice. To return the palette to the tool bar, click the close box, just as you do with any other window. Figure 10-4 shows a pen palette popped up from its icon, and it shows the same palette torn off, along with the other three pen palettes.

Patterns

Patterns can be applied to both fills and lines. The fill pattern palette and the line pattern palette are identical, so you have to be careful to choose from the fill pattern palette to create a fill, and the line pattern palette to affect your lines. You can also make your own pattern by editing an existing one. Skip ahead a bit to the section "Editing patterns, gradients, and textures" for instructions. By using a wide pen along with a pattern, you can create some nice patterned borders.

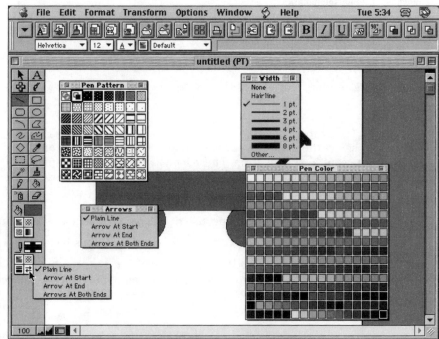

Figure 10-4:
Palettes pop up and tear off — take your pick.

Textures

Textures make a graphic look almost like a real object. The texture pop-up menu has 20 textures, some of which are different on the Mac and in Windows. (See Figure 10-5.) These textures can be edited, or you can create your own. We tell you how in the section, "Editing patterns, gradients, and textures." The texture pop-up menu is located below the paint bucket and color fill palette. Textures apply only to fills, not to lines.

Gradients

Gradients are another fill option to lend reality to your graphics. A *gradient* is a pattern that fades from one color to the next. Take a look at the gradient palette in Figure 10-5. You select a gradient like you select any other fill or line. However, like textures, gradients apply only to fills and not to lines. The 32 gradients can also be edited. For more on editing them, check out the next section.

Figure 10-5:
She's the daughter of Rosie O'Gradient, a regular, old-fashioned palette.

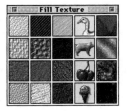

 Instead of selecting a new color from the fill palette, you can pick up a color that's already in your document. To pick up a color, click the eyedropper to select it, and then move the eyedropper into your document and until its tip is on the color you want to use. Click at that position to pick up this color as your new fill color. This newly selected color now appears in the fill sample area.

 You can also use the eyedropper to pick up a pen color. Just press the Option (Mac) or Alt (Windows) key as you click your desired color.

Line options

Two options available for your lines are width control and arrow heads. These options must be set before you create your line. Both options are pop ups on the line palette and work the same as the other palette pop ups.

✔ You can set the width of any line or border. You can turn off a border by selecting None. (You can do the same for a line, but what's a line with no line?) You can also make a border or line as wide as you like by selecting Other from the pop up and entering a width (in points).

✔ Arrows are available only with the straight-line tool. They are great for use in presentations and manuals to point out objects.

Editing patterns, gradients, and textures

If you want something more than the predefined patterns, gradients, or textures, this is the place for you to learn how to have it your way. (Does that burger place still let you do that?)

To edit patterns:

1. **Tear off the patterns palette (described in the previous section, "Borders, Lines, and Fills"), and double-click the pattern that looks closest to what you want.**

   This brings up the Pattern Editor and takes you directly into your pattern, which is ready to be edited. You also can choose Options⇨ Patterns to bring up the patterns palette, and then choose a pattern. By choosing a pattern close to what you want, you save some work. You now should see the Pattern Editor dialog box, shown in Figure 10-6.

Figure 10-6: Edit those patterns, mate — the Pattern Editor dialog box.

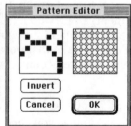

2. **Your pointer is your editing tool. Click anywhere in the left box of the Pattern Editor dialog box to turn pixels on or off. Each pixel toggles on or off when you click it.**

   The box on the left is an enlargement of your pattern; the box on the right is a full-size sample of your pattern. You can click the Invert button to change the black areas of your pattern to white and the white areas to black.

3. **When you are happy with your pattern, click OK.**

   Click the Cancel button to forget the whole thing and leave the existing pattern untouched.

To edit gradients:

1. **Tear off the gradients palette and double-click a gradient that's closest to what you want to use.**

   You also can choose Options➪Gradients to bring up the gradients palette, and then choose a gradient. Either way, you arrive at the Gradient Editor dialog box, just like the one shown in Figure 10-7.

Figure 10-7: You don't have to study hard to get a good gradient; you can make one yourself with the Gradient Editor dialog box.

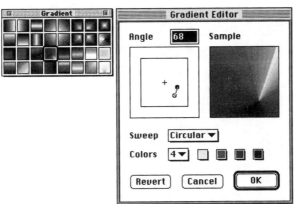

2. **Pick a number of colors from the pop-up menu.**

   You can have two, three, or four colors. Then, double-click each color's square to choose your colors.

3. **Next, use the Sweep pop-up menu to assign the sweep you want.**

   Sweep refers to the way the colors travel or dissolve into each other. You can select circular, starburst, or directional.

4. Click and drag each of the handles on the line that appears, and experiment with the effects.

The line and the movable points appear at the top left of the editor window. Your sweep determines what the line and points offer you in the way of adjustment. As you experiment, the area to the right shows you the effect you're creating.

5. When you have created the gradient of your dreams, click OK to place it in the palette.

Your new gradient replaces the one that you started with. If you stray too far afield and want to start over with the original gradient, click the Revert button. If you change your mind and decide that one of the preset gradients suits you fine, click Cancel to abort the mission.

To edit textures:

1. Tear off the textures palette and double-click a texture that's closest to what you want.

You also can choose Options⊅Textures to bring up the textures palette, and then choose a texture. Either way, you arrive at the Texture Editor dialog box, as shown in Figure 10-8.

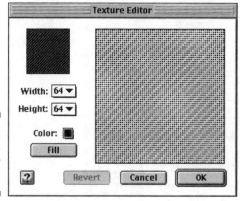

Figure 10-8:
The Texture
Editor
dialog box.

2. Before you start editing, select a repeat size to designate how often your pattern repeats.

A smaller size means the pattern repeats more often. This may give you a finer, more polished effect. Then you can begin editing by selecting a color from the color pop-up menu and then clicking the edit area to place the color. You can always place another color on top of an existing color, which replaces the first color.

3. **To fill your entire editing area with the color you select, click Fill.**

   To make major changes that have one main color, this option may be a good place to start.

4. **If you have a texture or picture that you want to use, copy it, return to the texture editor window, and then paste it with Edit⇨Paste.**

   Do you like your desktop? Take a screen shot of it and select a bit of it to paste.

5. **To remove everything and get a blank white sheet, choose Edit⇨Clear.**

6. **When you're happy with your texture, click OK to place it in the palette.**

   Your new texture replaces the one that you started with. But if you decide that you strayed too far afield and want to start over with the original gradient, click Revert. Or, if the original textures are beginning to look better to you, click Cancel.

While editing your palettes, you have the option of using the editor's Revert and Cancel buttons. After you close the edit box, you no longer have those options. You can't revert to the original pattern, gradient, or texture. The editing you did applies only to that document, though, so when you open a new document, you return to the default palettes. To remain in your current document and undo the fill change, you can use File⇨Revert to revert your document to the way it was when it was last saved.

If you like a certain texture and want to use it elsewhere, you can. Open the texture in the editor, and choose Edit⇨Copy. Now it's on your clipboard, waiting to go anywhere.

It's also possible to load custom color, pattern, gradient, and texture palettes. The palette appears in your current document only. Here's how to do it:

1. **Choose Edit⇨Preferences and select Palettes from the pop-up menu that appears.**

2. **Click the button for the type of palette you want to load.**

   You can choose from options to Use Standard, Load a palette, and Save a palette:

   - *Use Standard:* Reloads the default palette.

   - *Load a palette:* Takes you to the folder where ClarisWorks stores several premade palettes (see Figure10-9). Only palettes of the appropriate type are shown. You can load one of these palettes or navigate to where you store your own palettes. Double-click the palette you want to use, and then click OK. For colors, you have to select the editable 256-color palette to be able to load a palette.

     • *Save a palette:* Presents a typical Save dialog box and takes you to the Palettes folder in the ClarisWorks folder. This is a good place to save your palettes, so give it a name and click Save in that dialog box.

3. When you finish choosing your preferences, click OK.

If you decide you don't want to keep your changes, click Cancel.

Before clicking OK to leave Preferences, if you want the palettes you selected to always appear when you launch ClarisWorks and begin a new document, click Make Default.

Figure 10-9:
You're preference is our preference. Are you feeling earthy today?

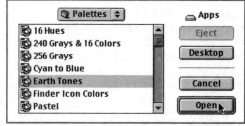

If you change a color palette while working in a document, you may be in for a surprise when you return to the document. All of the document's current textures and gradients change to reflect the colors in the new color palette. You can change the palette back, but images you have already placed may retain some color weirdness.

If you like the palettes that you've loaded, save your document as stationery to make those palettes available whenever you use that stationery.

Changing colors and filling in empty spaces

After you create your shapes, you can alter any solid colors or white areas (even those within patterns). For example, if you draw a rectangle while the fill color is set to white or another solid color, you can easily change the color later. You also can fill in the rectangle with a pattern, gradient, or texture. However, after you fill it with a pattern, gradient, or texture, only the white spaces or solid colored areas within that design can have the new fill applied. Any pattern, gradient, or texture is actually composed of solid colors — they just happen to all be mixed together. Therefore, you can point your paint bucket at any one area of color, and that area changes — whether it's one lone pixel or a large area.

 For an interesting effect, first fill an area with a texture or gradient, and then apply a solid color or gradient to the background or the solid areas within the pattern. Simply select the fill you want, select the paint bucket tool, and then click inside the area you want to fill.

 The very tip of the paint, spilling out of the bucket, is the *hot spot,* which is the part of the paint bucket that has to be inside the area you're filling. If you are working with a small shape, it is helpful to zoom in on the shape.

 Make sure the area you fill is completely closed. If even one missing pixel is missing from your object's outline, paint "leaks out" to fill the entire background on which the object is placed. That's the time for the trusty Undo command. Undo your work, zoom in, plug the leak, and then try again. You can set your shapes to close automatically with the Edit⇨Preferences command, if you want to avoid such problems.

Paint Mode

Paint modes affect what happens when you draw or paste one shape or line on top of another. Mac users can pick from three different settings to designate how new paint interacts with existing patterns underneath it. Windows users have only one of the following abilities (that is, tint):

 ✔ **Opaque:** This is the normal setting. In opaque mode, new paint covers anything underneath it. It's like working with oil paints. This is available only on the Mac.

 ✔ **Transparent pattern:** In this mode, any white space in your new shape is transparent. Whatever pattern is underneath the shape shows through in the white space. The rest of the colors work as they do in opaque mode. This is available only on the Mac.

 ✔ **Tint:** This mode mixes the new paint with any existing pattern under it. For example, if you paint a blue square over a red circle, the overlapping area is purple. Tint mode works like watercolors. A button for tint is located in the paint button area on the default button bar.

On the Mac, if you would rather not use buttons, you can change the paint mode by choosing Options⇨Paint Mode to access the Painting Mode dialog box.

Painting Freehand

To paint with freehand strokes, you have three tool choices. All three tools use the current fill colors, textures, and gradients to paint with. You can also combine patterns with colors to create an effect. Each tool also has a special option or function. These functions are mentioned only briefly here, but they are explained in detail later in this chapter, in the section "Hot Rod Your Tools."

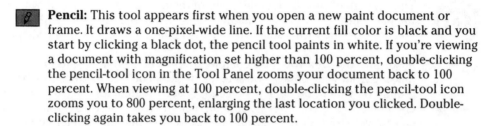

Pencil: This tool appears first when you open a new paint document or frame. It draws a one-pixel-wide line. If the current fill color is black and you start by clicking a black dot, the pencil tool paints in white. If you're viewing a document with magnification set higher than 100 percent, double-clicking the pencil-tool icon in the Tool Panel zooms your document back to 100 percent. When viewing at 100 percent, double-clicking the pencil-tool icon zooms you to 800 percent, enlarging the last location you clicked. Double-clicking again takes you back to 100 percent.

Brush: This tool paints with various brush shapes, including patterns. Double-clicking the brush-tool icon in the Tool Panel displays the Brush Shape dialog box. The brush can also act like one of those stamps that the kids love in their drawing programs. Instead of dragging the brush in your document as you would drag a brush while painting, just place the brush pointer, hold it still, and click. Instead of a line or area full of paint, you paint one focused area, as if you've used a stamp and stamp pad. You can paint or stamp textures, gradients, colors, and patterns.

After you apply a color to your document, the paint brush becomes a color-adjustment and blend tool. In the Brush Editor dialog box, select a brush size, and then choose an effect from the Effects pop-up menu. Your brush now lightens, darkens, tints, or blends the colors you brush over, depending on the effect you chose. Continuous brushing increases the effect. The section "Hot Rod Your Tools," later in this chapter, provides more information on the Brush Editor.

Spray can: This tool applies color, textures, and gradients with a spray-paint-like effect. The spray can is often used over a brick pattern for that graffiti-on-the-wall effect. The spray can also acts like a stamp, stamping its color, pattern, and so on as a rubber stamp would. Instead of dragging to spray within your document, keep the spray-can cursor still and press your mouse button to "spray" long enough for the texture, gradient, color, or pattern to fill in completely.

You can use the freehand tools to paint over other shapes, to create highlights and accents, or to perform detailed editing. Figure 10-10 shows a sample of how each tool paints.

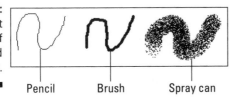

Figure 10-10:
The different strokes of the freehand paint tools.

Pencil   Brush   Spray can

Selecting Areas

The paint environment has three selection tools; which one you use depends on what you want to select.

 The selection rectangle or marquee tool: This tool selects rectangular areas. It's known as the marquee tool because after something is selected, a rectangle flashes around it, like a theater marquee. Everything inside the rectangle moves or is copied, including the white space, which *whites out* anything you move it over. Double-clicking the selection rectangle selects the whole document.

 The lasso: Yee-haw! You can rope any odd shape you can draw a line around. The lasso selects only colored pixels — not white ones — so you can leave a wide space around your art and be sure that you get it all. When you move something that is selected with this tool, it doesn't *white out* your other work. Therefore, unlike the marquee tool, this tool doesn't leave obnoxious white space around your art when you move or copy it to another document. The lasso tool automatically closes an open loop by drawing a straight line from the point where you release the mouse button to the point where you started the loop. Consequently, you should try to complete your loops to avoid having parts of your shape cut off by the straight line that the lasso tool inserts to complete an open loop. Double-clicking the lasso tool lassoes all colored pixels in the document.

 The magic wand: A true magician's tool, the magic wand is used to select any area that is all one color. For example, suppose you have a map of the United States that shows each of the states in a different color, and you want to select only Kentucky. Because all the states are different colors, clicking anywhere inside Kentucky with the magic wand selects the entire state.

Figure 10-11 shows examples of how each tool works.

 If you accidentally miss selecting part of the artwork and leave it behind when you move or copy the selection, use the Undo command, deselect the area, and try again. Undo to the rescue again!

Figure 10-11:
Selection
antics: how
each
selection tool
does its job.

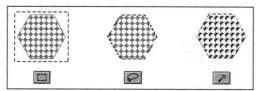

To position shapes precisely, show the graphics rulers by choosing
Format⇨Rulers. In the Rulers dialog box, click Graphics, and then click OK.

Erasing and Deleting

We all make mistakes. Here are three ways to fix the mistakes you make
while painting:

- ✔ **Use the eraser tool.** When you drag this tool over a colored area, it
  erases everything under it, causing the area to turn white. Double-
  clicking the eraser tool deletes everything.

- ✔ **Select and delete the unwanted area.** Use one of the selection tools
  discussed in the preceding section to outline an unwanted area; then
  press Delete or choose Edit⇨Clear.

- ✔ **Use the pencil tool to correct tiny flaws.** Zoom in to edit individual
  pixels.

Be careful about clicking the eraser tool. Remember that double-clicking the
eraser tool in the Tool Panel completely clears your document. Good thing
you have the Undo command to get everything back.

Check out Figure 10-12 for examples of how each of the three deleting
techniques works.

Figure 10-12:
Cut it out:
Tools for
deletion.

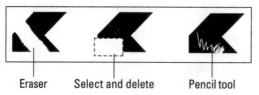

Eraser   Select and delete   Pencil tool

Hot Rod Your Tools

This section gives you the secret powers to customize and modify the paint tools for maximum performance!

Modifier keys

The modifier keys don't affect all the tools, but we let you know which tool each key works with and what it does.

Shift

The Shift key is the most widely used modifier key. It works like a straight edge or a level to help you make perfectly straight lines.

- ✔ The Shift key constrains lines to be exactly vertical, horizontal, or on a 45-degree angle.

- ✔ The Shift key also constrains ovals to be perfect circles, rectangles to be squares, and so on. It works with all the shape tools except the squiggle tool.

- ✔ The Shift key works with the pencil, brush, and spray can to constrain their output to be either horizontal or vertical, but it does not work for 45-degree angles.

- ✔ The Shift key constrains dragging a selected item so that the selection can move only sideways or up and down.

Option (Mac)/Alt (Windows)

Holding down the Option key (Mac) or Alt key (Windows) doesn't affect as many tools as the Shift key, but the tools that are affected perform some really cool functions:

- ✔ **Polygon and bezigon tools:** Using the Option or Alt key with these two tools enables you to paint irregular shapes. The polygon tool uses straight sides, and the bezigon tool uses curves. Option or Alt toggles between lines and curves, so that a shape can have both straight and curved sides.

- ✔ **Eyedropper:** Normally, you use the eyedropper tool to select the fill color by clicking a sample in your document. The Option or Alt key enables you to use the eyedropper to select a pen color.

- ✔ **Selection tools:** Holding down the Option or Alt key while dragging a selected area away from its original location copies the selection. It's a Copy/Paste shortcut.

Command (⌘)/Ctrl

With this modifier, the selection rectangle looks like a rectangle but works like the lasso. Only the colored pixels within the rectangle are selected. Dragging a rectangle usually is easier than enclosing a shape with the lasso, but the selection rectangle includes any white space in the new copy, whereas the lasso does not. This modifier enables you to use the selection rectangle, without copying the white space. The best of both tools!

Dialog boxes

Five of the paint tools have dialog boxes that can be used to change the way the tools perform. The dialog box for each tool is displayed by double-clicking its icon. The following list includes a description of the settings that you can change with each of these tools:

- **Round corners:** Double-clicking the round rectangle tool reveals a dialog box containing two choices for how it works: Round Ends or Radius (round corners). Radius is the standard option, which affects how round the corners are. You enter the radius of the curve for the corners (in points) in the box next to the Radius button. The larger the number, the more rounded the corner.

    The Round Ends option makes shapes that look like a rectangle with a semicircle stuck on each end. Normally, when you press Shift and draw with the round rectangle tool, you get a square with rounded corners; using the Round Ends option, the sides of the square are rounded, and you get a circle.

- **Modify arc:** How much of an arc would you like? Set it here. The arc angle lets you control how many degrees the arc covers; 360 degrees is a full circle, 180 degrees is a half circle, and 90 degrees is a quarter circle. Notice that although there is a space to enter the start angle, it's grayed out because the start angle has no effect in the paint environment. (Normally, start angle determines where the arc starts.) The outer edges of the arc always use the outline you select from the Line pop-up menu located below the pen. To apply the outline to the inside cut of the arc as well, click Frame Edges.

- **Number of sides:** Double-click the regular polygon tool to set the number of sides for your regular polygons. The default is 6 sides — you can have as few as 3 or as many as 40.

- **Brush shape and effects:** This is where you really can have fun with the paint brush. Double-click the paint brush or choose Options⇨ Brush Shape to bring up the Brush Shape dialog box and edit your brush. You can replace the standard round brush with any of the brushes shown in Figure 10-13. If none of those brushes suits you, click Edit to open the Brush Editor dialog box (see the right side of Figure 10-13), with which you can create your own brush shape. Use the pointer to edit the pattern of dots used for the brush, and then click OK.

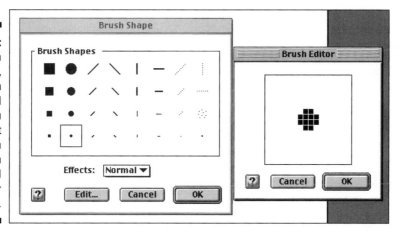

Figure 10-13:
Choose a
brush shape,
or make an
old frayed
one like you
used in art
class with
the Brush
Shape and
Brush Editor
dialog boxes.

You can also set up the brush as a color-adjustment and blend tool, from the Brush Editor dialog box. Select a brush size, and then choose an effect from the Effects pop-up menu. Your brush now lightens, darkens, tints, or blends the colors you brush over, depending on the effect you chose.

✔ **Spray Can:** And for our finale . . . double-click the spray can tool or choose Options⇨Spray Can. These options let you control the size of the dot produced by the spray can and the speed at which the paint sprays. The dot size can be from 1 to 72, and the flow rate ranges from 1 to 100. As the flow rate increases, the spray effect is more blotchy, similar to what's shown in the sample area in Figure 10-14.

You can try out your new settings in the sample area within the Edit Spray Can dialog box. Try a setting, use the Clear Sample Area button, and then try another. Ultimate convenience. Click OK when you're done.

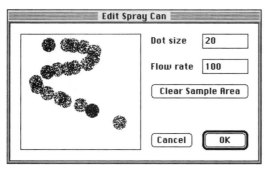

Figure 10-14:
I can't
believe it's
not spray
paint: the
Edit Spray
Can dialog
box.

Chapter 11
Special Effects with Paint

In This Chapter

▶ Warping, twisting, and distorting graphics

▶ Changing the size of the image

▶ Rotating, flipping, and other circus tricks

▶ Using color effects

This chapter is for those of you who aren't satisfied with average graphics. You're looking to create something really eye-popping, different . . . unusual. You want to know how to really push your pixels around and make your text and graphics look like they've been put through a taffy-puller. The special effects commands in the ClarisWorks paint environment all live in the Transform menu. They fall loosely into four categories: warping, resizing, rotating, and color manipulation.

Warping Your Graphics

You've designed your company logo, but it still doesn't look quite right to you. Maybe if the whole thing leaned to the right a little to make it more dynamic. . . . Or maybe you want to see the design stretching out toward the horizon. The commands in this section are all about twisting your artwork.

Distorting

The Distort command lets you pull the corners of a selected area out in any direction you want. To use this command, follow these steps:

1. **Using any of the selection tools, select what you want to distort.**

2. **Choose Transform⇨Distort.**

   Hollow handles, or white squares, appear at the corners of your selection. Click and drag them to stretch out your selection.

3. Drag the corner handles to reshape the selection.

Click once outside the selected area to make the distort handles go away. The graphic is still selected. If you decide that you liked the graphic better before, now's the time to use the Undo command.

Remember how you could pick up pictures from the newspaper with Silly Putty and stretch them out to make them look really strange? That's sort of what Distort does. We stretched out a sample newspaper column in Figure 11-1.

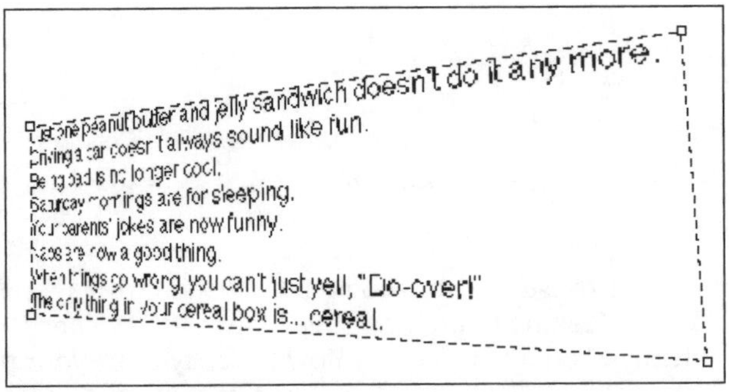

Figure 11-1:
It's not putty, you silly! It's the ClarisWorks Distort tool.

> Use the peanut butter and jelly sandwich doesn't do it any more.
> Eating a car doesn't always sound like fun.
> Driving a car doesn't always sound like fun.
> Being bad is no longer cool.
> Saturday mornings are for sleeping.
> Your parents' jokes are now funny.
> Naps are now a good thing.
> When things go wrong, you can't just yell, "Do-over!"
> The only thing in your cereal box is... cereal.

Putting it in perspective

The Perspective command lets you create the effect of extending your art toward the horizon. It works much like the Distort command:

1. Select any part of your painted area.

2. Choose Transform⇨Perspective.

The hollow handles appear at the corners.

3. Drag the handles to create the perspective effect.

The direction in which you first drag the handle determines how the perspective effect looks. Drag sideways to work with the top or bottom edge; drag up or down to work with the side. You can see examples of both in Figure 11-2.

Figure 11-2:
Perspective is all in how you look at it.

Shearing

Shearing is a techie term used by engineers and physics professors. What it amounts to is slanting. You know what happens if you open both the top and the bottom of an empty cereal box? If you look through it from end to end and smoosh the sides a bit, the rectangle turns into a parallelogram — that's kind of what you do with the Shear command. Shear works much like Perspective:

1. **Select whatever you want to shear.**

2. **Choose Transform⇨Shear.**

   You should see those now-familiar hollow handles.

3. **Drag the handles in the direction you want your graphic to slant.**

   Moving side to side slants the sides. Moving up and down slants the top and bottom. Keep it up until you are happy with the result.

You can make your artwork look like it's caught in a heavy wind, speeding along, or sliding down a hill in San Francisco, as in Figure 11-3.

Figure 11-3:
Celebrate
the Shear
command.

Resizing

You have two choices for resizing your artwork: by hand or by dialog box. The manual method enables you to resize your graphic any way you like. The Scale Selection dialog box lets you type in the percentage by which you want to scale your artwork.

To resize artwork manually, the quickest way to fit your artwork to a specific area, follow these steps:

1. **Select the part of your painting you'd like to resize.**

2. **Choose Transform⇨Resize.**

   Hollow handles appear at the corners of your selection.

3. **Drag a handle to reduce or enlarge the size of your selection.**

Hold down the Shift key as you drag to resize proportionally. That way, you don't squash or stretch the image.

To precisely resize something, use the Scale By Percent dialog box and follow these steps:

1. **Select the part of your document that you want to resize.**

   You can use any of the three ClarisWorks selection tools.

2. **Choose Transform⇨Scale By Percent.**

   This command brings up the dialog box shown in Figure 11-4.

Figure 11-4:
Scaling graphics is easier than scaling walls, as you can see by the simplicity of this dialog box.

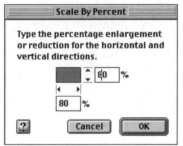

3. **Enter the percentage by which you want to scale your selection in the boxes next to the horizontal and vertical axes.**

   A number less than 100 reduces the graphic's size; numbers greater than 100 increases the graphic's size.

   Enter the same number in both percentage boxes to maintain the selection's proportion.

4. **Click OK to accept the change or Cancel to call off this resize thing.**

Rotating and Flipping

Rotating and flipping are really cool and sometimes very handy operations. You can flip, rotate, or free rotate your artwork.

Flipping

Flipping a graphic makes it a mirror image of itself. An image can flip sideways or up and down. Flipping is different from rotating a graphic. When you flip an image, it's actually reversed, as if in a mirror.

 To flip your graphic horizontally, follow these steps:

1. **Select the area you want to flip.**

2. **Choose Transform⇨Flip Horizontal.**

   Flip Horizontal flips the image from side to side as shown in Figure 11-5.

   If you decide you liked the image better before the flip, or you chose the wrong direction, click Undo right away, before you deselect the image.

 To flip your graphic vertically, follow these steps:

1. **Select the area you want to flip.**

2. **Choose Transform⇨Flip Vertical.**

   Flip Vertical flips the image up and down, as shown in Figure 11-5.

Figure 11-5:
Eggs over
easy —
with the flip
commands.

 ✔ Flipping an object once horizontally and once vertically does the same thing as rotating the image 180 degrees.

✔ Flipping twice in the same direction brings it back to its original position.

Rotating via a dialog box

Rotating literally turns the image around, rather than mirroring it. Using the Rotate dialog box allows you to precisely control the angle of rotation. This is extremely helpful when you have several objects (such as text blocks) that need to match. It also ensures you can rotate to exactly 45, 90, or 180 degrees. Keep in mind that at an angle larger than 180 degrees, the image will be turned upside-down.

1. **Select the image you want to rotate.**

2. **Choose Transform⇨Rotate.**

   In the Rotate dialog box, enter a number for the angle at which you want to rotate the selected image. You can type any number from 1 to 360.

3. **Click OK to rotate the image or Cancel to call it off.**

 The Rotate 90 degrees button is the fastest way to rotate a selected image. Click the button twice to rotate your image 180 degrees, three times for 270 degrees.

Free rotating

The Free Rotate command lets you rotate an image manually to any angle. This one is the most fun because you get to see what you're doing.

1. **Select the image you want to rotate.**

2. **Choose Transform⇨Free Rotate.**

   Hollow handles appear at the corners of your selection.

3. **Drag any handle in the direction in which you want the image to rotate.**

   The image pivots around its center in the direction you drag, as shown in Figure 11-6.

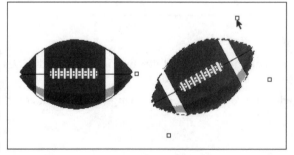

Figure 11-6: Have a ball with the Free Rotate command.

 To line up several images in paint mode: Use the pencil tool (or line tool) with the Shift key down to make a straight line. Use this line as a visual guide to align your images, but be sure to leave a little space between the line and your images. Erase it when you finish.

Color Tricks and More

The rest of the commands in the Transform menu let you manipulate your artwork by using color. These commands give you the flexibility to do quite a bit of editing after you have drawn your artwork. You can find a button for each of these in the default button bar.

The commands

Here's a quick breakdown of what these commands can do for you:

 ✔ **Fill:** Works kind of like the paint bucket tool. The major difference is that this command fills in the entire current selection without the limitations of the paint bucket. Absolutely any area you select is filled by this command. Use the magic wand tool to obtain control, and then use this command to easily change colors, patterns, textures, and gradients in your images.

 ✔ **Pick Up:** Breaks the ice at a singles event. Actually, this is a really cool command that lets you transfer the colors and patterns of an image to a selection that is placed on top of it. Kind of like lifting up newsprint with Silly Putty. Select the image or area you want to apply the effect to. Move it on top of the part of the paint image that you want to pick up. Click the button or choose the command. Your image/selection picks up the same painted image that it is on top of. Of course, you don't want to keep it on top of that other image. You just want to borrow (copy) the other image's pattern or color. While it's still selected, you can move it back where you want to use it.

 ✔ **Invert:** Changes black to white and white to black. Invert also transforms colors into their opposites. In an image with lots of colors, using this command is kind of like looking at the negative of a color photo. (Use this command selectively: If white is included, it'll turn black.) Just select and click.

 ✔ **Blend:** Makes the selected area look out of focus by blending colors into the neighboring dots, which can soften sharp edges in an image. It's the ClarisWorks version of smearing petroleum jelly on the lens. Just select the area to blend and click the button or choose the command.

 ✔ **Tint:** Want to look at your artwork through rose-colored glasses? This is the way to do it. The Tint command tints a selected area toward whatever color is selected in the fill sample area. Apply it several times to increase the effect. This effect doesn't apply when working in black and white.

✔ **Lighter/Darker:** These two commands work like the Tint command. They lighten or darken a selected image by adding more white or more black. Just select an area and click the button or choose the command. Apply it several times to increase the effect. This effect doesn't apply when working in black and white.

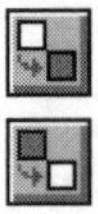

One last word about paint effects. . . .

Remember, part of the fun of the paint environment is playing and exploring your creativity. Try out these effects. Combine them and see what kinds of results you get. Experimenting gives you new ideas for how you can use these effects for your own needs.

As food for thought, check out Figure 11-7. We did it by combining several special paint effects to create a cool pattern, selecting the text, and then using Pick Up to transfer the pattern onto the text. You can also do this with a gradient, a scanned photograph, or anything else you can create.

Figure 11-7:
Create a graphic like this using your imagination and the Pick Up command.

Chapter 12
Draw, Pardner!

● ●

In This Chapter

▶ Drawing regular and freehand shapes

▶ Selecting and deleting shapes

▶ Setting up lines and fills

▶ Resizing and reshaping

▶ Setting drawing preferences

▶ Using text boxes and other frames

▶ Moving, aligning, and grouping

▶ Using clip art

● ●

*T*he object of drawing is to draw objects. Oops, the preceding sentence is a circular reference, and we wanted an *oval*. We better use the trusty Undo and try again. . . .

Whereas the paint environment involves manipulating individual pixels, the draw environment involves creating and manipulating shapes — or objects. Each object can be moved or changed individually at any time. Objects (shapes) can be compiled to create intricate graphics or can be used alone.

Skip back to Chapter 9 to review how drawing and painting compare or to obtain advice on when to use a draw document.

The draw environment also gives you the most flexibility to integrate other ClarisWorks environments — it's the best environment for including many different types of frames in your document. If you're new to environments and frames, check out Chapter 1.

Setting Up Your Draw Document

When you open a new draw document, you are greeted by a blank page, like the one in Figure 12-1. From there, you have a lot of control over how that page can look and act.

Notice the dots, or *graphics grid,* in the background, which helps you line up objects. The graphics grid appears only on-screen and never prints. Choosing Options⇨Hide Graphics Grid makes it invisible.

Sometimes, when you want to draw a graphic to an exact size, ClarisWorks instead resizes the graphic in increments. The object jumps from one preset size to another, skipping intermediate sizes. The *autogrid* causes this phenomenon by constraining the sizing or moving of shapes to a preset interval (such as an eighth of an inch). The autogrid helps you line up objects or draw consistent shapes, but it also limits you. To toggle the autogrid off or on, choose Options⇨Turn Autogrid Off/On or press ⌘-Y (Mac) or Ctrl+Y (Windows).

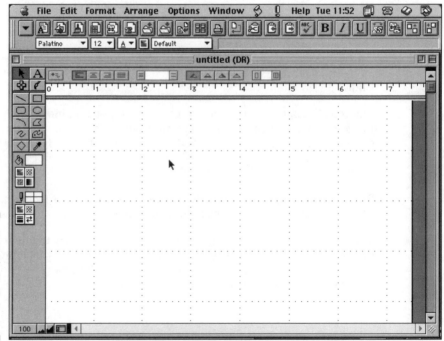

Figure 12-1:
Ready and
waiting —
a new
ClarisWorks
draw
document.

As you work, you may want to see how your document *really* looks. Choosing Window⇨Page View or clicking the optional Show Margins button enables you to see your margin area. Displaying a ruler along the top and right sides of your document enables you to see the size of your document or image in inches or other units of measurement. Choose Window⇨Show Rulers to display the rulers.

You can save a set of preferences as the default for all your draw documents. See "Saving as stationery" in Chapter 2 for more information on setting up default pages.

Drawing Tools

The graphics tools work the same way in the draw environment as they do in the paint environment, except that in the draw environment, the objects the tools create remain objects instead of being *painted in* or turned into individual pixels in the document. Once a shape is placed in the paint environment, it must be manipulated pixel by pixel. In the draw environment, the shape remains an independent object that can be moved, resized, filled with color, and so on at any time.

Because the tools for the draw and paint environments are basically the same, we don't explain them in detail in this chapter. Check out Chapter 10 for a detailed description of each tool.

- ✔ **The regular shape tools** are the line tool, the rectangle tool, the round tool, the oval tool, the arc tool, and the polygon tool. These tools create the basic building blocks of your artwork.

- ✔ **The freehand tools** allow you greater drawing flexibility than the regular shape tools. The freehand tools are the squiggle tool, polygon tool, and bezigon tool.

The polygon and bezigon tools are the two most powerful and overlooked tools in ClarisWorks. The secret to using these tools is to draw shapes that combine curves and straight lines — with help from the Option (Mac) or Alt (Windows) key. If you're using the bezigon tool, just press the correct key for your system, and the next segment will be a straight line. The polygon tool works in reverse, making the next segment of your shape a curve. Take a look at the examples in Figure 12-2. The shape on the left was drawn with the polygon tool. The shape on the right was drawn with the bezigon tool. To make a straight segment with the bezigon tool, hold down the Option (or Alt) key when you click both of the end points. If you hold down the key on only one point, that point end becomes a counterpoint for two opposite curves. See the section "Resizing, Reshaping, and Rotating," later in this chapter, for more information.

Normally, after you use a tool, the pointer switches back to the arrow pointer. To lock in a tool so that you can use it more than once, double-click its icon in the Tool Panel. The tools's icon turns black to let you know that you can keep using that tool until you select another tool. This works for any drawing tool.

Figure 12-2:
The U.S. Mail is brought to you by the polygon tool. The bone, thanks to the bezigon.

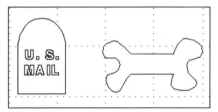

Selecting and Deleting

When your screen is cluttered from practicing with all the tools, you may be wondering how to get rid of some of the shapes you made. The draw environment doesn't have an eraser like the paint environment does. Instead, you select an object, and then delete it.

In the draw environment, all the selection techniques we describe here are performed with the arrow pointer (as Figure 12-3 illustrates).

Figure 12-3:
I think I'll take . . . this one! The arrow pointer in action.

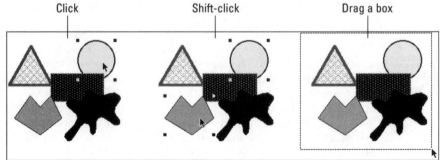

✔ Click any object to select it.

✔ To select several objects at once, press Shift as you click each object. You don't have to keep the Shift key pressed. You can release it, and then press it again to add another object to the selection.

✔ You can also select a group of objects by using the arrow pointer to drag a box (marquee) around the objects; only objects that are completely inside the box are selected, unless you press the ⌘ key (Mac) or Ctrl key (Windows) while dragging. In that case, any object your arrow pointer touches is selected.

✔ Use the Shift key to deselect one object in any group of selected objects, without deselecting the entire group: Press Shift and click the object you want to deselect.

✔ Notice that when an object is selected, you see its handles at its corners.

✔ To remove a selected object, choose Edit⇨Clear, Edit⇨Cut, or press Delete. Using Cut lets you Paste the object elsewhere. The other methods don't.

Copying

After you make a shape, you can save it and reuse it later. Before you can copy anything, however, you have to tell ClarisWorks what to copy. To select the object to copy, you can choose from two methods:

✔ **Copy and Paste:** Use this option when you want to copy an object to another document, to another part the document you're in, or to copy the object directly on top of the original. By now, you probably know that to copy, you either choose Edit⇨Copy or press ⌘-C (Mac) or Ctrl+C (Windows). Then, to paste what you copied, either choose Edit⇨Paste or press ⌘-V (Mac) Ctrl+V (Windows). Here are the secrets of pasting:

   • *Pasting to a different page:* If you are pasting to a page other than the one you copied from, click the location in the document where you want the object to end up. If you don't click before using the Paste command, ClarisWorks pastes the object into the center of your screen.

   • *Pasting to the same page:* If you are pasting to the same page that you copied from, you can make the copied object paste directly on the original by using the Paste command *prior to* clicking anywhere in the document. This is a great trick for creating drop shadows.

✔ **Duplicate:** A faster way to create a copy in the same spot as the original
is to use the Duplicate command. Just choose Edit⇨Duplicate, or press
⌘-D (Mac) or Ctrl+D (Windows). ClarisWorks places the duplicate copy
over the original, but slightly offset. Use Duplicate several times to
create a stack of objects. Duplicate doesn't leave a copy of the object
on the Clipboard, which comes in handy if you have other plans for the
Clipboard soon, or if you don't want to displace something currently on
the Clipboard.

Setting Up Lines and Fills

You can assign fill and line characteristics to an object at any time. Unlike
the paint environment, you don't *have to* set up the line and fill characteristics *before* you create the object to be able to change them later; in the draw
environment, you can assign and change the line and fill as often as you like.

Line settings apply to the border of an object or, if the object is a line, to the
line itself. You can change the color, pattern, and width of any line or border
in the draw environment. You can also add an arrowhead to the start, to the
end, or to both ends of any line made with the straight line tool.

Fill settings apply to the inside of a shape; they cannot be applied to straight
lines. If a shape is open, ClarisWorks draws an invisible line from the starting
point to the ending point of the shape and fills any areas enclosed by that
line. You can fill an object with a color, pattern, gradient (an area that fades
from one color to another), or texture. The patterns palette also includes a
transparent option, which makes the inside of the object clear, so you can
see whatever background is behind the object. Actually, there *is* no inside —
which means you have to click exactly on the object's outline to select it.

Styles for Draw Objects

You can really draw in style with ClarisWorks. Use the stylesheet palette to
save a set of object properties, such as the fill's color, pattern, gradient, or
texture, and the border's width, color, and pattern. After you set up a
custom style to reflect your format choices, you can apply that format to
any object in that document with just one step. You also can change the
format of all the objects that have this style simply by making changes to
the style — the objects update automatically.

For example, suppose you want your finished document to have several
objects with the same fill color and pattern, but you haven't decided what
pattern and color you want to use. In this situation, you can create a style

with a temporary fill pattern and color settings, and then apply that style to the shapes. Later, when you decide which pattern and color you want to use, just edit the style by changing the fill color and pattern.

You can create a style for graphics in the draw environment in the same way you create a style for text in the word-processor environment, except that you choose graphics settings rather than text settings for your style. (To find out about setting up text styles, see Chapter 5.) Here are a few tips that are specifically related to making a graphics style:

- A graphics style can include settings for the fill color; the color and pattern combination; the gradient or texture; as well as for the pen's thickness, color, or color-and-pattern combination.

- Select Basic as the style type in the New Style dialog box. Graphics styles are always Basic styles, not Paragraph, Outline, or Table.

- When you are editing the style, you can select a new color, pattern, texture, and so on by clicking the attribute you want to change and selecting the new properties from the tool bar and button bar. Just bring the style editor's S pointer over to the pen or fill pop-up menus and select the attributes you want.

Resizing, Reshaping, and Rotating

Don't you hate when you don't leave enough room to fit your house on the map you've drawn for a party invitation? Everyone runs into situations where they need to adjust a graphic a bit. Resizing and reshaping graphics is what the ClarisWorks draw environment is all about. Any draw object can be sized to your heart's content. One of the main reasons for choosing the draw environment over the paint environment is the ability to rearrange your graphics easily. There are plenty of arrangement tools and options.

Resizing

You can resize an object in three ways: by dragging, by using the Scale Selection dialog box, and by using the size palette.

Dragging

Use the arrow pointer to select the object, and then drag any of the handles to enlarge or reduce the object's size. If you select several objects at the same time, they all are affected when you resize, even though you only select and drag one handle. The other handles tag along proportionally. Figure 12-4 shows the resize process. You can easily distort an object this way. To maintain the proportions, hold down the Shift key as you drag.

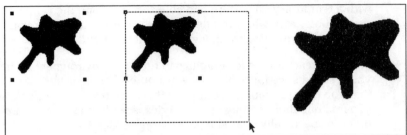

Figure 12-4:
It's not a
drag to
resize
objects.

Scaling

Scaling enables you to reduce or enlarge an object to a specific percentage of its current size. Here's what you do:

1. Use the arrow pointer to select the object(s) you want to resize.

Be careful not to select extra objects or they are also scaled.

2. Choose Arrange⇨Scale By Percent.

This brings up the Scale By Percent dialog box, shown in Figure 12-5.

3. Enter the percentage by which you want to resize the object.

You can resize horizontally (sideways), vertically (up and down), or both. To maintain the object's current proportions, type the same number in both boxes.

4. Click OK to resize the object.

Remember that if you aren't happy with how the resized object turns out, use the Undo command and try again.

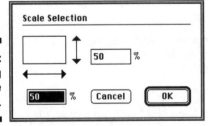

Figure 12-5:
Scaling
by the
numbers.

Resizing with a palette

If you want an object to be a precise size, use the size palette to reduce or enlarge the object:

1. **Select the object with the arrow pointer.**

2. **Choose Options⇨Object Size to call up the size palette.**

3. **In the boxes with the double-headed arrows, enter your choice of horizontal and vertical measurements, as shown in Figure 12-6.**

4. **Click the arrow next to the measurement, or press Return to make the change.**

You can also use the size palette to position an object at a precise location on the page. The top four boxes are used to set how far you want the object to be placed from the left, top, right, or bottom margin.

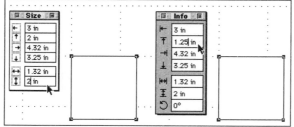

Figure 12-6: If you need an object to have exact dimensions, use a palette.

Reshaping

The most powerful graphics feature in ClarisWorks is the capability to reshape draw objects. Reshaping lets you change any object by manipulating the points and lines that define its shape.

Note: You can reshape only freehand shapes, regular polygons, arcs, and round rectangles. Reshaping does not work on regular rectangles, ovals, and straight lines.

Reshaping freehand objects

To reshape an object, either add the optional button to your button bar and click it, or choose Arrange⇨Reshape or press ⌘-R (Mac) or Ctrl+R (Windows). This puts you in reshape mode. The pointer changes to a crosshair with a box in the middle, and all the anchor points that make up your shape are visible. There are the two kinds of anchor points:

✔ **Corner anchor points:** These points are marked by a square. They appear at the ends of straight line segments and at the corners where two straight lines meet.

✔ **Curve anchor points:** These anchor points are marked by a circle and control where the bend of the curve changes.

Figure 12-7 shows the reshape pointer and a shape with both corner anchor points and curve anchor points. To change the shape of the object, just click an anchor point and drag the point to a new location.

You also can change the way a line bends around a curve anchor point by using the control handles that appear when you click a curve anchor point, as shown in Figure 12-7. Drag either handle to change how the line bends around the anchor point. Experiment by pivoting and stretching the control handle. Figure 12-7 shows the same object before and after adjusting a control handle.

Control handle   Corner point

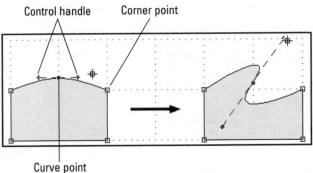

Figure 12-7:
Take control of your curve anchor points with control handles.

Curve point

You also can reshape objects in the following ways:

✔ **Add anchor points:** Click anywhere along the object's border with the reshape pointer to add an anchor point. This process lets you add sides to your shape.

✔ **Delete anchor points:** Click an anchor point with the reshape pointer and press Delete. This makes curves smoother because there are less controls affecting the curve. Use the other control handles to reshape your line. Using fewer anchor points not only creates a smoother line, it also speeds up printing because there is less for ClarisWorks to tell your printer.

 ✔ **Smooth out the sharpness of a polygon or a bezigon:** Click the anchor point with the reshape pointer to select it, and then either add the optional Smooth button to your button bar and click it, or choose

Edit⇨Smooth or press ⌘-(on Mac or Ctrl+(in Windows — the open parenthesis key. This actually changes the corner anchor point to a curve anchor point. To make the control handles appear on these curves so you can work with them, you press Option (Mac) or Alt (Windows). You can also smooth multiple anchor points or the whole object by selecting them before you use the Smooth command.

✔ **Sharpen the smoothness of a bezigon or make a polygon even sharper:** This changes the curve point to a corner anchor point. Click the anchor point with the reshape pointer to select it, and then either add the optional Unsmooth button to your button bar and click it, or choose Edit⇨Unsmooth or press ⌘-) (Mac) or Ctrl+) (Windows). (That keyboard command is the close parenthesis.)You also can sharpen the smoothness of multiple anchor points or the whole object.

Figure 12-8 shows you how a blob becomes a valentine heart when we change two curve anchor points to straight-line anchor points.

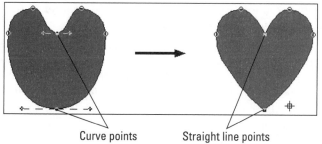

Figure 12-8:
We love changing anchor points.

Curve points   Straight line points

Reshaping round rectangles and arcs

You reshape round rectangles using the Corner Info dialog box and reshape arcs using the Arc Info dialog box. In the draw environment, you must create a round rectangle or arc before you can modify it. This contrasts with the paint environment in which you must specify the settings first and cannot edit the shape once it is made. To bring up the Corner Info dialog box or the Arc Info dialog box, double-click the object. The Corner Info dialog box is exactly the same as in Chapter 10. The Arc Info dialog box is described next (see Figure 12-9).

Rotating

ClarisWorks can rotate any object or frame to any angle from 0 to 360 degrees — and even create a mirror image by flipping it.

Start angle 0   Start angle 45   Start angle 25
Arc angle 90   Arc angle 90   Arc angle 150

Figure 12-9:
Change the
Start angle
and Arc
angle in the
Arc Info
dialog box
to produce
various
arcs.

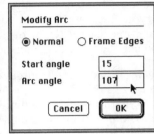

Modify Arc

◉ Normal   ○ Frame Edges

Start angle   [15]
Arc angle   [107]

[Cancel]   [OK]

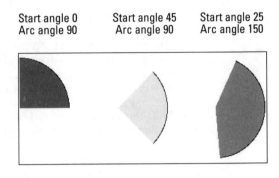

 ✔ **Flip Horizontally:** You can flip any draw objects or frames. To flip an object horizontally, either add Flip Horizontal button to the button bar and click it, or choose Arrange⇨Flip Horizontally. Flipping in the draw environment works the same way as in the paint environment, so take a look at the section "Rotating and Flipping" in Chapter 11 for examples of how the flipping commands work.

 ✔ **Flip Vertically:** To flip your draw objects or frames vertically, either add Flip Vertical button to the button bar and click it, or select Arrange⇨ Flip Vertically. We covered this in the paint environment, so take a look at the section "Rotating and Flipping" in Chapter 11 for examples of how the flipping commands work.

 ✔ **Rotate 90 degrees:** You can use the Rotate 90° command to rotate a draw object or frame clockwise in 90-degree increments. The Rotate 90° command is a button, so you have easy access to it. Click twice to rotate 180 degrees or three times to rotate 270 degrees.

✔ **Free rotate:** You can *free rotate* any frame or object — that is, rotate in one-degree increments from 0 to 360. You can do this in either of two ways: by dragging or by designating a specific angle:

- *To rotate by dragging:* Either choose Arrange⇨Free Rotate or press Shift-⌘-R (Mac) or Shift+Ctrl+R (Windows) to turn on Free Rotate mode, which changes your arrow pointer to an *X,* as shown in Figure 12-10. Click any shape or frame, and then drag the handles at the corners to rotate it. You see an outline of the shape as it moves. Free Rotate stays on until you select another tool. You can turn Free Rotate off the same way you turn it on. Try rotating some text for effect. Then try editing it. (Wait until you see how your text pops into line to edit and then rotates itself again!)

- *To rotate to a specific angle:* Choose Options⇨Object Size to show the size palette. Click the object or frame that you want to rotate, type the angle in the bottom box on the palette, and then click the arrow next to the box or press Return. Figure 12-10 shows where to type the angle.

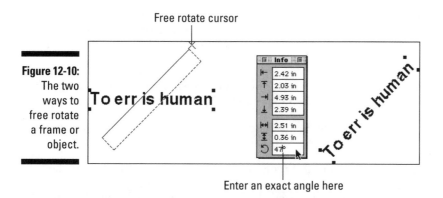

Free rotate cursor

Figure 12-10:
The two
ways to
free rotate
a frame or
object.

Enter an exact angle here

Setting Drawing Preferences

The behavior of some of the draw tools is determined by the preferences
you set for the draw environment. To get to the graphics preferences,
choose Edit⇨Preferences. The Preferences dialog box appears. If you are in
a drawing document when you select preferences, you are taken straight to
the graphics choices. Otherwise, use the Preferences pop-up menu to select
Graphics preferences.

The Graphics Preferences dialog box is shown in Figure 12-11.

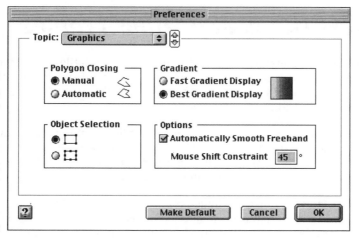

Figure 12-11:
And your
preference
is? Changing
the prefer-
ences that
affect how
the drawing
tools work.

Here's how the graphics preferences break down:

✔ **Polygon Closing:** You can select Manual or Automatic closing. Manual
enables you to draw open shapes; double-clicking finishes the shape
wherever you double-click. For a closed shape, you finish by clicking

back at the starting point. Automatic closes any shape you create by drawing a line from your ending point to the starting point. With Automatic, you can make an open shape only with the squiggle tool.

✔ **Object Selection:** You can choose to display four or eight handles when an object is selected. The four extra handles in the middle of each side let you move each side individually when you resize an object.

✔ **Gradient:** Choosing Best is, of course, best. But if objects filled with a gradient seem to take a long time to redraw or print, choose Fast.

✔ **Automatically Smooth Freehand:** This check box controls how the squiggle tool works. If this box is checked, the squiggle tool draws shapes made up of many small curves. If the box is not checked, the squiggle tool draws shapes made up of many tiny, straight lines.

✔ **Mouse Shift Constraint:** If you hold Shift while drawing a straight line and pivot the end of the line around the starting point, the line clicks into place at various places around the circle. The angle you type in this box determines the angle at which the line clicks into place. This option also affects how regular polygons appear on-screen.

When you finish changing the preferences, click OK to set these preferences for your current document. To make these the default settings in every new draw document, click Make Default. To keep the original settings of the dialog box, click Cancel.

Using Text Boxes and Other Frames

One of the reasons the draw environment is so versatile is the ease with which you can place and manipulate text, spreadsheets, and paint frames. The frame tools at the top of the Tool Panel enable you to create frames and edit the information inside them.

Within a frame, you have all the same capabilities that you have in that type of document. When you work inside a frame, you actually switch to that environment. For example, when you edit text inside a text frame, the menus change to the menus available in the text environment.

If you're working in a draw document that has lots of different kinds of frames, and your menus seem messed up, you probably are inside one of the frames. To return to the drawing environment, click the arrow pointer icon in the Tool Panel.

To make simple captions for your drawings, click the text tool to select it. Bring your I-beam cursor over to your document; then click and drag to create a free-floating text frame. Type your text and format it any way you want. To do more fabulous, complex things with columns of text or text wrapped around graphics, check out Chapter 13. If you need help formatting text, check out Chapters 5 and 6.

Moving, Aligning, and Grouping

After you create and set up some shapes, you need to know how to move them around on the page to fine-tune your drawing. This section shows you how to move objects "by hand" and how to use align tools so that your drawing looks sharp. After the shapes are in place, you find out how to join them together as a group so that you can deal with the whole drawing as one object.

Moving

Everything you always wanted to know about moving objects but were afraid to ask:

✔ **Moving methods:** You have three ways to move objects in the draw environment: by dragging, by using the keyboard, or by using the size palette.

  • *Dragging:* The most obvious way to move objects around the screen is to use the arrow pointer to drag them to a new location. Nothing tricky here.

  • *Using the keyboard:* If you need to move your object more precisely than you can do by dragging it, you can select the object and use the arrow keys on the keyboard. The arrow keys move the object one pixel at a time or one unit on the autogrid at a time.

  • *Using the size palette:* Moving objects with a palette works the same way as resizing them with this palette: Just type how far you want the object to be from the left, top, right, or bottom margin of your document. To bring up the size palette, select Options⇨ Object Size. Moving objects this way lets you specify a precise position on the page.

✔ **Autogrid:** Dragging and keyboard navigation are affected by the autogrid. Autogrid may sound like an L.A. freeway at rush hour, but it's actually an invisible grid that makes your objects move across the screen in set increments. The autogrid is useful for drawing consistent shapes and for making objects line up evenly, but it also prevents you from drawing a shape smaller than a grid increment or moving an object just one or two pixels at a time.

  • *To toggle the autogrid off or on:* Choose Options⇨Turn Autogrid Off/On or press ⌘-Y (Mac) or Ctrl+Y (Windows).

- *To set the autogrid increments:* Choose For<u>mat</u>⇨<u>R</u>ulers to bring up the Rulers dialog box. The autogrid is based on ruler settings, so to change the autogrid increments, type a new number in the Divisions box and then click OK. The smaller the divisions, the smaller the autogrid's increments.

- *To snap-align existing objects:* If you want objects that were drawn with the autogrid off to snap to the nearest grid point, select the object, and then either choose Arrange⇨<u>A</u>lign To Grid or press ⌘-K (Mac) or Ctrl+K (Windows).

✔ **Layers:** You may have noticed that objects can overlap each other. Each draw object or text block exists in its own layer. Each new object is added in front (also called on top) of any existing layers. When one object covers another, you need to shuffle the layers. Four commands enable you to move objects in front or in back of others. The two most commonly used commands have buttons on the default palette. The other two are optional buttons. You can also find commands for all four in the Arrange menu. The commands are:

- *Move Forward:* Moves up the currently selected object one layer toward the front. The keyboard shortcut is Shift-⌘-+(Mac) and Shift+Ctrl++(Windows) — that's a plus sign. This is a default button.

- *Move To Front:* Moves the selected object in front of all other layers. This is an optional button.

- *Move Backward:* Moves down the currently selected object one layer toward the back. The keyboard shortcut is Shift+⌘- (Mac) — that's a hyphen — or Shift+Ctrl+-(Windows). This is a default button.

- *Move To Back:* Moves the currently selected object in back of all other layers. This is an optional button.

For example, say you're creating a logo. You begin with text for your company name. Then you add a big oval. Next a small graphic. Your text is in back and you need it in front so use the Move Forward button twice, or use Move to Front for faster action. If you can't see it, select the oval and use the Move Backward or Move to Back command.

You also can use these commands to hide objects behind other objects. For example, you may have a logo you don't want to have show. Just send it behind something. (Or create a shape to put over it.) This is the ClarisWorks equivalent of sweeping the dust under the rug, except there's no bump to trip over.

Aligning

If you want your objects to line up perfectly, the alignment tools have you covered. You have six commands, all buttons on the default palette, to make the various options handy. If you prefer, you can use the Align Objects dialog box instead. Whichever method you use, first select the objects you want to align. Then click the button or buttons to do the alignment or call on Arrange⇨Align Objects to summon the dialog box.

✔ **Align Top:** This aligns all selected objects along their top-most edges.

✔ **Align Bottom:** This aligns all selected objects along their bottom-most edges.

✔ **Align Left:** This aligns all selected objects along their left edges.

✔ **Align Right:** This aligns all selected objects along their right edges.

✔ **Align Centers Horizontally:** This aligns all selected objects along an imaginary horizontal line that goes through each object's center.

✔ **Align Centers Vertically:** This aligns all selected objects along an imaginary vertical line that goes through each object's center.

Grouping

Grouping lets you link several objects together to be treated as one object. This option comes in handy when you are making any kind of graphic that is a composite of several objects. Grouping ensures that objects stay together relative to one another during resizes and moves. To group objects, just follow these steps:

1. **Select the objects you want to group together.**

   You can either drag a selection box around the objects with the arrow pointer or click each object as you hold the Shift key down.

2. **Either place the optional button on your button bar (see the Appendix) and click it or choose Arrange⇨Group or ⌘-G (Mac) or Ctrl+G (Windows).**

Your objects are now grouped. You may notice that all the individual selection handles have been replaced by selection handles for the group as a single object, as shown by the ClarisWorks Architecture Library image in Figure 12-12.

To bust up this cozy situation and work on one of the objects individually, select the group, and then choose Arrange⇨Ungroup. ClarisWorks clip art and other graphics programs allow you to ungroup and work with each element.

Figure 12-12:
The same
objects
before and
after the
Group
command.

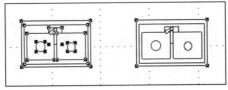

Joining

Joining lets you link together two freehand objects to make one single object. This option is different from the Group command because the two objects can't be "unjoined." Joining takes place with Reshape mode on. Here's how you join two objects:

1. **Select the first object.**

2. **Either place the optional button on your button bar (see the Appendix) and click it or choose Arrange⇨Reshape or press ⌘-R (Mac) or Ctrl+R (Windows).**

3. **Cut or copy the object to the Clipboard.**

4. **Select the second object.**

   Normally, the Join command attaches the starting point of the object on the Clipboard to the ending point of the object you just selected. If you want to connect the starting points of both objects, click the starting point of the object you just selected. Both of these options are shown in Figure 12-13.

5. **Either choose Edit⇨Paste or press ⌘-V (Mac) or Ctrl+V (Windows).**

   Notice in Figure 12-13 that the object that was pasted assumes the fill and line settings of the other object.

6. **Either choose Arrange⇨Reshape or press ⌘-R (Mac) or Ctrl+R (Windows) to turn off reshape mode when you finish. (Or click the button if you've added it.)**

You can use this process to join several copies of the same object together to form a border or a pattern.

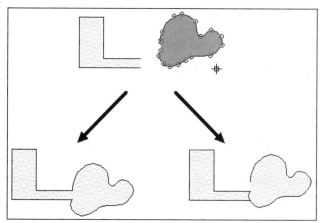

Figure 12-13: The objects at the top are going to be joined. On the left, they are joined end point to starting point, and on the right, starting point to starting point.

Locking

To make an object or frame stay put, you can select it and use Arrange➪ Lock. Locking is like nailing down the object on your page, because a locked object can't change or move — that is, until you use the Unlock command. In an intricate image, locking an object that you don't want affected makes it easier to select and change the objects around it. You know something is locked if it has gray handles. Note, however, that frames work a bit differently: You can't move or resize them, but you *can* change their contents, which is very handy.

Many stationery and Assistant documents have locked frames and objects. If you see gray handles when you select an object or frame, use the Unlock command to move or resize it.

Inserting Graphics

One old saying says "a picture is worth a thousand words." Images can add a lot to a document. Another old saying says "Why reinvent the wheel?" And you don't have to, thanks to clip art. Clip art is any graphic or image that has no copyright or includes the copyright holder's permission for public use. It can be scanned images of old advertisements or cartoons created especially for use in computer documents. You can paste clip art into your document as is or you can use clip art as a starting point for your own art by customizing it with your own artistic touch.

ClarisWorks comes with scads of clip art. This section first looks at traditional methods of inserting graphics into your document and then looks at Libraries, where you can find loads of clip art.

Pasting and inserting

Here are three ways to add art to your document:

✔ **The copy-and-paste method:** Open the clip art document you want to use and copy the image. Return to your document and paste the image from the clipboard into your document.

✔ **The Insert method:** Click the Insert button on the default palette or choose File⇨Insert to go to the Open, or Open/Save dialog box (see Chapter 2); then you navigate to the clip art document that you want to use. When you pick a document, the image is placed directly into your document.

✔ **The drag-and-drop method (Mac only):** You can drag any object from one open document right into another open document, even between (drag-aware) applications. Or you can drag a closed ClarisWorks document onto an open document's page, which places the contents of the ClarisWorks document right into your document. This also works with some other documents created by other programs. (In Windows, this procedure opens the closed document instead of adding its contents to the open one.)

If you're on a Mac, you can use the Create Preview button in the Open/Save dialog box to preview the image before you place it into your document.

After you have an image in your document, you can move it and resize it just like any other object. The art may appear in a paint frame, depending on the document format. If the art is composed of several objects grouped together, you can even ungroup these objects and modify the image — or just use certain pieces.

When buying clip art, keep in mind that while ClarisWorks can use just about any common graphic file format, you need to get your art in the format that prints best on your target printer. If you have a PostScript printer or use PostScript interpreter software with your printer, such as StyleScript (from Infowave), you can use EPS format. (We love StyleScript.) On other printers, EPS files don't look as good as their promise. You may prefer bitmapped formats, such as TIFF, or object formats, such as PICT (more common on Macs).

Using ClarisWorks Libraries

ClarisWorks comes with 32 libraries of ready-to-use clip art images, stored in ClarisWorks Libraries. A ClarisWorks Library is a unique palette, provided to you to browse and place graphics and text into your ClarisWorks documents. The palette also contains controls for adding, organizing, and displaying graphics. Libraries can hold draw objects, paint images, spreadsheet cells, frames, QuickTime movies, and images from other applications' libraries.

To open an existing library, such as the one in Figure 12-14, select the Library by name from the Library submenu of the File menu. The Library has its own set of menus and controls to view and name objects, and to save changes to them:

> ✔ Use the palette's View menu to see images By Name or By Object (in miniature). When viewing a list by name, click an image's name to preview that image in the top of the palette.

> ✔ Search a Library by name, enter the word(s) you seek in the Name field at the bottom of the palette, and then click Find. To reveal the search part of the library palette, click the triangle at the lower-right corner.

> ✔ Alphabetize your library by choosing Alphabetize from the palette's View menu.

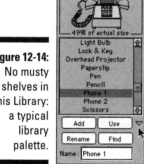

Figure 12-14:
No musty shelves in this Library: a typical library palette.

To use an image from a Library, just drag it into your document, or click the image or name, and then click the Use button.

You can also create your own libraries to hold frequently used images, such as company logos, borders, or stock images. You can even store text. Here's how:

1. **Choose File⇨Library⇨New to open an empty Library, ready to fill.**

2. **Select an image from any open document and either drag it into the palette's window or click the palette's Add button.**

   This adds the image to the Library. You can also cut or copy an image from another application and use the Paste command in the palette's Edit menu to add images.

3. **Enter a name in the Name field, and then click Rename to give the image a name.**

   If the Name field isn't showing, click the arrow at the bottom of the palette, as shown in Figure 12-14. Naming is optional — and helpful.

4. **Repeat Steps 2 and 3 to add additional images at this time.**

   You can always add images later if you like.

5. **Choose File⇨Save or File⇨Save As from the library palette.**

   This saves your library for later use. You can save libraries anywhere, but to have them show up in the File menu's Library submenu, save to the ClarisWorks Libraries folder (in the ClarisWorks folder).

Use the Group command on images that are made up of several objects before you try to add the image to a library. Otherwise, all the objects in the image are added separately.

Chapter 13

The Lowdown on Page Layout

. . . .

In This Chapter

▶ Discovering the basics with an envelope template

▶ Adding pages to a draw document

▶ Turning on rulers

▶ Linking frames

▶ Wrapping text in a draw document

▶ Using headers, footers, and page numbers

. . . .

*P*age layout is an area where ClarisWorks really struts its stuff. In preceding chapters, we talk about placing various elements into various documents, but here we put it all together to create great-looking, high-end documents. You may be thinking, "Hey, I don't see a page-layout option when I open a new document." That's because you use draw documents for page layout. The draw environment is a natural for page layout because it lets you combine different frames and graphics and has the tools you need to make everything look the way you want it to. We start with a simple exercise — making an envelope — and then work our way up to the big stuff.

Page Layout Basics: The Envelope Template

Making an envelope template is a great way to demonstrate the basics of page layout. In this case, the *page* we lay out is an envelope.

Here's an overview of the process: First, we set up the page size and margins. Next, we add a company logo — a graphic element. Finally, we put in the return address and some generic text to stand in for the addressee — the text elements. Okay, here we go:

1. Open a new ClarisWorks draw document.

Click the button, or choose File⇨New and pick Draw Document in the New Document dialog box.

2. Choose File⇨Print Setup (Windows) or File⇨Page Setup (Mac).

Figure 13-1 shows the Page Setup dialog box (Mac version), which lets you tell ClarisWorks you want your document page to be the size of an envelope. Your document setup dialog box looks different depending on the platform and printer you are using and, with a Mac, what version of the printer software. Set the page size for envelope (Comm 10 or Monarch) and that you are using landscape (horizontal) orientation, like the settings shown in Figure 13-1. Click OK when set.

You should now see an envelope-sized draw document on your screen.

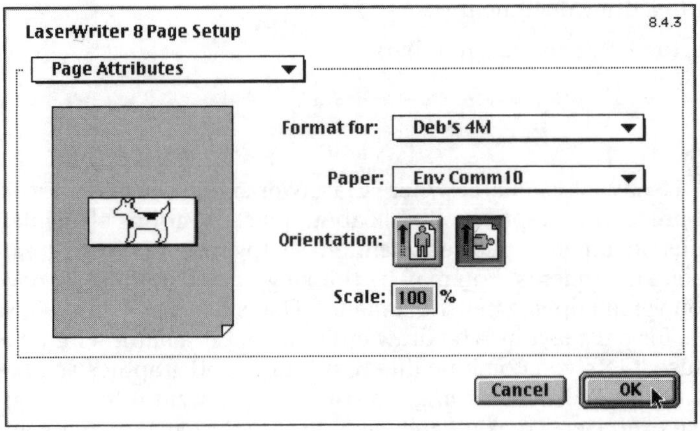

Figure 13-1:
Make sure
the size is
set for
envelope
and the
orientation
is
landscape.

LaserWriter 8 Page Setup   8.4.3

Page Attributes ▼

Format for: Deb's 4M ▼

Paper: Env Comm10 ▼

Orientation:

Scale: 100 %

Cancel   OK

3. Choose Format⇨Document.

Verify that the top, bottom, right, and left margins are set to 0.25 inch or less. The small margins let you place your return address way up out of the way in the corner.

The exact measurements depend on your printer — most printers need at least a ¹/₄-inch margin. Some need ¹/₂ inch. Also make sure/the document is only one page across and one down. Click OK when you finish.

4. To see the whole page on-screen, including the margin area, choose Window⇨Page View or press Shift-⌘-P (Mac) or Shift+Ctrl+P (Windows).

If you prefer to use buttons, remain in the current view and add the show/hide margins button (top) to your button bar and click it. The margin area shows up as white. Then the show/hide page guide button (bottom), which is also optional, adds a hard line view of the margins. With these buttons, or with page view on, you can see the envelope exactly as it looks when it's printed. These are two helpful buttons.

The grid of dots does not print out; it's there only to help you place objects on the page. You can turn it off anytime.

5. **(Optional) Add a graphic for your company logo.**

For this example, we paste in a preexisting logo copied from another file. Other instructions for inserting graphics are in Chapter 12. If necessary, resize your graphic to fit it in the corner of the envelope.

6. **Use the text tool to create a text frame for your return address in the upper-left corner, and then type your return address and format it in your favorite font.**

Text formatting information is in Chapter 5.

7. **Repeat Step 6 to make a text box for the addressee information in the middle of the envelope and type some placeholder information as shown in Figure 13-2.**

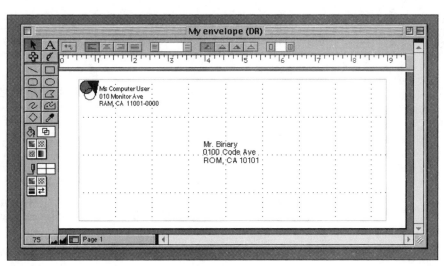

Figure 13-2:
The envelope template with everything in place. Just a couple more steps to finish everything off, and you're done!

The Address Envelope Assistant

The Envelope Assistant and Address Envelope Assistant combo is another way to create and address your envelopes — if you don't need anything fancy. Before you can make this Assistant work correctly, you must do two things:

✔ **You must use the Envelope Assistant in the New Document dialog box at least once before you can use the Address Envelope Assistant.**

The Address Envelope Assistant gets the return address and the envelope size information from the settings you picked with the Envelope Assistant. If you haven't used the Envelope Assistant yet, go to the Assistant button bar and click the icon for Envelope. (Or choose File⇨New, click

Start with an Assistant or Stationery, and double-click to use the Envelope Assistant.) You only have to follow these steps once to set the information — unless at some point you want to change your return address or envelope size.

✔ **In your document, select the address you want on the envelope before you select the Address Envelope Assistant.**

After you select an address, choose Help⇨ClarisWorks Assistants and click Address Envelope Assistant. If no address is selected, a message appears telling you that you need to select an address. Your envelope appears in a new untitled document window.

If you like the formatting from the return address and want the same formatting here, select it as an object, paste it here, and then change the words. Make sure you have at least five lines in the address text box for long addresses.

8. **After everything is where you want it, choose Edit⇨Select All or press ⌘-A (Mac) or Ctrl+A (Windows) to select everything. Choose Arrange⇨Lock to lock it all into place.**

You can still change the text in the address boxes, but you can't accidentally move the boxes.

9. **Give your envelope template a name you can remember.**

10. **Save the document as stationery so you always work with a copy, leaving the original untouched by choosing File⇨Save As and setting the document type to stationery.**

If you save the stationery document to the ClarisWorks Stationery folder, your envelope template will be available in the stationery list when you open a new document. If you prefer, create your own folder, call it Templates or something else you like, and save all your templates there. Place the folder in your ♦ menu (Mac) or Start menu (Windows).

Now that you have set up this template, anytime you need to print an envelope, all you do is open a copy and fill in the address information. It's fastest to copy the address from the document you plan to send inside the envelope and paste it here.

Adding Pages to Your Draw Document

To lay out longer documents, such as a double-sided flier or a newsletter, the first thing you want to do is add pages to your draw document. The number of pages is controlled in the Document dialog box. (The Windows version of the dialog box is shown in Figure 13-3.) Choose Format⇨ Document to bring up this dialog box.

Figure 13-3:
Add pages, set margins, and control how your document looks on-screen with the Document dialog box.

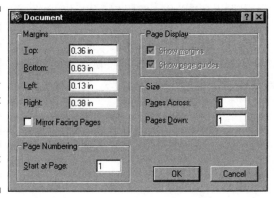

In the appropriate fields, type in the number of pages across and down for your document; the pages are added when you click OK.

Most people like to enter **1** in the Pages Across setting so they can scroll downward to the next page. If you have two or more pages across and several down as well, the page numbering proceeds from left to right until the rightmost page is reached and then moves down to the next row starting from the left side again.

If your monitor is large enough to display two pages at once, you may want to make your document two pages across when you are working on a newsletter or other document that has double-sided or facing pages. If you can't fit two pages on the screen, try zooming out to 75 percent.

Text and Graphics Rulers

Rulers help you work with objects and frames. There are two kinds of rulers: graphics and text. Graphics rulers show you where objects and frames are located on the page. A graphics ruler goes along the side as well as along the top. The text ruler is the same as it is in the text environment: It lets you control the settings inside the text frames on your page. The text ruler lets you change line spacing, set tab stops, and control alignment. Check out Chapter 5 for more information about formatting text.

To show the graphics rulers, click once on the selection arrow tool to make sure you are in draw mode and then choose Window⇨Show Rulers or press Shift-⌘-U (Mac) or Shift+Ctrl+U (Windows). The graphics rulers appear at the top and left edges of your document, as shown in Figure 13-4.

To change the unit of measurement or the ruler's divisions, choose Format⇨Rulers, to bring up the Rulers dialog box shown in Figure 13-4. ClarisWorks rulers can reflect inches, centimeters, millimeters, picas, and points. You can also use the Rulers dialog box to change from the graphics ruler to the text ruler, and vice versa: Click the appropriate button in the Ruler Type box and click OK.

Figure 13-4:
Rulers, rulers everywhere. The Rulers dialog box in front of a draw document with the rulers visible.

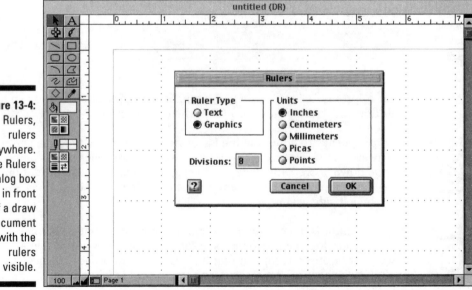

You can also change rulers by changing environments, hiding the rulers, and then showing them again.

Linked Frames

Kinda sounds like a magic trick, huh? No sleight of hand here. Linking text frames lets you automatically flow text from one frame into another. This capability lets you create columns of text that continue across several columns, even to another page. You can also use frame links to show several different views of a spreadsheet or paint frame in the same document. Linking frames lets you recycle a paint graphic or spreadsheet data without using several copies of the same frame and making your document into a huge file.

You can create as many groups of linked frames in a document as you like. And, of course, you can mix linked and unlinked frames within your document.

Linking text frames

Linked frames are special text frames that form a chain. When the first frame fills up, any extra text flows into the next frame in the chain, or hangs out waiting until you create one. You can link as many frames as you want by adding to the end of the chain. Sorry, you can't add frames in the middle or at the beginning. But you *can* delete from the beginning or middle — the text just reflows.

You can turn an existing frame into a linked frame or create an empty linked frame. Existing frames or chains can't be linked to each other, though. Instead, paste all the text into the first existing frame of one chain and create new frames from there. With this stuff in mind, we show you two ways to create these magic linking things.

Magic is easy, once you know the trick. To link an existing frame:

1. **Select the existing text frame; then choose Options➪Frame Links.**

2. **Click once on the continue indicator at the bottom of the frame.**

    Now ClarisWorks knows to flow the text, linking to the next frame you create. Your arrow pointer turns to a special I-beam.

3. Use the I-beam to create another frame by clicking and dragging to define the area.

The outline of your first frame becomes invisible, but because there's text there you know where it is. When you click the text, you can see the frame.

4. Repeat Steps 2 and 3 to add more frames to the chain.

You always click the last continue indicator to create a new link.

5. Go back to Options⇨Frame Links to turn off frame links when done.

Your arrow pointer returns to normal.

To create a new empty frame as your first linked frame is no harder. Nothing up your sleeves? Just follow these steps:

1. Choose Options⇨Frame Links.

This lets ClarisWorks know you are creating linked frames.

2. Select the text tool from the Tool Panel. Click the mouse and drag to create a new text frame.

3. Type any text into this frame as a placeholder.

The frame becomes invisible while you are creating the new frame it links to.

4. Click outside the frame.

You're back in the draw environment, leaving the frame selected, as Figure 13-5 shows.

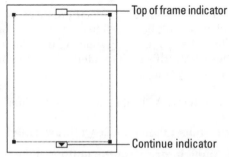

Figure 13-5:
A new frame ready to be linked. Notice the indicators at the top and bottom.

Top of frame indicator

Continue indicator

5. Click once on the continue indicator at the bottom of the frame.

Now ClarisWorks knows to flow the text, linking to the next frame you create. Your arrow pointer turns to a special I-beam.

6. Use the I-beam to create another frame by clicking and dragging to define the area as usual.

Your first frame becomes invisible, but your placeholder helps you see where it is.

7. Repeat Steps 5 and 6 to add more frames to the chain.

Always click the last continue indicator to create a new link.

8. Go back to Options⇨Frame Links to turn off frame links when done.

Your arrow pointer returns to normal.

To align your text fields, you can select them and use the Align Object buttons or commands. You can also use the rulers and the graphics grid to help with positioning. To select the ones you want to work with, hold down the Shift key and click once on each frame (called Shift-clicking) or drag the arrow pointer to surround the entire area (marquee technique). Notice frames are only visible when selected.

You can add text to the linked frames by typing, pasting, or using the File⇨ Insert command, just as for regular text frames. When there's more text than fits in the chain, the last frame shows a text overflow indicator like the one in Figure 13-6.

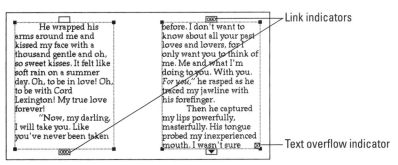

Figure 13-6:
Flood!
These linked
frames are
overflowing!

When you see the overflow indicator, you have three choices:

- ✔ Add another linked frame to the chain for the excess text.
- ✔ Make the existing frames bigger to display more text.
- ✔ Make the text a smaller point size so more words fit in the same space.

After you create a layout you like — even with empty linked frames — you may want to save it as stationery. See Chapter 2 for more on stationery documents.

Wrapping text in a draw document

You can have one or more linked text frames surround one or more objects and have the frame text wrap around the objects. The trick to wrapping the text around the graphic is setting the text up as a frame link. Regular text frames just lie there over or under your objects. Remember, you have to select the graphic and set it to have the text wrap around it. There's a button for irregular text wrap — the most exciting — on the default button bar and optional buttons for regular and unwrap. You can also use Options⇨ Text Wrap. We talk about text wrap in the word-processing section of this book.

Linking spreadsheet and paint frames

Linked spreadsheet and linked paint frames work a bit differently from linked text frames. Instead of making the information flow from one frame to another, linked spreadsheet or paint frames let several frames use the same information or image, like having more than one window looking at the same information. Suppose you want to use a paint image that takes up 25K of hard disk space. Using five copies of the image adds 125K to the document's size, whereas sharing one copy of the same image among five linked paint frames adds only 25K.

Another advantage to linking paint or spreadsheet frames is that any change you make in one frame shows up in all the rest of the frames in the chain. For example, suppose you're using linked frames to show a small spreadsheet at several places in your document. If you need to change a number, all you have to do is make the change in one frame. The change shows up in all the linked frames that show the same cells. If the frames weren't linked, you would have to manually change the same number every time you used that spreadsheet in your document.

To add linked frames to an existing paint or spreadsheet frame:

1. **Select the frame with the arrow pointer.**

2. **Choose Options⇨Frame Links to turn on frame links mode.**

   This lets ClarisWorks know that you are going to add a linked frame. You should now see a continue indicator at the bottom of the frame.

3. **Click once on the continue indicator.**

   Refer back to Figure 13-5 to refresh your memory as to what the indicator looks like.

   Your arrow pointer is now a spreadsheet tool.

4. Click and drag to create a new frame linked to the first.

If you want to add more linked frames, click the continue indicator on the frame that you want to link to and drag another frame.

After you have all the linked frames you need for that spreadsheet or paint frame, you can resize and arrange them on the page.

The top of each new paint or spreadsheet frame starts where the last linked frame leaves off. Take a look at Figure 13-7 to see what we mean.

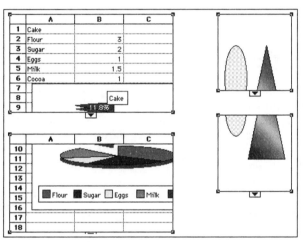

Figure 13-7:
Linked
paint or
spreadsheet
frames pick
up where
the last one
left off,
unless you
specify
otherwise.

If you want to have a different part of the paint image or spreadsheet displayed in a linked frame, you can specify what part of the document appears in the upper-left corner of the frame, which is known as the origin. You set the origin as an intersection of pixels for paint frames or as a specific cell for a spreadsheet frame. You type this information into the dialog box you bring up by choosing Edit⇨Frame Info. Figure 13-8 shows the dialog boxes for both paint and spreadsheet frames.

If you want all the linked frames in your document to show the same part of the image or spreadsheet, set the origin of each frame to the same number, typically 0,0 for paint frames or A1 for spreadsheet frames.

For paint frame · · · · · · For spreadsheet frame

Figure 13-8: Frame and glory! Use the Modify Frame dialog box to set what appears in a frame.

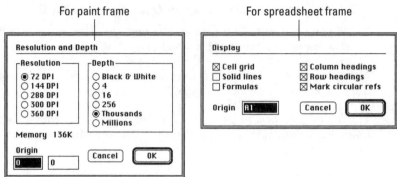

Opening frames

Opening a frame always reminds us of Alice stepping through the looking-glass. Because spreadsheet and paint frames are like windows looking at what may be larger documents, you need a way to see the whole image or spreadsheet. ClarisWorks lets you open up a frame into its own separate full-sized document window so you can see and edit all of a frame's contents, not just the visible parts. You do this by following these steps:

1. **Click once on a paint or spreadsheet frame to select it.**

2. **Choose Window⇨Open Frame.**

You can now view and edit whatever is in the frame as if it were a separate document. After you click the Close box on this new window, any changes you made show up in the frame. Easy as pie.

To have a chart show up inside a spreadsheet frame instead of in a separate frame, as it usually would, open the spreadsheet frame first, and then make the chart. Either way, the chart updates if you change the numbers in the spreadsheet.

When you open a paint frame, you see a document that's the same size as the frame you opened. If you have several frames linked together, the window shows a document that is as tall as all the frames stacked one on top of the other and as wide as the widest frame. You can change the size of the paint area by choosing Format⇨Document. See Chapter 10 for more information on resizing paint documents.

Headers, Footers, and Page Numbers

You can add a header or footer to your draw document just as in a text document. Using a header or footer lets you put all the information that needs to appear on every page of your document in one place. The perfect example is page numbers.

Now, technically, you can put a page-number placeholder in any text frame in a draw document. The only problem is that if you have a five-page document, you have to create five text frames, one on each page, and make sure that they all line up to get those page numbers in the same place on every page.

Why not use a header or footer, which lets you add the page number once and have it show up on every page? Remember, headers and footers are actually text frames. You can put anything in a header that you can put in other text frames — text, placeholders for page numbers, time, date, or graphics. You can even put in a spreadsheet frame if that's your idea of the perfect header or footer. Take a look at Chapter 5 for a complete rundown on headers and footers.

Chapter 14
Presenting Presentations

● ●

In This Chapter

▶ Presentations — what are they?

▶ Presentation tips

▶ Using a master page

▶ Movies

▶ Slide show controls and options

● ●

*R*emember when your presentations were considered *professional* just because you drew a *visual* to add dimension? These days, kids are using computer presentation software to do the "what I did on my summer vacation" bit.

A ClarisWorks presentation is an electronic slide show — but you don't have to take photos. Instead, you get to make your slides because the slides are actually pages of your ClarisWorks documents. You even get to have your show run on automatic — if you want. But that's not all. You also get to use movies and sounds. For added effect, you can print your slides as overhead transparencies or as handouts.

ClarisWorks enables you to create presentations that look every bit as professional as the expensive productions dished out by corporate high-brows at the annual marketing meeting — only yours will be a lot easier to put together. The presentation counts — not the cost of the software that creates it.

Laying Out a Presentation

Draw documents are the natural choice for presentations, thanks to their layout flexibility. However, you can use any type of document for presentations — except a telecommunications document. Word-processing documents are fine for presentations, too. Whatever type of document you decide to use, making a presentation is easy.

Perhaps more important than the power of the presentation software is the look and feel of your slides. As you design yours, keep these suggestions in mind:

- Keep it simple. Don't overwhelm and confuse your audience with zillions of colors, backgrounds, and words.

- Use the same background for all slides to keep attention focused on the information.

- Use a clean, readable font and keep the wording simple and brief.

- Let your speech provide the details; the slides are merely your outline.

- Light text on a dark background shows up well. A good color combination is white or yellow text on a blue background.

- Align design elements and text well. If misaligned, they look sloppy. Take advantage of the rulers, the graphics grid, and the alignment button commands in ClarisWorks.

- Design a master page first. Set up all the information you want on every page, such as a background design and company logo.

- Reveal your points one by one, building on each. Transparent slides let you do this.

- Create your handout's contents as you create your show and then hide the handouts by making them invisible during your presentation. Put each handout next to the slide it goes with to help you remember which handout goes with which slide.

- Use the Presentation Assisant to build a sample presentation and check out how it is set up.

Actually, the best place to build your presentation is the Presentation Assistant. There are plenty of style choices that you can customize by using the draw tools and techniques explained in Chapters 12 and 13. You can open the Assistant from the New Document dialog box or from the Assistants button bar, which you select from the arrow at the left of any button bar.

The best page setup for displaying slides on a computer screen is a letter-sized page in the wide or landscape orientation. Use the Page Setup (Mac) or Print Setup (Windows) dialog box to set this.

Editing Master Pages

A master page is not a novice page that's been promoted, but the page full of all the elements common to each page in your presentation. Master pages are an option only from within draw documents — one of the main reasons for using drawing documents. In other environments, your document can grow to several pages, but you are limited to placing common elements within your header or footer. There's no way to add a common element in the middle of the page — unless you have a lot of patience and time to waste.

Most often, you use a master page to add a colored background and other stuff like a company or school logo, a theme, a title, page numbering, and dates. You use a master page for any element that you want to appear on every slide.

To add elements or edit a master page, follow these steps:

1. Choose Options⇨Edit Master Page.

The page indicator at the bottom of the window reports that you're on the master page. A check mark also appears next to the Edit Master Page command in the menu. Additionally, the text blocks disappear.

2. Edit away!

All the drawing, painting, and layout stuff covered in Chapters 10–13 comes into play here.

3. When you finish, choose Options⇨Edit Master Page again to return to your other pages.

To view your slides complete with their backgrounds, turn on *page view*. Turn it off again to hide the master page elements. You turn page view on and off by choosing Window⇨Page View or pressing Shift-⌘-P (Mac) or Shift+Ctrl+P (Windows).

On some pages, your master page elements may not be appropriate. For example, on your title page, a page number may seem silly, or the header may be redundant. You can't remove the element, so instead you mask it. Use your drawing tools to create a shape that covers it up; then set the color of it to match the background color.

Elements on the master page cover the graphics grid when you edit slides in page view. Use Window⇨Page View to turn off page view so that you can see the grid. If you prefer to see the background graphics, use the line tool (constrained with the Shift key) to draw temporary guide lines, either on the individual page or the master page. Just remember to delete the lines when you're finished.

Adding Movies

How would you like to make your slide show into a state-of-the-art digital sound and video spectacle? It's a cinch with QuickTime whether you're on Mac or Windows. (Windows users also have the choice of using Microsoft Video for Windows — AVI. Mac users can also include QuickTime VR.) Movies can have video, sound, or both. Just drop in a couple of clips and your audience will think you're the presentation queen or king.

Movies are added just like any other image. You can copy and paste them from another document, or use File⇨Insert. On the Mac, you can also drag the clip right onto the slide. See Chapter 12 for more about working with images.

You can move, align, and resize movies, just like any other draw objects. QuickTime movies have a small film icon, or *control badge,* in the lower-left corner. Clicking the control badge displays a VCR-style control bar for full video control. Double-clicking the movie also plays the clip. Figure 14-1 shows both states of the control badge and controls. AVI movies also have a control badge, but clicking it plays the video instead of exposing further controls.

Figure 14-1:
Quick,
Robin, to
the
QuickTime
controls!

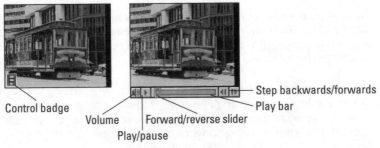

Step backwards/forwards
Play bar
Control badge
Volume
Forward/reverse slider
Play/pause

Mac users, you have a hidden way to control a video's speed and direction. Hold down Control and click and hold one of the step buttons (it doesn't matter which). A speed slider appears. Drag the slider to adjust the video's direction and speed. Placing the slider near the center mark plays the video in slow motion. Moving the slider toward the outside plays the video faster in that direction.

Note: If the QuickTime movie is pasted in line with text, the control badge has no effect. Instead, double-click the movie to play it. In order for the QuickTime controls to work, cut the movie and paste it back as a floating object.

QuickTime movies — the easy way

If you're not set up to record your own movies, you can round up quite a collection of royalty-free movies. BMUG, a computer user group, sells a two-CD set with hundreds of royalty-free movies, still images, and sounds in a full range of content. Call BMUG at (800) 776-2684 or (510) 549-2684. AMUG, the Arizona Mac User's Group also sells a set. They're on the web at AMUG.org. You may also find miscellaneous clips for sharing at your local user group (another reason to join your local user group). The LAMG's BBS has a folder full. It's in Los Angeles but accessible to members via the Web. For information, check out LAMG.org.

To add sound or music to your ClarisWorks presentation, place a QuickTime movie that has no image, just a soundtrack. To get that soundtrack, you can create your own or convert a track from an audio CD (honoring royalties and rights).

Most music is copyrighted. There are two kinds of copyrights, one for the music and lyrics, marked by ©, and one for the performance, marked by ℗. Even classical music recorded by some unknown Slavic orchestra can have a performance copyright. Music on CDs that have no copyright notice on the CD or liner notes may still be copyrighted. To be safe, check with the music publisher before you use any music in a presentation.

Controlling the Show

And now the moment you've been waiting for: seeing your slide show. After you get a few slides ready, you'll want to test the presentation and see how it runs. Just choose Window⇨Slide Show, and up pops the Slide Show dialog box shown in Figure 14-2.

Using the Slide Show dialog box

The Slide Show dialog box lets you control how your slides and movies behave. There are three main sections.

Figure 14-2:
Let the
show begin:
the Slide
Show
dialog box.

Order and visibility

The Order section lets you control the slide order. It also lets you turn your slides transparent or hide them. To change the order in which any slide appears in the presentation, drag it up or down in the list. This capability is great if you forget about some information and make the slide as an after-thought. That is, the slide may be out of place at the end, so you can move it into position later.

Each click on the icon next to each slide number changes its visibility. If it's Opaque, it becomes Transparent, Transparent becomes Hidden, and so on, in a circle. Hiding slides is a great way to include your handout notes in your presentation. Put them on every other slide and make those slides hidden when you run the presentation.

Slide options

Slide options give you control over how your slide show looks and runs:

- **Fit to Screen:** Fits the pages of your document to the size of your screen.

- **Center:** Centers your page on the screen. (Boy, we're being so informative aren't we? Telling you all this stuff you couldn't figure out on your own.) This option is useful if Fit to Screen is not checked and your document pages are smaller than the screen.

- **Show Cursor:** Keeps the cursor visible while the slide show is running. Some people like to use the cursor as an on-screen pointer; others find it distracting.

- **Fade:** The one special effect in ClarisWorks. The screen fades to black out of each slide and then fades in with the next. It's not in the Windows dialog box because it's available only on the Mac.

- ✔ **Loop:** Shows your presentation over and over until the audience finally gets the point.

- ✔ **Advance Every:** Sets your presentation to run by itself. This feature is handy for timed presentations or self-running slide shows.

- ✔ **Background:** Specifies a background color for the slides if you didn't use a master page. This option is useful for presentations made from text documents.

- ✔ **Border:** Sets a color for the area around the edges of the slide. Your slide has a border if Fit to Screen is not checked and your pages are smaller than the screen. A border and background of the same color have the effect of a screen-sized slide with a solid-color background.

QuickTime options

The QuickTime options box is where you tell ClarisWorks how you want QuickTime movies to play back during the slide show. Of course, you have to have QuickTime installed. (It comes on the ClarisWorks Office CD in case you don't already have it.)

- ✔ **Auto play:** Makes all QuickTime movies start playing as soon as the slide appears on-screen.

- ✔ **Simultaneous:** Plays all movies on a slide at once, when the slide appears on-screen. This is available only if Auto play is checked.

- ✔ **Complete Play Before Advancing:** Makes each QuickTime movie play to the end before advancing to the next slide. If you're advancing your slides automatically, your viewers won't be impressed to see the slide change in mid-movie.

To have a sound-only QuickTime movie play while another video QuickTime movie plays, be sure to check the Simultaneous box. Also make sure that the volume in the video movie is all the way down so there won't be problems with the sound playback.

Moving through the slide show

After you set the options in the Slide Show dialog box, you can click Start to begin the presentation. Or you can click Done to save the settings and return to the document. Cancel puts the settings back as they were before you opened the dialog box.

After you save the settings, you can go right into the presentation by clicking the Start Show button. Or, if you like to do things the hard way, press Option (Mac) or Ctrl (Windows) when you choose Window⇨Slide Show. Not as fast, but it bypasses the dialog box.

After you start the slide show, you have lots of options for controlling it. Table 14-1 spells them out for you.

Table 14-1	How to Make Things Happen in a Slide Show
To Make This Happen	*Do This*
Move forward to the next slide	Click the mouse button or press →, ↓, Page Down, Return, Enter, Tab, or the spacebar.
Move backward to the previous slide	Press ←, ↑, Page Up, Shift+Return, Shift+Enter, Shift+Tab, or Shift+spacebar.
Play a QuickTime Movie	Click the movie once.
Pause or resume a QuickTime movie	⌘-click or Option-click the movie (Mac) or Ctrl+click or Alt+click (Windows).
Stop a QuickTime movie	Click the movie once.
Move to the beginning of the slide show	Press the Home key.
Move to the end of the slide show	Press the End key.
Stop the slide show	Press q, Esc, ⌘-. (period)(Mac) or Ctrl+.(period)(Windows) or ⌘-Q (Mac).

When you exit the slide show, you end up back at the Slide Show dialog box. Click Cancel or Done to dismiss the dialog box.

Whew! Armed with all that information, you should be able to put together a presentation with little ol' ClarisWorks that'll knock the socks off your audience.

Part IV
Working with Numbers: It All Adds Up!

In this part . . .

Remember when spreadsheets were long white scrolls of paper that ran to the floor as a half-blind, near-sighted, bespeckled man sat hunched over, eyes glazed, quill pen in hand? Okay, maybe we've gone back too far.

Remember when spreadsheets were long, perforated pages of hard-to-read numbers?

For us in-the-mode computer owners, those stacks are a thing of the past. Spreadsheets make numbers much easier to deal with. They back up onto a tiny disk, instead of taking up shelves of cabinet space. They can be colorized, sorted, moved around — handled any which way we want — just to make them easier to see. Then there's the ultimate: turning them into charts so they're really easy to understand! Not the kind of chart it takes posterboard and a whole pack of markers to slave over. This is the kind where you drag your mouse once, click one button, and voilà — there it is!

Numbers are still numbers and that's not very exciting to most of us. But they're certainly easier and more fun these days with things like ClarisWorks around to help us.

If you're not into numbers right now, don't worry about this section. But when the time comes, we're here for you, ready to bring you into the groove of the spreadsheet.

Chapter 15
Spreadsheets 101

• •

In This Chapter

▶ Using a spreadsheet for the proper purpose

▶ Selecting in spreadsheets

▶ Manipulating data

▶ Picking preferences

• •

S preadsheets are hopelessly tied to the geeky image of the computer user who plays with numbers all day and has tape in the middle of inch-thick glasses. The truth is, spreadsheets are cool! Maybe we could start a bring-a-friend-a-spreadsheet campaign to spread the word on spreadsheets. Or maybe we're being overzealous. Hmmm. . . .

Deciding When to Use a Spreadsheet

When most people think of spreadsheets, they think of Microsoft Excel. But most people never use half of the capabilities of a spreadsheet such as Excel. For most purposes, everything you need a spreadsheet to do happens to be right here in ClarisWorks.

Visions of dreary bookkeeping duties, like balancing your checkbook or setting up a company's financial statements, are probably dancing in your head. (Or, more likely, lurking rather than dancing.) Actually many people also get a lot of mileage out of spreadsheets as calendars and schedules. We've even seen spreadsheets used to create games like Yahtzee and 21.

Spreadsheets are really good for working with numbers. You can use them to keep financial information and statistics, to record tax information, or to record and chart data for a chemistry experiment. Hey, speaking of charts, ClarisWorks can make you any kind of spiffy-looking chart or graph you want based on numbers in your spreadsheet. You don't even have to type any complicated formulas to create your chart; just click a button.

Working with Cells, Rows, and Columns

Spreadsheets are made up of rectangular containers called cells. The cells are stacked on top of and next to each other to form a grid. A horizontal line of cells is a *row*. A vertical stack of cells is a *column*. Rows are labeled with numbers, starting with 1. Columns are labeled with letters, starting with A. Each cell has a name based on the intersection of the row and column where the cell is located. The cell at the upper-left corner of the spreadsheet is A1. Figure 15-1 points these things out to you. You can assign cells friendlier names. We show you how in Chapter 16.

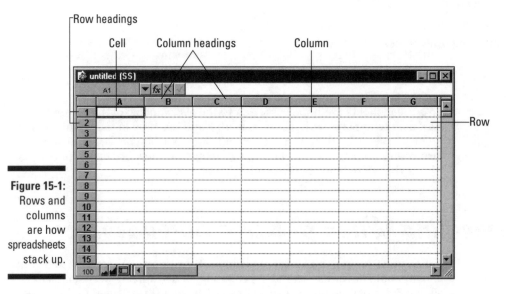

Figure 15-1: Rows and columns are how spreadsheets stack up.

Selecting a single cell

As always on the computer, you have to select something before you can do anything to it.

To select a single cell, you need a microscope and very tiny tweezers — if you're in a biology lab. In a ClarisWorks spreadsheet, you just click a cell to select it.

When a cell is selected, you see a dark border — called the selection box — around it. For example, B3 is selected in Figure 15-2. When you first open a new spreadsheet, cell A1, the cell in the upper-left corner, is selected. In the spreadsheet environment, you can move to your next selection by pressing keys. Table 15-1 lists the keys that move the selection box and in which direction they move it.

Table 15-1	**Moving the Selection Box with the Keyboard**
Press This Key	*To Move in This Direction*
Tab	Move right one cell
Return	Move down one cell
Shift+Tab	Move left one cell
Shift+ Return	Move up one cell
→, ←, ↑, ↓	Move one cell in the direction of the arrow (if the cursor is visible in the entry bar, press Option [Mac] or Ctrl [Windows] and the arrow)

Selecting a range of cells

You can only select cells that are next to each other in a rectangular block so a selected block is always in a rectangular shape, even if it's only one row high or one column wide. You never see a T-shaped group of selected cells.

There are two ways to select a block of cells:

✔ **Dragging:** Just position the plus-sign pointer in one corner of the block you want to select; then click and hold down the mouse button while dragging to the opposite corner. The block of cells highlights, like those in Figure 15-2.

✔ **Shift-clicking:** Click once in one corner of the block you want to select; then press Shift and click once on the cell in the opposite corner diagonally. This is especially useful for selecting a block of cells that is larger than your screen or for any large block, because you avoid dragging long distances.

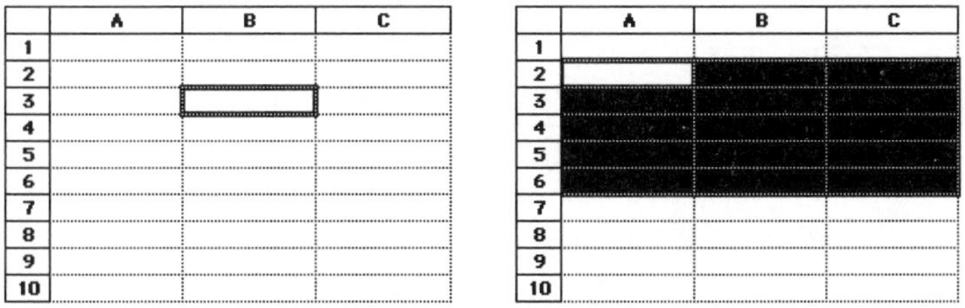

Figure 15-2:
On the left, a single cell is selected; on the right, a block of cells is selected.

Selecting columns and rows

To select an entire column or row all the way out to the uncharted nether regions of the spreadsheet edge, just click the row or column heading. That's a lot of cells for just one click.

Selecting the whole spreadsheet

Do you wanna select the whole thing? If you really, really, really want to select every row and every column, here's how: Click the little box in the very top-left corner, where the row and column headings meet.

Many people get extremely frustrated when they try to select a block of cells because they can't get that one silly cell in the corner to select. Or, at least they think they can't. Truth is, they did. It just doesn't turn black. Think about it: If you want to enter information into a cell when you have a group selected, which cell would it go into? All of them? Nope, just the one that stays white. In fact, this feature makes entering information into a block of selected cells really easy. So don't worry about that one silly cell; you got it.

Entering Data

Entering information into a spreadsheet is different from any other ClarisWorks environment. Instead of typing directly into a cell, you type in the entry bar at the top of the window, as shown in Figure 15-3.

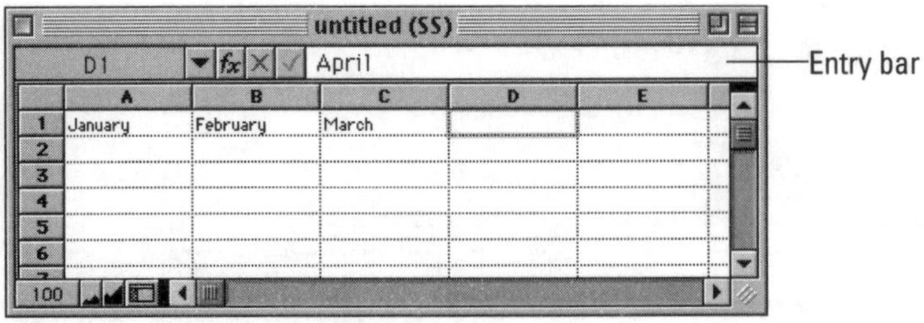

Figure 15-3:
All
characters
enter at the
entry bar on
the top,
please.

	A	B	C	D	E
1	January	February	March		
2					
3					
4					
5					
6					

D1 ... April ——Entry bar

untitled (SS)

After you type in your information, click the Accept button — the one with the check mark on it — to enter the information into the selected cell. To delete the information in the entry bar, click the Cancel button — the one with the X on it. You can save time by pressing Enter, Tab, or Return — or by selecting another cell. (Each has a different effect after entering your data. More on that subject soon.)

If you've used a spreadsheet before, you have probably been frustrated by having to manually select the cell at the top of the next column when you get to the bottom of the one you are in. The same thing applies to rows. The $100 tip is to first select the group of cells you're working with. Then when you press Return at the bottom of the first column, the selection box moves back to the top of the next column for you. If you're working in rows, when you press Tab at the end of a row, the selection box pops to the beginning of the next row.

Setting Preferences

We all have our preferences. Movies, soft drinks . . . and now you have a spreadsheet action preference, too.

The spreadsheet section of the ClarisWorks Preferences dialog box lets you set how the Enter and arrow keys behave when you enter information into a cell or move the selection box around. (That's the Enter key on the number pad.) Take a look at your options, shown in Figure 15-4.

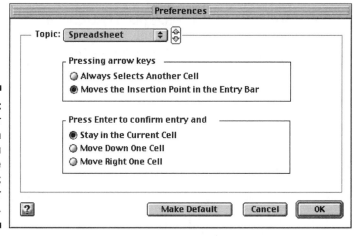

Figure 15-4:
The Enter key can take you anywhere or nowhere; whatever you prefer.

Choose Edit⇨Preferences to arrive in this window. If you don't land at spreadsheet options, use the pop-up menu to get here. The options here are pretty self-explanatory. Changing them helps if you're used to another spreadsheet. Most people change the arrow keys so that they move to the next cell. ClarisWorks is preset to have the arrow keys move the cursor within the entry bar when the cursor is there, and to move from cell to cell when it's not. To have the arrow keys always move between cells, select Always Selects Another Cell, and use the mouse to move your cursor through the text within the entry bar.

Editing

After you're finished and looking at the big picture, you may find some errors. To edit the contents of a cell, use the entry bar, just as when you entered the information. You can select, Delete, Copy, and Paste in the entry bar, just like in a text frame. Remember to enter your changes by clicking the check mark or pressing Enter on the number pad, or selecting another cell with the keyboard or mouse. Any of those actions enters the updated information into the cell.

If you are working on a spreadsheet that someone else made and you click a cell, the entry bar may contain a bunch of gobbledygook that starts with an equals sign. Don't panic — that's a formula. Find out more about formulas in Chapter 18. All you need to know for now is that the gibberish is telling ClarisWorks how to come up with the number you see in the cell. It's best to leave it alone until you check out Chapter 18.

Moving Data

ClarisWorks provides three ways to move the contents of cells in spreadsheets. Each way involves first selecting the cells you want to move.

If you move the contents of a block of cells into another block of cells that already have stuff in them, the information that was at the destination gets replaced. If you don't want to lose information, make sure that your destination cells are empty.

To move the contents of a cell or cells, do one of the following:

- ✔ Select the cells you want to move, hold down ⌘-Option (Mac) or Ctrl+Alt (Windows) and click in the cell where you want the upper-left corner of the selected block of cells to appear. This is absolutely the fastest way to move the information in a selected block of cells.

- ✔ Select a cell or group of cells and use the old copy (or cut) and paste routine. Just cut or copy the selection and click the upper-left corner cell where you want the just-cut or just-copied block of cells to appear. Then paste. Copy and paste is the only method that places the cell data in the Clipboard.

- ✔ If you like dialog boxes, try this: After you select the cells to move, choose Calculate⇨Move. In the dialog box that appears, type the name of the cell where you want the upper-left corner of the selected block of cells to appear. Then click OK, or cancel the move with the Cancel button.

Filling Cells

Filling cells is a shortcut for typing the same thing over and over in a series of cells. It's also faster than copying and pasting, pasting, pasting. . . .

Fill Down and Fill Right

Suppose you're working on the spreadsheet in Figure 15-5, and you know the next ten entries are all 50 cents. Just enter 0.50 in the first cell, select it along with the next nine cells, and choose Calculate⇨Fill Down. Want to fill the next nine cells to the right instead? The Fill Right command has you covered. When you have to enter the same information repeatedly, fill it instead!

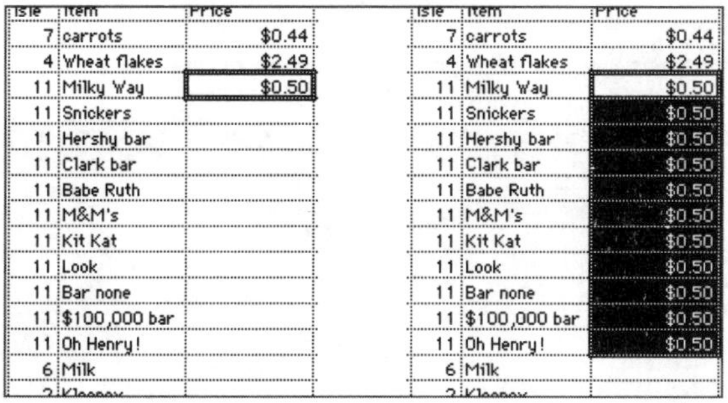

Figure 15-5:
Yo Phil! It's easier with Fill.

Isle	Item	Price		Isle	Item	Price
7	carrots	$0.44		7	carrots	$0.44
4	Wheat flakes	$2.49		4	Wheat flakes	$2.49
11	Milky Way	$0.50		11	Milky Way	$0.50
11	Snickers			11	Snickers	$0.50
11	Hershy bar			11	Hershy bar	$0.50
11	Clark bar			11	Clark bar	$0.50
11	Babe Ruth			11	Babe Ruth	$0.50
11	M&M's			11	M&M's	$0.50
11	Kit Kat			11	Kit Kat	$0.50
11	Look			11	Look	$0.50
11	Bar none			11	Bar none	$0.50
11	$100,000 bar			11	$100,000 bar	$0.50
11	Oh Henry!			11	Oh Henry!	$0.50
6	Milk			6	Milk	
2	Kleenex			2	Kleenex	

Fill Special

Fill Special is a smart fill. It auto-fills a selected group of cells with sequential information such as times, days of the week, or month names. Simply fill in one or two entries of the sequence, and Fill Special guesses the pattern for the rest of the selected cells.

For example, suppose you're a student creating a schedule of your classes each day of the week. As Figures 15-6 and 15-7 show, Fill Special creates a schedule for you.

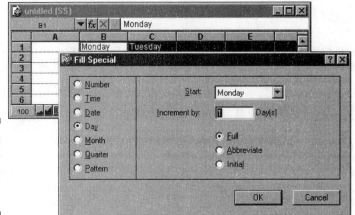

Figure 15-6:
Fill Special
fills in the
days of the
week.

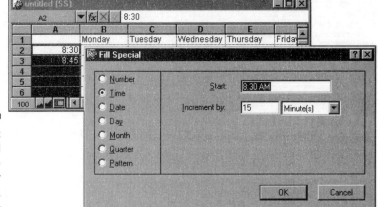

Figure 15-7:
Fill Special
fills in the
times for
each day.

The spreadsheet in Figure 15-6 shows the seeds of a schedule. The first row, where the days of the week go, is selected. Calculate⇨Fill Special brings up the Fill Special dialog box below the selected cells. After the days are filled in, it's time to move on to the times. As Figure 15-7 shows, the times in the first column are selected, along with the next 35 or 40 cells down, and Fill Special works its magic again, knowing to complete the times in fifteen-minute intervals. Use Fill Special to complete any row or column of information that advances in regular increments.

Chapter 16
Formatting Spreadsheets

- -

In This Chapter

▶ Formatting numbers

▶ Formatting text

▶ Sorting stuff in spreadsheets

▶ Changing rows and columns

▶ Changing display options

▶ Setting print options

- -

Do you remember spreadsheets as vast expanses of numbers, repeating endlessly with the same blandness as yesterday's oatmeal? They don't have to be like that. (Our kind of oatmeal is pretty cool.) You can use lots of clever formatting tricks to help people see that those numbers are actually important.

Formatting Numbers

What better place to start than with how you get your numbers to look the way you want? While we're at it, format dates and times, too — because they're all affected by the same dialog box, shown in Figure 16-1. You find this dialog box by choosing Format⇨Number or Shift-⌘-N (Mac) or Shift+Ctrl+N (Windows), but don't go there until you select the numbers you want to format. (Actually, thanks to buttons, you may never go there anyway.)

Number formats

The left side of this mega-format dialog box is for numbers of any kind. With these options, you get to decide how the numbers in the selected cells look. Explaining the details of this side of the dialog box is much easier with a table, so here ya' go. Table 16-1 explains the various number formats.

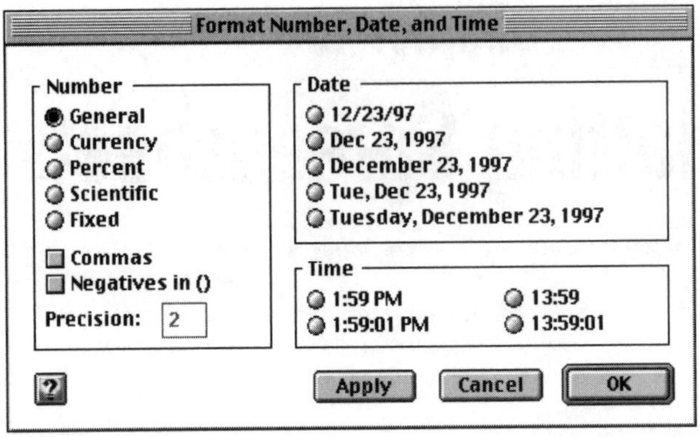

Figure 16-1:
Numbers
can be in
fine form
thanks to
this Format
dialog box.

Table 16-1	**Various Number Formats and What They Do**	
Button	*Format*	*What It Does*
No button	General	The standard number format — for example, 25.1415. This format displays as many decimal places as you enter — as long as they fit in the cell. If all the decimals don't fit, ClarisWorks converts the number to scientific notation.
 [icon]	Currency	Automatically puts a dollar sign in front of the number and inserts decimal points, such as $25.14.
 [icon]	Percent	This format automatically adds the percent sign to the number and multiplies your number by 100.
 [icon]	Scientific	Automatically displays the number with one digit to the left of the decimal point and as many digits to the right as you specify in the Precision box — for example, 2.51e+1.
No button	Fixed	Rounds numbers to however many decimal places are set in the Precision box, such as 25.14.

The following three options appear below the number formats in the
Number section of the dialog box:

✔ **Commas:** This option inserts commas after every three digits to show thousands, millions, and so on. Check this box to turn on the option, or click the button that appears on the default button bar. The button turns on the formatting, but it can't be used to turn off the formatting. To turn off comma formatting, you must uncheck the option in the Format Number dialog box.

 ✔ **Negatives in ():** This option puts parentheses around negative numbers — as bookkeepers do. If this check box is unchecked, negative numbers appear with a minus sign. The button for this is optional, so you can put in on your button bar if you tend to use it. You can use the button to turn on this formatting but not to turn it off. To turn it off, use the Format Number dialog box.

 ✔ **Precision:** This number dictates how many digits appear to the right of the decimal point. It affects all number formats. The default is 2, so if you don't change it, all numbers with more than two decimal spaces are rounded to hundredths, such as 25.14.

Date formats

 You have five formatting options for showing dates, which are shown in the Date section of Figure 16-1. Your choices range from showing dates in numbers only (as in 3/15/95), to showing the day and month completely spelled out (as in Wednesday, March 15, 1995). The button for this cycles through the five formatting choices. It's optional, so you can put it on your button bar if you like. Or, you can open the Format Numbers dialog box and select the option you like best. The longest date formats don't fit in a standard-sized cell. The upcoming section "Inserting and Resizing Rows and Columns" explains how to make room for the longer date formats.

Time formats

 As the Time section of Figure 16-1 shows, you can choose from four formatting options for displaying the time: regular or military time formats, with or without seconds. The button for this cycles through these time format options. Add it to your button bar if you like, or you can use the Format dialog box.

Formatting Cells

Here's where you get to change the font, style, and other formatting options for your cells. Formatting lets you make important totals or labels stand out in your spreadsheet.

Text styles

Spreadsheets have all the text-formatting options that are available in the text environment. However, these options take a back seat to number functions in spreadsheets, and therefore are found in submenus of the Format menu, as are the text color and alignment options. To apply a different font or style, first select the cells you want to change, and then choose the new font, style, size, color, or alignment. You don't have to go to the Format menu for these things. They are all located on the ruler and button bar.

It's bound to get you one of these days — you'll go to some menu to pick some option of function, only to find that the option isn't there. After all these years, it still happens to us. If this happens to you, remember to take a look at the shape of your pointer or at which frame tool is selected. Then, switch environments if you need to, or check the other menus.

Default font

Let's face it: Arial and Geneva are not the most exciting typefaces in the world. But they're destined to fill every cell in your spreadsheet unless you tell ClarisWorks otherwise. Spreadsheet documents can have a default font that is different from the default set for Text Preferences. It's so easy to change the default spreadsheet font that we aren't even going to bore you with a picture. To set your font to something you actually want to look at:

1. **Go to Options⇨Default Font.**

2. **Choose a new font from the scrolling list.**

3. **Type a new point size in the Size box.**

4. **Click OK (or Cancel to call it off).**

When you change the font, even the text that you already entered in the spreadsheet cells changes to the new default font and size. The exception is when you have already applied a new font or size to certain cells: Any custom formatting you apply overrides the new default settings.

Changes to the default font apply to that spreadsheet only. To make it universal for all your spreadsheets, set the default font in a blank spreadsheet and make a stationery from it. See Chapter 2 for a tip about this.

Text wrap

What happens when you enter more text into a cell than it can hold? Normally, one of two things happens:

✔ If the cell to the right is empty, the text stomps right over it.

✔ If the cell to the right has something in it, any text you type that doesn't fit in the cell gets cut from view.

 Because neither of those options is too pretty, set up the cell so that, when it's full from left to right, the text wraps around to a new line. To turn on text wrap for a cell, just select the cell and click the text wrap button — found hanging out on your default button bar, or go to Format⇨Alignment⇨Wrap. After wrapping a cell, adjust the row height so that all the text is visible. There's an optional button that makes this adjustment a breeze, which is mentioned in the upcoming section "Inserting and Resizing Rows and Columns."

Figure 16-2 shows the same cell unwrapped and wrapped.

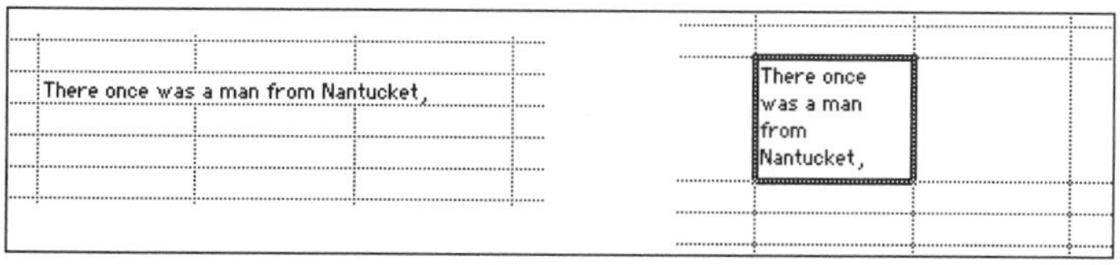

Figure 16-2:
Wrapping
text in a cell
is like
coloring
inside the
lines.

There once was a man from Nantucket,

There once
was a man
from
Nantucket,

Cell color

A nice, colorful background spices up even the most mind-numbing financial statement. ClarisWorks comes with table styles that format your whole spreadsheet and add uniform color quickly. These styles are available in the stylesheet palette. To add color and patterns to your cells manually:

1. **If the Tool Panel is not showing, click the Tool Panel button at the bottom left of the spreadsheet window.**

2. **Select the cells you want to colorize.**

   Just like they did to those old movies.

3. **Use the Fill and Pen pop-up menus to choose a color, fill pattern, and border color.**

   In case you're wondering, gradients and textures don't work in spreadsheets. For more about cell borders, see "Adding Borders, Gridlines, and Headings," later in this chapter. See Chapter 12 for more information on using the fill and pen palettes.

For added effect, apply different colors to highlight groups of information, or try alternating colors in odd and even columns or rows.

Spreadsheet styles

After you format your spreadsheet cells the way you want them, you can save your formatting as a style that you later can apply to other areas of your spreadsheet. You use the stylesheet palette to do this. You can find the details of how to create a style in Chapter 5, but here's a tip on making styles for spreadsheets.

You use the table style type to create a new spreadsheet style. A table style has many substyles that can have separate formatting for odd and even rows or columns, top and bottom rows, and the outside columns. Because of this, set up an example of the formatting you want in your style, and then use the Inherit Document Selection check box in the New Style dialog box to copy your formatting into the new style.

Sorting

Suppose you just put together a spreadsheet to track how many boxes of cookies each Girl Scout in your troop has sold. Besides the total number of boxes sold, you need two other lists from the spreadsheet: an alphabetical list the girls can check to make sure you have the correct number of boxes they sold, and a list that shows the top ten sellers for number of boxes sold. You can get both of these lists from the same spreadsheet by using the spreadsheet environment's built-in sorting feature:

1. **Select all the data in the spreadsheet that you want to sort.**

   In the Girl Scout example, make sure you select all cells that contain data. If you select only the names of the girls and not the number of boxes they sold, only the names are sorted, and you scramble the information about which girl sold how many boxes.

2. **Choose Calculate⇨Sort.**

   This brings up the Sort dialog box, shown in Figure 16-3.

3. **Choose the range, order keys, and direction, and then click OK to sort:**

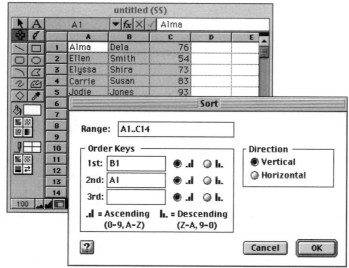

Figure 16-3:
Sorting your
Girl Scouts,
made easy.

- *Range:* Range lets you verify and change the selected range of cells. The number to the left of the two dots is the cell in the upper-left corner of the range. The number to the right of the two dots is the cell in the lower-right corner. If the range doesn't reflect what you want to sort, select again in the spreadsheet or enter the correct cell names in Range.

- *Order Keys:* The order keys tell ClarisWorks what to sort, and how to sort it. In the Girl Scout example, to sort alphabetically by last name, the first cell to contain a girl's last name is in the 1st order key box. The Ascending button to the order key's right tells ClarisWorks to sort A to Z. If Descending is selected instead, the names sort from Z to A. The 2nd order key box creates a subsort. For example, after the list sorts the Girl Scouts by their last name, if two of the girls happen to have the same last name, the subsort then sorts those two girls' first names in alphabetical order. By having three sort levels, a spreadsheet can cover the whole district, sorting first by troop, then by last name, and then by first name.

To sort by the number of boxes sold, starting with the most boxes, enter C1 for the 1st order key in descending order and leave the other two order keys blank. If two or more girls sell the same amount of cookies, you can subsort by last name, and even use the first name as the third level sort.

- *Direction:* If you have the spreadsheet set up so that each row contains one set of information, such as a Girl Scout's first name, last name, and boxes sold, select Vertical. If each column is one set of information — as in the daily schedule shown in Figure 15-7 in Chapter 15 — select Horizontal.

Inserting and Resizing Rows and Columns

Have you ever realized partway through a spreadsheet project that you really, really need to add another set of information? ClarisWorks figures this will happen to somebody sooner or later, so it makes it easy to sneak those extra rows or columns into your spreadsheet. (Do it when no one is looking and they'll never know.) We're about to show you how to add those after-thoughts to your spreadsheet (before you get in trouble with the boss for leaving them out). While we're at it, we'll show you how to resize cells, because you're bound to find that the standard cell sizes don't cut it for your project.

Inserting

Okay, it happened. You just found that vital piece of information that *needs* to be in the middle of your spreadsheet. Cool . . . you get to insert a column.

To show you how, we use the Girl Scout cookie example from the previous section. Say you forgot to include the troop number for each girl and need to add it between the last name and the number of boxes sold. To perform this trick, follow these steps:

1. **Cells are inserted to the left, so select the column to the right of where you want to insert the new column. In this case, select column C (see Figure 16-3).**

2. **Click the Add rows or columns button right on the default button bar.**

   Or, either choose Calculate⇨Insert Cells or press Shift-⌘-I (Mac) or Shift+Ctrl+I (Windows).

   Here's the trick: If you select the column by clicking the column head (the letter C in this case), the column pops in. But, if you only select some cells in the column — by dragging through the cells — a little Insert Cells dialog box pops up, asking whether you want to shift the selected cells to the right or down. Full control. Make your choice, which for this example is to the right. Of course, you need to click OK, too.

New rows are inserted above the row(s) you select. Inserting a new row works the same except, if asked, you select Shift cells down.

The number of rows or columns that you select is the number of rows or columns that are inserted. To add two rows, select two rows.

Resizing

You can resize rows and columns in three ways. Regardless of which method you choose, to resize several columns or rows at once, making them exactly the same size, first select all the rows or columns you want to resize.

Resizing with the mouse

To resize visually, use the mouse. Move the plus-sign pointer over the row number or column letter area and then over the line between the row or column to be adjusted. The pointer changes to a line with two arrows, as shown in Figure 16-4. After the pointer changes, drag the gridline to make the row or column larger or smaller.

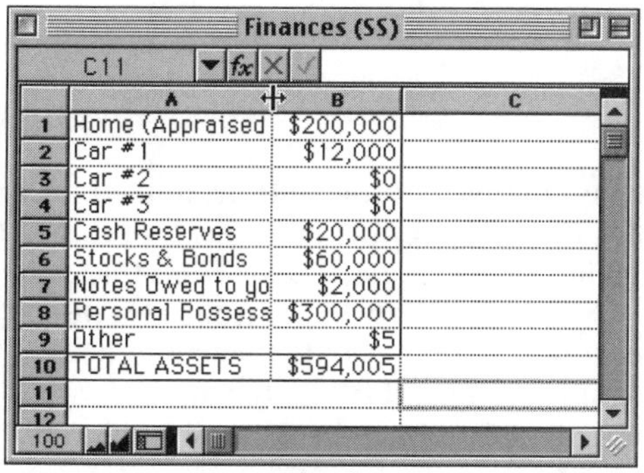

Figure 16-4:
The double-
arrow
pointer
resizes
rows and
columns.

	A	B	C
1	Home (Appraised	$200,000	
2	Car #1	$12,000	
3	Car #2	$0	
4	Car #3	$0	
5	Cash Reserves	$20,000	
6	Stocks & Bonds	$60,000	
7	Notes Owed to yo	$2,000	
8	Personal Possess	$300,000	
9	Other	$5	
10	TOTAL ASSETS	$594,005	
11			
12			

Finances (SS) — C11

Resizing with buttons

To quickly make cells fit the text that is inside them, you can place either of the two optional buttons on your button bar and use them. (See the Appendix to discover how to add buttons to any button bar):

 ✔ You can automatically resize a single selected cell to the correct height to fit its contents. If several cells are selected, this button makes them all the height of the tallest cell in the group.

 ✔ As you can with height, you can automatically resize widths. If one cell is selected, automatic resizing makes the cell wide enough to fit that cell's contents. If several cells are selected, automatic resizing sets the width of all of them to the width needed by the fullest cell.

Resizing with the dialog box

If your column and row headers are hidden so that the numbers and letters don't show, you can't use the mouse method. In that case, or if you need exact control over your heights and widths, the dialog box option gives you control in points, as font sizes are measured (one inch = 72 points):

1. **Select the row or column to resize, or just select one cell in that row or column.**

2. **Choose Format⇨Column Width or Row Height.**

3. **In the dialog box that appears, enter a measurement in points, and then click OK.**

Adding Borders, Gridlines, and Headings

One good way to call attention to or categorize a number is to put a border around it. You probably also want a line above your totals or below your column titles. Speaking of headings, you may not want the column and row headings to appear in your spreadsheet, or the cell grid for that matter.

Borders

 A border is only a click away. Just select the cells around which you want to put a border, and then click a button. A button for each option is located on the default button bar, making selection very easy. Each button clearly illustrates its effect, so you can easily find the buttons you need. One button puts a border around the whole perimeter of the selected cells. (That's the one shown here as an example.) The rest of the buttons let you place a border only on the left side of each selected cell, on the right, on the top, or on the bottom. To place a border on the top and bottom, click both of those buttons — more than one is okay. These are toggle buttons, so if a border is on, clicking the button again turns it off.

If you prefer, you can select Format⇨Borders and use the Borders dialog box to check off your options, but that requires extra steps.

Gridlines

Gridlines can be effective — or distracting. Whichever you prefer, you're in control with optional push-button action, or the Options⇨Display dialog box. The grid does print, by the way. Unlike borders, gridlines affect the entire spreadsheet.

Here's the inside scoop on grids:

✔ To remove gridlines from view, either take advantage of the optional button shown here, or uncheck Cell grid in the Display dialog box.

✔ For solid gridlines, place the button shown here into your button bar and click it. Cell grid must be turned on for the lines to appear as solid, so this button has no effect when you turn off the gridlines. In the Display dialog box, Cell grid has to be checked for this to be an option.

✔ To get back to normal dotted lines, turn on the grid (clicking the button or checking the option), and then, if solid lines are turned on, click the solid-line button to turn them off (or uncheck Solid lines in the dialog box).

If you use solid gridlines, you won't be able to see any black borders around cells. Colors will show, though (if you have a color computer and monitor).

Headings and other display settings

Column and row headings are a big help while working in a spreadsheet, but you probably don't want them in a presented document, on a table, or as a part of such items. (Headings are the A B C . . . and 1 2 3 . . . at the top and side of your spreadsheet.)

You can turn off both top and side headings with the optional button shown here, or you can control them individually with the Display dialog box by unchecking the Column Headings or Row Headings box or both boxes.

You can use column and row headings on the screen but keep them from printing out. Three check boxes appear in the Print dialog box when you print a spreadsheet: Print Column Headings, Print Row Headings, and Print Cell Grid. All three boxes are normally checked. Uncheck the appropriate box to keep the headings or cell grid from printing. On the Mac, these options aren't directly in view. Select ClarisWorks from the pop-up menu below your printer's name to get to this set of options.

If you explore the Display dialog box, you may notice two check boxes that we haven't discussed. They deal with spreadsheet formulas. The Formulas check box is checked if you want a cell to display the actual formula rather than the result of the formula. Normally, it's unchecked. The Mark circular refs check box helps you track down problems in your formulas. If two or more cells refer to each other, which causes an error, these cells are marked to call your attention to the problem. By default, this is checked.

Using Titles, Page Breaks, and Print Ranges

What do titles, page breaks, and print ranges have in common? They all are used to set up how your spreadsheet pages look on-screen and in print.

Locking titles

Have you ever had your column titles scroll out of sight while you are working on a long spreadsheet, leaving you with no idea of what kind of information is in each column, without having to scroll up and down to see the titles? Not fun? Then you'll love Lock Title Position. It prevents your column titles from scrolling out of sight. To lock column titles in place:

1. **Select the cells that contain the column or row titles.**

2. **Choose Options⇨Lock Title Position.**

    A check mark appears next to this command when the titles are locked.

Now when you scroll, the row containing your titles is always at the top of the window. The same applies for scrolling sideways when you have locked row titles. The locked titles also print out as the first row or column on every page — excellent for multipage spreadsheets, so you don't have to shuffle through the pages to find the top page every time you forget what information a particular column contains.

There are two drawbacks, though. One is that you can't have both a column heading and a row heading locked. You must chose one or the other. The other drawback occurs when your titles aren't in the top row or left-most column. In that case, locking the titles also locks the rows or columns above or to the left of them as well. You can avoid this simply by splitting the window with the pane controls. See Chapter 2 for more information about splitting a window.

Unchecking Lock Title Position unlocks the titles, whether they are selected or not.

If you want information to appear on every page of a printout of your spreadsheet, such as your name, the date, or a title for the spreadsheet, just insert a header or footer. Choose Format⇨Insert Header or Insert Footer. These commands change to Remove Header and Remove Footer after a header or footer is added. Choosing one of these commands switches your spreadsheet to page view, where you can edit the contents of the header or footer. See Chapter 5 for more information on headers and footers.

Page breaks and new pages

ClarisWorks puts in an automatic page break when you fill up enough cells to run into a margin. If you want to insert a page break before the default, here's what you do:

1. **Select the cell to appear in the lower-right corner of your new page.**

2. **Choose Options⇨Add Page Break.**

   This puts a page break at the right of the selected cell and below it. Page breaks show up as dashed lines that intersect at your corner cell.

To remove a page break, select the same cell (at the intersection of the dashed lines) and select Options⇨Remove Page Break.

You don't actually add new pages to a spreadsheet. Instead, you add columns and rows. Spreadsheet documents are normally 40 columns by 500 rows. To add more, choose Format⇨Document and type new numbers into the Size area of the Document dialog box. Spreadsheet frames are 10 columns by 50 rows. To increase the size of a frame, you first have to open it as a separate window by selecting Window⇨Open Frame. Then select Format⇨Document and enter your new numbers into the Size area of the Document dialog box.

If your document is printing more pages than you planned, try choosing Options⇨Remove All Breaks. This deletes all manual page breaks; it does not remove automatic page breaks inserted by ClarisWorks. Also try resetting the print range, described next.

Print range

The Print Range dialog box limits the printing of large spreadsheets to just the parts you want. As shown in Figure 16-5, this dialog box lists two options: print all cells containing data and print just a specified range of cells. Bring up this dialog box by choosing Options⇨Set Print Range.

Figure 16-5:
The Print
Range
dialog box
can save
you paper.

To print a range of cells, you can either select the cells you want to print before calling up the Print Range dialog box, or enter the cell range into the box. If you want to enter your range, type the name of the cell that's in the upper-left corner of the range, followed by two periods and the name of the cell at the lower-right corner of the range.

To print all cells containing *any* information, select All cells with data.

You can set a print range to include blank cells. This is handy if you want to print a list or schedule and leave blanks to be filled in later by hand.

If your document prints out on too many pages, try selecting just the cells that you want to print, and then set the print range to those cells.

Chapter 17

Charting — Pictures from Numbers

In This Chapter

▶ Introducing chart types

▶ Creating a chart

▶ Customizing a chart

▶ Resizing, moving, or deleting your chart

▶ Making charts from spreadsheet frames

C harts are fun — or at least a lot more fun than creating spreadsheets, in our humble opinion. Charts let you represent sterile numbers in a lively, visual way that people can relate to. You may stare at columns of numbers for ages before spotting a trend that you would spot in an instant with a chart. Most people think better in pictures than in numbers.

These charts are especially fun because they are tied to your spreadsheet, which means they change automatically whenever you change your data!

Getting to Know the Types of Charts

ClarisWorks has 12 chart types to choose from. Each type has at least three variations. Using these variations separately or together, you can make hundreds of different-looking charts. On top of that, you can make other modifications to further customize a chart. The trick to choosing a chart is finding one that displays your data the way you want it and helps people notice what you want them to see. The Chart Options dialog box, shown in Figure 17-1, presents the different chart types for you to select from.

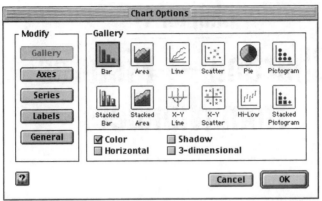

Figure 17-1:
All these
chart types
make it
easy sailing
in this
uncharted
territory.

Here's a quick breakdown of each chart type and its possible uses:

✔ **Bar/Stacked Bar:** Bar charts have one bar grouping for each category of data. The number of bars in the group depends on how many figures you have for each category. A variation of the bar chart is the stacked bar chart. Instead of showing a group of bars, this chart stacks them all on top of each other. For example, then you could include bars for three companies showing total earnings over three years; each bar could be broken down into three different colors or patterns to show earnings for each year.

✔ **Area/Stacked Area:** An area chart is good for emphasizing how quantities change over time. An area chart shows the quantity data as the area under a line — one line for each category. The stacked area chart stacks each series of data on top of each other, so that you get a total amount for each category, broken down by series.

✔ **Line/X–Y Line:** Line charts are made up of points and lines. Each line is created by connecting points. These points begin at the intersection of the chart's X-axis (horizontal) and Y-axis (vertical). Usually, the X-axis is a time interval and the Y-axis is the variable that the chart illustrates (interest rates, temperature, and so on). You see this kind of chart on the news all the time when there's talk about falling interest rates or skyrocketing inflation over a particular time period. Line charts make it very easy to see a trend in a series of data.

An X-Y Line chart takes a line chart one step farther by allowing for negative numbers. As depicted in the button for this chart, the 0 point is in the middle of the chart in order to show the negative numbers.

✔ **Scatter/X–Y Scatter:** A scatter chart is a lot like a line chart, except no line connects the points on the chart. The X–Y scatter chart works the same as the X–Y line chart, without the lines. A scatter chart helps emphasize data points rather than an overall trend.

✔ **Pie:** A pie chart is as American as apple pie. Pie charts graphically display data percentages in relation to 100 percent of a whole pie. This type of chart is useful for showing, for example, how much of your income you blow on different expenses.

✔ **Hi–Low:** This chart uses two sets of numbers for each data point to show high and low points. It's good for tracking stocks or commodities.

✔ **Pictogram/Stacked Pictogram:** This is like bar and stacked bar charts, but with a twist: You get to add a picture inside the bars. For example, this is the kind of chart *USA Today* and *Newsweek* use to show weapons buildups, with little tanks stacked on top of each other.

Making a Chart

You build a chart from the data in your spreadsheet, so the first step in making a chart is to select a block of spreadsheet cells. Most chart types use whatever is in the upper-left cell as a title. The labels along the left side and across the bottom (the axis labels) come from the first row and the first column. Figure 17-2 shows a block of selected cells and the rows and columns that become labels on the chart.

After you select the cells that contain the data you want in your chart, the quickest way to make a chart is to click one of the chart buttons, shown in Figure 17-3. There's a button for every type of chart described in the preceding section. Most of the buttons are even on the default button bar, just waiting around for you to use. Five less commonly used buttons lie waiting as options. By coincidence, the buttons all match their chart types. Compare the buttons with the Chart Options dialog box and you see what we mean.

If you don't see these buttons, they may be hidden. Move your mouse to the bottom of the button bar until your pointer becomes a double-headed arrow. Click and drag downward to expand the number of rows on your bar. (If the bar is at the side of your screen, the grow arrows appear at the inside edge and you drag inward.)

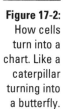

Figure 17-2: How cells turn into a chart. Like a caterpillar turning into a butterfly.

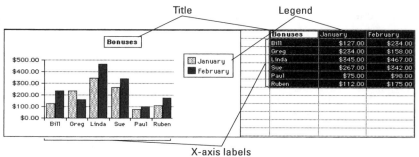

Figure 17-3:
Buttons are
the fastest
way to
make
charts.

Not all of the chart buttons are on the default bar. Some are optional. To learn how to add optional buttons to your button bar or make your own custom button bar, see the Appendix.

If you select a chart that you don't have enough data for, ClarisWorks tells you or you get a chart that says `Not enough chart data`. If this happens, delete the selection and try another, or look more closely at your selection or data.

If you prefer to use the menus or the keyboard to make your chart, select your cells and then either choose Options⇨Make Chart or press ⌘-M (Mac) or Ctrl+M (Windows). This takes you to the Gallery section of the Chart Options dialog box, shown back in Figure 17-1. Click the type of chart you want; then click OK to create the chart.

Modifying a Chart

After you see your chart on-screen, you may want to change it. To modify a chart, you get to bring up the Chart Options dialog box, but you get to do it a whole new way — by double-clicking the chart. Of course, you can always use the menus: Edit⇨Chart Options.

Chart type and variations

Flip back to Figure 17-1 for a look at the Chart Options dialog box. Notice the check boxes at the bottom of the Gallery section. Depending on the type of chart you are working with, you should see three to five check boxes with different options for your chart. You can use these options alone or in combination to give each type of chart tons of different looks. Here's what the options do:

 ✔ **Color:** This turns the color on and off in your chart. It substitutes black-and-white patterns for colors in bars, pie pieces, and other filled areas.

✔ **Horizontal:** This changes the orientation of the chart to horizontal. For example, with this option turned on, bar charts have the bars grow from left to right rather than bottom to top.

✔ **Shadow:** This adds a drop shadow behind the chart elements for a 3-D effect.

✔ **3-dimensional:** This adds depth to chart types, when available. It actually draws a representation of a 3-D object. For example, if you check the 3-dimensional box for a bar chart, the bars are actually drawn as 3-D boxes rather than flat bars. It's not available for pie charts.

✔ **Square grid:** This is for X–Y line and X–Y scatter graphs only. It uses a grid that shows both negative X and Y values, so the origin, or center point, is in the middle.

✔ **Scale multiple:** This is for pie charts only. Pie charts make a new pie for each series of data in a category. This shrinks pies so that they all fit in the chart window.

✔ **Tilt:** This is for pie charts only. It tilts the pie instead of showing the normal top-down view. Try it along with shadow for a 3-D look.

Other chart options

You may have noticed the five buttons on the left side of the Chart Options dialog box. Each button takes you to an area of that dialog box. Table 17-1 describes what each area does for your chart. You can access certain areas of the dialog box directly by double-clicking the related part of your chart; these double-click shortcuts are included in Table 17-1.

Table 17-1   The Five Areas of the Chart Options Dialog Box

This Area	*Does This*
Gallery	Lets you choose a chart type and variations. Double-click the chart background to get here.
Axes	Lets you modify the axis labels, set intervals, set tick marks, and more. You can go directly to this area by double-clicking either axis.
Series	Lets you modify how some or all of the data series are displayed. You can add a label to the data. Most important, this area lets you change a series to a different type.

(continued)

Table 17-1 *(continued)*

This Area	Does This
Labels	Lets you set up how and where you want the title and legend to appear — or not to appear. Also lets you add a drop shadow to the title and legend boxes or have them print sideways to sneak them in on the side. Double-click the title or legend box to come directly to this area.
General	Controls which cells are used for the chart, and whether the data series are in rows or columns — that is, do the numbers in your spreadsheet progress left to right (rows) or top to bottom (columns)? Also lets you use numbers in the first row or column as labels.

Changing colors and line width

How would you like to change the colors ClarisWorks picks out for your chart? You can change the fill color and pattern of bars in a bar chart, the thickness and pattern of the line that surrounds the bars, or the border and fill settings for any data series in any type of chart. To change the color or pattern of a data series:

1. **With the chart selected, click the box in the legend next to the data series you want to change.**

   A small circle appears in that box, indicating that any changes will affect that data series.

2. **Use the color controls in the Tool Panel to select a new setting for that data series.**

   Use the pen to do outlines. Use the color, pattern, texture, or gradient to change the filled-in areas, just like changing a draw object.

Updating the chart with new numbers

Your chart is actually tied to the spreadsheet cells that created it. When you change the information in those cells, the chart is automatically updated. You can even add more cells to the chart range. Just use the General area of the Modify Chart dialog box to enter the new range. The tie-in ends, though, when you cut the chart. Copies of your chart also are not linked to the originating spreadsheet.

If you cut your chart and then paste it anywhere, it loses its link to the spreadsheet cells it was created from, so the chart isn't updated when changes are made in those cells. Instead, the chart becomes a group of draw objects that you can change manually if you want. If you need the chart updated, the best way is to make a whole new chart.

Adding your own picture to a pictogram chart

One of the best-looking chart types is the pictogram chart, especially when you add your own picture. To create your own pictogram chart, follow these steps:

1. **Choose Edit⇨Copy, ⌘-C (Mac), or Ctrl+C (Windows) to copy a draw or paint graphic.**

2. **Bring up the Modify Chart dialog box and then click Series to go to the Series area, shown in Figure 17-4.**

   For fastest access, double-click the box next to the series label in the legend to get to the Series area.

Figure 17-4: ClarisWorks really stacks up when you are making custom charts.

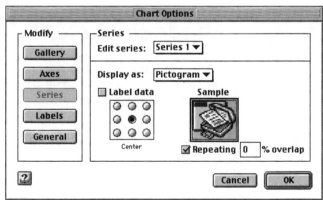

3. **If the series is not already displayed as a pictogram, choose Pictogram from the Display As pop-up menu.**

4. **Click the Pictogram Sample area.**

   A dark square surrounds a selected sample.

5. Paste your graphic.

Click the Paste button, select Edit⇨Paste, or press ⌘-V (Mac) or Ctrl+V (Windows).

If you want the pictogram to be stacked in the bar, check Repeating. Otherwise, the graphic stretches or shrinks to fit the bar.

Resizing, Moving, and Deleting Charts

In a way, a chart is a big draw object. You can move, resize, or delete it, just like any other rectangle you make with a draw tool. A chart floats above the spreadsheet in its own layer, like a draw object:

✔ **To move your chart:** position the pointer anywhere inside its border, hold down the mouse button, and drag the chart to a new location.

✔ **To resize your chart:** drag any corner handle. The objects in the chart are resized to fit within the new border.

✔ **To delete your chart:** click it to select it; then either press the Delete key or choose Edit⇨Cut or Edit⇨Clear.

Making Charts in Other Document Types

Charts can be made in any type of document that lets you make a spreadsheet frame, except a paint document. That leaves text, draw, and database (in layout mode), in addition to spreadsheet documents. Normally, when you make a chart from data in a spreadsheet frame, the chart appears in the document in its own layer, separate from the spreadsheet frame. Don't worry — the chart is still linked to the data in the spreadsheet frame.

To have the chart appear inside the frame with the spreadsheet, open the frame — Window⇨Open Frame — before you make the chart.

After you cut the chart, its links to the spreadsheet cells that created it are severed. Copies are never connected. They are separate draw objects.

Chapter 18

Making It All Add Up with Formulas and Functions

In This Chapter

▶ Adding with AutoSum

▶ Naming fields

▶ Entering formulas

▶ What are functions?

▶ Referring to cells in a formula

*H*ere's a scary thought: Spreadsheet formulas come pretty close to actually programming your computer. You actually type in calculations you want the spreadsheet to make.

Don't worry if this sounds a little daunting. We start by showing you a really important formula — and it's really easy.

First, a couple of definitions are in order. A *formula* is a series of instructions that tells ClarisWorks to make a calculation. Formulas get entered into cells. A *function* is a predefined shortcut for doing complex calculations that you can include in your formula to make life easier. A formula can include functions that help it perform your calculation.

The AutoSum Shortcut — First and Finest

The majority of math in spreadsheets seems to be the adding of columns or rows full of numbers — sometimes incredibly long rows full of numbers. If this is as far as you want to go with spreadsheet formulas, you're just about finished with your lesson for today. Lesson one and only — the AutoSum button.

AutoSum automatically adds up a row or column of numbers, dumping the result into an empty cell at the bottom of the column or at the end of the row. All you have to do is select the cells to add and click AutoSum on the default button bar. Here's how:

1. **Select the cells you want to add (the range), along with an empty cell at the end to hold the result (see Figure 18-1).**

2. **Click AutoSum.**

   The result appears in the empty cell.

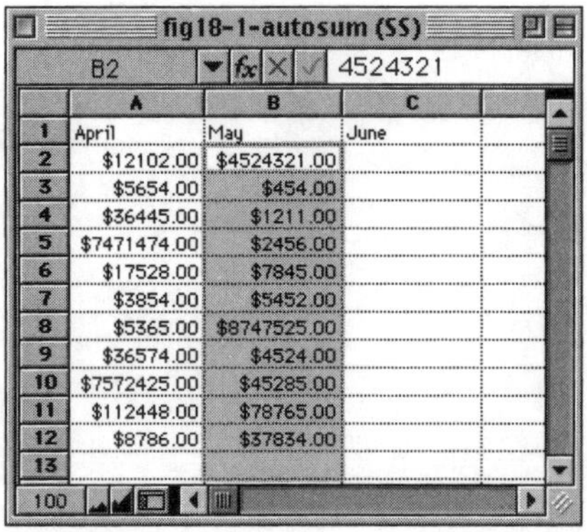

Figure 18-1:
Totals with
a tap —
on the
AutoSum
button.

	A	B	C
1	April	May	June
2	$12102.00	$4524321.00	
3	$5654.00	$454.00	
4	$36445.00	$1211.00	
5	$7471474.00	$2456.00	
6	$17528.00	$7845.00	
7	$3854.00	$5452.00	
8	$5365.00	$8747525.00	
9	$36574.00	$4524.00	
10	$7572425.00	$45285.00	
11	$112448.00	$78765.00	
12	$8786.00	$37834.00	
13			

fig18-1-autosum (SS)

B2 — 4524321

AutoSum actually creates a formula that adds the range of cells you selected and places the result in the empty cell. If you change a number in one of the cells, the total updates automatically as long as you have the Auto Calc option checked in the Calculate menu.

You can use the AutoSum shortcut to fake your way through most of what you are likely to do with a spreadsheet. If you need to do more complex calculations with formulas, keep reading.

Warning: Thinking zone ahead

The rest of this chapter should be marked with the Technical Stuff icon. Using formulas in a spreadsheet is pretty heady stuff. If there's any way to get out of doing this math stuff, find it. But if you're into math or can get into trying, you'll get used to this stuff and, who knows, maybe even come to love it.

Here's some good news: If you took Algebra in high school and wondered, "What good is this going to do me in the real world?" — you finally have the answer.

Entering Formulas

Here's the number one rule of formulas: They always start with an equal sign (=).

This rule is set in stone. If it doesn't start with an equal sign, it's not a formula. The equal sign tells ClarisWorks that a formula follows. Remember it this way: "The number you see in this cell equals the result of this formula."A typical formula looks like =A1+A2. This formula adds the contents of cell A1 to the contents of cell A2 and displays the result in the cell containing the formula.

Math operations

You can do basic math in formulas, as well as more complex things. Table 18-1 offers a list of some math calculations you can do, the symbols they use, and the order in which each calculation happens in the formula. Remember from high school Algebra all those parentheses around parts of long, complicated equations? Remember how it really mattered where those parentheses went and what parts went where? This is that stuff: Right here, right now. The order in which calculations happen affects the result of the calculation. For example, the result is different if you add first and then multiply versus if you multiply and then add.

Table 18-1	Math Operations in ClarisWorks Formulas	
To Do This Operation	*Use This Symbol*	*Order in Which ClarisWorks Performs This Kind of Operation*
Divide number by 100 (percent)	%	1
Raise a number to a power (exponent)	^	2
Multiply	*	3
Divide	/	3
Add	+	4
Subtract	–	4

Operations that have the same order number are evaluated from left to right. You can change the order of calculations by using parentheses. If parentheses are present in a formula, ClarisWorks calculates the contents of the innermost set of parentheses first and works its way out. They're really handy for simplifying what you're doing.

Entering cell references

The easiest way to tell ClarisWorks which cell you want to use in your formula is to click it. Anytime the cursor is in the entry bar and you click a cell, the name of that cell is added into the entry bar. For example, to get =A1+A2 to appear in the entry bar, type an equal sign, click cell A1, type a plus sign, and then click cell A2. If you want a range of numbers, just drag across the range and select them and the range appears in your formula.

Of course, you can always type in a cell name, but clicking the cell eliminates any typing errors that may sneak in.

Naming your cells

In standard spreadsheet language, instead of calculating something like "Total Income" minus "Total Expenditures," you normally end up with something like =D97–M84. The first way is a tad more friendly and easier to track, though, isn't it? Claris thought so, too, so they let us name our cells. Nice and friendly.

To name a cell, follow these steps:

1. **Select the cell (or range of cells) to be named.**

2. **Click the arrow in the entry bar and choose Define Name.**

   It calls up the Define Named Range dialog box as shown in Figure 18-2.

3. **Name your cell and then click Define.**

   This one has the same name as the heading, but yours doesn't have to.

Notice in Figure 18-2 that the cell reference is A1. It's in the top corner — the left-most element of the entry bar. After the cell is named, selecting that cell presents its name instead of its column and row address.

You can also select an entire range of cells and give them one collective name. Notice that the Edit Names dialog box in Figure 18-3 shows a range of cells called "Monthly total."

Click 1   Click 2

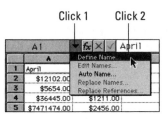

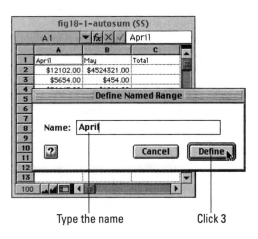

Figure 18-2:
You can
name that
cell in three
clicks.
Naming
your cells is
easy and
makes
spreadsheet
work more
friendly.

Type the name   Click 3

Editing cell names

Whether you make a mistake naming your cell or just want to change it for
clarity, you can do so easily, by following these steps:

1. Click the arrow in the entry bar and select Edit Names.

The Edit Names dialog box, shown in Figure 18-3, comes up.

2. Click once on the name to be changed.

That name appears in the Name field below the list of named cells.

3. Enter your new name and click Modify.

If you want to change more names, repeat Steps 2 and 3. If not, click
Done.

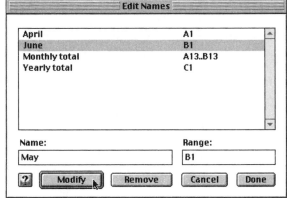

Figure 18-3:
Changing
your cell
names is as
easy as
changing
your mind.

Creating your formulas becomes much easier now. While you're in the entry bar creating your formula, you can pick a cell by name instead of scrolling all around looking for it. More about formulas is coming up.

From now on, when you want to go to a named cell, just select its name from the pop-up menu on the entry bar. You're there in a zip.

You can also reassign a name from one cell or cell range to another. For example, say you give the name "Holiday" to cells G3..G5 and then check a calendar and realize your mistake. You can switch the name "Holiday" to refer to G8..G10. Reassigning a name is similar to editing a name, except that you change the cell address in the Range field, ignoring the Name field. To assign a range of fields enter the first cell address, type two periods, and the last cell address.

Using Functions

At the beginning of the chapter, we said that a function is a built-in shortcut for doing complex math calculations in spreadsheet formulas. One of the best examples of a function is the SUM function. If you want to add up the contents of ten cells, instead of typing **=A1+A2+A3** and so on, you can type **=SUM(A1..A10).** This format automatically adds up the contents of the ten cells. AutoSum uses the SUM function in this way.

ClarisWorks has over 100 built-in functions that fall into eight general categories: Business and Financial, Date and Time, Information, Logical, Numeric, Statistical, Text, and Trigonometric.

The best way to add a function to your formula is to use one of the built-in ClarisWorks functions. Enter your formula until you get to the place where you want a function. Then click the fx button in the entry bar. The Paste Function dialog box, shown in Figure 18-4, appears. Scroll through the list and select the function and then click the OK button. The function appears in your formula where the cursor was.

We'd love to tell you all about each of those functions, but that goes way beyond the scope of this book. The online help is pretty good about explaining all of them. ClarisWorks includes an entire "Alphabetical list of functions" in the Help feature. Enter that in the index to find it, or from the Paste Function dialog box, click the Help icon, and it takes you almost right to it. Anytime you want to do a complex calculation, take a look to see if ClarisWorks provides a function that does it for you.

These three functions give you some ideas about what you can do with a spreadsheet. If this stimulates your imagination, you can find more information about these and other functions in the online Help system.

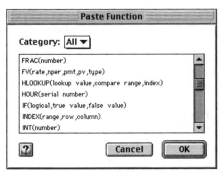

Figure 18-4:
Even the
funkiest
function is
just a click
away.

- ✔ **AVERAGE:** This function works just like the SUM function, except that it calculates the average value of the contents of a range of cells. A typical AVERAGE function in a formula looks like this: =AVERAGE (A1..A10). AVERAGE is probably the second-most-used ClarisWorks function.

- ✔ **IF:** This function tests to see if a condition is true or false; it returns one value for true and another for false. This one function opens the door for a spreadsheet to make decisions based on the data in the spreadsheet. For example, you can have it check to see if it's Wednesday and, IF it is, have it then recalculate all prices in a list to reflect a 10 percent discount. This is one powerful function.

- ✔ **MACRO:** This function lets a spreadsheet activate a macro you've recorded. It lets ClarisWorks pull its own strings. The combination of the IF and MACRO functions is what enables people to make games in spreadsheets.

Functions can be extremely powerful tools for manipulating data in a spreadsheet. By using the right functions, you can have a spreadsheet make decisions based on the data you enter. The possibilities are limited only by your imagination. We've seen spreadsheets that do everything from play blackjack to analyze stock trends.

Relative versus Absolute References

To create your own formulas, you need to know how to specify which cells you want your formula to use for its calculations. For example, looking at the formula that AutoSum puts into cell B26, you see something like =SUM(B15..B25). This formula tells ClarisWorks to add up the sum of the contents of cells B15 through B25 and put that number into the cell containing the formula.

However, if you copy and paste that formula into another cell, the range changes to reflect the move. That's because the formula uses a relative reference to decide which cells to add. What really happens is that the formula tells ClarisWorks to add up the total of the ten cells above the cell containing the formula. If you paste the formula into cell C26, it changes to =SUM(C15..C25); in D26 it would be =SUM(D15..D25); and so forth.

Relative references make a formula portable so that you can easily use it in another part of your spreadsheet. Relative references are the standard way of setting up formulas in ClarisWorks because they give you so much flexibility to copy and paste the formula to other parts of a spreadsheet.

Absolute references refer to a specific cell and don't change when moved. To make a cell reference absolute, all you have to do is put a dollar sign in front of each part of the cell name — for example, B26. If you put B26 into a formula, that formula always gets the contents from cell B26, no matter where the formula moves in the spreadsheet.

You can also mix the reference types to constrain just the column or row, like $B26, or B$26. The first example is constrained to column B, but the row reference changes as the formula moves up or down. The second example is constrained to row 26, but the column reference changes as the formula is moved right or left.

Part V
Working with Files: Smoothing Out the Rough Edges

The 5th Wave   By Rich Tennant

"IT'S A SOFTWARE PROGRAM THAT MORE FULLY RE-FLECTS AN ACTUAL OFFICE ENVIRONMENT. IT MULTI-TASKS WITH OTHER USERS, INTEGRATES SHARED DATA, AND THEN USES THAT INFORMATION TO NETWORK VICIOUS RUMORS THROUGH AN INTER-OFFICE LINK-UP."

In this part . . .

Databases are magic. They make all the boxes full of business cards disappear, leaving in their place one slim, nonexistent (sort of) file. Amazing. They also take hours of redundant writing, copying, pasting, and such and do it all for us over and over with a few clicks of a button. They make labels and sorting and all kinds of stuff just go away.

But the word — *database* — sounds kind of techy and scary, doesn't it? We thought so too — once upon a time. But now we're cool and fearless, storing anything we can in these great things. But it's no fun to be cool and fearless alone. We want you there, too.

In this part, we show you what databases are and what they can do for you. You see how to enter, sort, and find information in a database; how to create a database; how to print records; and how to make your own form letters to send out to your friends during the holidays. Databases give you more scope for your genius!

Try 'em. We think you'll like 'em.

Chapter 19

Your Rolodex Revisited — Database Basics

In This Chapter

▶ Deciding to use a database document

▶ Creating records (not what you do at a recording studio)

▶ Defining (not irrigating) fields

▶ Understanding database modes (the database *modus operandi*)

▶ Getting your information in and putting some order to it

▶ Getting your information back out again and using it

▶ Using shortcuts for searching

*T*he database environment is one of the most overlooked and underused parts of ClarisWorks, but this environment has a lot of power. The ClarisWorks database environment is brought to you by the publisher of FileMaker Pro, the most popular database on the Mac, which is gaining a wide following in Windows as we write this. This chapter shows you how to get to first base with databases (and what not to do on a blind data).

Deciding When to Use a Database

Databases are used to collect and store information. A perfect example of a real-world database is the card catalog at the library. You remember card catalogs, don't you? They had all those funny little drawers filled with cards listing each book by title, author, or subject. Why don't you see those old catalogs anymore? Most libraries have put the card catalog on a computer using a database program; computerized card catalogs are easier to update and save paper.

The card catalog is a collection of similar information: Each card has spaces for the author, title of the book, publisher, and so on, which makes it a perfect candidate for a database. You can use a database for any collection of information with similar items, such as:

- ✔ An address list (the most popular use for the database environment)
- ✔ A job/client file
- ✔ A recipe file
- ✔ A catalog of your videotape collection
- ✔ A list of which Versace suits go with which Chanel handbags

The database environment has the power to produce sophisticated reports about the data it contains. In this chapter, we show you the basics so you can enter information into an existing database, such as the name-and-address list provided with ClarisWorks, and organize the information the way you want it.

The best way to learn about databases is to play with an existing one. If you don't happen to have one, you can create one easily by using the Name and Address Assistant. While you're it, instead of just playing around with it, why not use it for real. You can use it as is or customize it in any way.

You can only use the database environment in a database document. There is no such thing as a database frame.

Database Records

A database *record* is a set of information. To go back to the card catalog example, one card is the equivalent of one database record. A record is like a form you fill out and file into the database. After you enter your information, you can sort the records or search for records that contain specific items.

You can think of the records in the database as cards in a stack. You can arrange them alphabetically, by number, by date, and so on. You can even separate a group of cards from the stack and just work with the smaller group. Figure 19-1 shows you a sample database record.

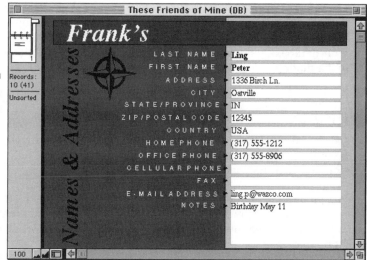

Figure 19-1:
This
database
contains
several
addresses,
each one in
its own
record —
like this
one.

Database Fields

Each database record is made up of several pieces of information. Each of these pieces is a *field*. Every record in the same database has the same fields. A field can contain text, a number, a date, multimedia, a formula that makes a calculation based on information in other fields, or a field that summarizes other data.

Take another look at Figure 19-1. See the different spaces for each piece of information? Those are the fields in that database. When you enter information in a database, you type it into fields. You find out more about fields in Chapter 20, which is about designing a database.

Browse, Find, and Layout Modes

The ClarisWorks database environment has four modes: browse, list, find, and layout. Each mode lets you work on a different aspect of the same database document, and each has its own tools and commands. The following list describes these modes:

 ✔ **Browse mode:** This is where you or your user enters, views, and sorts data.

✔ **List mode:** This is an alternative to browse mode. It lets you view all the records in your database in a spreadsheet-like list made up of columns and rows. Use list mode for a quick overview of all the information in your database. You can also quickly find and select individual records in list mode.

 ✔ **Find mode:** This allows you to search for records containing specific information. After you have a found set, you can save that set and work just within that set.

 ✔ **Layout mode:** This is your design mode, which is where you create new layouts for viewing your records in a new way, modify existing layouts, or delete layouts you don't want anymore.

 You can get into any mode by clicking its button in the button bar, by using a keyboard shortcut, or by selecting the mode from the Layout menu. Layout is an odd name for that menu because layout is also a mode of its own. Don't let that confuse you.

Entering Data

Whenever you enter data or work with data in any way, make sure you are in browse or list mode. One way to be sure you're in browse or list mode is to look at the left side of your ClarisWorks window. At the top of the controls is a *Record book* — your control for moving through records. In browse or list mode you can see a bookmark at the right of the Record book, as shown back in Figure 19-1. In the other modes, the bookmark doesn't show. We talk about the Record book and bookmark's functions very soon.

To enter browse mode, click the button, choose Layout⇨Browse, or use Shift-⌘-B (Mac) or Shift+Ctrl+B (Windows).

You can also work with data in list mode, although traditionally all fields of information aren't in the layouts that are used for lists. To enter list mode, click the button, choose Layout⇨List, or use Shift-⌘-I (Mac) or Shift+Ctrl+I (Windows).

Adding a new record

 The first thing you want to do is add a new, blank record to hold your information. The easiest way to accomplish this is to click New Record on the button bar. If you prefer, you may choose Edit⇨New Record or press ⌘-R (Mac) or Ctrl+R (Windows).

When a new record is similar to the information in an existing record, choose Edit⇨Duplicate Record to copy that record. Doing so puts you in the new, duplicate record. Just change any information that's different. This is very handy when entering corporate contacts because many people have the same corporate address. There is no button to duplicate a record. The keyboard shortcuts are ⌘-D(Mac) or Ctrl+D (Windows).

Deleting records

 To remove a record forever, select it by clicking anywhere in its background, and then use the Delete button or choose Edit⇨Delete Record. When you delete a record, all the information contained in its fields is deleted. If your sample database comes with any fake data, use the Delete Record command on those records — after you've seen how the system works or replaced it with a few records of your own.

Filling in text fields

When a new record appears, the cursor is in the first field. Type the information for that field. The fastest way to move from field to field within a record is by pressing the Tab key. You can also click any field with the arrow pointer to position the cursor in it. To move back a field, use the mouse or press Shift+Tab.

 Pressing the Return key in a field adds a line to that field — which is not what you want to do unless you are starting a new paragraph! On-screen, the extra line may cover up another field, but that's the least of it. An extra return messes up your labels, envelopes, merges, and more. As in word processing, pressing the Return key is a habit to be broken. If you press the Return key by mistake, use Backspace or Delete to remove the extra line. Do it right away, before you have to waste hours trying to figure out what's wrong later.

Using multimedia fields

To place media (stills or movies) in this frame, you use the browse mode, as with all other data entry. For media, it is best to move your movies into the same folder as the database before you insert the movies. This saves you a lot of grief when it comes to moving your database or passing it to another computer.

To insert still images, select the multimedia field, choose File⇨Insert, navigate to the desired image, and then click Insert (this button says Open in Windows). Your still image is now part of the database. That's it. You're done. If you're working with movies, read on for everything you need to know.

To insert QuickTime movies — and AVI (Audio/Video Interleave) movies, too, if using Windows — select the multimedia field, choose File⇨Insert, navigate to the desired movie, and then click Insert (this button says Open in Windows). Your movie is now part of the database. Your QuickTime or AVI movie now appears in the field, waiting to be played. However, you must have QuickTime installed on the computer for a QuickTime movie to play (and in Windows, you need Microsoft Video for an AVI video to play). If you don't have QuickTime/Microsoft Video installed, the image shows but doesn't play when clicked. To run a movie, double-click anywhere in the frame.

In Windows: To easily locate and select an AVI file, select Microsoft Video from the Files of Type listbox. For QuickTime movies, select QuickTime movie. ***On the Mac:*** To easily locate and select a movie, select QuickTime from the Show pop-up list.

It is best to store media files in the same folder as the database because ClarisWorks must find the file in order to play it. ClarisWorks doesn't actually embed the media file into the database — it would swell your files beyond belief. Instead, it uses *pointers* to files. Pointers to files are relative to the location of the database. If you move the database, the path to that file breaks, and ClarisWorks asks you to locate that file and gives you an Open dialog box when you try to play it. If you keep the media in the same folder, the path doesn't break. This also ensures that, when moving the database to another computer, you move all necessary media files.

Other movie types can also be inserted but, with each of these, remember that they are limited to one platform and don't work on the other platform.

- ✔ On the Mac, you can place QuickTime VR. You can insert it using the same steps as a regular QuickTime movie. In the database, it plays and functions the same as anywhere else — double-click the image and your cursor becomes a small circle. Move the circle to move around in the image.

- ✔ In Windows, you can also place or point to OLE objects. However, in the case of movies, because you need the movie player, using OLE ends up being the same as using File⇨Insert. This is because the true strength of OLE is in allowing editing of your movies and embedding the movies in the database. Embedding doesn't happen in a ClarisWorks database due to potential bloating of your database. We suggest you don't use OLE for movies with the ClarisWorks database as there are no true benefits.

- ✔ Another OLE option for Windows users is to create a new object. Frankly, like the option to call upon an existing file, you really gain no benefit by inserting a movie this way within ClarisWorks.

Navigating through a database

As your database becomes larger, moving from record to record becomes more of a hassle. Your best navigation tool is the Record book, shown in Figure 19-2. You can also use the scroll bar if you're in list mode or showing multiple records at once.

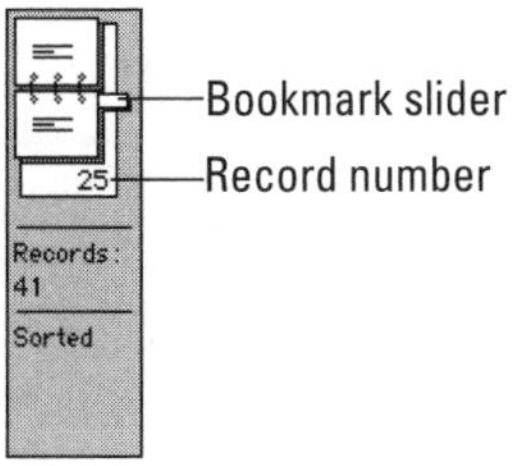

Figure 19-2:
The Record book's bookmark and record number move you between records.

—Bookmark slider
—Record number

Records: 41
Sorted

Click the top page of the Record book to move back a record. Click the bottom page of the Record book to move forward a record. Use the slider to move past many records quickly. To move the slider, click and drag it. In the lower-right corner of the Record book, you see the record numbers change, telling you where you are. You can also select the record number and type another number in its place and then press Enter to get to that record. (Windows users: Use the Enter key on your number pad.) The numeric Enter key is safer than the Return key when dealing with data, because the Return key creates a new, often unwanted, line when you're in a field.

Importing data from other databases

Another way to enter information into a database is to import it from a database created by another application, like FileMaker Pro. You can import data from any file that ClarisWorks can read, including other ClarisWorks files and the file types we list in Step 1, below.

To import a database document from another application:

1. **Open the ClarisWorks database into which you want to import the data.**

   You can add to a database that has existing records or add data to a blank one.

2. **Choose File⇨Insert. Select ASCII, DFB, DIF, SYLK, or Works as the files you want to show (depending on the type of database you're trying to open).**

   (If you're not sure what the file type is, try each.) Navigate to the location of the document you want to insert, select it and click Insert.

   If you don't see the file, open the file in the application that created it and export the document or records you want by saving them or exporting them as one of the formats that ClarisWorks can import: tab-delimited (ASCII), DBF, DIF, or SYLK format. Then return to Step 2.

3. **Choose File⇨Insert. Navigate to the document you created in Step 1, select it and click Insert.**

   This action brings up the Import Field Order dialog box shown in Figure 19-3. The left side of the dialog box shows the data in the file you are importing. The right side of the dialog box shows the fields in your ClarisWorks database document.

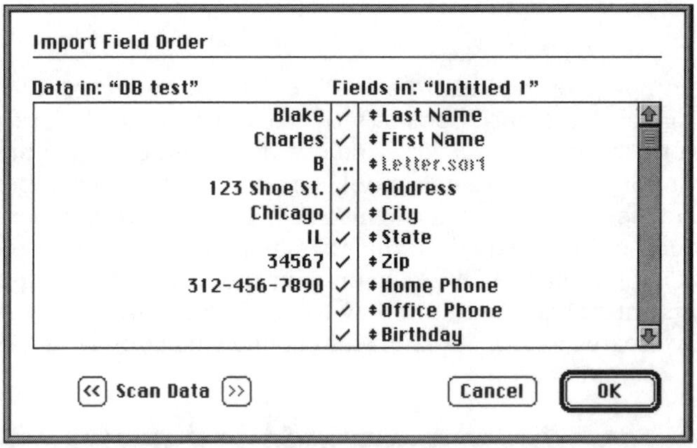

Figure 19-3:
Ever wanted
to try your
hand at the
import
business?
Try the
Import Field
Order dialog
box and see
how you
like it.

Import Field Order

Data in: "DB test"   Fields in: "Untitled 1"

Blake	✓	✦ Last Name
Charles	✓	✦ First Name
B	...	✦ Letter.sort
123 Shoe St.	✓	✦ Address
Chicago	✓	✦ City
IL	✓	✦ State
34567	✓	✦ Zip
312-456-7890	✓	✦ Home Phone
	✓	✦ Office Phone
	✓	✦ Birthday

[«] Scan Data [»]   [Cancel]   [OK]

4. **Drag the fields on the right side of the dialog box up or down so that they match up with the data on the left side.**

   Check marks identify fields that will be imported. Fields that won't be imported have three dots instead. You don't have to import the data from every field: Click in that column to add or remove a check mark.

   If your destination database doesn't have enough fields to import all the data, you can cancel the import process and add more fields to your database. See Chapter 20 for more information on adding fields.

5. **When you are happy with the matchup, use the Scan Data buttons to verify a few records.**

   Make sure that the data is going into the correct fields.

6. **Click OK to import the data.**

You can also export data from ClarisWorks by saving a database document as an ASCII text file or by using another commonly used data interchange file format such as DBF, DIF, or SYLK. Doing so lets you use your database with another application, like FileMaker Pro or Excel. ClarisWorks provides many filters for exchanging data with other software. If you need a refresher on how to save a document in a different format, pop back to Chapter 2.

Sorting

Sorting is one of the things databases do best, which is why you use a computer instead of a card catalog. Want to alphabetize by a last name field? Just a few clicks or so, and a few seconds later, you have your alphabetized list. How? You've got a few choices. The really fast way is by using a button. For more control, you can use Organize➪Sort Records, which we show you soon.

Button sorts

✔ **Sort Ascending:** To quickly sort one field from A–Z, position your cursor in that field (within any record in the set) and click Sort Ascending in the default button bar.

✔ **Sort Descending:** To sort from Z–A, position your cursor in that field (within any record in the set) and click Sort Descending in the default button bar.

✔ **Sort Again:** To use the field and order that were used by the last sort to sort the records again. This is most useful after you set up a sort order that includes subsorts, by using the longer method of sorting, which we cover in a moment.

These buttons work only on records that are visible in the database. Hidden records are not sorted.

The Sort Records dialog box has some benefits. Suppose you had to sort by Last name in ascending order (A–Z). Then suppose some people had the same last name. With this dialog box, you can place the First name field second in the sort to sort records that have the same last name alphabetically by first name. With this in mind, take a look at the next sort option.

Saved sorts

To set up a sort you can save and reuse, take advantage of the Fast Report pop-up menu to create a named sort. Besides being reusable, named sorts also have the advantage of being able to subsort other fields, unlike the buttons one field sort ability. To create a named sort:

1. **Find the set of records to be sorted.**

2. **Choose New Sort from the Sort pop-up menu on the Tool Panel, as shown in Figure 19-4.**

   This brings up the Sort Records dialog box, also shown.

Figure 19-4: Use the Sort pop-up menu to create a named sort.

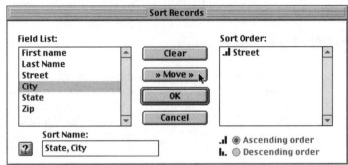

3. **Name your sort in the lower-left corner.**

4. **Set up a sort.**

   • From the scrolling Field List on the left, click once on the field you want to sort on, and then click Move (or double-click the field). This moves the field to the Sort Order list on the right.

   • With the field name still selected in the Sort Order list, click the Ascending or Descending button to set the order of the sort.

   For text, A–Z is ascending, and Z–A is descending. For numbers, ascending is 1-2-3 . . . and descending is 10-9-8. . . .

   • Add any fields you want for a subsort by repeating the last two steps as many times as necessary. You can also select items in the Sort Order list and use Move, or double-click the items, to remove them from the sort.

5. **Click OK to save the sort.**

   Your named sort now appears at the bottom of the Sort pop-up menu on the Tool Panel, as in the pop-up menu on the right in Figure 19-4.

To use your named sort, just choose it from the Sort pop-up menu on the Tool Panel, shown in Figure 19-4. To change your sort later, use Edit Sorts from the Sort pop-up menu to choose a named sort and change how it sorts your records.

For faster sorting action, here are a couple of field selection tips:

- ✔ To select several contiguous field names from the Field List at once, press Shift and click the first and last item, or drag over several items while holding down Shift.
- ✔ To select noncontiguous items, press ⌘ (Mac) or Ctrl (Windows) and click each item.

To print mailing labels, you can sort by state, zip code, last name, and first name to group your labels by state and zip with all names in each zip code in alphabetical order. You can have as many items in the Sort Order list as there are fields in your database.

As you sort records, be aware that their numbers change relative to any found set and sort. Don't count on them to remember where a record is. They are not for record identification. For that, you use a serial number field, as discussed in Chapter 20.

The Sort command ignores hidden records and those not part of the current found set. If you want to search just a subset of your database, hide the ones you don't want to include. You can use Organize➪Hide Unselected or the Hide Unselected Records button (shown to the left of this paragraph) to exclude them. Then do the search.

You can do a Find to pick out a subgroup of records for your search. Check out the next section in this chapter to see how the find mode works.

Old sorts

The final sort option has the least benefit and is the oldest way to sort. You get to it but using Organize➪Sort Records. It works the same as a named sort but you don't get to name it, save it, and reuse it. We just want to point it out to you so you don't go through all the trouble to set it up only to find that you can't save it.

Finding

You can flip through your database manually when you need information, or you can use the find mode to search for specific information.

Find mode

To enter find mode, click the Find Mode button, or choose Layout⇨Find.
The keyboard shortcuts are Shift-⌘-F (Mac) or Shift+Ctrl+F (Windows).
In find mode, you see what looks like a new, blank record. This is actually a
Find Request form, like the one shown in Figure 19-5. Type the information
you want to find into the appropriate field.

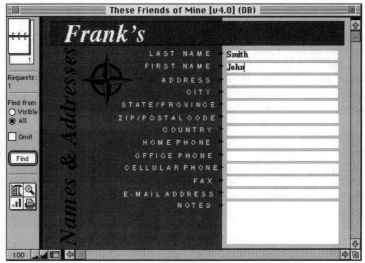

Figure 19-5:
To find
something
in a
database,
please fill
out this
form.

Narrow your search

Take a look at the left of the Find Request form in Figure 19-5. It has a couple
of options to help you with your search. At the bottom is the Omit check
box. If you select this box, ClarisWorks finds all the records that don't match
the information you typed into the fields on the form.

You also have the choice of searching all records in the database or just the
visible records. When records are found that match your search criteria, all
other records in the database are hidden. You can use one find session after
another to keep narrowing down the possibilities. For example, you can first
find all records that contain the name John; then type in your state, check
the Omit button, and do another search to find all the Johns outside your
state. That way, you can easily find your friend John who moved out of state,
even if you don't remember which state he moved to.

You can further narrow your search by filling in more fields. That way, you
can search for records that contain John in the first name field, Utah in the
state field, and Smith in the last name field. This search yields only records

for the John Smiths who live in Utah that you have in your database. The more fields you fill in, the fewer records your search turns up.

Broaden your search with multiple requests

You can use multiple Find Request forms to broaden your search to find more records. One of the examples I just cited lets you narrow your search to records with a first name of John and the state of Utah. What if you want to find all your friends named John and all your friends who live in Utah at the same time? You can use multiple Find Request forms to create a search that finds John in the First Name field or Utah in the State field. Here are the steps to follow:

1. **Enter find mode (use the button, menus, or keyboard).**

2. **Type your first search criterion in the appropriate field on the Find Request form.**

3. **Choose Edit⟿New Request or press ⌘-R (Mac) or Ctrl+R (Windows).**

4. **Enter the second search criterion in the appropriate field on the new Find Request form.**

5. **Repeat Steps 3 and 4 to add as many request forms as you need.**

   ClarisWorks displays the number of request forms in this search next to the word Requests on the left side of the window. Remember, the more forms you add, the broader your search.

6. **Click the All or Visible button to search the database.**

Save your search

You can set up a search to save and use later without re-creating the search forms. This is called a named search. To create a named search, follow these steps:

1. **Choose New Search from the Search pop-up menu on the Tool Panel, shown in Figure 19-6.**

Figure 19-6:
The Search
pop-up
menu.

2. **In the dialog box that appears, type a name for your new search.**

3. **Use the techniques described on the last couple of pages to create a search.**

4. Click the Store button that appears in the Tool Panel or press Enter to save the search.

Your new search now appears at the bottom of the Search pop-up menu on the Tool Panel.

To use your named search, just choose it from the Search pop-up menu.

Match records

This section is only for people needing massive database searching power. Pregnant women and people with heart conditions should skip this section.

The Match Records command is like the find mode on steroids. You can actually use the Match Records command to find all records that meet the following criteria:

✔ Contains *barb* somewhere in the First Name box

✔ Has a last name that starts with *L*

✔ Was entered before last Tuesday

✔ Has an address that's the square root of the zip code

If you need the really big guns for your search, you've come to the right place. Just take a look at the Enter Match Records Condition dialog box in Figure 19-7. Sheesh, even the name of the thing is scary.

Figure 19-7:
Fear the mighty Enter Match Records Condition dialog box!

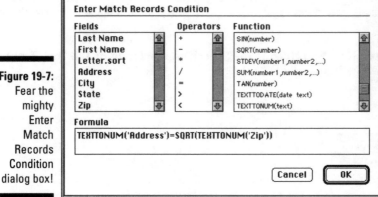

Unlike a Find search, the Match Records command does not hide records that don't match the search criteria; the Match Records command selects all matching records instead. Match Records searches only on visible records, so if you want to search your whole database, choose Organize⇨ Show All Records or press Shift-⌘-A (Mac) or Shift+Ctrl+A (Windows) before you search.

In the bullet list above, we mention finding records where the address is the square root of the zip code. The formula in Figure 19-7 does just that. That's right — a formula. To make the most of the Match Records command, you have to build your own formula to tell ClarisWorks what to look for. Is this yucky enough for you yet? All this formula stuff goes way beyond the scope of this book. We just thought we'd show it to you so that you can see what you are missing.

If you type your own formulas, remember to enclose the text in double quotes. Field names need to be enclosed in single quotes. Don't forget to close your parentheses.

Searching Shortcuts

Four buttons are available to let you do one-click searches in your database. All four require that you use an existing record as an example to let Claris-Works know what you want to search on. All you do is click a field that contains the information you want to use, and then click one of these buttons:

- ✔ **Match Equal:** Finds all records that have matching information in the selected field.

- ✔ **Match Not Equal:** Finds all records that don't match the information in the selected field.

- ✔ **Match Less Than:** Finds all records that have information that is less than the information in the selected field.

- ✔ **Match Greater Than:** Finds all records that have information that is greater than the information in the selected field.

For greater than and less than, letters at the beginning of the alphabet are considered less than letters at the end. If you select a field containing text that starts with C and then click Match Less Than, only records containing text that starts with A or B in the selected field will be found.

Like the Match Records command, these buttons search only visible records. To search your whole database, show all records before you click the button.

Opening other databases to use in ClarisWorks

ClarisWorks can directly translate and open databases that were created in several other programs. Simply open the other database using the File➪Open command, select database as your document type, and choose ASCII, DFB, DIF, SYLK, or Works in the File Type box, depending on the type of database you're trying to open. (If you're not sure what the file type is, try each.) When it opens, save the file as you normally would. Databases that can be opened directly include Microsoft Works database files and any other database that uses DBF as its format, including dBASE.

This is an excellent feature that makes it a breeze to work with other people's files. When you need to open another database type, try this method first. There's no harm in trying. If the database can't be translated by ClarisWorks, it simply won't show in the Open dialog box when you try to select it. To open a database that won't directly translate or to add records to your existing database, use the data from a database and import the data as we show you in the section, "Importing data from other databases."

To open a database that won't directly translate, open the file in the other application and export the database or records you want to use in ClarisWorks by saving them or exporting them as tab-delimited (ASCII), DBF, DIF, or SYLK format. Then follow the steps mentioned above to open the file.

Chapter 20

Designing a Database

• •

In This Chapter

▶ Figuring out what you want your database to do

▶ Categorizing your information into fields

▶ Choosing the right type of field

▶ Changing field options

▶ Laying out a database (a left hook is usually effective)

▶ Adding special parts that summarize your data when you print

• •

*D*o you keep all your really important information on little slips of paper that always get lost? Well, if you do, maybe you should think about making a custom database to organize and sort all your little slips. Having important client information, that superb casserole recipe, or all your research notes at your fingertips is much nicer than having to go through all the pockets of your dirty clothes looking for that one scrap of paper with the vital information on it.

Creating a ClarisWorks database can be easy at the simplest level, but you can get into some fairly heavy stuff. For ease, your best bet is to use an Assistant or stationery — at least to get started. Remember, the JIAN business templates that come with ClarisWorks were designed with ease and efficiency in mind. Plenty of other templates abound. The ClarisWorks User Group (www.cwug.org), local Mac User Groups (www.apple.com), and other computer user groups are sources for database templates. The Claris Web site (www.claris.com) leads to an entire list of products related to their software.

That all said, doing it yourself is really cool. So why not take a stab at it?

Planning It Out

The first step in creating a database is planning. Sure, you can always go back and add things later, but if you plan beforehand, you won't have to go back and move data around to fix things. Ask yourself these kinds of questions as you design your database:

✔ **What will you be using the database for?** Will you be using it mostly on-screen, or do you want to organize information for printed reports or labels? Make the form fit the function.

✔ **How many fields do you need to put information in?** Make a list of all the information items you want to include. Split items into their smallest parts, like using a first name and a last name field rather than just a name field. It's much easier to join information together later than to pick out different items in one field.

✔ **What kind of information are you going to store?** A database for storing research notes for a term paper will be quite different from a recipe database.

✔ **How do you want to access the information?** You can add more fields for keywords or categories that can help you sort or find information in the database. For example, do you want to look up a recipe by a type of ingredient or by the number of people it serves?

✔ **Do you want to include special fields that automatically enter the date, time, or serial number for a record?** How about using a pop-up menu to limit entries in a field to a preset list? (More about these special field options in the section called "Mastering Special Field Types.")

✔ **How many different layouts do you need?** Do you want one layout for entering data and another for printing out the contents of your database? How about a layout for printing labels? Actually, this isn't so important because you can always add layouts later. See the section "Laying Out the Database," later in this chapter, for more information on layouts.

If you don't understand what some of these questions mean, keep reading; the technical ones are explained in this chapter. After you get an idea of what you can do with a database, jot down your answers to these questions and sketch out how you want the layout to look. Visualizing what you want before you sit down at the computer makes the design process much easier.

Defining Fields

Where paper forms would have blanks, database records have fields. Before you can enter information into a database, you have to create the blanks to hold the information. Each record is made up of several fields into which you enter the information in the database. The first step in making a new database is telling ClarisWorks how many and what kinds of fields you want.

The first thing you see when you open a new database document that isn't based on stationery or an Assistant is a Define Database Fields dialog box like the one in Figure 20-1. After all, you don't have a database until you have a place to put your data.

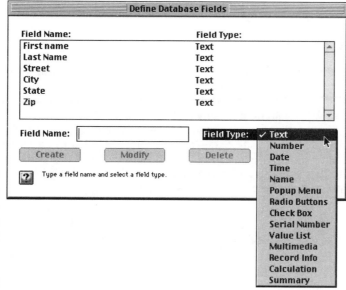

Figure 20-1:
The Define
Fields
dialog box
and all the
field types.

Here's how to create your database fields — after you read about each field type:

1. **Name your Field in the Field Name area.**

2. **Select the type of field you want from the Field Type pop-up menu.**

   We go over those in a moment.

3. **Click Create to define the field.**

   Depending on the type of field you picked, you may see an Options dialog box at this point. You can choose options for your field now or come back to it later. Click OK in the Options dialog box to create the field.

   The field now appears in the list at the top.

4. **Repeat Steps 1 through 3 to define all the fields in the database.**

5. **Click Done when you finish adding fields.**

   Don't worry about closing this dialog box. You can always come back to it. In fact, even the best designers do.

Mastering Basic Field Types

You may be wondering, "What are all those different types of fields for?" So we've got the lowdown on each one right here. After we explain each field, we go over the options for the field and how to use them.

Text fields

Text is the general format for most information. You can put almost anything in a text field, including numbers. However, if you enter numbers into a text field, ClarisWorks sees them as text, so they sort as text (1, 11, 12, . . . 2, 21, . . .) rather than numerically (1, 2, 3, . . .), and you can't do calculations with those numbers, such as figuring elapsed time. (It is possible to convert this text into numbers to use in a calculation, but that requires a special function to convert them to numbers. Chapter 18 has more information on functions.) By the way, a text field can hold up to 1,008 characters, depending on the text formatting within it.

Number fields

To have a number automatically be formatted as currency or automatically include commas, use number format. Also use this field type if you want to use the contents of the field for a calculation in another field. No text can be put in a number field, so if you're using the field for zip codes, it wouldn't work when you came upon a Canadian address. Don't even try a phone number here. The dash is illegal.

Date fields

The advantage of a date field is the ability to use it in calculations. Whether you have the user enter a date or you take advantage of the auto-enter ability, you can have this field help you know when invoices are overdue, when something has expired, and so on. The user can type the date numerically, or enter something like Aug 12 and have ClarisWorks convert it to 8/12 automatically. As a convenience, you don't have to enter the year when hand entering a date. ClarisWorks assumes the current year and adds it for you. If your date is not for the current year, be sure to enter the year. For example, enter 8/12/93.

You can set the date field to have the date appear in any of the standard date formats when it prints. We cover that in the section called "Laying Out the Database," later in this chapter. Several validation options are also available. See the section that follows for these options.

Time fields

This field type acts just like the date field except it is used to store and calculate time rather than dates. It also has validation options, discussed in the upcoming section.

Name fields

This is for entering a first and a last name in the same field. No database developer worth anything would let you do that, though. What happens when you want a mail merge that says "Dear Mr. Smith"? You can't. And "Dear Mr. Bob Smith" doesn't cut it. The only thing you may want to use this field for is to have it automatically enter the user's name, which is the name ClarisWorks sees from your computer setup. If people share the computer that the user's name is stored on, it isn't always accurate, but you can still use it to have an idea of who is entering what in your system.

Don't use the name field to place names, except to auto-enter the user's name. For all other names, create these regular text fields: a first name field, a last name field, and, optionally, fields to hold prefixes and suffixes such as Dr. and III.

Serial number fields

This field lets you automatically number your database records. This is a database creator's *must*. Never create any database without giving each record its own permanent, unique ID number. A unique ID number allows you to find the order in which you originally entered your data even after you've sorted and re-sorted your data. All you have to do is sort on the serial number field. You can also use this list to quickly find if a record has been deleted because that serial number is no longer present. Someday you'll thank us for this advice.

You may also use this field type to assign customer or invoice numbers. If you've been using a paper-based system and are switching to a database, you can even start your numbers where the paper system left off.

Only numbers can be entered in a serial number field. Upon creation, it automatically enters the number 1 in the first field you created, continuing to increment record numbers by one. (The second field is 2, then 3, and so on.) You can click the Options button and change this numbering system in the Options dialog box. In Next Value, enter the number to give the next record you create. In Increment, enter how much higher the subsequent numbers should be.

Record info fields

You can set up record info fields to automatically insert the time or date when the record was created or modified; or, you can also keep track of the person who modified your database. You *always* want to record the date created and date modified so you can find out how current your information is. You can also enter a record info field that allows you to find out who made changes to your data so you can discuss the accuracy of the changes with that person. Used in this way, record info fields are troubleshooting aids. You can also use record info fields in a message-taking or note-taking database because this data type can time- or date-stamps your messages or notes for you.

Multimedia fields

The coolest! This field can hold most graphic formats, QuickTime movies, AVI movies for Windows, and QuickTime VR for the Mac. That means it can display a picture — or movie — that can be played inside your database! There's nothing special or fancy about creating this type of field. Its power is in the types of files it can contain. The field has no options or special settings. Just create the field, size it to your liking in the layout, and enter browse mode later to place your media or image files. We discuss file placement options and considerations in Chapter 19.

You can use this field type to do all kinds of cool things. For example, you can make photo ID employee badges right from your employee database. Or, if you have a company catalog, you can store videos of the items you carry, distribute the database for customers to view, or create a print catalog. In the print catalog, one frame of the video shows so that customers can still see an image of the item.

Setting Options for Fields

As you define your fields in the Define Database Fields dialog box, you can set up options for making them enter information automatically or verify that user input meets your criteria. These are some of the bells and whistles of databases.

Each type of field has its own set of options that enhance its functionality. Create one of each and explore to get the idea. Figure 20-2 shows an Options dialog box (this one is for the text field called "First name").

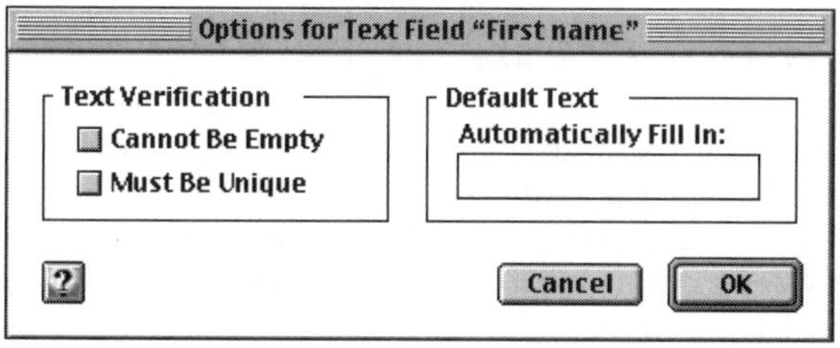

Options for Text Field "First name"

┌─ Text Verification ─────┐ ┌─ Default Text ──────────┐
│ ☐ Cannot Be Empty   │ │ Automatically Fill In: │
│ ☐ Must Be Unique   │ │ [   ] │
└─────────────────────────┘ └─────────────────────────┘

[?]   [Cancel] [OK   ]

Figure 20-2:
Your first
options
dialog box.

The options are:

- **Automatically Enter:** When any new record is created, whatever you enter in this option box is auto-entered for you. For example, in regular text field you may expect that someone lives in New York, so this option can auto-enter **NY** in a state field. If they don't live in New York, just change it. If they do, you save a lot of typing. In a date field this can enter the date for you. In a serial number field it can enter the next serial number for you. And so on.

  Automatic data entry of some sort or the other is available for the following field types: text fields, number, date, time, name, serial number, and record info fields.

- **Cannot Be Empty:** This option forces the user to enter something in the field (or the user can't do anything else). Put a check mark by this one to put it into action. If it makes you crazy, come back and turn it off. This option is available for the following field types: text, number, date, time, name, and serial number fields.

- **Current Date:** This option automatically enters the date and is only available for the date field type.

- **Current Time:** Current Time automatically enters the time. This option is available only for time fields.

- **Must Be Unique:** This makes sure you don't have two records with the same exact information (or it won't let you go on). Put a check mark by it to turn it on. This option is available for the following field types: text, number, date, time, name, and serial number fields.

- **Range:** Use this option to specify that a number be within a range that you specify. This is good for inventory control, invoices, or even ages. This option is available for number, date, and time fields.

- **User's Name:** User's name enters the name ClarisWorks sees in your computer setup. Although not always right because people share computers, you can use it to have an idea of who is entering what in your system. This is for name fields.

Auto-enter data and data validation only work in a field if the option is on when the field is created or if the information is entered at a time that the option is on. Turning these options on after the fact doesn't retroactively look at, change, or enter data.

Mastering Special Field Types

The following fields are created in the same dialog box as the others but each has a specific look to it and all are for entering predefined data. You enter this data as you create your database, so the user is limited to the choices you provide. Database people call predefined data *value lists*. You predefine values for your users to choose from via the Options dialog box.

Pop-up menu and radio button fields

Pop ups and radio buttons have the same effect. Both pop ups and radio buttons force your users to select one choice from your value list. The main difference between pop-up menus and radio buttons is the amount of room each takes up on-screen. Radio buttons allow the user to see all choices at a glance while a pop-up menu shows only one until it's clicked to reveal the rest of the values. These fields are life-savers. Just imagine a database where you or your staff enter plain text. One day someone writes LA in the City field. The next person writes L.A., while someone else writes Los Angeles. If you search for "LA," you miss those other entries. A value list limits the deviations by standardizing entries.

To set up a pop up or radio button field, follow these steps:

1. **Select the field in the Define Fields dialog box and click Options to bring up a dialog box like the one in Figure 20-3.**

    This is important: ClarisWorks starts you off with two place-holders. You want to change the preentered values or you look like a goofy monkey when users see Item 1 in their list of choices.

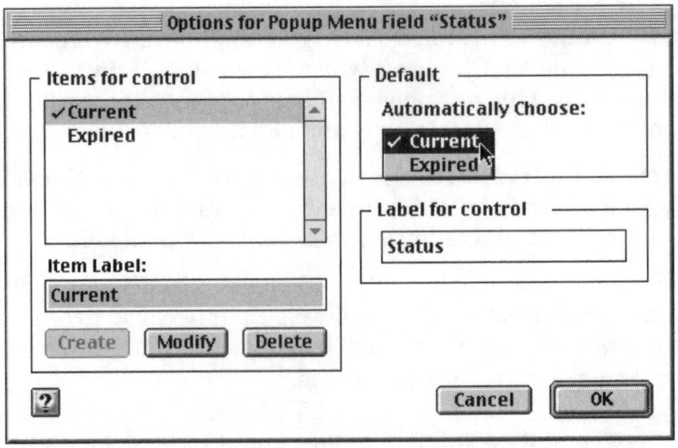

Figure 20-3:
Whatever your values, you can make them pop by creating a pop-up window.

Options for Popup Menu Field "Status"

- Items for control
  - ✓ Current
  - Expired
- Item Label:
  - Current
  - Create | Modify | Delete
- ?

- Default
  - Automatically Choose:
    - ✓ Current
    - Expired
- Label for control
  - Status

Cancel | OK

2. Click on Item 1 **in the Items For Control box to select it, and then type your first value.**

The first value shows up in the Item Label field.

3. Click Modify.

This changes Item 1 to your value. Do the same for Item 2.

4. Continue entering as many values as you like by simply entering the value in the Items For Control box and clicking Create after entering each one.

When they're all created, click pop up in the Default section of the dialog box and select the one you want to have appear automatically. You may want to make a value that says Pick one please so people know to select one, and you know whether they did or not. The last section of the dialog box shows you the name of the field you are working in.

Value list fields

This list would be more aptly called a Scrolling List, but alas, it's not. It works almost like the other value-list types, having users select from a scrolling list, except that it gives you the opportunity to allow the user to type anything else in the field as well — with control. By checking Alert for Unlisted Values, a warning appears: The value entered is not in the accepted list, asking whether to Continue, Accept (the value and move on), or accept it and Add to List. Continue allows the user to try another entry. If the old value is left, the box keeps reappearing. Additionally, you can demand the value not be left empty and/or be unique. The warnings pop up when the user exits the record, not the field.

Check box fields

This creates a field where the user either checks or unchecks the value. It is limited to one value, not a list. You determine whether the value is initially checked or not. The word the user sees by the check box is whatever you enter in the Label For Check Box area of the Options dialog box, not the name of the field.

Laying Out the Database

After you define your fields, they show up on a generic record, stacked one on top of another. This arrangement may suit your purposes just fine, or you may want to rearrange things according to your own taste.

Fields that (kind of) think for you

There are two kinds of fields that you can set up to perform some function or manipulation to your database information and display the result. These are Calculation fields and Summary fields.

Calculation fields

The content of a calculation field is the result of a formula you create for the field — such as searches for matching records and spreadsheets. When you create a calculation field, the Formula dialog box appears. If you haven't thought of a formula yet, just put two quotation marks there to keep the field defined. You can write yourself a message between the quotation marks if you like. Not all calculations are numeric. The figure below shows a

concatenation of text — it joins together the contents of two text fields. This power is very handy. The concatenation shown below also happens to be one of the handiest and most often-used database calculations around.

Summary fields

A summary field is a special calculation field that accesses data from several records at once. Use a summary field to compute totals and averages for all the records in the set you are working in. Summary fields are handy to include on printed reports. Summary fields are odd birds — their results show only on-screen in Page View or when you print. For more information on narrowing your search, see Chapter 19.

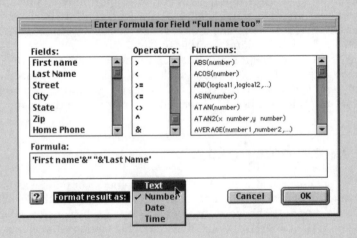

 If you want to change the way a record looks, you need to use layout mode. You can turn on layout mode by clicking the button shown in the left margin or by using Layout⇨Layout. You may also use the keyboard shortcuts: Shift-⌘-L (Mac) or Shift+Ctrl+L (Windows).

Layout mode works just like the draw environment and gives you access to all the draw and frame tools by replacing the status area at the left of the database window with the standard Tool Panel. Everything in layout mode is treated as a draw object, including the fields and their labels, as shown in Figure 20-4. Anything you do to one record appears on all records.

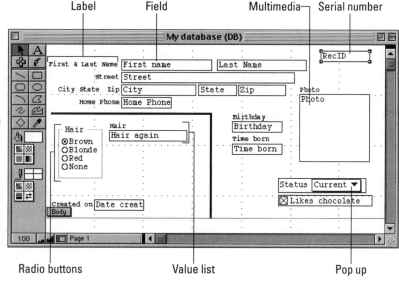

Label   Field   Multimedia— Serial number

Radio buttons   Value list   Pop up

Figure 20-4: Working on a database. Working — but not looking good yet.

In layout mode, the name of the field is displayed in the box representing the field. The field label appears in a separate text frame. The names in the field disappear when you switch back to browse mode.

Labels are not attached to any particular field and do not affect the field's contents. As you move fields around, make sure you move the label as well. You can change the label for a field to anything you like — the label is just a text frame. Most people use labels to tell users what data belongs in each field. Notice how we connected three labels together when we placed the city, state, and zip fields next to each other.

If you want to change the way a number, date, or time appears in a field, double-click the field to bring up the Format dialog box. Remember, you can't change the text formatting in all types of fields by double-clicking, but you can always use the commands in the Format menu.

You can draw graphics or add clip art to the background to make it more lively. You may want to put colored rectangles behind different groups of fields to make them stand out more. Be as creative as you like — you can do anything in a database layout that you can do in a draw document.

You can make a colored background for the layout by drawing a colored rectangle that covers the whole record area. Choose Arrange⇨Move to Back to put the rectangle behind the fields, labels, and other graphics. You can also use the Arrange buttons. We discuss these buttons and other techniques you can use to design your layout in Chapters 12 and 13.

When you color the background, the fields appear as white. If you want them to blend in with the background, select the field and use the fill tool to make it transparent.

If you want a larger area for your record, drag down the line labeled Body to make more room. A record can be as large as you like, but for entering information, make sure it all fits on the screen. It's better to switch layouts than to scroll. Database designers create one layout for each group of data and place it logically. Here are some ways to get fields into and out of your layout:

- ✔ To remove a field from a layout, select the field and press the Delete key.
- ✔ Choose Layout⇨Define Fields to create new fields, or to change existing fields to other types or alter values.
- ✔ Choose Layout⇨Insert Field to add an existing field to a layout.

Figure 20-5 shows you what the sample database looks like after a background and some graphic accents have been added.

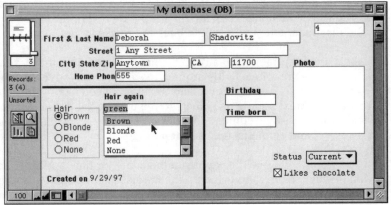

Figure 20-5:
The same database — what a difference some color and lines make.

Adding Summary Reports for Printing

Databases can have more than one layout. All the layouts in a database share the same information, and you can enter information into the database in any layout. Layouts are just different ways of viewing the same information. For example, your address database can have one layout to make it easy to enter data on the screen, another layout that you use to print a phone list, and yet another layout for printing address labels. The data entry layout would include all the fields in the database, arranged to make entering data easy. The layout used to print the phone list just has the name and phone number fields on a short body; it should be easy to read when printed. The address label layout needs to fit on standard laser labels and needs to include only fields with address information.

Most databases have at least one layout used only for printing a report of the records. A handy thing to include in a layout for printing reports is a section that sums up the information in the records. Summary parts let you include things like totals or averages either for all the records in a database or for certain subsets of records.

Summary parts do not show up in browse mode unless you have page view turned on. They're designed to be printed out with the report of the database, not to be viewed on-screen. You can use page view to preview what your report will look like when printed.

Adding a grand summary part

Actually, there are two kinds of grand summary parts: the Leading Grand Summary part, which appears once at the very beginning of a report, and the Trailing Grand Summary part, which appears once at the end of the report.

You use grand summary parts to create totals, averages, or summaries of information for the entire database. An example is a Trailing Grand Summary part that contains a summary field totaling the sales figures from every record in a database. Using that summary field, you can print a monthly sales report that has the total sales for the month printed at the end of the report — the Trailing Grand Summary. Or, if you want the good news right up front, you can use a Leading Grand Summary part.

To add a grand summary part:

1. **Click the button to switch to layout mode, choose Layout⇨Layout, or press Shift-⌘-L (Mac) or Shift+Ctrl+L (Windows).**

2. **Choose Layout⇨Insert Part.**

   This brings up the Insert Part dialog box shown in Figure 20-6.

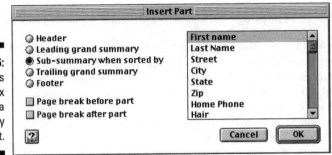

Figure 20-6:
Use this
dialog box
to insert a
summary
part.

3. **Choose Leading Grand Summary or Trailing Grand Summary.**

4. **Click OK to insert the part.**

In addition to adding a summary part, you have to add a summary field to your database that includes a formula to get a total or an average. Then use the Insert Field command to put the summary field onto your layout. Although you can place the summary field anywhere in the layout, putting it in the summary part makes the most sense.

To get a total or an average for a certain field across all records in a database, create a summary field using the SUM or AVERAGE function that uses a field name for its input, like this: SUM(<field name>). Typical formulas look like this: SUM('Amount') or AVERAGE('Count'). Of course, you can create formulas to show anything you like in a summary field.

Adding a sub-summary part

A sub-summary part lets you get subtotals or other information for a subgroup of sorted records. The sub-summary part works like the grand summary part, except that it appears before or after every subgroup of records instead of at the beginning or end of the whole database. Also, the sub-summary part shows up only when your database has been sorted.

Adding a sub-summary part is a bit different from adding a grand summary part. We step you through it:

1. **Click the button to switch to layout mode, choose Layout⇨Layout, or press Shift-⌘-L (Mac) or Shift+Ctrl+L (Windows).**

2. **Choose Layout⇨Insert Part.**

   This brings up the Insert Part dialog box (refer back to Figure 20-6).

3. **Choose Sub-summary When Sorted By.**

   Pick a field from the scrolling list on the right. The sub-summary appears in the report only when the database has been sorted by the field you pick here.

4. **Click OK.**

5. **A dialog box appears asking you whether you want the sub-summary above or below the subgroup of reports. Select one to place the part into your layout.**

To get something to print out in the sub-summary part, you need to insert a summary field and create a formula for that field. Skip back to the end of the previous section, "Adding a grand summary part," for a tip on a couple of commonly used formulas.

A sub-summary appears only if the database is sorted by the field you specified when you inserted the sub-summary part.

Understanding header and footer parts

There's a difference between header and footer parts in a database layout and regular headers and footers. A database can have both layout and regular headers and footers, and each does something different. There are four fundamental differences between layout header and footer parts and regular headers and footers:

- ✔ Layout header and footer parts can contain summary fields with formulas for summarizing field information. Regular headers and footers can't.

- ✔ Layout header and footer parts appear only on pages printed using the layout that contains them. Regular headers and footers appear on every page printed with any layout in the database.

- ✔ Layout header and footer parts use the draw environment. Regular headers and footers use the text environment.

- ✔ You add layout header and footer parts in layout mode. You add regular headers and footers in browse mode.

Also, a regular header appears above a layout header part, and a regular footer appears below a layout footer part.

Here's a special treat! Figure 20-7 shows you a sample layout that contains all the parts covered in this chapter.

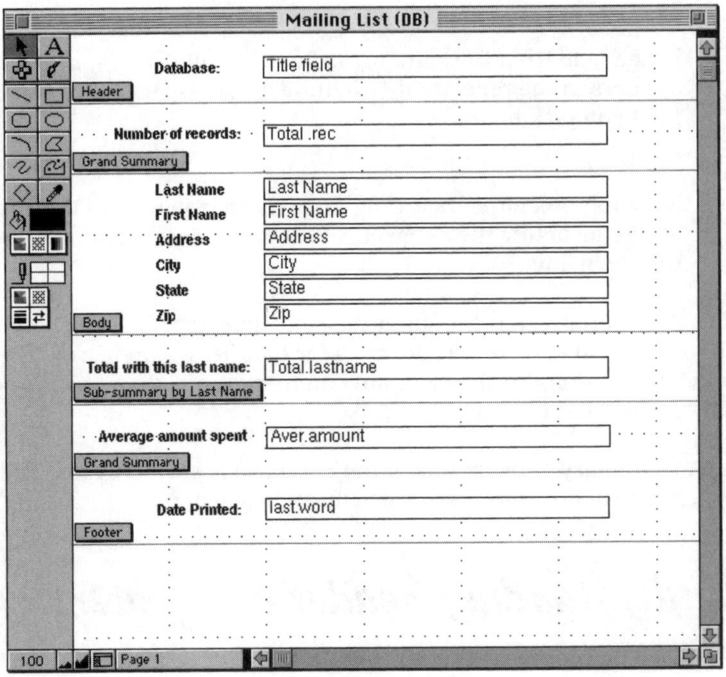

Figure 20-7:
Covering all
the bases:
This layout
has every
possible
part.

Chapter 21
Printing a Database

• •

In This Chapter

▶ Adding layouts to your database just for printing

▶ Printing labels

▶ Using standard labels

▶ Working with custom label layouts

▶ Closing up space when you print a layout

▶ Using ClarisWorks reports

• •

*W*hat do you do with the data in a database? Well, you can look at it on-screen, or you can print it. This chapter deals with the second option. Usually, you want things to print out a little differently than how you see them on the computer. Sometimes, a lot differently. Take labels, for example: You've got to take the address information that fills up practically your whole screen and cram it onto a one inch label. That job calls for a new layout.

Adding Layouts for Printing

The first thing to do if you want to use a different layout for printing is add a new layout to your database. After you add a new layout, you can set up the way you want your report to print out. To add a new layout for printing, just follow these steps:

1. **Access the Layout pop-up menu from the Tool Panel, as shown in Figure 21-1, and choose New Layout.**

   The New Layout dialog box appears, as shown in Figure 21-2.

   Another method to get to the New Layout dialog box is to choose Layout⇨New Layout.

Figure 21-1:
Get your
layouts
here! The
Layout pop-
up menu on
the Tool
Panel.

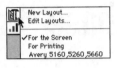

Figure 21-2:
The path to
a new
layout
starts with
the New
Layout
dialog box.

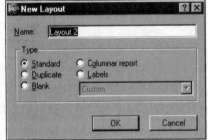

2. **Enter a name for your layout in the <u>N</u>ame field within the New layout dialog box.**

3. **Select a layout type from the available layout options.**

   You have several layout options from which to choose:

   - *Standard:* This layout option is the standard layout; it stacks the fields one on top of another and places all fields on the layout.

   - *Duplicate:* This layout option copies all the formatting of the current layout into the new layout.

   - *Blank:* This layout option is — you guessed it — empty, zilch, nada, the big nothing.

   - *Columnar report:* This layout option tries to arrange all the fields you specify onto a single horizontal line. It includes a header part that contains the field labels so when you print, you get a page with column titles across the top and each record represented by a single horizontal row of data. This is good for printing large databases.

   - *Labels:* This layout option has a pop-up list of many, many label options. Most of the rest of this chapter explains how to work with this type of layout.

4. **Click OK to add the new layout to your database.**

If you choose Columnar report or Labels, then when you click OK, the Set Field Order dialog box appears. Choose which fields you want to use in the layout and in what order you want them to appear. Figure 21-3 shows the Set Field Order dialog box.

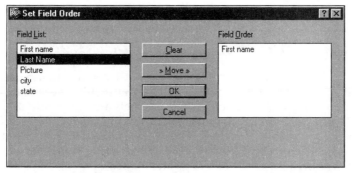

Figure 21-3:
Get your
fields in
order with
the Set
Field Order
dialog box.

To set up the fields for your new layout, click a field in the Field List, and then click Move — or just double-click the field in the first place. This action adds the field to the Field Order list on the right. Remove items from the Field Order list by selecting them and clicking Move to put the fields back into the Field List. (The Move button is smart. It changes direction.) You can also hold down Shift, and then click and drag to select several items in either list and move them all at once. When the Field Order list looks the way you want, click OK to add the layout to your database document.

Most new layouts need some tinkering. Check out "Laying Out the Database" in Chapter 20 for more information.

Printing Labels

These days, laser and inkjet labels come in a bewildering array of sizes, colors, and shapes. You can get labels for everything, including audiocassettes and videocassettes.

ClarisWorks comes with premade layouts for more than 50 popular sizes and shapes of Avery labels. You can also make your own custom sizes. Look for the 8 1/2-by-11-inch sheets of self-sticking labels that say they are laser printer or inkjet safe.

The easiest way to add a new label layout is to use the Create Labels Assistant, which steps you through the process of setting up a label layout. It's so easy to use, you could skip the rest of this chapter — but don't! This is your introduction to creating new layouts regardless of the layout. Anyway, you can find the Create Labels Assistant under the Help menu when you select ClarisWorks Assistants.

Using standard Avery label layouts

The quickest and easiest way to set up a label layout is to use one of the premade layouts for Avery labels. Of course, you should have the labels first so you know which layout to create. Avery labels are the standard. They all have a product number that identifies them. The label choices in Claris-Works correspond to that code. These days, many other label vendors note the same code on their packages, too. Follow these steps to create your new layout specifying one of these label standards:

1. **Bring up the New Layout dialog box using the pop-up menu in the Tool Panel, or Layout⇨New Layout.**

2. **Choose Labels as your Type, and then select the product number for your labels from the pop-up list under the Label option.**

3. **Click OK.**

4. **In the Set Field Order dialog box that appears, choose which fields you want on your labels, and then click OK.**

You may have to move and resize the fields to get them to fit on the label. See the section "Closing Up Space When You Print," later in this chapter, for information on how to make text slide over and eliminate empty space between fields.

Be sure to get the right labels for the printer you'll be using. Using a label with the wrong adhesive or design may be hazardous to your printer's health. All labels are clearly marked for use with laser, ink jet, or impact printers.

The best tip ever for printing labels is to use calc fields. (We talk about calc fields in Chapter 20, in case you need more information.) Create one calc field as a complete name field. Create another to compile any separate street address fields. Make a third to concatenate the city, state, and zip fields. Now you have only three fields to align.

If the information at the edges of your labels gets cut off, use the Document dialog box to set the margins for the layout as close to the edge as your printer allows. Choosing Format➪Document brings up the Document dialog box. If things still get cut off, adjust the layout to leave more room around the edges. Depending on the type of printer and platform you use, you will probably get a message telling you what to do if you have a problem with information being cut off.

Customizing label layouts

If you can't find the product number that matches your labels or if your labels don't have a matching number, make a custom label layout by following these steps:

1. **Bring up the New Layout dialog box (refer to Figure 21-2).**

   Use the pop-up menu in the Tool Panel, or choose Layout➪New Layout.

2. **Name your new layout.**

3. **Choose Labels as the Type, and then choose Custom from the pop-up list and click OK.**

   This brings up the Label Layout dialog box shown in Figure 21-4.

Figure 21-4:
Use any size labels you want by making a custom layout with the Label Layout dialog box.

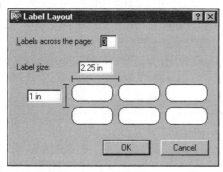

4. **Enter three pieces of information about your labels: the number of labels across the page, the label width, and the label height; then click OK.**

5. **In the Set Field Order dialog box that appears, choose which fields to include, and then click OK.**

When you measure the label width and height, measure from the edge of the label to the beginning of the next label, including any blank space in between. You can make up for the extra space between the labels by leaving room around the edges of the fields in your layout.

If you want to use your custom label layout again in other databases, save a blank copy of the database document containing the layout as a stationery document. See Chapter 2 for more information on working with stationery.

After you create a layout, it appears in the Layout menu or in the pop-up menu on the Tool Panel. The Edit Layouts command also appears in both places. You can use Edit Layouts to change the layout name at any time.

Closing Up Space When You Print

You can set up a layout to slide text up or over to close up blank space in a field when you print. How you actually get this feature to work can be a bit confusing, so we clear that up right here.

Here's how you close up space between fields for printing a layout:

1. **Choose Layout➪Edit Layouts.**

   The Edit Layouts dialog box (shown behind the Layout Info dialog box in Figure 21-5) appears.

2. **Select the layout to edit and click Modify.**

   The Layout Info dialog box, shown in Figure 21-5, appears.

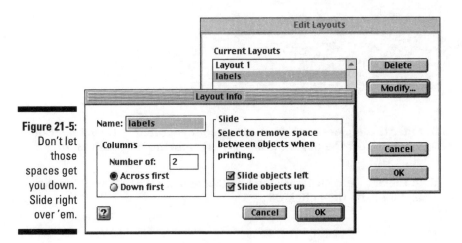

Figure 21-5: Don't let those spaces get you down. Slide right over 'em.

3. Check the box next to one or both of the slide options.

Here's the tricky part: The fields must meet the following conditions for sliding to work:

• Fields only slide left toward other fields the same size or larger. A field can't slide toward one even slightly shorter than itself. Fields can also slide up — but not toward another field that's even slightly narrower than itself.

• The fields need to be precisely aligned at their top edges to slide left and at their left edges to slide up.

• The fields can't touch or they won't slide.

These idiosyncrasies can work to your advantage to prevent some fields from sliding. For example, if you don't want a field to slide left, make it slightly larger than the field to its left.

Using Reports

The FastReport feature lets you select a named sort, a named search, and a specific layout to use together to create a custom set of information from your database. See Chapter 19 for more information on named sorts and searches.

To create a new report, choose New Report from the Reports pop-up menu on the Tool Panel, as shown in Figure 21-6. This brings up the New Report dialog box shown next to it.

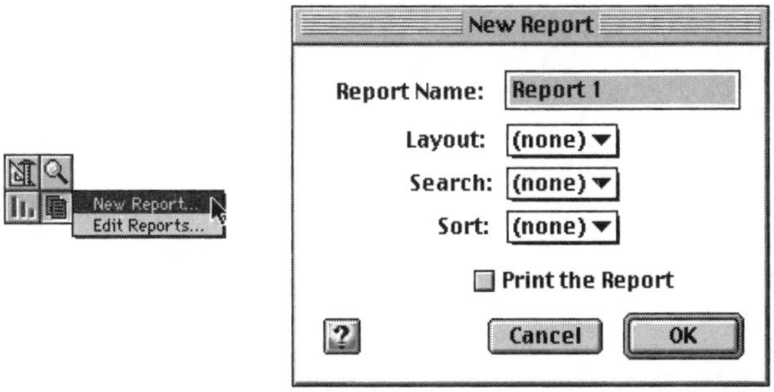

Figure 21-6:
This report just in —
easy access and easy reports are alive and well in ClarisWorks.

New Report

Report Name: Report 1

Layout: (none) ▼

Search: (none) ▼

Sort: (none) ▼

☐ Print the Report

Cancel   OK

Give your report a name, and then choose the layout, sort, and search options for your report. Check the box next to Print the Report for your report to automatically print when selected. Then click OK. Your report now awaits you at the bottom of the Reports pop-up menu.

Chapter 22

Mail Merge — It's One Cool Trick

In This Chapter

▶ Understanding mail merge

▶ Setting up a merge document

▶ Selecting records for the merge

▶ Performing the merge

▶ Printing your merge

*H*ave you noticed that since the computer has become popular, everyone is sending you personalized sweepstakes letters? That's mail merge at work. But it's a really tacky example of it. We just used it because we know you can all relate to it. Mail merge is actually a powerful tool for creating *good-looking* personalized business letters, invoices, and more.

What Is a Mail Merge and What Can It Do for Me?

If the phrase *mail merge* only conjures up images of dozens of postal trucks weaving together on a crowded freeway, you probably need an explanation of what this is all about. A mail merge is what happens when you take a form letter or a similar document and insert information from a database to print large numbers of "personalized" documents.

You may be wondering if this can really help you.

Have you ever had to send out newsletters by printing separate labels and sticking one on every single newsletter? Or, have you had some other mailing for which you had to print the labels, sort through piles of letters, and match the labels up with the correct letters — sticking a label on every single letter? With mail merge, you can print the address right on the newsletter or letter!

Have you ever created a price list from an inventory database, looking at the inventory information and retyping it into your price sheet? Or copying and pasting it in? By merging, you can avoid reentry of information.

And, of course, don't forget the good old holiday cards or letters. In this busy world of information overload, you may just want to save hours every year by merging the same *special* holiday greeting to every member of your family. Of course, you want to personalize it with a few custom fields inserted.

So . . . do you think it sounds good? When you see how this works, you'll probably think of a few things you can use it for. Or maybe not. Either way, this chapter tells you how to set up and print a mail merge.

Creating a Merge Document

You can merge data into any word-processing document, a text frame in a drawing document (like the one shown in Figure 22-1), or a spreadsheet document.

Create your document as you normally would, setting it up exactly as you want it to look. Enter anything that the merged data won't enter for you — anything you want to appear in every document. You don't have to leave gaps for the text to merge into. When you tell the mail merge palette you want a field, it inserts a placeholder that grows or shrinks to fit the information being added. You don't have to enter any special codes either. ClarisWorks does that for you.

Selecting Records to Print

ClarisWorks uses whatever records are visible in the database at the time you give the Print Merge command. It also uses them in the order they happen to be sorted in.

In the database, use the Find or Match Records command to select a group of records that you want to use for the merge. It's a good idea to set up a named search and/or sort. If you use the Match Records command, make sure that you also hide unselected records (Organize➪Hide Unselected), so that only the selected records are visible. To use every record in the database, click the Find All button or choose Organize➪Show All Records. See Chapter 19 for more about the Find and Match Records commands.

Finally, sort the records you selected into the order in which you want them to print.

Merging the Data

After you have the merge document ready, choose which database you want ClarisWorks to pull information from. The database has to be open to pull data from it, so if it isn't open, open it now.

To select the database, make the merge document the active window. Then select File⇨Mail Merge. This brings up the standard Open dialog box in Windows, or a very basic Open dialog box on the Mac.

Navigate through your hard drive until you see the database. Select it and click OK. If you don't see your database, perhaps it isn't open. Click Cancel. Locate and/or open the proper database, make sure it's saved, and try again.

After you select a database, the mail merge palette, shown in Figure 22-1, appears. This is your tool for adding the placeholders into your document, to choose a different database for the merge, or to print the merged documents.

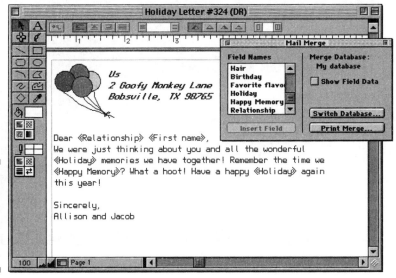

Figure 22-1:
The mail merge palette; a magic portal.

You can move between your letter and the palette. Position the cursor in the document where you want a placeholder inserted, and then move back to the palette. Scroll through the list of field names on the left, click to select the field you want to insert, and then click Insert Field. ClarisWorks inserts the placeholder at the point where your cursor is placed in the document. The placeholder appears as the field name you chose surrounded by double angle brackets, as shown in Figure 22-1. Go back to the document, type any spaces or punctuation you may need, and then — leaving the cursor where you want the next field's data to appear — return to the palette to select the next field. You can also simply double-click the field name instead of clicking Insert Field.

Do you prefer to work with real data instead of field placeholders? All you need to do is check the Show Field Data option in the palette and you see your actual field contents. With this checked, you can move through your records to see how each document will look once the merge takes place. You can see the information from any record by typing a number into the Record box or by using the arrows. Figure 22-2 shows the same letter with real field data from record number two showing. Notice the difference between the two palettes. Figure 22-3 shows the same palette for Windows, also set to to show real field data.

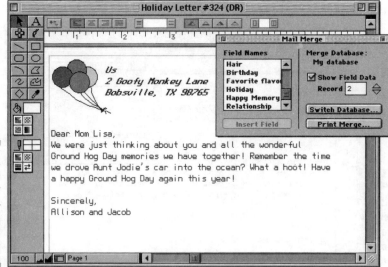

Figure 22-2: That same letter again — this time with "live" data.

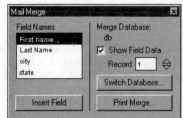

Figure 22-3: The Windows mail merge palette, also set to show "live" data.

And now, some memorable merge facts:

- ✔ You can insert any type of field in your database except summary fields.
- ✔ Fields do not have to be visible on the layout to be inserted.
- ✔ You can use the same field multiple times in your document. In our example, we placed the holiday field twice.
- ✔ You can insert up to 246 fields.
- ✔ Each field can have up to 1,000 characters (or fewer characters if they contain formatting).

Any font or formatting you apply to the placeholder affects the way the text from the database prints out. Apply the formatting you want to the whole placeholder, including the brackets at both ends.

Save the changes to your merge document after you insert all the placeholders. It will remember the database and can be used over and over.

Printing Merged Documents

Now for the moment of truth. All that's left is to actually print the merged documents. If you're still in the mail merge palette, click Print Merge. If you've left the mail merge palette and saved the merge document, open the merge document again, and follow these steps:

1. **Choose File⇨Mail Merge to bring up the mail merge palette.**

2. **Click the Mail Merge button on the palette.**

   This brings up the standard Print dialog box. See Chapter 2 for general information on printing documents.

3. **Click Print and away you go!**

   Sit back and watch your printer spew out all those customized printouts. There's nothing quite like the feeling of pulling off your first successful mail merge.

Before you print a mail merge with tons of records, test it by printing a small group of hand-selected records. That way, you can make sure that all insertions work as they should and that all the text is formatted correctly. Print one page as a test before you commit to a huge print job, such as your entire holiday mailing.

Part VI
Working with the World: Reaching Out and Touching Someone

The 5th Wave   By Rich Tennant

Buddy Diskk COMPUTER COMEDIAN

"INFORMATION SUPER HIGHWAY? THEN WHY DO I ALWAYS SEEM TO BE BEHIND AN OLD PICK-UP WITH A 2400 BAUD ENGINE?"

In this part . . .

Whether you're a Net junkie, or a Net novice, you find that working with the Internet couldn't be easier than with ClarisWorks Office. ClarisWorks integrates your Web capabilities right into your ClarisWorks documents, launching your Web Browser for you with the simple click of a ClarisWorks button.

Want to establish your presence on the Web? ClarisWorks allows you to save your ClarisWorks documents as HTML files ready to be put on the Web. If that weren't enough, ClarisWorks Office comes bundled with Claris Home Page Lite, a Web authoring utility that allows you to quickly and easily set up great Web pages.

Have you ever had your car break down and only had a pocket knife to fix it? In a pinch, you can make that pocket knife do some pretty amazing things; just like the old ClarisWorks Communication environment. It's not the sexiest communication tool on the block, but it works in a pinch.

Chapter 23

Connecting to the World the ClarisWorks Way

● ●

In This Chapter

▶ Accessing the Internet

▶ Setting up a Web browser

▶ Push button Web connectivity and e-mail

▶ Netscape Navigator basics

▶ ClarisWorks terminal emulation

● ●

*T*hat old saying about needing to be well connected to get ahead in this world has taken on new meaning since the Internet went public. And they thought no man was an island before all this! These days, no computer's an island either. Whether you are using ClarisWorks as an office-based business tool, a lone computer-based business tool, or for your own use, you'll find that ClarisWorks makes Internet connectivity a lot easier. In this chapter, we take you on an exploration of all ClarisWorks connectivity options. And because you may be new to the Web, we show you Netscape Navigator, the number-one Internet browser.

First Things First — Getting Internet Access

This chapter is all about how ClarisWorks takes you to the Web quickly and efficiently — with the click of a single button. However, before you go anywhere on the Web or do anything like send e-mail or post your Web pages to the Web, you need to have a physical connection to the Internet. It's like dialing a phone. You can press all the numbers you want, but if the phone isn't connected to the phone company's network, you can't actually make a call. Similarly, your computer needs to be connected to the Internet.

About that ISP. . .

Realizing you may not already have an ISP waiting in the wings, the ClarisWorks people invited two national ISPs — Earthlink and Netcom — to join your ClarisWorks Office package. You find installers for each of these ISPs on the ClarisWorks Office CD.

Mac OS8 also comes with an entire Internet-connection package that guides you through the setup of an account and provides several ISPs to choose from. On the Windows side, the Internet Connection Wizard allows you to enter your ISP's information or sign up with a default provider.

If your computer is on an office network and your company provides Internet access, you can connect through the network. You don't need an ISP; skip the rest of this section. Ask your network manager to help set up your computer for Internet access.

 If you have a home account, you don't have your own dedicated connection like people using a network at the office; you have a *dial-up connection,* which is a modem connection over your phone line. Your Web browser can't display the Web site you want to see until you establish a modem connection to your ISP (Internet Service Provider) first. We bring this up because your interaction from ClarisWorks to the Web requires you to have that Internet connection established. If you're on a dial-up account, you need to remember to connect your modem to your ISP's modem. And don't forget to disconnect when you're done!

 Many ISPs offer unlimited Internet access. Some people abuse this, keeping their connections open for hours at a time, which prevents others from having a turn to use that modem. To allow others to connect, the ISP needs to buy more modems and more phone lines. ISPs have to pay for those modems and phone lines, which drives up their costs, and therefore your fees. Instead, like a phone, call in, connect, do what you need to do, and then disconnect. *Please.* By the way, if you don't disconnect while you aren't using the Internet, you not only ruin it for the rest of us, but also risk being switched to a higher fee schedule. You also tie up your phone line so no one can call you.

One-Click Web

Throughout this book, we show you buttons for doing most of the common ClarisWorks tasks. Now it's time to introduce the Internet buttons and links — your one-click paths to Cyberspace. You have several ways to travel through Cyberspace using ClarisWorks. ClarisWorks can simply open your browser, or it can take you to a specific destination. You can even tell ClarisWorks what destination to take you to.

You need to have a Web browser and a connection to your ISP to use the ClarisWorks Web connection abilities. If you don't have a browser to launch, clicking the button doesn't do anything. If you aren't connected to the Internet, clicking all the Web connection objects in the world doesn't do anything more than launch your Browser to an empty page.

Having a Web browser doesn't mean you own the rights to it. Check the licensing agreement. For example, if you install an ISP package that installs Netscape Navigator, you have the right to use it only as long as you are a customer of that ISP. Please respect all software license agreements.

Launching your browser

One way to get to the Web is by clicking the Launch Browser button, which launches your browser. Of course, you really want to go to the Web. And the Launch Browser button delivers — as long as you are connected to your ISP at the time. If you're not connected to your ISP and don't have your computer set up to connect you automatically, this button simply launches your browser to a blank page, which may be a little anticlimactic. To set up your computer to connect automatically, check out the sidebar, "For your Internet connection convenience."

So where in the World Wide Web does clicking this Browser button take you? That's a good question. It takes you to whatever page your Browser calls home. Each Browser has a *default home page,* or starting Web page, which you can change in the Browser's preferences. You can hang out at this home page as long as you like. Or you can head to any place you want. We show you how to get around the Web in Netscape later in the section on Netscape.

Visiting a Web site

There are tons of sites to visit on the Web, so aptly, ClarisWorks gives you lots of ways to get to them. You can use a preset button or link, or even travel free-flight (so to speak) by jumping a ride on any *URL* (Web site address) written in your document, whether it's a link or not. ClarisWorks has three ways to connect to a Web site:

✔ **Click the Open URL button:** Select a *URL,* or Web address, and then click the Open URL button. Your browser is called into action taking you directly to the site you highlighted. The Open URL button is not available in paint or draw environments because you can't select text in them, but it is available in a database because you can have URLs in the fields. The Open URL button is also available from any text frame or document, including a text frame within a drawing document.

For your Internet connection convenience

You can set your dial-up connection to connect automatically when you call upon your Browser. This way clicking any Web button in ClarisWorks is guaranteed to take you to your destination.

On a Mac, this is actually done by your PPP software (Point to Point Protocol) which controls your dial-up. Choose ⬛⇨Control Panels, then to either PPP or FreePPP. Select the Options button, wherever that is. Then check the button that says something about connect automatically. This can be great — or drive you crazy. The strike against it is that every single time you launch any Web-accessing program it starts to connect, and sometimes you just don't want to! If it makes you crazy, go back and turn off the option.

In Windows, if you use the native Windows Dial-Up Networking, here's the drill: Double-click the My Computer icon, double-click the Dial-Up Networking folder to open it, and then click the connection to your ISP to highlight it. Choose Connections⇨Settings. On the General tab, you can select either Prompt to Use Dial-Up Networking or Don't Prompt to Use Dial-Up Networking. If you select Prompt to Use Dial-Up Networking, Windows automatically checks to see if you have a connection established when you try to launch an Internet application. If it finds that you do not have a connection, it attempts to create a connection with your ISP. If you want to manually establish the connection each time or don't want a connection at all, select Don't Prompt to Use Dial-Up Networking.

✔ **Click a link:** Click a link, or hypertext link to be exact, and your browser pops up and delivers you directly to the linked page. It couldn't be easier, could it? Links in ClarisWorks are not limited to text. They can also be graphics. To learn how to make your own links see Chapter 24.

 ✔ **Click a custom button:** This is a button that you set up yourself to take you to a particular site. If you have any sites you go to on a regular basis, you'll love this capability. You can even give it its own icon. Is the wisdom you glean from the site destined to become a part of a document? Great! Launch the site while you're in that very document. That way it's waiting for you, ready to take all the information you can paste into it as you visit the Web site. If you're running an office, small business, or classroom, you can create entire button bars full of all types of custom buttons, with as many as you want to take your users to the Web.

TECHNICAL STUFF

Changing your default browser

In case you want to use a Browser other than Netscape, which ClarisWorks is preconfigured to call upon, here's how to switch Browsers.

In Windows:

In ClarisWorks, select Edit⇨Preferences, then select Communications. Where it says ClarisWorks Web browser, click Change to, then select your preferred browser.

On a Mac, follow these steps:

1. **Select the Internet button bar.**

   You do this by clicking the arrow on the left of your current button bar.

2. **Click the Internet Config button on your Internet button bar.**

   Internet Config, is a separate little public domain program that enables your Internet settings and preferences to be accessible by almost any other Internet application. Internet Config should open to a window called Internet Preferences which is just a bunch of buttons. This window is shown in the figure below.

3. **Click Helpers to open the Helpers dialog box.**

   Helpers are pointers to the applications you want your Internet applications to call upon. There is a Helper to help with each function of Internet access.

4. **Scroll to** `http`**, select this line, and then click Change to open the Add Helper dialog box.**

   The http Helper is the application that's called when you request an address that begins with *http*. So the http Helper is your Web browser.

5. **Click the Choose Helper button.**

   This brings up an Open dialog box.

6. **Navigate to the Browser you want, then click Open.**

   The Open dialog box disappears.

7. **In the Add Helper dialog box, click OK; then close that window using the close box in the top-left corner.**

8. **Making sure Internet Preferences is the active window, select File⇨Save and then File⇨Quit.**

Note: Internet Config is going to end up on your Mac all over the place, just like SimpleText. They all reference the same preferences, which are called Internet Preferences and live in your Preference folder within your System folder. It's okay to trash your extra copies, but for the sake of ClarisWorks, keep the copy ClarisWorks installs. (This is the copy inside the ClarisWorks folder.)

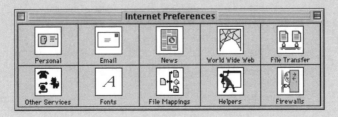

Internet buttons, by the way, don't have menu or keyboard equivalents. As usual, the most often used Internet buttons appear on the default bar; however, ClarisWorks also offers an Internet-specific bar that provides the full set of Internet buttons. Click the arrow at the left of the button bar to select it. Oddly, some seemingly universal buttons, such as launching your browser or e-mail, are not defaults. You can add these and other buttons to your button bar. See the Appendix to find out how to do that.

Launching Your E-Mail Application

 Regular mail is great for lots of stuff, but e-mail is immediate and lets you send information that can be copied and pasted. With the Launch Email button, you get to your e-mail program any time, from any environment, no matter what you're doing in ClarisWorks, with just the click of a button.

On the Mac, Claris Emailer Lite is preconfigured to launch as your e-mail program. Since OS8 comes with Claris Emailer Lite and you can download it from the Claris Web site (www.claris.com) for free, it may be your e-mail software of choice. If you don't have Claris Emailer Lite, clicking the Launch Email button has no effect. If you prefer another e-mail program, such as Claris Emailer 2.0 or Eudora, follow the directions in the "Changing your default browser" sidebar, except this time, select mailto in the helper list. While you're in Internet Config, set up your e-mail address, if you haven't already. In the main Internet Config window, click Email; then enter the information you agreed upon with your ISP. Save it and quit.

When you click the Launch Email button in ClarisWorks for Windows, the e-mail program launched is Microsoft Exchange (called Windows Messaging on NT machines). Unlike the browser-launching button, there is no option to change e-mail programs within Preferences. If Microsoft Exchange is not installed, clicking the button has no effect. (You can go into Windows Setup and install it from your original Windows disc.) If Microsoft Exchange is installed but you haven't yet set up a profile, Exchange prompts you to either choose a profile or set up a new one.

Customizing Your Button Bar for the Web

If you're using ClarisWorks in a business or classroom environment, you'll have a field day with custom buttons when it comes to using the Web.

For example, suppose you have an assistant at work who each day, needs to go to a specific Web site. You can create a button to take your assistant directly to that site.

To create a custom button to take you to a specific Web site:

1. Select New Button from the arrow on the button bar.

The New Button dialog box, shown in Figure 23-1, appears.

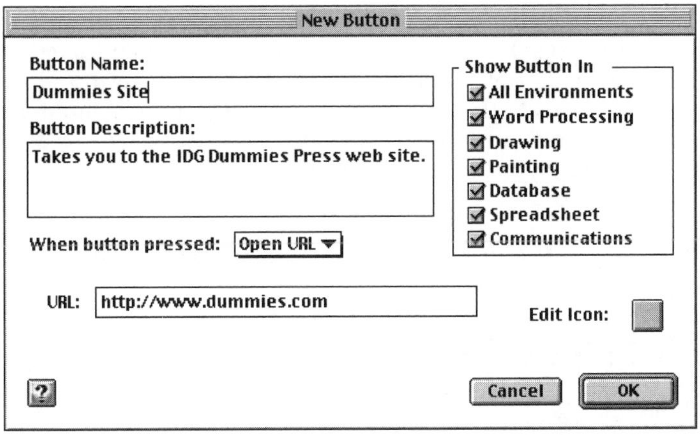

Figure 23-1:
Making a
custom
button to
get to the
*...For
Dummies*
Web page.

```
┌───────────────────────────── New Button ─────────────────────────────┐
│                                                                       │
│  Button Name:                        ┌─ Show Button In ────────────┐  │
│  ┌─────────────────────────────┐     │ ☑ All Environments          │  │
│  │ Dummies Site                │     │ ☑ Word Processing           │  │
│  └─────────────────────────────┘     │ ☑ Drawing                   │  │
│  Button Description:                  │ ☑ Painting                  │  │
│  ┌─────────────────────────────┐     │ ☑ Database                  │  │
│  │ Takes you to the IDG Dummies │     │ ☑ Spreadsheet               │  │
│  │ Press web site.             │     │ ☑ Communications            │  │
│  │                             │     └─────────────────────────────┘  │
│  └─────────────────────────────┘                                     │
│  When button pressed:  [ Open URL ▼ ]                                 │
│                                                                       │
│  URL: ┌────────────────────────────────┐                             │
│       │ http://www.dummies.com         │         Edit Icon: [  ]     │
│       └────────────────────────────────┘                             │
│  [?]                              [ Cancel ]   [ OK ]                 │
└───────────────────────────────────────────────────────────────────────┘
```

2. Enter a name for your new button in the Button Name box.

In our example, our button takes us to the Dummies Web site, so we name our button **Dummies Site**. This is the name that shows in the balloon or pop-up text when you rest your mouse on that button without clicking.

3. Enter a description for your button in the Button Description box.

A good description helps you remember the button's function later. The description also shows in the button bar's info bar when you place your mouse pointer over that button.

4. Choose the When Button Pressed pop-up menu, and choose Open URL.

This tells ClarisWorks you are creating a button that takes you directly to a Web site. (The URL is the address of that Web site.) Notice you now have a field in which to enter the URL.

5. In the URL field, enter the full address you want to go to when this button is pressed.

In our example we entered the full address of the *...For Dummies* Web site (www.dummies.com).

6. In the Show Button In panel, select the environments in which you want this new button to show.

If you want your Web site buttons to show at all times, check every environment as we did in this example.

7. Double-click the blank gray Edit Icon button to design your button.

A mini painting window comes up, as shown in Figure 23-2. You can design your button in the painting window, or copy an image from somewhere and paste it in. Without closing this dialog box, we visited the . . .*For Dummies* site and used our computer's Screen Capture command to select and capture a part of the Dummies logo that we thought made a nice button to remind us of the button's function. Then we came back to the editor window and used the computer's Paste command to paste it in. Remember to get permission to use other people's art and to respect the copyright.

8. Click OK to close the dialog box.

You now have a custom button to take you to this site.

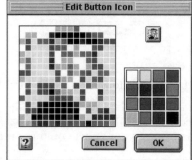

Figure 23-2:
Editing a
custom
button.

To put this button on an existing button bar or learn how to create you own new button bar, see the Appendix.

Taking custom buttons one step farther, you can create entire button bars dedicated to each person in your office, depending on the jobs each performs. In a school computer lab, you can create a button bar for every class taught, or for each grade.

You can create buttons that

✔ Play a macro you've recorded.

✔ Open a document.

✔ Launch an application.

✔ Run a script (Mac only).

Check out the Appendix for more on creating and editing custom buttons.

In addition to being more efficient, custom Web buttons also reduce the chances of users ending up at the wrong Web site — or wandering along the way.

Netscape Navigator

We told you how to launch your Web browser, so it's only fair that we help you use it. By getting around in a browser, you can get around the Web. The browser is the interface that displays all the various images, text, hyperlinks, multimedia files, and Java programs on the Web as individual Web pages. A browser insulates you from all that techy stuff. All you need to know is to look under your browser's menus to find a command for what you want. We show you the basics here. By the way, we're showing you Netscape Navigator Version 3 because, as of this writing, it's the market leader for this technology, and it's the browser you get if you sign up with EarthLink or Netcom — the ISPs on the ClarisWorks Office CD.

Getting to your first site

At the top of the Netscape Navigator 3 window is a large button bar, as shown in Figure 23-3. Under that is a very long, white field labeled Location. That's the key to getting where you want to go. To get to a site, you type the URL (Web address) of your destination, and then press Return or Enter (number pad) to send the URL off through your modem and on to the highways and byways of the Web. Within moments (or longer, depending on the speed of your modem), your request finds its way to the server you sent it to, which, in turn, returns the page you requested. You can enter a new URL there at any time.

If you select a URL in your ClarisWorks document and click the URL button, or click a live URL link, you should be at the page you requested. That will be the address that shows in the location field.

Where do you go from here?

If you haven't ventured past your start page, you may be wondering what all the hype is about. Well, the start page is only the beginning. Fasten your seat belt and return your tray table to its upright and locked position. Stow your carry-on luggage. You thought the Concorde was fast? Try making the New York to Paris run in about three seconds. Most Web pages contain *hyperlinks,* which, when clicked, zoom you to another page, maybe next door, maybe halfway around the world. The following list should get you off the ground:

- **Links**: On the Web, an underlined word is an indication of a link (technically, *hypertext link*), such as <u>Click me!</u> Move your pointer over any underlined word and look at the bottom left of your browser window. You should see a URL there. By the way, you need to click only once.

- **Buttons**: It's common to make a button-type image to indicate a link. Buttons do the same thing as links. They just look nicer.

- **Images**: Any image — graphic or photo — can be a link. Images that are links are called *imagemaps*. Imagemaps are really cool and look great. The way to tell whether an image is a link is to look at the address box in the bottom of the browser. If the image is a link, the link's address is displayed there. Why images? For fun. For effect. Maps are usually links, each region taking you to something about that area.

Returning to a site

It's easy to go to one page to look for something, follow a link, and then another . . . until you have no idea where you are. You need to get back to that first site, but how?

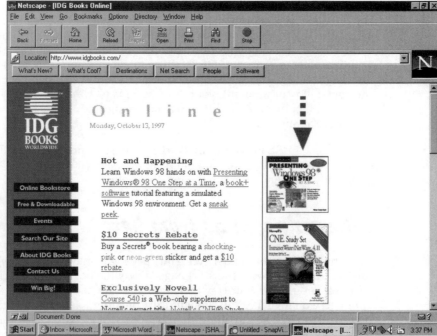

Figure 23-3:
Stopping by the IDG home page on the way to the . . .*For Dummies* site. . . .

✔ Somewhere in the menus is one that tracks your wanderings. It's called Go in Navigator 3. The first place you visited (as they say in Cyberspace) is at the bottom of the list. Select any location from the list and you'll return there. With any luck, you'll be able to recognize your site by the name in the list. Sometimes those name are rather mystical. The designer of the page controls how the location name appears and not all are savvy when it comes to naming.

✔ Windows users can also follow another audit trail. All URLs you type into the location field are recorded. To return to any of those sites, click the downward pointing arrow to the right of the location text box. It keeps a list of visited sites from session to session that expires according to your General Preferences settings.

✔ Another option is the Back button. It's one of those large (huge?) buttons at the very top of the browser window. Each time you click it, it takes you back one site visit. A site visit, by the way, is a visit to a site. In Web lingo you *visit* sites and are counted as a *visitor*.

Is it déjà vu or have you really been there before? In a site full of links, how do you know if you've followed a link already? As a courtesy, links change color when you click them. In Preferences, you can control how long a link stays that second color. In Navigator 3, it's called Links Expire.

Bookmarks

Your bookmarks are here to stay. (Unless you delete the file, they're stored in your hard drive.) Bookmarks even carry over when you update to a newer version of the browser. The only warning to give you about bookmarks is that they seem to multiply faster than rabbits. Very quickly, you won't be able to find anything because your list will be so long. The good news is that they can be organized. Bookmark organization can be crafted into a fine art. Here are the tools to start your work:

✔ **Creating a bookmark:** Bookmarks are easy to make. When you arrive at a site that you like and want to return to, go to the Bookmark menu and select Add Bookmark.

✔ **Organizing bookmarks**: Somewhere in the menus, you find a command that helps you organize your bookmarks. In Navigator 3, it's <u>Window</u>⇨ <u>Bookmarks</u>. This command, wherever you find it, brings up a separate window and a new set of menus. Somewhere amongst those menus, there's a menu that lets you create new folders and those separator lines that you see in menus. It's the Item menu in Navigator 3. Create as many folders as you want, then move your bookmarks into them. Moving bookmarks works just like moving any file on your hard drive.

Unearthing the Communications Package

Welcome to Jurbasic Park, where you take a ride back to a time long ago, when dinosaur-sized computers inhabited the earth. Oh no! Something's gone wrong! They've gotten loose, and . . . we can't bear to say it . . . *they're text-based!*

The communications environment within ClarisWorks for the Mac is Old Faithful, dating back to the dark ages of the computer world. (About 6 years in human years.) It serves little purpose now if you have access to the Web and all that fancy stuff. You can't do anything with communications software that can't be done better with a Web browser.

The ClarisWorks telecommunications environment is terminal-emulation software. It lets a large, central computer (usually a mainframe) think your computer is a *generic terminal,* or a monitor and keyboard hooked to it that uses the central computer for all its processing power. This allows your computer to send and receive text — that's text only — from other computers.

A ClarisWorks communications document stores your settings for remote computer dial-up. The document stores information such as modem speed, phone numbers, and so on. It also records the text exchanged in your session. Like using a new document for each letter you write, you use a new document each time you connect. For frequent use, you can create and open stationery.

It's also possible to use ClarisWorks to connect directly to another computer. You can transfer files directly from your computer to your friend's. This is covered in the ClarisWorks User's Guide. Instead of taking up more of your pages here, we refer you to the User's Guide for more on direct connections, including computer-to-computer hook ups via cable (which you really, *really* won't ever need). If you read this part of the guide, it's definitely time to get back to the present.

ClarisWorks doesn't install a communications program in Windows. Instead, it calls up HyperTerminal, which is part of the Windows installation, to handle this communication. If HyperTerminal isn't installed, you can specify another such program in the Communication Preferences. The whys and wherefores of HyperTerminal are beyond the scope of this book; check out Andy Rathbone's *Windows 95 For Dummies,* 2nd Edition, published by IDG Books Worldwide, Inc.

Chapter 24

Publishing for the World Wide Web

In This Chapter

▶ Overview of a Web page

▶ Creating your Web page with ClarisWorks

▶ Creating your Web page with Claris Home Page Lite

*Y*ou've browsed the Web, gotten to know what's out there, seen what you like — and more important, what you don't like. Now it's time to establish your own presence on the Web. Ready, here you go. . . .

The Secret Life of a Web Page

Things are not always as they appear. That's the secret of magic — and of any Web page's magic. Actually, it's the secret of any word-processing document, too. Just as there are invisibles hiding in your word-processing document, there are even more hidden codes in a Web page. Imagine if you had to learn all those codes before you could even type a letter to your mom? Luckily, when it comes to both Web pages and word-processing documents, Claris does the work for you, embedding the codes each time you select a font attribute, set the alignment with the ruler, or do anything else to your pages.

Back in ancient times — a couple of years ago — in order to create a Web page, you had to enter all those codes by hand. Fortunately, once again, Claris makes things simple, so you no longer have to learn these codes. You can study these codes if you want to, but because Claris takes care of them for you, you won't be bothered with them here — at all. You're busy. You want a Web site, not a programming education.

"Those codes" are called HTML tags, and the language that brings those codes to life is called HTML, or *Hypertext Markup Language*. The text you view is actually hanging out between a bunch more text that you don't see. This hidden text is the HTML tags, which hide between these pointy brackets: ⟨ ⟩. These tags are all over the place, telling your browser the size at which it should show text on your page, where to align, when to start a new paragraph, and so on.

ClarisWorks Office gives you two ways to create a Web page: You can turn any word-processing document into a page simply by doing a Save As, or you can use Claris Home Page Lite, a separate program included in the ClarisWorks Office bundle. This chapter looks at both options so that you can decide which program to use, and when to use it.

Before you begin to build any Web site, ask your ISP what file-naming conventions to observe. Generally, keep the name short, and don't use spaces or other special characters. You definitely need to add ".htm" or ".html" as the extension so the browsers know it is an HTML file and can find it. Your ISP can tell you which extension to use.

Creating Web Pages with ClarisWorks

ClarisWorks is great for creating Web pages, because you can publish any existing documents to the Web. Here's the deal: Almost anything you can toss into your word-processing document can be part of your Web page. A few things are simply ignored. Nothing is unsafe or bad. Create your word-processing page, and you have your Web page. That's it. All you do is choose File⇨Save As, select HTML, give it a precise title adding .htm or .html to the end; then click Save. And, of course, transfer it to your Web site.

Before you begin any Web page or Web site project, create a folder to house all elements of it. Have one folder for each Web site. For each site, also make another folder called Raw Graphics, or such, in which to place your artwork. By keeping the pieces of art, you'll be able to change the art later. Using folders and saving elements make life much easier when it's time to edit your pages.

Adding elements

A Web page can be straight text, or full of charts, tables, multimedia, and graphics. It can contain simple text links, or it can have any object act as a link (which is called a button). Once you have your Web page created and your text input, you can jazz it up; after all, who wants a humdrum Web page? The following sections give you pointers on how to bring your Web page to life.

The capability to assign a font to a Web document is rather new and is of questionable value. After all, you have no way of knowing what fonts are on your viewers' computers. HTML is constantly evolving to deal with this type of issue, but for now, the ClarisWorks solution is to translate any fonts you place in your document into the default font for your computer when it saves your page as HTML. If you're using your document within ClarisWorks, design to your heart's content (but with taste) when it comes to using fonts. However, if you're designing solely to save it as a Web page, don't waste your time worrying about fonts.

Font attributes

For the sake of good design, whether you are designing your document for ClarisWorks or for the Web, stick to using bold and italic fonts for emphasizing words. They look classy and translate well into HTML. You can use any attribute listed in the Style menu, but the rest probably won't make it through the translation.

Text alignment translates fine — except justification, which becomes flush left (normal).

Tables

ClarisWorks tables make it through the HTML translation well. You definitely want to use them — not only for the typical reasons mentioned in Chapter 7 and in the spreadsheet chapters, but also for reasons you may have never thought of before. Tables are a main source of placement control on the Web. In Chapter 5, we explain how to use tabs in word-processing. On the Web, you get to forget about all that stuff and use tables instead. Suppose you want a stair-step effect — the first line of text at the left, the next line farther right, the third even farther right. Normally, tabs would do the job. However, on the Web, each tab just translates into a single space. Thus, to achieve the same result, create a table and place your text in the boxes to match the positioning you want. Then, turn off all the borders so the text looks more natural. ClarisWorks spreadsheets can't contain graphics, though, so this layout method won't work with graphic elements. See Chapter 7 for more about tables.

 If you already created your text table with tabs, just click the text-to-table conversion button to make an instant table. Because tables are actually spreadsheets, this text becomes a spreadsheet and you enter the spreadsheet environment when you double-click it to make adjustments to your table.

Bulleted or numbered lists

One of the most effective ways to present information is to use a bulleted or numbered list. To create a list, enter at least some of the list's contents, pressing the Return key after each line. Then select one of the list styles from the Style pop-up menu below the button bar. You can also use the Stylesheet to define your own. After the style is applied, you can continue to add to your list by placing your cursor at the end of the last character in the list and pressing Return to carry the style down to the next line (as in any word-processing document). See Chapter 8 for more on lists. All list styles translate perfectly and look great on the Web.

Images

Images placed as objects (floating frames) are not translated to HTML. Place your graphics inline with the text to be included in translation to the Web page. Most image formats are supported by ClarisWorks. In other words, you can place a picture saved as PICT, TIFF, or EPS, and ClarisWorks calls its file translators into action to make the picture work in the document. The Web requires that images be one of two specific formats: GIF or JPEG. As you create your page, graphics remain in their original formats or the formats to which ClarisWorks translated them. When you save your page as HTML, ClarisWorks translates the images into the required GIF or JPEG. For more on inserting graphics, see Chapters 7 and 12.

ClarisWorks translates all the images you place on your page, whether inserted, pasted, or created, into separate graphic files when you save your page as HTML. ClarisWorks names these graphics sequentially: html1.gif, html2.gif, and so on. This is where having a separate folder for your page comes into play. You definitely want all of these files to be kept together with your page, or the images will not be found and used when viewed on the Web.

QuickTime videos — movies

You can insert a QuickTime Movie (.mov files in Windows) just as you insert any other graphic. It looks just like a graphic, displaying the first frame of the video, but has a small filmstrip icon in the lower-left corner. Clicking that icon brings up its control strip. You should recognize the standard-style video controls from VCRs and tape recorders. The controls work the same too. Click outside the video area and the controls disappear. Windows users can also insert Microsoft Video (.AVI) files.

Other page elements

Table 24-1 shows you how common word-processing page elements translate to HTML and end up looking on the Web.

Table 24-1	Effects of HTML Translation
Before Translation	**After Translation (in HTML)**
Inline frames	Remain in the correct place. Spreadsheet frames become HTML tables.
Text frames as objects (floating)	Totally ignored
Drawings/paint frames (floating)	Move to the closest side margin
Soft return or column break	Line break , which begins a new line without space between
Soft hyphen	Totally ignored
Header or footer	Headers show at the start, footers at the very end — both with a horizontal rule to separate them from the rest of the page. Only the first section's header and footer are recognized. The others are ignored.
Footnotes/endnotes	Become numbered end notes
Page and section breaks	Become horizontal lines
Auto-enter date/time	The time that the document was saved
Footnote indicator	Becomes a link to the endnote and is turned into a superscript number in parentheses
Auto-enter page number	Doesn't work — numbers just become generic number sign (#)

Don't use such special characters as <, >, &, ;, and / on your page. These characters are part of HTML code.

You can learn — and affect — how ClarisWorks translates your documents into HTML by clicking the HTML-translation preferences button.

Adding a background

Backgrounds do a lot for a Web page. You can select a color for your background or use a graphic.

To use a color for your background:

1. **Click the HTML-translation preferences button.**

2. **Choose Export Preferences (Basic) from the pop-up menu.**

3. **Select a color from the pop-up menu labeled Color.**

To use a graphic for your background:

1. Click the HTML-translation preferences button.

2. Select Export Preferences (Basic) from the pop-up menu.

3. Click Set Background Image.

This brings up an Open window and takes you directly to the ClarisWorks Library image. Select an image from this library or navigate to your own graphic.

Backgrounds don't show up in the document; they appear only in Preview. To get an idea of how your page looks on the Web, click the Preview button.

To remove a background, return to HTML-translation preferences as in Steps 1 and 2 above; then select None from the pop-up menu.

Creating links

Links can take your readers to another location on the Web, to another place within the document they are already in, or to another page within your site. You can assign text as the link, or have an object do the job. Objects that are links are called buttons. Whether you link from text or objects, the method is the same. (ClarisWorks also lets you make links to other documents, but these links aren't appropriate on the Web because your regular documents are on your hard drive, not at the Web site.)

Linking to a URL

The easiest way to create your links is with buttons. If you don't want to use buttons, go to the section "Using the links palette to create links," later in the chapter. To create a link using a button:

1. Select the object or text that will be your link, as in Figure 24-1.

2. Click the new URL link button on the default (or Internet) button bar.

The new URL link window pops up. If your link is text, your selected text is automatically entered as the link's name. Change it if you want. If your link is a graphic, enter a name for the link.

3. Enter the URL to link to.

Click in the URL field and type your destination. To link to a location on the Web, enter the address, or *URL*, for that location. (URL stands for *Uniform Resource Locator*.) Your selected text becomes underlined, which tells your readers that this is a link. The Links dialog box, shown in Figure 24-2, automatically pops up, showing the links you have created for that document. That's it. You have a link.

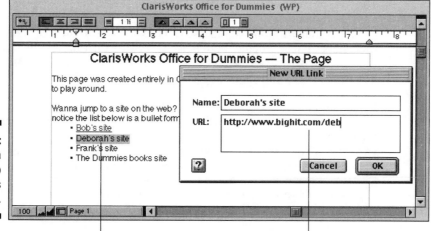

Figure 24-1:
Creating a
URL link to
Deborah's
Web site.

Select the text you want to link.   Enter the Web address (URL).

Figure 24-2:
The links
dialog box.

 From a hard drive, ClarisWorks always attempts to connect to a link if it's
live. For the purposes of ClarisWorks, a live link is a Web address that you
want treated as a link rather than as editable text. If the link is live, Claris-
Works calls up your browser — launching it if it isn't already running — and
takes you directly to that location. For a link to act as a link rather than as
text, though, the live links feature must be turned on for that link. If this
feature is not on, click the button to turn it on. You know a link is live when
your cursor turns to a hand and globe when over the link.

 To edit the words in the link, click the Live Links button to turn off document linking. Otherwise, clicking those words brings up the Web site — or at
least tries to. *Note:* Editing the words that link is different from editing the
link, which is the destination to which your reader jumps.

Tip: You don't have to be on the Web to use links. You can also link to another document in the word-processing environment. First select the text or object that you want to link. Next, click the New Document Link button; then click Choose Document. Finally, select the destination document from the Open (Open/Save) dialog box. The text that you selected changes into a link to the document you chose.

Linking to another part of your document is a bit different. First, you need to define the destination, which ClarisWorks calls *book marking.* Then you create the link and tell it to link to the bookmark. Again, we show you the easiest way to create links — with buttons. To use the palette instead, see the next section, "Using the links palette to create links."

1. **Select the object or text your link will jump to.**

 2. **Click the New Book Mark button on the default (or Internet) button bar.**

The New Book Mark window pops up. You can see this window, along with the selected text the bookmark refers to, in Figure 24-3.

3. **Enter a name for this bookmark.**

If your bookmark is text, your selected text appears as the name. Change it if you want. In Figure 24-3, we call our bookmark `Top of Page` so we know where it jumps to.

Figure 24-3:
A book-mark at the top, named to reflect its location, not text.

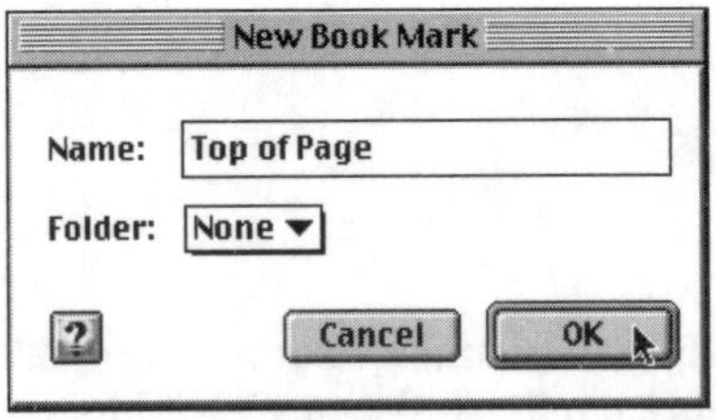

```
┌─────────── New Book Mark ───────────┐
│                                      │
│  Name:  │ Top of Page            │   │
│                                      │
│  Folder: │ None ▼ │                  │
│                                      │
│  │?│        ( Cancel )   ( OK ▸ )    │
│                                      │
└──────────────────────────────────────┘
```

4. **(Optional) In the Folder pop-up menu, select a folder to store your bookmark in.**

5. **Click OK.**

 If you find that the number of bookmarks within your document is getting out of hand, create folders and store the bookmarks by topic. To create a folder, open the links palette, select Book Mark from the pop-up menu, select New Folder from the palette's Special menu, name the new folder, and then click OK. To move a bookmark into a folder, select the bookmark, select Edit Book Mark, and select the folder from the Folder pop-up.

6. Select the object or text that will be your link.

7. Click the New Document Link button on the default (or Internet) button bar.

The New Document Link window pops up, as in Figure 24-4. (This is the same one as for linking to separate documents. It does double duty.)

Figure 24-4:
Linking to another part of your document.

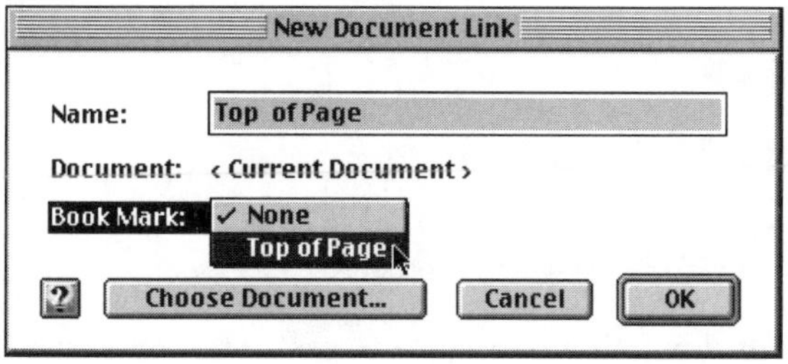

New Document Link

Name: **Top of Page**

Document: ‹ Current Document ›

Book Mark: ✓ None
Top of Page

? Choose Document... Cancel OK

8. Enter a name for this link.

If your link is text, your selected text appears as the name of the button. Change it if you want.

9. Select your destination bookmark from the Book Mark pop-up menu.

10. Click OK.

Using the links palette to create links

For those of you who like to do things the hard way, here's how to use the links palette to create your links:

1. Select the object or text that will be your link.

2. Select Window⇨Show Links Palette or press Shift-⌘-M (Mac) or Shift+Ctrl+M (Windows) to bring up the palette.

3. Select the kind of link you're creating from the pop-up menu at the top.

Figure 24-5 shows a new URL link being created in the links palette.

4. In the Links menu of the Link dialog box, select New.

The words that follow New depend on the type of link being created. In Figure 24-5, the New is New URL Link. The New URL Link window pops up with your selected text as the name. Change the name if you want. Otherwise, the cursor is waiting in the URL field.

5. Enter the URL to link to.

Figure 24-5:
Creating a
link with
the links
palette.

Testing a link

After you create your link, it's a good idea to test it to make sure it takes your readers where you want them to go. Testing is the same for all types of links. To test a link, follow these steps:

1. **If Live Links is not already on, click the Live Links button on the default (or Internet) button bar.**

   You know links are live when your cursor changes to a hand and a globe as you move it over the link.

2. **Click the link.**

   Your link should perform as expected. See the instructions for creating each type of link.

Editing a link

If you find your link doesn't take your readers where you want them to go, or if you change the link's destination, you need to make changes. Editing is the same for all types of links. To edit a link, follow these steps:

1. **Select** W**indow⇨Show Lin**k**s Palette or press Shift-⌘-M (Mac) or Shift+Ctrl+M (Windows) to bring up the palette.**

2. **Select the kind of link you're editing from the pop-up menu at the top.**

3. **In the Links menu of the Links dialog box, select Edit.**

   The words that follow "Edit" depend on the type of link being created. The Edit URL Link window pops up.

4. **Make any changes and click OK, or cancel the action if you decide it's fine as is.**

In the Links palette's menu, selecting Special⇨Sort by Position may make it easier to locate a link you're seeking to edit.

Saving your document as a Web page

As you design your page, save it first as a regular ClarisWorks document. Use the Preview button to preview it in your browser as often as you like. When you're ready, do one last regular save to keep the normal ClarisWorks document safe. Then choose File⇨Save As and select HTML as the type in the pop-up menu. Give your page a short name including the extension ".html" or ".htm" at the end. Be sure to ask the host of your Web site what type of name you should give your pages. Some computers still use the | 8.3 format. (That's 8 characters, followed by a period and three more characters.)

When you save your document as a file type (like HTML), ClarisWorks retains that file type in the document type pop-up list until you either change the type again or restart ClarisWorks. Be careful of this as you save your documents or you may inadvertently overwrite a file. Unless you happen to have the document saved under a different name, an overwritten file is gone. Honest. You have no way to get it back except to completely re-create it.

If you haven't saved to a specific folder, there's a chance you have several versions of the same stuff all over the place. If so, make a new folder, open the original ClarisWorks document, and save as HTML again — this time to the known folder. Use this copy and recycle/trash the rest.

You can change the name of the folder, but don't change filenames.

Creating Web Pages with Claris Home Page Lite

The official name of this software is Claris Home Page Lite, but it's tiring to say the full name. For the rest of the chapter, we just call it Home Page.

Just realize that it's actually the Lite version. The full version does a few more things. The biggest difference is that, with the full version, you can view and edit the actual HTML code. There's upgrade information on your ClarisWorks Office CD.

Home Page is a program designed specifically for creating Web pages. While a full treatment of Home Page is beyond the scope of this book, we can give you enough information to make a good start. For more information, check the on-screen help that comes with it, which is pretty decent. If you come across anything grayed out, that feature is available only in the full version.

As with any document, save it the moment you create it. The first time you save your page, you are prompted to give it a name. This is the name that appears at the top of the Browser window when people visit your site. It is separate from the actual name of your document. The name you use for your actual document must be within the specifications of your Web site host. Check with your ISP to find these conventions. For now, it doesn't matter much; you can rename the file before you transfer it to the Internet.

A new page is plain and gray, like the one in Figure 24-6. (The two dialog boxes shown come up as needed. They are open for this screen shot just to show you.) You can begin by pasting in existing text or by typing your own. Or, if you like, begin with an image. It's up to you.

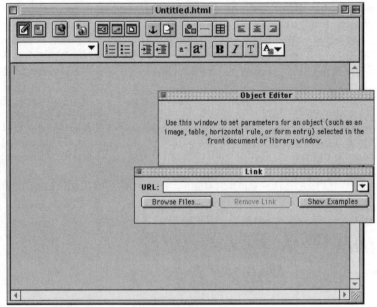

Figure 24-6:
A Web page waiting to happen — with Claris Home Page Lite.

Telling your story with text

The text tool is a default — you don't have a choice of tools. If the cursor is flashing, just begin typing. As with word processing, you can select your text attributes as you go, or you can get your words down first and then go back later and select the text to which you want to apply the attributes. But, unlike word processing, when making a document to publish on the Web, fewer attributes are available to apply. Your basic choices are bold, italic, teletype (which mimics the old computer-style font), and color. Other attributes don't convert well for the Web.

The best way to get your message across in print is to stylize it. In a word-processor, you may be used to being able to change fonts and do almost anything to text. But, unlike word-processing documents that are often designed to be set in stone when they are printed, Web pages are designed to be transported through Cyberspace and to be viewable anywhere. Therefore, HTML documents have their own set of font styles. Home Page provides these preset styles for your convenience.

Paragraph styles

You can select any of these basic paragraph styles from the pop-up menu, shown in Figure 24-7, or from the Format menu. Paragraph styles apply to the entire paragraph. As always on a computer, you have to select something before you can change it, so select your text before applying any style to it.

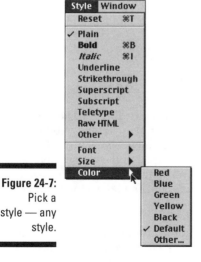

Figure 24-7: Pick a style — any style.

Here are the styles you can use in Claris Home Page:

- **Normal:** This is the default paragraph setting. Selecting it sets your text back to no formatting.

- **Preformatted:** This sets your text to show as monospaced, as opposed to the computer norm of having proportionately spaced characters. Using this style helps your text look the same on your viewer's computer as you set it up to on your own. The use of tables to maintain columns and rows is rapidly taking over.

- **Address:** This sets your text to the traditional style for e-mail addresses on the Web — italics.

- **Headings 1-6:** These headings represent relative text sizes. Heading 1 is the largest font size — the one to use at the top level of your headings. Heading 6 is the smallest font size.

- **Bullet List:** Creates a bullet at the beginning of each line you create when you press Return. Use bullets when there's not a specific order for the information in your list. There's also a button you can click to apply this style.

- **Numbered List:** Creates a new number at the beginning of each line you create when you press Return. You won't see the numbers until you preview in your browser. Instead, you see pound signs in each line. There's also a button you can click to apply this style.

- **Term:** This is another type of list style. It's a mid-sized font with no space between new paragraphs.

- **Definition:** Again, this is another list style. It's a mid-sized font with no space between new paragraphs.

Saying it with pictures

The strength and popularity of the Web stems from its ability to serve graphics and multimedia. Your pages don't stand much chance of being looked at, much less taken seriously, if they don't have visual appeal. Graphics come in all forms on the Web. For example, you can use them to divide pages or turn images into buttons that can take your vistors around your site. It's a cinch to add and work with graphics so take a look and give it a whirl.

Home Page allows you to add any of the major graphics file formats: JPEG or GIF, which are the formats of the Web, and PICT (Mac) or BMP (Windows), which are the standard for their respective platforms. Home Page automatically converts PICTs and BMPs to GIF for you. When you preview your page, if an image doesn't show up, don't panic. You can't see JPEG files while previewing within Home Page, unless you have QuickTime installed. But they do show up in the browser preview.

To insert a graphic, place your cursor where you want the image to end up; then use Insert⇨Image, locate and select the image in the Open (Open/Save) dialog box, and click Open. Mac users can also open their graphics folder and drag the graphic's file right onto the page. It still converts and still lands at the cursor's position.

Movies are among the coolest elements of a Web page and they're just as easy to add as regular graphics. Just select Insert⇨QuickTime movie on a Mac or in Windows; then use the Open dialog box to locate and select the movie. Windows users can also add AVI movies by choosing Insert⇨Plugin.

Copy each graphic to your Web page's folder before you add it to your page. This ensures that it will always be found by your page when it's on the Web.

Editing graphics

Most of Home Page's controls for editing graphics are located in the Object Editor dialog box. Just double-click any graphic to call it up. You can also click to select the image, and then click the Object Editor Tool, but that takes more effort, as does using the menus.

Alternate labels

It's a good idea to give each image an alternate label — words that appear when graphics are turned off or the image can't be found by the browser. They're a nice courtesy and are easy to add. Whenever you double-click an image to open the Object Editor, the cursor awaits you in the Alt label box. Just type a few descriptive words. By the way, programs that read aloud for those who can't see make excellent use of your alternate tags.

Interlacing and transparency

Have you visited a page and waited forever while the image loaded from top to bottom? It takes too long and you have no idea what you're waiting for. Interlaced images are a better alternative.

To have your image come in interlaced, double-click the image to bring up the Object Editor. Click the Set button next to the words Transparency and Interlace. This brings up a window titled by the name of your graphic. Click the Interlace button at the top of this window. As you move your mouse pointer over each button you learn what it does. To make parts of the image invisible, so that the image better fits the look of the page, click the Transparency button, and then use the eye-dropper cursor that is provided to click any parts of the image that you want to be transparent.

Graphics as links

Pictures can do more than add a nice touch to a Web page. They can also act as links to take your visitors anywhere else on your page, in your site, or on the entire Internet. Any image can become a link. Simply enter the URL for that destination in the field marked Default URL; then press Enter. (It's the only text field so it's not hard to find.) When your URL is entered, just close the window. That's it.

Alignment and borders

You also want to align your graphic and adjust its border width. To do so, double-click your image to bring up the Object Editor. Then set the width of the line that shows around your graphic, change the number in the field marked Border. The default is frameless, so the field is blank. A larger number creates a 3-D-frame effect. Alignment controls where the image sits in relation to the field it is in or the line of text it is on. It moves the image up and down, not side to side. To move your image sideways, use the text alignment buttons located at the top of the main window.

Resizing

Resizing is a bit finicky. The key point to know about resizing is that pixels set a definite size for your image, while setting a percentage sizes the image as a percentage of the browser window's size. As a guideline, for a standard 14-inch monitor, 580 to 600 pixels is a safe total width. To adjust the size of a graphic double-click it to bring up the Object Editor; then click the tiny arrow to reveal the sizing controls.

Background colors and images

Choosing Edit➪Document Options brings up the dialog box you need to add your background color or image.

✔ For a solid color, double-click the color where it says Background color, and then pick a color. Then click OK. For Mac users with OS8: When the system's Color Picker comes up, scroll to HTML colors and select your choice of colors from there, which consist of the 216 Web-safe colors.

✔ To use an image, click the Set button next to Background Image; then navigate to your desired image and double-click it, or click Open. Then click OK.

From Edit➪Document Options, you can also control the color of the links on your page.

Tables

 Tables are definitely stronger in Claris Home Page Lite than in ClarisWorks. If you have text on the page already, place your cursor below the text, click the table button, and then select and drag your text into the cells where you want it. If an extra paragraph mark comes in for some reason, just delete it. If you don't have text on your page already, make the table and enter your text. These tables can also hold graphics and are a cinch to resize. To edit a table, double-click its border. An Object Editor comes up. You can also resize the entire table or portions of it by clicking the outside border and dragging.

For something really cool, copy some text that you have set up with tabs to align as a basic table. Paste it into Home Page and — instant Web table!

Linking

 Text that acts as links are always important to include on a Web page. They allow your visitors to get around within your site and to jump to other sites. Graphic links are fun but, sometimes, you want to make navigation options perfectly clear to your guests. To create a text link, select the text to be linked, and then click the Link Editor button at the top of the page. In the dialog box that opens, enter your target URL, and then press Enter on the number pad to close the window. The Show Examples button provides useful address models. Browse Files lets you find and link to another document on your hard drive. But remember, your computer won't be on the Web for the link to find it later.

Previewing

 You can see a quick preview within Home Page or have it launch your browser to show you how it really looks on the Web. Click the Preview button for a quick preview from within Home Page. For a more accurate idea of how your page will look on the Web, you'll want to preview the page in a browser. To see how it looks in your default browser, click the Preview in Browser button. Each browser, and each version of each browser, has its own way of interpreting HTML, so the more browsers that you preview your page in, the better. You can preview you page in any browser that's installed on your hard drive. To do so, save your page and close it. Then drag your page onto the icon, alias, or shortcut of your browser. Keep an alias or shortcut of each browser handy on your desktop for easy access.

Saving your Claris Home Page Web page

When you save your Claris Home Page Lite document, it is automatically saved as an HTML document. Each image should be in your project folder before you add it to your Web page so they should all be in that folder awaiting upload to the Web. All of your images must be transferred to your Web host along with your page or pages. You probably have all you need with Claris Home Page Lite to get your document to the Web. Contact your ISP for the exact method to transfer your Web pages.

Part VII
The Part of Tens

The 5th Wave — By Rich Tennant

"WHY DON'T YOU TAKE THAT OUTSIDE, HUMPTY, AND PLAY WITH IT ON THE WALL?"

In this part . . .

The Part of Tens is a Dummies tradition. They're fun, but don't let that fool you. These lists contain little snippets of wisdom.

Take a look. They're easy, fun, and informative.

Chapter 25

Ten Real-Life Uses for ClarisWorks

● ●

In This Chapter

▶ Making magic

▶ Writing screenplays

▶ Running a raffle

▶ Printmaking

▶ Managing projects

▶ Running sports teams

▶ Running a graphic design business

▶ Creating fundraising calendars and material

▶ Doing public relations

▶ Publishing a book

● ●

*W*e know that ClarisWorks is a serious business tool that does a great deal. But sometimes its uses pop up in places that surprise even us. This chapter is one of our favorites because it can surprise you, make you laugh, and stimulate your imagination.

Make Magic

Magic Bob Weiss wasn't into having to learn how to use his PowerBook. It was old and outdated when he got it, and it didn't even run the latest software. But then Bob got ClarisWorks (Version 2.1!) and Magic Bob's computer was magical. Bob even had it *making* magic — literally. He actually used ClarisWorks to create his own magic effects. For example, he had a special card trick in which he let a volunteer pick a vacation destination — having already predicted the volunteer's choice of destinations. He used the drawing environment to design the cards for this part of the trick. Then he printed these drawings on his inkjet printer. These drawings became part of his illusion when he glued the printout into place and laminated it with his home laminator. Bob invents specialized magic for various companies and products. Between the drawing, painting, and word-processing environments, he creates quite a bit of his magical apparatus, most of which we can't even begin to describe — and wouldn't be allowed to because it's a secret. Oh yeah, on a more down-to-earth level, he used the drawing environment to fully produce the newsletter for the Los Angeles chapter of the magic club for which he serves as president, to create signs for the magic shows he runs, and to do his correspondence and invoices (on his custom letterhead).

Write Screenplays

You don't need an expensive script-writing program to write a great screenplay. Attorney-turned-writer Mark Treitel had already spent more than $200 on dedicated commercial programs when he was given ClarisWorks. Using the word processor, he realized its style control was all he ever needed or is likely to need, and he kicked himself for spending all that money. (Remember, he's a struggling writer.) With a few tweaks to the stylesheet, he has formatted scripts for features, TV sitcoms, and dramas, as well as animation. Plus, he uses the Mac's text-to-speech function to hear his dialog read back to him. Seinfeld has never sounded so funny as when spoken by *Zarvo,* the Mac's voice for speech.

Run a Raffle

Professional database developer, Leonard Horthy did the Los Angeles Macintosh Group a great favor when he created a database to manage their entire giant raffle. As prizes are donated, they are entered into the database and automatically assigned a number, which is marked on the prize. As prizes are won, a button puts the operator in find mode to enter the prize number and bring up the record for that prize. All the raffle operator needs to do is enter the winner's name. At the end of each hourly drawing, the operator simply hits the button that runs Leonard's macro, switching to a nicely designed layout and putting the database into slide show mode. Because drawings are frequent, the database is copied to another machine so it can continue to run as new prizes are drawn.

Printmaking

LA-based artist Gayle Gale calls ClarisWorks "a printmaker's dream." She uses the painting environment to produce her full print line, from her wearable art to fine art that hangs in galleries. For example, after she paints an image, she reduces it down to postage-stamp size, places it into the drawing environment, and prints directly on sticker paper to create her line of stickers. By printing on transfer paper, she creates iron-on art to integrate into all sorts of wearable art, including purses. By printing on high-gloss paper, she creates frameable prints. With card stock, she makes greeting cards. But that's just the start. Gayle tries to print on anything. She has an entire line of salable art — all created in ClarisWorks.

Manage a Project

At Internet Outfitters, an Internet solutions firm in Santa Monica, California, all project management is done in ClarisWorks. The database environment is the central focus. Each new job is entered and each task is assigned a number. Several layouts are then accessed in which employees do time management; maintain a contact list; and provide detailed task reports, status check lists, and a deliverables checklist. Correspondence is, of course, done in the word-processing environment.

Run Sports Teams

Bob LeVitus (yes, one of your authors) always finds time for his kids and their sports teams. ClarisWorks is part of these teams all the way. The soccer team's roster is in a database, allowing Bob to use mail merge to generate awards, certificates, and mailings. Of course, the Certificate Assistant helps with those certificates, as do the clip art Libraries. (Bob's a writer, not an artist.) The spreadsheet environment is home to the scheduling, stats tracking, and substitution grid.

Run a Graphics Design Business

Sharon Rubin, art director, graphic designer, and partner for Essanee Unlimited, Inc., uses ClarisWorks in several ways. She uses the word-processing capabilities to prepare all the copy for the video boxes and all ancillary marketing collateral that she designs for a major video distributor. As a professional painter, she also uses ClarisWorks to maintain her art catalog, track exhibitions, and create invoices. And, of course, she uses ClarisWorks for her correspondence.

Create Fundraising Calendars and Materials

Donna Shadovitz turns to ClarisWorks for many things when her freelance editing lands her in full document-creation jobs. Although much of what she does is writing, she does it within the drawing environment. For example, she recently did the ads for a fund-raising calendar — the kind that has large local ads at the top and the month at the bottom. Each ad was done as a new drawing document with several text blocks and graphics freely placed. Later, the pieces were all compiled. By the way, she also does her own business cards in the drawing environment.

Do Public Relations

One famous restaurant was frustrated by having to use several different programs to do their PR — until they discovered ClarisWorks. They couldn't believe one inexpensive program could do everthing when so much was already invested in software that clashed and didn't do the job. ClarisWorks pulled it off, though. Clients' special requests are maintained in a database. Those who wish to be contacted are faxed a special flyer, merged into the drawing-based document, when their favorite foods are in season. The database is searched by zip code to invite local customers to events or offer specials. Other software is used to do the faxing, but macros automate the process, making the task an easy one.

Publish a Book

Publishing a cookbook is another great fundraiser. Collecting recipes in the ClarisWorks database is easy. You can collect all types of recipes in one database, and then search and find only those you want in any particular book and sort them in the order in which they should appear. To handle the layout, create another layout in the database or export the text into a word-processing document. The word-processing environment can handle different left and right pages, intelligent page numbering, graphics stylishly placed, and so on.

Chapter 26

Ten Ways ClarisWorks Tries to Drive You Crazy, and How to Stay Sane

● ●

In This Chapter

▶ My menus changed

▶ My button's gone

▶ My computer keeps changing programs

▶ My text has all these *&%#$! symbols

▶ My whole line's formatting changed

▶ My printer keeps printing a blank page

▶ My text won't line up

▶ My letters are all squished together

▶ My two-page spreadsheet prints on 20 pages

▶ My fields won't slide on mailing labels

● ●

*I*n general, ClarisWorks is an easy program to use. However, at times something just seems crazy and you don't have time to joke around. We put together a list of some more frustrating situations so you can get on your merry way.

Arrgh! What Happened to the Menus?

Ah . . . the anguished cry of a new ClarisWorks user. Just when you think you have a handle on where the commands are, the menus change. Menus morph when the blue ranger (or you) switches environments, usually by clicking a frame or draw object.

To morph back, click the body of your document (sometimes you have to click twice) to return to the main environment, or inside the frame (sometimes twice) to get back to the frame's functions and menus.

Where Did My Button Go!?

A minute ago, you saw the button you needed and now it's gone or it's moved. No, it's not time to get your eyes checked — just time to check your cursor. Like the menus, buttons come and go as you change functions. Why have a bloated menu four rows long full of stuff you don't need? Follow the preceding advice and you'll be fine.

Some Other Darned Program Won't Leave Me Alone!

You've entered your text and formatted it perfectly, but you want to change a few words. All you want is to place your text cursor, but instead Netscape keeps popping up. Netscape (or whatever browser you've chosen) isn't feeling unloved and making a play for your attention. You're asking for it! That text is a link and by clicking it, you're calling up the Web page. Or you're linked to another program and keep calling it to the front. The solution is to turn off Live Links so the text acts like plain text again. A button in the default button bar is just waiting to help. (Links are a new feature and it got us a few times, too.)

What Are All These *&%#$! Symbols in My Text?

So you've discovered the normally invisible formatting characters: dots between words, bent arrows at the ends of paragraphs, and the like. They exist to help you see what you're doing, but sometimes they interfere with your thoughts. Sanity is just a click away, in the default button bar, looking like the funny *P* your teachers put on your papers to tell you to begin a new paragraph. Or take the long route by choosing Edit⇨Preferences, selecting Text in the pop-up menu, and unchecking Show Invisibles. Mac users can also press ⌘-; (semicolon) — remember the key with the most dots controls the dots.

My Whole Line's Formatting Changed

You deleted a few words or lines and now an entire paragraph has gone berserk. Suddenly, your once-normal words are centered, huge, or red, eh? Actually, you deleted more than words or numbers. You deleted the invisible paragraph symbol that told the paragraph above how to look. With that symbol gone, the paragraph took on the formatting of the next paragraph symbol it found. The immediate solution is to hit the Undo button — the one picturing a document with an arrow pointing backward. (You may also choose Edit⇨Undo, or click ⌘-Z or Ctrl+Z.) The moral of this story is to watch carefully what you select. If you see highlighting, something is being selected, even if it is invisible. You may want to turn on your invisibles while you work. (See "What Are All These *&%#$! Symbols in My Text?" for more on invisibles.)

My Printer Keeps Printing a Blank Page

You've written a one-page letter in a word-processing document, but your printer keeps printing an extra blank page. Those sneaky little invisibles are at it again — but you unwittingly put them up to it! You've actually created that second page yourself — and it isn't blank. It's just that everything you typed is invisible! Place your I-beam cursor at the end of your text and drag downward. See all those invisible characters you're highlighting? Delete them and you'll be back to one page. To make turning those little minxes visible easier, see "What Are All These *&%#$! Symbols in My Text?" earlier in this chapter.

My Text Won't Line Up

You just spent *hours* typing to create a form you need *now,* and you can't get the text to line up evenly. You have probably gone and gotten spacey on us — using the spacebar to line up your columns. The problem is that spaces and letters are intelligently (proportionately) spaced so that no two lines are alike (unless they are 100 percent identical). The only way to ensure that things line up exactly is to use tabs. See Chapter 5 for how to add tab stops.

My Letters Are All Squished Together

Suddenly, all the characters on your screen are almost on top of each other and you can barely read anything. We bet you've turned on Fractional Character Widths. This feature allows characters to print most perfectly (except on the old dot matrix machines). Your screen's image (resolution) isn't as fine as the printer's though, so the letters all pile up. The solution is easy: choose Edit⇨Preferences, select Text in the pop-up menu, and uncheck Fractional Character Widths. If you really like the printed effect, turn on Fractional Character Widths just before printing. By the way, not all monitors squish the letters.

My Two-Page Spreadsheet Prints on 20 Pages

Is your two-page spreadsheet printing in little chunks spread over about 20 pages? One of two things has happened: Either you didn't set a print range, or you have extra page breaks telling ClarisWorks that you want 20 itty-bitty pages.

Try these two solutions: Select only the cells that you want to print and then choose Options⇨Set Print Range. The range you selected shows in the range box. Click OK. To remove unwanted page breaks, choose Options⇨Remove All Breaks. You can always add some back, if you like.

My Fields Won't Slide on Mailing Labels

Having the fields slide over to fill empty space when printing mailing labels from a database is a great feature, but getting it to work right is very, very tricky.

Solution: Make sure that the fields on your layout meet all three of the following conditions:

- ✔ A field can't slide left toward another field that is even slightly shorter than itself. A field can't slide up toward another field that is even slightly narrower than itself. Fields only slide toward other fields that are the same size or larger than they are.

- ✔ Fields need to be precisely aligned at their top edges to slide left and at their left edges to slide up.

- ✔ Fields can't touch. Fields that touch won't slide.

Appendix

Buttoning Up

• •

*B*utton bars are powerful and convenient in their natural state, but they can be even more powerful when you customize them. By now we figure you're well versed in ClarisWorks. You know what it does. You know what you want it to do. And you're ready to tweak your button bars and even add your own buttons. This Appendix shows you how to customize your ClarisWorks environment.

Editing Button Bars

One of these days, you may find yourself wanting a button that doesn't appear on the default button bars that come with the environments in ClarisWorks. Maybe not today, maybe not tomorrow, but soon, and for the rest of your life. When this happens, you'll know that you have ClarisWorks in your blood. Here's looking at you, kid. To edit a button bar, follow these steps:

1. **To the left of the buttons on the bar is a pop-up button marked with a down-pointing arrow. Click it and choose Edit Button Bars.**

   Your button bar is listed.

2. **Click the one to edit and click Modify, or just double-click the one to edit.**

   The bar you choose appears at the top of your screen as the active bar and the Edit Button Bar window opens. On the left is a box containing all the buttons currently on your bar.

3. **Select the category you want to take buttons from.**

4. **Double-click the button to be added.**

   Keep repeating Steps 3 and 4 until you get what you want.

5. **When you finish, click OK and Done.**

To delete a bar, choose Edit Button Bars, select the one you want to remove, and then click Delete.

Creating a new bar is like editing an existing one, so follow the steps outlined above for editing a button bar. Just select New Button Bar instead of Edit Button Bar. Begin by entering a name for your new bar. A new empty bar appears at the top of your screen. Any buttons you add appears there. Continue until it's complete, and then click OK and Done.

Creating New Buttons

To add a new button, follow these steps:

1. **Select New Button from the Button bar selection list.**

   A dialog box appears, giving you a choice of the kinds of buttons to add. Select your type from the pop-up list.

2. **Name your new button.**

3. **Give the button a description so you can remember it much later.**

4. **For each type of button, you do something different to add it. Here's what each does and how to add it:**

   • *Play a macro you've recorded:* For this one, you need to record the macro first. All macros appear in a pop-up list. Select one.

   • *Open a document:* Click Select Document and navigate until you reach the one to have open.

   • *Launch an application:* Same as opening a document, except you select a program instead.

   • *Open a URL:* Enter the URL in the field that appears.

   • *Execute a script (Mac only):* Same as opening a document, except you select a script instead.

4. **Check off the environments you want this new button to show in.**

5. **Click the blank button by Edit Icon now if you want.**

   If you don't edit the button now, it appears as a plain gray button. Blank buttons aren't much help. However, you also get to give it a description, which shows in the information bar when you mouse over it.

6. **Click OK.**

You can move any button's position by pressing ⌘-Option (Mac) or Ctrl+Alt (Windows) as you drag the button.

Creating an Icon

Click the blank button by Edit Icon to create or edit an icon. Use this button editor as you would any painting program. See Chapter 10 for more information on painting. Basically, you click Color to select a color, and then use your pointer to click in any square you want to apply that color to. Click OK when you finish.

You can use the Paste command to paste a design that's already been created and copied. You can even copy and paste a few character of text.

To go back to a button to edit it later, select Edit button. Only your own buttons may be edited. It isn't possible to edit a button made by Claris.

Index

• A •

About ClarisWorks,
    Windows, 41
About help, Mac, 38
Accept button, spreadsheet
    data entry, 212
access providers, Internet,
    297–298
actions, undoing last, 31, 56, 335
Add Column button, 90
Address Envelope Assistant, 45,
    188
aliases, Macintosh, 20
align on tabs, 75
align tab, table creation, 109
alignments, baseline, 61
Alt key (Windows)
    command conventions used in
        book, 3
    tool modifiers, 152
anchor points
    adding/deleting, 172
    shape objects, 171
    smoothing, 172–173
Application menu,
    Macintosh, 19
Arc Info dialog box, 173
arc tool, 137, 152
arcs, reshaping, 173
area charts, 232
arrow heads, line options, 142
arrow pointer tool, 27, 104
Assistants
    accessing, 44
    Address Envelope, 188
    described, 15, 44–45
    Envelope, 188
    Help menu, 45
    Mac help, 39
    Make Table, 109–111
    Presentation, 200
    stationery listing, 43
Assistants button bar, 25
attributes, text formatting,
    65–66

Autogrid, 164, 177–178
AutoSum button, spreadsheet
    calculations, 239–240
AVERAGE function, 245
Avery labels, printing, 283–286

• B •

background colors, database
    layouts, 276
backgrounds
    Claris Home Page Lite, 324
    Web publishing, 313–314
Backspace key, text deletion, 55
balloon help, buttons, 26
bar charts, 232
baseline alignment
    Equation Editor formula, 61
    graphics, 105–106
Basic style
    application methods, 69–70
    described, 68
    naming conventions, 69
bezigon tool, 138, 165
bindings, document gutters, 88
blocking text, described, 73
bold text, 65
book publishing, ClarisWorks
    use, 332
Bookmark menu, help topics, 41
bookmarks
    database modes, 252
    database navigation, 255
    folder organization, 316
    help system, 41
    Netscape Navigator, 307
    Web publishing links, 316
    Web sites, 307
borders
    frames, 105
    graphics, 324
    painting, 138–139
    selection box, 210
    spreadsheet cells, 226

browse mode, databases, 252
browsers
    default home page, 299
    launching, 299
    licensing agreements, 299
    live links, 315
    Netscape Navigator, 305–307
    previewing pages before
        publishing, 325
    switching between, 301
    testing links, 318
    URL access methods, 299–302
Brush Editor dialog box,
    152–153
brush tool, 148
Bullet style, bulleted lists, 78
bulleted lists
    hanging indents, 77–78
    outlines format, 123
    Web publishing, 312
button bars
    Assistants, 25
    button addition, 338
    button positioning, 338
    chart buttons, 233–234
    Default, 25
    editing, 337–338
    Internet, 25
    Internet customization,
        302–305
    moving on-screen, 25
    point size selections, 67
    text alignment, 71
buttons
    balloon help, 26
    creating, 338
    custom Internet, 303–305
    described, 16
    hiding/displaying, 26, 334
    icon selections, 339
    interface, 25–26
    positioning, 338
    toggling, 24
    ToolTips, 26

• C •

calculation fields, database design, 274
Cancel button, spreadsheet data entry, 212
captions, tables, 116
cell blocks, selecting, 113
cell formatting
  colors, 221–222
  default font, 220
  saving as style, 222
  text styles, 220
  text wrap, 220–221
cells
  absolute versus relative references, 245–246
  AutoSum calculations, 240
  borders, 226
  content editing, 214
  data sorting, 222–224
  described, 210
  fill down, 215
  fill right, 215
  fill special, 215
  fill techniques, 215–216
  formula display, 227
  formula naming conventions, 242–244
  formula references, 242
  moving data between, 214
  print range settings, 229–230
  range selection, 211, 214
  selecting, 113
  selection techniques, 210–211
  single cell selection, 210, 214
center alignment, described, 71
center-aligned tabs, 75
Change All button, find/replace search cautions, 98
characters
  curly versus smart quotes, 64
  filled tabs, 76–77
  Fractional Character Widths, 336
  fractional widths, 64
  invisible formatting, 64, 79, 334
Chart Options dialog box, 231–236

charts
  3-dimensional, 235
  color editing, 234, 236
  creating, 117–118, 233–234
  deleting, 238
  document types, 238
  double-click shortcuts, 235–236
  drop shadows, 235
  grids, 235
  horizontal display, 235
  information updating, 236–237
  labels, 233
  line widths, 236
  modifications, 234–238
  moving, 238
  picture insertion, 237–238
  resizing, 238
  titles, 233
  types, 231–233
check box fields, database design, 273
check list format, outlines, 124
Claris Emailer Lite, 302
Claris Home Page Lite, 16
  background colors/ images, 324
  graphic borders, 324
  graphical links, 324
  image alignment, 324
  image insertion, 322–324
  image labels, 323
  image sizing, 324
  included features, 319–320
  interlaced images, 323
  link creation, 325
  paragraph styles, 321–322
  previewing before publishing, 325
  QuickTime movies, 323
  saving as HTML file, 326
  supported graphics formats, 322–323
  table insertion, 325
  text entry, 321
  transparent images, 323
  upgrade information, 320
ClarisWorks
  closing, 36
  cross-platform functionality, 2

  environments, 9–15
  functionality, 1
  Internet connectivity, 16
  opening a document on startup, 20
  seamless integrated, 10
  starting, 17–18
  uses, 329–332
  version information, 38, 41
ClarisWorks Assistants.
  See also Assistants
  Mac, 39
  Windows, 41
ClarisWorks DR Options stationery, 34
ClarisWorks Libraries, 105, 183–184
ClarisWorks Stationery folder, 34
clicking, described, 54
clip art, ClarisWorks Libraries, 183–184
Clipboard
  charts, copying/pasting, 117
  graphics, copying/pasting, 182
  images, copying/pasting, 104–105
  objects, copying/pasting, 107
  pictogram chart picture insertion, 237–238
  shapes, copying/pasting, 167–168
  spreadsheet cells, cutting/ copying/pasting, 214
  text, cutting/copying/pasting, 57–59
  textures, copying/pasting, 145
colors
  cell formatting, 221–222
  chart modifications, 234, 236
  Claris Home Page Lite, 324
  database layout, 276
  font, 67
  paint selections, 139–140
  Web page backgrounds, 313–314
columns, 90–92
  AutoSum calculations, 240
  described, 210
  headings, 227

hiding/showing row headings, 115–116
hyphenations, 101
inserting, 224–225
locking/unlocking titles, 228
print range settings, 229–230
resizing, 225–226
row height/width settings, 114–115
selecting, 113
selection techniques, 212
Columns dialog box, 91–92
Command (Cmd) key, Mac
keyboard shortcut conventions used in book, 3
tool modifiers, 152
commands
Arrange⇨Align Bottom, 179
Arrange⇨Align Centers Horizontally, 179
Arrange⇨Align Centers Vertically, 179
Arrange⇨Align Left, 179
Arrange⇨Align Right, 179
Arrange⇨Align To Grid (Cmd/Ctrl+K), 178
Arrange⇨Align Top, 179
Arrange⇨Flip Horizontally, 174
Arrange⇨Flip Vertically, 174
Arrange⇨Free Rotate, 179
Arrange⇨Group (Cmd/Ctrl+G), 179
Arrange⇨Lock, 181
Arrange⇨Move Backward, 178
Arrange⇨Move Forward, 178
Arrange⇨Move To Back, 178, 276
Arrange⇨Move To Front, 178
Arrange⇨Reshape (Cmd/Ctrl+R), 171, 180
Arrange⇨Rotate 90 degrees, 179
Arrange⇨Scale By Percent, 170
Arrange⇨Ungroup, 179
Bookmarks⇨Edit Bookmarks, 41
Calculate⇨Fill Down, 215
Calculate⇨Fill Right, 215

Calculate⇨Fill Special, 215–216
Calculate⇨Insert Cells (Shift+Cmd/Ctrl+I), 224
Calculate⇨Move, 214
Calculate⇨Sort, 222
Calculate⇨Sort⇨Direction, 224
Calculate⇨Sort⇨Order Keys, 223
Calculate⇨Sort⇨Range, 223
conventions used in book, 2–3
Edit⇨Chart Options⇨ 3-dimensional, 235
Edit⇨Chart Options⇨Color, 234
Edit⇨Chart Options⇨ Horizontal, 235
Edit⇨Chart Options⇨Scale multiple, 235
Edit⇨Chart Options⇨Shadow, 235
Edit⇨Chart Options⇨ Square grid, 235
Edit⇨Chart Options⇨Tilt, 235
Edit⇨Clear, 86, 150, 167
Edit⇨Copy (Cmd/Ctrl+C), 57, 104, 167
Edit⇨Cut (Cmd/Ctrl+X), 57, 107, 167
Edit⇨Document Options, Home Page, 324
Edit⇨Duplicate (Cmd/Ctrl+D), 168
Edit⇨Duplicate Record (Cmd/Ctrl+D), 253
Edit⇨Insert Date, 85
Edit⇨Insert Equation, 60
Edit⇨Insert Page #, 85
Edit⇨Insert Time, 85
Edit⇨New Record (Cmd/Ctrl+R), 252
Edit⇨New Request (Cmd/Ctrl+R), 261
Edit⇨Paste (Cmd/Ctrl+V), 58, 105, 167
Edit⇨Preferences, 63, 79, 145, 175, 213
Edit⇨Select All, 73, 81
Edit⇨Smooth (Cmd/Ctrl+( ), 173
Edit⇨Undo (Cmd/Ctrl+Z), 56, 335

Edit⇨Undo Move, 113
Edit⇨Unsmooth (Cmd/Ctrl+)), 173
Edit⇨Writing Tool, Mac, 64
Edit⇨Writing Tools⇨ Auto-Hyphenate, 101
Edit⇨Writing Tools⇨ Check Document Spelling (Cmd/Ctrl+=), 93
Edit⇨Writing Tools⇨Check Selection Spelling, 94
Edit⇨Writing Tools⇨Edit Hyphenation Dictionary, Mac, 101
Edit⇨Writing Tools⇨ Select Dictionaries, Windows, 101
Edit⇨Writing Tools⇨ Thesaurus (Shift+ Cmd/Ctrl+Z), 100
File⇨Document Summary, 36
File⇨Exit (Ctrl+Q), Windows, 36
File⇨Export Styles, 70
File⇨Import Styles, 70
File⇨Insert, 105, 182, 202, 253, 256
File⇨Library, 105
File⇨Library⇨New, 184
File⇨Mail Merge, 291
File⇨New, 19
File⇨Open, 21
File⇨Page Setup, Mac, 92, 186
File⇨Print (Cmd/Ctrl+P), 34, 41
File⇨Print Setup, Windows, 92, 186
File⇨Quit (Cmd-Q), Mac, 36
File⇨Revert, 31, 136
File⇨Save (Cmd/Ctrl+S), 32
File⇨Save As, 310, 319
Find (Cmd/Ctrl+F), 41, 96
Find Again (Cmd/Ctrl+E), 97
Format⇨Alignment⇨Wrap, 221
Format⇨Borders, 226
Format⇨Column Width, 114, 226
Format⇨Copy Ruler (Shift+Cmd/Ctrl+C), 81
Format⇨Descent, 61, 105

(continued)

commands *(continued)*
Format⇨Document, 86, 88, 189, 229
Format⇨Insert Break, 84
Format⇨Insert Footer, 228
Format⇨Insert Footnote (Shift+Cmd/Ctrl+F), 88
Format⇨Insert Header, 228
Format⇨Insert Section Breaks, 86
Format⇨Number (Shift+Cmd/Ctrl+N), 217
Format⇨Number⇨Commas, 219
Format⇨Number⇨Negatives in ( ), 219
Format⇨Number⇨Precision, 219
Format⇨Paragraphs, 80
Format⇨Row Height, 114, 226
Format⇨Rulers, 150
Format⇨Scale by Percent, 106
Format⇨Section, 86–87, 91
Format⇨Tab, 76
Help⇨ClarisWorks Assistants, 88
Insert⇨Footer, 86
Insert⇨Header, 86
Insert⇨Images, 323
Layout⇨Browse (Shift+Cmd/Ctrl+B), 252
Layout⇨Define Fields, 276
Layout⇨Edit Layouts, 286
Layout⇨Find (Shift+Cmd/Ctrl+F), 260
Layout⇨Insert Fields, 276
Layout⇨Insert Part, 277
Layout⇨Layout (Shift+Cmd/Ctrl+L), 274
Layout⇨List (Shift+Cmd/Ctrl+I), 252
Match Records, 262
Object⇨Size, 174
Options⇨Add Page Break, 229
Options⇨Brush Shape, 152
Options⇨Default Font, 220
Options⇨Display, 115
Options⇨Edit Master Page, 201
Options⇨Frame Links, 191

Options⇨Gradients, 143
Options⇨Hide Graphics Grid, 164
Options⇨Lock Title Position, 228
Options⇨Make Chart (Cmd/Ctrl+M), 234
Options⇨Object Size, 171
Options⇨Paint Mode, 147
Options⇨Patterns, 142
Options⇨Remove All Breaks, 229
Options⇨Remove Page Break, 229
Options⇨Set Print Range, 229
Options⇨Spray Can, 153
Options⇨Text Wrap, 106, 194
Options⇨Textures, 144
Options⇨Turn Autogrid Off/On (Cmd/Ctrl+Y), 164, 177
Organize⇨Hide Unselected, 259
Organize⇨Show All Records (Shift+Cmd/Ctrl+A), 263
Organize⇨Sort Records, 257–259
Outline⇨Move Left (Shift+Cmd/Ctrl+L), 120
Outline⇨Move Right (Shift+Cmd/Ctrl+R), 120
Outline⇨New Topic Left (Cmd/Ctrl+L), 120
Outline⇨New Topic Right (Cmd/Ctrl+R), 120
Page Setup, 31
Print Setup, 31
Revert, 30
Set Default Printer (Cmd-L), Mac, 35
Stack Windows, Mac, 24
Style⇨Plain Text, 66
Tile Windows, Mac, 24
Transform⇨Blend, 161
Transform⇨Darker, 162
Transform⇨Distort, 157
Transform⇨Fill, 161
Transform⇨Flip Horizontal, 159
Transform⇨Flip Vertical, 159
Transform⇨Free Rotate, 160

Transform⇨Invert, 161
Transform⇨Lighter, 162
Transform⇨Perspective, 156
Transform⇨Pick Up, 161
Transform⇨Resize, 157
Transform⇨Rotate, 160
Transform⇨Scale by Percent, 158
Transform⇨Shear, 157
Transform⇨Tint, 161
Undo, 31
Window⇨Bookmarks, Navigator, 307
Window⇨Open Frame, 196, 229, 238
Window⇨Page View (Shift+Cmd/Ctrl+P), 165, 186, 201
Window⇨Show Links Palette (Shift+Cmd/Ctrl+M), 317
Window⇨Show Rulers (Shift+Cmd/Ctrl+U), 70, 165, 190
Window⇨Show Stylesheet (Shift+Cmd/Ctrl+W), 68, 82, 124
Window⇨Show Tools (Shift+Cmd/Ctrl+T), 111
Window⇨Slide Show, 203
Window⇨Slide Show⇨Advance Every, 205
Window⇨Slide Show⇨Background, 205
Window⇨Slide Show⇨Border, 205
Window⇨Slide Show⇨Center, 204
Window⇨Slide Show⇨Fade, Mac, 204
Window⇨Slide Show⇨Fit to Screen, 204
Window⇨Slide Show⇨Loop, 205
Window⇨Slide Show⇨Show Cursor, 204
Window⇨Tile, Windows, 24
Windows⇨Show Tools, 26
Windows⇨Stack, Windows, 24
Word Count, 99

communications
  described, 13
  text-based, 308–309
  when to use, 20
components, book, 4–6
control badge, QuickTime
    movies, 202
controls
  pane, 24
  Tool Panel, 24
  view, 23–24
  zoom, 23–24
conventions, used in book, 2–3
copyrights, music/lyrics, 203
corner anchor points, 172
Corner Info dialog box, 173
Create Labels Assistant, 45
cross-platform functionality, 2
Ctrl key
  keyboard shortcut conven-
      tions used in book, 3
  tool modifiers, 152
curly quotes, preference
    settings, 64
cursors
  I-beam, 28, 51–52
  insertion point, 50
  keyboard positioning
      techniques, 52–53
  Mac versus Windows PC,
      51–52
  mouse positioning techniques,
      51–52
  text insertion, 28
curve anchor points, 172
custom label layouts, print
    setup, 285–286
custom palettes, creating,
    145–146

• D •

dash fills, filled tabs, 76–77
data
  database entry conventions,
      252–257
  mail merge, 291–293
  spreadsheet entry, 212–213
  spreadsheet sorting, 222–224
  table entry, 111–112

database design
  automatic field date/time
      entry, 271
  automatic record data entry,
      271
  calculation fields, 274
  check box fields, 273
  field insertion/deletion, 276
  field number range, 271
  field option settings, 270–271
  field types, 267–270
  fields, 266–273
  forced field data entry, 271
  information gathering, 265–266
  layout mode, 273–277
  pop-up fields, 272–273
  question list, 266
  radio button fields, 272–273
  summary fields, 274
  summary reports, 277–280
  template sources, 265
  unique records, 271
  user name entry, 271
  value list fields, 273
databases
  adding/deleting records,
      252–253
  Avery label printing, 283–286
  blank space printing
      guidelines, 286–287
  bookmarks, 252
  browse mode, 251
  copying records, 253
  criteria searches, 260–262
  data entry conventions,
      252–257
  described, 12–13
  document merging, 15
  exporting data, 257
  field sort selection guidelines,
      259
  field types, 267–270
  find mode search, 259–264
  Hide Unselected Records
      button, 259
  importing data, 255–257
  information items, 250
  label layouts, 285–286
  mail merge printing, 293
  mail merge record selection,
      290

mail merges, 289–294
Match Equal button, 263
Match Greater Than button,
    263
Match Not Equal button, 263
Match Not Less Than button,
    263
match records search,
    262–263
media file pointers, 254
modes, 251–252
multimedia record fields,
    253–254
navigation techniques, 255
print field selections, 283
printing, 281–288
printing layout options,
    281–283
Record book, 252
record fields, 251
records, 250–251
reports, 287–288
saving search requests,
    261–262
saving sorts, 257–258
search shortcuts, 263
searches, 259–264
Sort Again button, 257
Sort Ascending button, 257
Sort Descending button, 257
sorting, 257–259
supported external types, 264
supported file types, 256
when to use, 20, 249–250
date fields
  automatic entry, 271
  described, 268
date formats
  preference settings, 64
  spreadsheets, 219
date stamps, 85
dates
  automatic database field
      entry, 271
  placeholders, 85
decimal points, align on tabs, 75
decimal tab, table creation, 109
Decrease Font Size button
    (Shift+Cmd/Ctrl+<), 67
Decrease Line Spacing button,
    79–80

Default button bar, 25
Define Database Fields dialog
  box, 267–271
Define Named Range dialog
  box, 243
Delete key, Mac versus
  Windows PC, 55
Design Science, Equation Editor,
  60–62
dialog boxes
  navigating, 21–22
  paint tools, 136, 152–153
dial-up connections, Internet
  access, 298, 300
Dial-Up Networking, Windows,
  300
diamond format, outlines, 123
dictionary, spell checker
  additions, 95
Display dialog box, 115–116
Document dialog box, Windows,
  90, 189
documents
  chart creation, 117–118
  column settings, 90–92
  creating, 18–20
  draw setup, 164–165
  draw/paint combinations,
    132–133
  environment selection, 19–20
  environment type uses, 19–20
  equation insertion, 60–62
  facing page formatting, 87–88
  finding/replacing text, 96–99
  first-time save, 32
  folder storage guidelines, 32
  footers, 85–86
  footnotes, 88
  gutters, 88
  headers, 85–86
  I-beam cursor positioning,
    51–52
  image insertion, 103–108
  inline image placement, 104
  insertion point cursor, 50
  launching when starting
    ClarisWorks, 20
  line spacing, 79–80
  mail merges, 289–294
  margin settings, 89–90
  merging, 15

multiple copy printing, 35
object placement, 104
opening existing, 20–22
outlines, 119–126
page additions, 189
page formatting, 84–92
page guides, 89–90
page numbering, 84–85
page range print selection, 35
page setup, 31
paper size/orientation
  settings, 92
paragraph spacing, 80–81
paragraph styles, 82–84
passwords, 15, 36
previewing before opening, 22
printing, 34–35
save versus save as, 33
saving, 32–34
saving as HTML file, 310, 319
saving as stationery, 33–34
spell checking, 93–95
stationery, 42–43
style copying, 70
switching between, 25
switching between in
  full-screen mode, 25
table creation, 108–111
table data entry, 111–112
table formatting with
  spreadsheet environment,
  112–117
text formatting, 63–92
text selection techniques,
  53–55
text wrap, 51
viewing multiple, 24
Web page elements, 310–313
word count, 99
word processing, 49–62
wrapping text in draw, 194
dot fills, filled tabs, 76–77
dragging, described, 54
draw
  advantages/disadvantages,
    131–132
  aligning objects, 179
  anchor points, 171–172
  Autogrid, 177–178
  ClarisWorks Libraries, 183–184
  copying/pasting shapes,
    167–168

document page addition, 189
document setup, 164–165
document text wrapping, 194
fill settings, 168
freehand tools, 165
gradient settings, 176
graphics insertion, 181–184
grouping objects, 179–180
joining objects, 180–181
line settings, 168
locking objects, 181
margin area viewing, 165
object layers, 178
object movement methods,
  177–178
object selection settings, 176
object styles, 168–169
polygon closing settings,
  175–176
preference settings, 175–176
regular shape tools, 165
reshaping objects, 171–173
resizing objects, 169–171
rotating objects, 173–175
selecting/deleting shapes,
  166–167
text boxes, 176–177
tools, described, 29, 165–166
when to use, 130
drawing
  described, 11
  versus painting, 129–133
  when to use, 19
drop shadows, charts, 235

• E •

Earthlink, 298
Edit Button Bars button, 337
Edit Layouts dialog box, 286
Edit menu, described, 31
Edit Names dialog box, 243
Edit Spray Can dialog box, 153
Edit Style window, 83
e-mail
  accessing, 302
  text formatting
    conventions, 65
embedded frames, 14
em-space, described, 73

End key, document
navigation, 53
Enter (Return) key
accepting spreadsheet cell
data entry, 212
computers versus typewriters,
50–51
versus text wrap, 60
Enter Match Records Condition
dialog box, 262
entry bar
cell content editing, 214
spreadsheet data entry,
212–213
Envelope Assistant, 188
envelopes
graphic addition, 187
logos, 187
margin settings, 186–187
page layout, 185–189
environments
charts, 231–238
combined draw/paint, 132–133
common menus, 30–31
communications, 13, 308
databases, 12–13, 249–294
described, 14
draw, 129–133, 163–183
draw, versus paint, 129–133
drawing, 11
frame integration, 13–15
Internet, 297–326
mail merge, 289–294
menu morphing, 30, 333–334
paint, 11–12, 129–153
presentations, 199–206
selecting, 19–20
spreadsheets, 12, 209–246
telecommunications, 308
text preference settings, 63–65
Tool Panel display differences,
26–27
Web publishing, 309–326
word processing, 10–12,
49–118
Equation Editor, 16, 60–62
eraser tool, 150
error messages
Not enough chart data, 234
The value entered is not in the
accepted list, 273

excluded characters, Web
publishing, 313
eyedropper tool, 141, 151

• F •

facing pages, formatting, 87–88
fields
automatic data entry, 271
automatic date/time entry, 271
calculation, 274
check box, 273
database design, 266–273
database print selection, 283
database records, 251
date, 268
described, 251
forced data entry, 271
forcing unique, 271
importing, 255–257
keyboard navigation, 253
labels, 275
mailing label positioning, 336
multimedia, 253–254, 270
number, 268
number ranges, 271
option settings, 270–271
pop-up menu, 272–273
radio button, 272–273
record info, 270
search criteria, 260–262
serial number, 269
sort selection guidelines, 259
summary, 274
text, 268
text entry, 253
time, 269
value list, 273
file formats, saving work in, 33
File menu, described, 30
files
first-time save, 32
HTML, 310, 326
media pointers, 254
saving in other formats, 33
saving over previous
version, 33
fill palette, 29, 138–139
fill pattern palette, 140
Fill Special dialog box, 216
filled tabs, 76–77

fills
draw settings, 168
gradient, 141
Find command, help system
topic search, 41
find mode
accessing, 260
database information search,
259–264
databases, 252
Find Request forms
multiple requests, 261
search criteria, 260–262
Find/Change dialog box, 96
first line indent marker, 72
flipping graphics, 158–160
floating objects, frames, 14
folders
bookmark organization, 316
ClarisWorks stationery, 34
document folder storage
guidelines, 32
hierarchy navigation, 21–22
My Documents, Windows, 32
System, Mac, 32
fonts
color selections, 67
default settings, 65
point measurements, 67
sizing, 66–67
spreadsheet formatting, 220
style editing, 67
Web publishing, 311
footers, 85–86
page layout, 197
spreadsheet, 228
summary reports, 279–280
footnotes, 88
Format dialog box, 217–219
formulas
absolute versus relative cell
references, 245–246
AutoSum calculations, 240
baseline alignment, 61
cell display, 227
cell naming conventions,
242–244
cell references, 242
defined, 239
Equation Editor, 60–62
math, 241–242

forward delete key, Mac, 55
fractional character widths,
    enabling/disabling, 64, 336
frame tools, 27–29, 136
frames
    borders, 105
    creating with Option/Alt-drag
        technique, 28
    described, 13–15
    embedding, 14
    environment integration,
        13–15
    floating objects, 14
    linking, 191–196
    object selection tech-
        niques, 27
    opening, 196
    page number placeholders,
        197
    paint/spreadsheet links,
        194–196
    spreadsheet editing
        techniques, 28
    spreadsheet insertion, 229
    text boxes, 176–177
    text selection techniques, 28
free-floating inline images, 108
freehand objects
    joining, 180–181
    reshaping, 171–173
freehand painting, 148–149
freehand tools, 165
FreePPP, Mac, 300
Frequently Asked Questions,
    Mac, 38
full-screen mode, switching
    between windows, 25
functions
    defined, 239
    Equation Editor, 60–62
    spreadsheet conventions,
        244–245
fundraising calendars/materials,
    Donna Shadovitz, 332

• G •

Gale, Gayle, printmaking,
    330–331
Go to Page dialog box,
    accessing, 24

Gradient Editor dialog box, 143
gradient fills, 29
gradients
    described, 141
    draw settings, 176
    editing, 143–144
grand summary parts, summary
    reports, 277–278
graphics
    arrow pointer techniques, 27
    baseline alignment, 105–106
    Claris Home Page Lite, 322–324
    ClarisWorks Libraries clip art,
        183–184
    distortion effect, 155–156
    distortions, 155–157
    document insertion, 103–108
    drag-and-drop insertion,
        Mac, 182
    draw document insertion,
        181–184
    drawing versus painting,
        129–133
    envelope addition, 187
    flipping, 158–160
    free rotation, 160
    handles, 27
    hyperlinks, 324
    library creation, 184
    modifying, 107–108
    perspective effect, 156
    resizing, 106, 157–158
    rotating, 158–160
    shearing, 157
    supported types, 182
    text wrapping around, 106–107
    Web publishing background,
        314
graphics design business,
    Sharon Rubin, 331
graphics formats, Claris Home
    Page Lite supported types,
    322–323
graphics grid, draw document,
    164
Graphics Preferences dialog
    box, 175
graphics rulers, 190–191
gridlines, spreadsheets, 226–227

grids
    Autogrid, 177–178
    graphics, 164
    spreadsheets, 227
    X-Y charts, 235
gutters
    described, 88
    text wrap styles, 106–107

• H •

handles, graphic object, 27
hanging indents, 77–78
hard drives
    folder navigation, 21–22
    live links, 315
Harvard format, outlines, 123
headers, 85–86
    hiding/showing table column/
        row headings, 115–116
    page layout, 197
    spreadsheet, 228
    summary reports, 279–280
headings, spreadsheet column/
    row, 227
Help Contents, Mac, 38
Help Contents, Windows, 41
Help Index, Mac, 38
Help Index, Windows, 41
Help menu, 37–42
    Assistants, 45
    bookmarking topics, 41
    Claris technical support, 42
    Macintosh elements, 38–40
    printing topics, 41
    sticky notes, Mac, 42
    version information, 38, 41
    Windows elements, 41
help system
    balloon help, 26
    ToolTips, 26
Hide Unselected Records
    button, databases, 259
hierarchy, folders, 21–22
hi-low charts, 233
hollow handles, graphics
    distortions, 157
Home key, document
    navigation, 53
home pages, browsers, 299

Horthy, Leonard, raffles, 330
hot spot, tool point, 147
HTML (Hypertext Markup
    Language), 310
HTML files
    Claris Home Page Lite, 326
    saving documents as, 310, 319
HTML-translation preferences
    button, 313–314
hyperlinks, described, 305–306
HyperTerminal, Windows, 308
hypertext links, 65, 300
hyphenations, 101

● *I* ●

I-beam cursor
    text position indicator, 51–52
    text tool, 28
icons
    creating, 339
    used in book, 6
IF function, 245
imagemaps, hyperlinks, 306
images
    Claris Home Page Lite, 322–324
    copying/pasting, 104–105
    database field insertion,
        253–254
    document insertion, 103–108
    free rotation, 160
    library creation, 184
    object-like behavior, 104
    pictogram chart insertion,
        237–238
    resizing, 106, 324
    text wrapping around, 106–107
    text-like behavior, 103
    transparent, 323
    Web publishing, 312
Import Field Order dialog
    box, 256
Increase Font Size button
    (Shift+Cmd/Ctrl+>), 67
Increase Line Spacing button,
    79–80
indent markers, 72
indents, 72–73
    first line, 73
    hanging, 77–78
    whole paragraph, 73

Infowave, StyleScript, 182
inline images
    described, 103
    document placement, 104
    making free-floating, 108
Insert Footnote Assistant, 45,
    88–89
Insert Part dialog box, 277–278
insertion point cursor, 50
interface
    buttons, 25–26
    common menus, 30–31
    described, 22
    draw tools, 29
    fill palettes, 29
    frame tools, 27–29
    page indicator, 24
    paint tools, 29
    pen palettes, 29
    Tool Panel toggle, 24
    tools, 26–29
    view controls, 23–24
    zoom controls, 23–24
interlaced images, 323
Internet
    access methods, 298–302
    access providers, 297–298
    browser selections, 301
    browser startup, 299
    button bar customization,
        302–305
    Claris Home Page Lite, 319–320
    Claris Tech Support Home
        Page access, 42
    dial-up connections, 298, 300
    e-mail access, 302
    hyperlinks, 305–306
    hypertext links, 300
    imagemaps, 306
    Netscape Navigator, 305–307
    Open URL button, 299
    PPP (Point to Point
        Protocol), 300
    URL access methods, 299–302
    Web publishing, 309–326
Internet button bar, 25
Internet connectivity, 16
Internet Outfitters, project
    management, 331
Introduction to ClarisWorks,
    Mac, 39

Introduction to ClarisWorks,
    Windows, 41
invisible characters
    blank page printing, 335
    find/replace search, 98–99
    hiding/displaying, 64, 334
    showing/hiding, 79
ISPs (Internet Service Provid-
    ers), 297–298, 310
italic text, 65

● *J* ●

JIAN Business*Basics*, Stationery
    collection, 43–44
joining, freehand objects,
    180–181
justified alignment,
    described, 71

● *K* ●

keyboard shortcuts
    Align to Grid (Cmd/Ctrl+K),
        178
    Autogrid (Cmd/Ctrl+Y), 164,
        177
    Browse mode (Shift+
        Cmd/Ctrl+B), 252
    Cmd/Ctrl+S, 32
    conventions used in book, 3
    Copy (Cmd/Ctrl+C), 57, 104,
        167
    Copy Ruler (Shift+Cmd/
        Ctrl+C), 81
    Cut (Cmd/Ctrl+X), 57
    Decrease Font Size
        (Shift+Cmd/Ctrl+<), 67
    Document Spell Check
        (Cmd/Ctrl+=), 93
    Duplicate (Cmd/Ctrl+D), 168,
        253
    Exit (Ctrl+Q), Windows, 36
    Find (Cmd/Ctrl+F), 96
    Find (Shift+Cmd/Ctrl+F), 260
    Find Again (Cmd/Ctrl+E), 97
    Footnote (Shift+Cmd/
        Ctrl+F), 88
    Free Rotate (Shift+Cmd/
        Ctrl+R), 174

(continued)

keyboard shortcuts *(continued)*
Group (Cmd/Ctrl+G), 179
Hyphenation (Cmd/Ctrl+-), 101
Increase Font Size (Shift+Cmd/Ctrl+>), 67
Insert Cells (Shift+Cmd/Ctrl+I), 224
Layout mode (Shift+Cmd/Ctrl+L), 274
Links Palette (Shift+Cmd/Ctrl+M), 317
List mode (Shift+Cmd/Ctrl+I), 252
Make Chart (Cmd/Ctrl+M), 234
Move Backward (Shift-Cmd/Ctrl+-), 178
Move Forward (Shift+Cmd/Ctrl++), 178
Move Left (Shift+Cmd/Ctrl+L), 120
Move Right (Shift+Cmd/Ctrl+R), 120
New Record (Cmd/Ctrl+R), 252
New Request (Cmd/Ctrl+R), 261
New Topic Left (Cmd/Ctrl+L), 120
New Topic Right (Cmd/Ctrl+R), 120
Number (Shift+Cmd/Ctrl+N), 217
Page Break (Shift-Enter), Mac, 84
Page Break (Ctrl+Enter), Windows, 84
Page View (Shift+Cmd/Ctrl+P), 201
Paste (Cmd/Ctrl+V), 57, 105, 167
Print (Cmd/Ctrl+P), 34
Quit (Cmd-Q), Mac, 36
Reshape (Cmd/Ctrl+R), 171, 180
Rulers (Shift+Cmd/Ctrl+U), 190
Section Break (Option-Enter), Mac, 86
Section Break (Shift+Ctrl+Enter), Windows, 86
Selection Spell Check (Shift+Cmd/Ctrl+Y), 94

Set Default Printer (Cmd-L), Mac, 35
Show All Records (Shift+Cmd/Ctrl+A), 263
Show Stylesheet (Shift+Cmd/Ctrl+W), 82, 124
Show Tools (Shift+Cmd/Ctrl+T), 111
Smooth (Cmd/Ctrl+( ), 173
Spell Check Word (Cmd/Alt+number), 94
text alignment, 71
text selection techniques, 54–55
Thesaurus (Shift+Cmd/Ctrl+Z), 100
Undo (Cmd/Ctrl+Z), 56, 335
keyboards
draw object movement techniques, 177
Mac versus Windows PC, 50
outline topic rearrangement, 121–122
resizing spreadsheet columns/rows, 225–226
spreadsheet selection techniques, 210–212
text document navigation techniques, 51–53
text selection techniques, 54–55
word processing text entry, 50

• L •

labels
Avery, 283–286
chart, 233
custom layouts, 285–286
database printing, 283–286
field, 275
outlines, 123–124
Web page images, 323
landscape orientation, 31, 92
lasso tool, 149
layers
draw object, 178
reordering objects, 178
Layout Info dialog box, 286
layout mode

accessing, 274
background colors, 276
database design, 273–277
databases, 252
elements, 275
field insertion/deletion, 276
layouts
Avery labels, 284–286
blank space printing guidelines, 286–287
database printing, 281–283
label, 285–286
presentations, 199–200
leading, described, 79
left alignment, described, 70
left-aligned tabs, 75
left indent marker, 72
legal format, outlines, 123
LeVitus, Bob
Mac OS 8 For Dummies, 4
sports team management, 331
libraries, ClarisWorks Libraries, 183–184
line charts, 232
line pattern palette, 140
line spacing, 79–81
line tool, 137
line widths, charts, 236
lines
arrow heads, 142
drawing, 168
width controls, 142
linked frames, 191–196
links
book marking, 316
Claris Home Page Lite insertion, 325
editing, 318–319
graphical, 324
hypertext, 65, 300
Links palette, 317–318
live, 315
spreadsheet/paint frames, 194–196
testing, 318
text frames, 191–193
troubleshooting, 334
URL, 314–317
Web publishing, 314–319
links dialog box, 315

Links palette, 317–318
list mode, databases, 252
lists, bulleted, 77–78
Live Links
  troubleshooting, 334
  Web publishing, 315
locked objects, 181
logos, envelope addition, 187

• *M* •

Macintosh
  Application menu display, 19
  browser selections, 301
  Claris Emailer Lite, 302
  ClarisWorks startup, 17–18
  ClarisWorks Stationery
    folder, 34
  document alias, 20
  drag-and-drop graphics
    insertion, 182
  forward delete key, 55
  FreePPP, 300
  Help menu elements, 38–40
  System folder, 32
  video controls, 202
  versus Windows PC
    keyboard, 50
  Word Services, 64
MACRO function, 245
magic wand tool, 149
magical products, Bob Weiss,
  329–330
mail merge palette, 291–292
mail merges
  data merges, 291–293
  described, 289
  document creation, 290
  printing, 293
  record selection, 290
  when to use, 289–290
mailing labels
  field positions, 336
  printing, 259
Make Table Assistant, 45,
  109–111
margins, 89–90, 186
marquee (selection) rectangle
  tool, 149
master pages, presentations,
  200–202

match case, find/replace
  search, 97
Match Equal button,
  databases, 263
Match Greater Than button,
  databases, 263
Match Less Than button,
  databases, 263
Match Not Equal button,
  databases, 263
math formulas, spreadsheets,
  241–242
measurement units
  em-space, 73
  line spacing, 79–80
  margins, 89–90
  points, 67
  rulers, 190
menu bar, point size
  selections, 67
menus
  environment common, 30–31
  morphing, 30, 333–334
merges, database/
  documents, 15
Microsoft Exchange, 302
Microsoft Video for Windows
  database field insertion, 254
  presentations, 202–203
mistakes, undoing last action,
  31, 56, 335
modes, database environment,
  251–252
modifier keys
  keyboard navigation, 51–52
  tools, 151–152
Modify Chart dialog box, 237
Modify Frame dialog box, 196
mouse
  clicking, 54
  column settings, 91
  dragging, 54
  draw object movement
    techniques, 177
  object selection
    techniques, 27
  outline topic rearrangement,
    121
  pop-up palettes, 139
  resizing objects, 169

resizing spreadsheet columns/
  rows, 225
shift constraints, 176
spreadsheet editing
  techniques, 28
spreadsheet selection
  techniques, 210–212
text document navigation
  techniques, 51–52
text selection techniques,
  28, 54
movies
  database field insertion, 254
  presentation addition, 202–203
multimedia fields, 270
multimedia, database field
  insertion, 253–254
My Documents folder,
  Windows, 32

• *N* •

name fields, user name
  entry, 271
named searches, saving,
  261–262
named sorts, database records,
  257–258
Netcom, 298
Netscape Navigator, 305–307
  bookmarks, 307
  hyperlink types, 306
  location field, 305
  returning to previously visited
    sites, 306–307
  version numbers, 305
New Book Mark button, Web
  publishing, 316
New Button dialog box, 303–305
New Document dialog box, 18
New Document Link button,
  Web publishing, 316–317
New Layout dialog box, 282
New Report dialog box, 287–288
New Style dialog box, 69
number fields, described, 268
number formats, spreadsheets,
  217–219
Number style, bulleted lists, 78
numbered lists, Web
  publishing, 312

numbers
field range, 271
footnotes, 88
page, 84–85
numeric format, outlines, 123

• O •

Object Editor dialog box, Home
Page, 323
objects
adding/deleting anchor
points, 172
aligning, 179
anchor points, 171
cutting/pasting, 107
document placement, 104
draw styles, 168–169
floating, 14
gradient fills, 29
grouping/ungrouping, 179–180
handles, 27
joining, 180–181
layers, 178
locking, 181
moving, 177–178
reordering layers, 178
reshaping, 171–173
resizing, 169–171
rotating, 173–175
scaling, 170
selecting/deleting, 166–167
selection settings, 176
size palette adjustments, 171
smoothing/sharpening, 173
text wrapping around, 104
OLE objects, database field
insertion, Windows, 254
opaque mode, 147
Open dialog box, Windows,
21–22
Open URL button, 299
Open/Save dialog box, Mac,
21–22
Option key (Mac), tool
modifiers, 152
orientation, page printing, 92
Outline style, 68
outlines
collapsing/expanding
subtopics, 122–123

custom styles, 124–126
elements, 119
formats, 123–124
labels, 123–124
moving subtopics, 120
rearranging topics, 121–122
setup, 120
subtopic creation, 120
oval tool, 137

• P •

page breaks
inserting, 84
spreadsheets, 229
Page Down key, document
navigation, 53
page formatting
columns, 90–92
facing pages, 87–88
footers, 85–86
footnotes, 88
headers, 85–86
margins, 89–90
numbers, 84–85
orientation, 92
page guides, 84, 89–90
paper size, 92
sections, 86–87
page guides, 89–90
page indicator, 24
page layout
draw document page
addition, 189
envelopes, 185–189
footers, 197
headers, 197
linked frames, 191–196
page numbering, 197
text frame links, 191–193
page numbers, 84–85, 197
Page Setup dialog box, Mac, 186
Page Up key, document
navigation, 53
page view, viewing slides, 201
pages
print selections, 35
spreadsheet insertion, 229
paint
advantages/disadvantages,
131–132

borders, 138–139
color selections, 139–140
custom palette creation,
145–146
editing shapes, 146–147
erasing/deleting mistakes, 150
fill palette, 138–139
freehand painting, 148–149
gradient fills, 141
line options, 142
modes, 147
opaque mode, 147
Pattern Editor, 142–143
patterns, 140
pen palettes, 139
selection tools, 149–150
shape tools, 137–138
special effects, 155–162
spreadsheet frame linking,
194–196
tearing off palettes, 140
textures, 141
tint mode, 147
tool dialog boxes, 136, 152–153
tool modifier keys, 151–152
transparent pattern mode, 147
when to use, 130–131
paint brush tool, 152–153
paint bucket tool, 146–147
paint tools, described, 29
painting
described, 11–12
versus drawing, 129–133
erasing/deleting mistakes, 150
freehand tools, 148–149
selecting/deleting mistakes,
150
when to use, 19
palettes
ClarisWorks Libraries, 183–184
custom creation, 145–146
fill, 29, 138–139
fill pattern, 140
line pattern, 140
Links, 317–318
mail merge, 291–292
object sizing, 171
pen, 29, 139
pop-up, 139
stylesheet, 68–70
tearing off, 140

pane controls, interface, 24
paper, sizing, 31
paper size, selecting, 92
Paragraph dialog box, 80
Paragraph Sorter Assistant, 45
paragraph styles, 68, 82–84, 321–322
paragraphs
copying rulers between, 81–82
Enter (Return) key, 50–51
hanging indents, 77–78
indenting, 72–73
spacing between, 80–81
text formatting, 70–84
whole paragraph indents, 73
passwords
changing, 36
document, 15, 36
Pattern Editor dialog box, 142–143
patterns
editing, 142–143
fills/lines, 140
pen palette, 29, 139
pencil tool, 148
pictogram charts, 233, 237–238
pictures, copying/pasting into documents, 104–105
pie charts, 233, 235
placeholders
database fields, 272–273
date/time stamps, 85
find/replace search, 97
mail merge data, 292
page numbers, 197
Pogue, David, *Macs For Dummies,* 5th Edition, 20
pointers
Mac versus Windows PC, 51–52
media files, 254
points, described, 67
polygon tool, 137–138, 151, 165
polygons, closing settings, 175–176
pop-up field, database design, 272–273
pop-up palettes, described, 139
portrait orientation, described, 31, 92

PPP (Point to Point Protocol), Mac, 300
precedence order, spreadsheet math formulas, 241–242
Preferences dialog box, 63–65, 213
draw environment, 175–176
spreadsheets, 213
text-formatting, 63–65
Presentation Assistant, advantages, 200
presentations
action controls, 206
design guidelines, 200
layouts, 199–200
master page editing, 200–202
movie addition, 202–203
slide order/visibility options, 204–205
slide show startup, 203–206
slide viewing in page view, 201
soundtrack copyrights, 203
Start Show button, 205
Preview button, Web publishing, 314
Print Range dialog box, 229
printers
selecting as target, 35
troubleshooting blank page print, 335
printing
Avery labels, 283–286
blank page troubleshooting, 335
blank space guidelines, 286–287
custom labels, 285–286
database layout design, 281–283
databases, 281–288
documents, 34–35
help system topics, 41
landscape orientation, 31, 92
locked column/row titles, 228
mailing labels, 259
merged documents, 293
multiple copies, 35
page range selection, 35
paper size options, 31
portrait orientation, 31, 92

reports, 288
spreadsheet column/row headings, 227
spreadsheet header/footer, 228
spreadsheet range settings, 229–230
spreadsheet troubleshooting, 336
target printer selection, 35
printmaking, Gayle Gale, 330–331
project management, Internet Outfitters, 331
properties, default style, 69
public relations, ClarisWorks use, 332
publications
Mac OS 8 For Dummies, Bob LeVitus, 4
Macs For Dummies, 5th Edition, David Pogue, 20
Windows 95 For Dummies, 2nd Edition, Andy Rathbone, 4

• Q •

questions, database design, 266
QuickTime
auto play slide show, 205
BMUG royalty-free movie URL, 203
Claris Home Page Lite insertion, 323
complete play before advancing, 205
control badge, 202
database field insertion, 254
presentation videos, 202–203
previewing documents before opening, Mac, 21
simultaneous play, 205
slide control options, 205
soundtrack insertion, 203
Web publishing, 312
QuickTime VR, database field insertion, Mac, 254
quotes, curly versus smart, 64

• R •

radio button fields, database design, 272–273
raffles, Leonard Horthy, 330
Rathbone, Andy, *Windows 95 For Dummies,* 2nd Edition, 4
readers, author's assumptions, 3–4
Record book, database navigation, 252, 255
record info fields, 270
records
  adding, 252–253
  automatic data entry, 271
  copying, 253
  described, 250–251
  fields, 251
  find mode search, 260–264
  importing, 255–257
  mail merge print selection, 290
  match search, 262–263
  multimedia fields, 253–254
  navigation techniques, 255
  print field selections, 283
  sorting, 257–259
  text field entry, 253
  unique, 271
rectangle tool, 137
regular polygon tool, 138, 152
regular shape tools, 165
Remove Column button, 91
reports
  databases, 287–288
  printing, 288
  summary, 277–280
reshape mode, objects, 171–173
Return (Enter) key, computers versus typewriters, 50–51
right alignment, described, 70
right-aligned tabs, 75
right indent marker, 72
Rotate dialog box, 159–160
rotating graphics, 158–160
round rectangle tool, 137, 152, 173
Row Height dialog box, 114–115
rows
  AutoSum calculations, 240
  described, 210

headings, 227
height/width settings, 114–115
hiding/showing headings, 115–116
inserting, 224–225
locking/unlocking titles, 228
print range settings, 229–230
resizing, 225–226
selecting, 113
selection techniques, 212
Rubin, Sharon, graphics design business, 331
rulers
  copying/pasting between paragraphs, 81–82
  graphics, 190–191
  measurement units, 190
  showing/hiding, 190
  text, 190–191
Rulers dialog box, 190

• S •

Save dialog box, 32–34
Scale By Percent dialog box, 158, 170
scaling
  described, 157–158
  objects, 170
scatter charts, 232
screenplays, Mark Treitel, 330
seamless integration, 10
searches
  database shortcuts, 263
  databases records, 259–264
  help system, 41
  invisible formatting characters, 98–99
  match case find/replace, 97
  match records, 262–263
  placeholder find/replace, 97
  saving, 261–262
  synonyms, 99–100
  TechInfo Database, 42
  text, 96–99
  whole word match, 97
Section dialog box, 87, 91–92
sections, page formatting, 86–87
selection (marquee) rectangle tool, 149

selection box, spreadsheets, 210
selection tools, 149–150
  Command/Ctrl modifiers, 152
  Option/Alt modifiers, 151
sentences
  indenting, 72–73
  text formatting, 70–84
serial number fields, 269
Shadovitz, Donna, fundraising calendars/materials, 332
shape tools, 137–138
shapes
  adding/deleting anchor points, 172
  anchor points, 171
  copying/pasting, 167–168
  editing after painting, 146–147
  moving, 177–178
  reshaping, 171–173
  selecting/deleting, 166–167
  smoothing/sharpening, 173
shearing, special effect, 157
Shift key
  text selection techniques, 54–55
  tool modifiers, 152
Shift+Tab key, field navigation, 253
shortcuts, Windows PC, 20
Show Balloons, Mac, 38
Show/Hide Invisibles button, 25, 74, 79
size palette, draw object movement techniques, 177
Slide Show dialog box, 203–206
slide shows
  action controls, 206
  starting, 203–206
slides
  viewing in page view, 201
  viewing order options, 204–205
smart quotes, preference settings, 64
Sort Again button, databases, 257
Sort Ascending button, databases, 257
Sort Descending button, databases, 257

Sort dialog box, 222–223
Sort Records dialog box, 257–258
sorts
  database records, 257–259
  field selection guidelines, 259
  hidden records, 259
  saving, 257–258
  spreadsheet data, 222–224
soundtracks, presentation addition, 203
spacebar
  text alignment cautions, 335
  word processing text alignment avoidance, 59
special characters, Web publishing excluded, 313
special effects
  3-dimensional charts, 235
  chart drop shadows, 235
  free rotation, 160
  graphics distortions, 155–157
  rotating/flipping graphics, 158–160
  scaling graphics, 157–158
  slide fade to black, Mac, 204
  tilted pie charts, 235
Spell Check button, 94
spell checker, 93–95
  canceling, 95
  entire document, 93
  text block, 94
  user dictionary additions, 95
  word list selections, 94–95
Spelling dialog box, 94
sports team management, Bob LeVitus, 331
spray can tool, 148, 153
spreadsheet tool, 28
spreadsheets
  absolute versus relative cell references, 245–246
  Accept button, 212
  AutoSum button, 239–240
  borders, 226
  Cancel button, 212
  cell content editing, 214
  cell formatting, 219–222
  cell range selection, 211, 214
  cell references in formulas, 242–244

cells, 210
chart creation, 233–234
chart information updating, 236–237
column/row headings, 227
column/row insertion, 224–225
column/row selection, 212
columns, 210
creating frames with Option/ Alt-drag, 28
data entry, 212–213
data sorting, 222–224
date formats, 219
described, 12
editing techniques, 28
elements, 210–212
entry bar, 212–213
filling cells, 215–216
formatting, 217–230
formula display, 227
formula entry, 239, 241–244
functions, 239, 244–245
gridlines, 226–227
header/footer information printing, 228
hiding/displaying headings, 227
math formulas, 241–242
moving data between cells, 214
number formats, 217–219
page breaks, 229
paint frame linking, 194–196
preference settings, 213
print range settings, 229–230
printing column/row headings, 227
resizing columns/rows, 225–226
rows, 210
selecting entire, 212
selection box, 210
single cell selection, 210–211
styles, 222
table formatting, 112–117
time formats, 219
titles, 228
troubleshooting print problems, 336
when to use, 20, 209

squiggle tool, 138, 176
stacked area charts, 232
stacked bar charts, 232
stacked pictogram charts, 233
Start Show button, presentations, 205
stationery
  ClarisWorks DR Options, 34
  constant element creation, 34
  described, 15, 42–43
  envelope template creation, 185–189
  JIAN Business*Basics* collection, 43–44
  listing types, 42–43
  saving document as, 33–34
sticky notes, help system, Mac, 42
Style menu
  described, 68
  text attributes, 66
styles
  application methods, 69–70
  Basic, 68–70
  copying between documents, 70
  creation, 68–70
  default properties, 69
  described, 68
  draw objects, 168–169
  editing, 82–83
  exporting/importing, 70
  naming conventions, 69
  outlines, 120, 124–126
  paragraph, 82–84
  spreadsheet, 222
  undoing, 66
  wrap, 106–107
StyleScript, 182
stylesheet palette, 68–70
sub-summary part, summary reports, 278–279
subtopics
  collapsing/expanding, 122–123
  outlines, 119
SUM function, 244
summary fields, database design, 274
summary reports
  database design, 277–280

(continued)

summary reports *(continued)*
  grand summary parts, 277–278
  headers/footers, 279–280
  sub-summary part, 278–279
symbols
  footnotes, 88–89
  indent markers, 72
synonyms, Thesaurus, 99–100
System folder, avoiding when
    saving documents, Mac, 32

• T •

Tab dialog box, 76
Tab key
  accepting spreadsheet cell
    data entry, 212
  field navigation, 253
  first line text indents, 72–73
  tab stop settings, 74–77
  text alignment, 59
tab markers, displaying, 74
tab stops
  default settings, 74
  filled tabs, 76–77
  modifying, 77
  setting, 75–76
  table creation, 108–109
  types, 74
table formatting
  cell block selection, 113
  cell selections, 113
  column selections, 113
  quick tips, 113
  row selections, 113
Table style, 68
tables
  captions, 116
  Claris Home Page Lite, 325
  creating, 108–111
  data entry, 111–112
  formatting, 112–117
  hiding/showing column/row
    headings, 115–116
  Make Table Assistant, 109–111
  positioning, 116–117
  row height/width settings,
    114–115
  scratch creation, 111
  undoing accidental move, 113
  Web publishing, 311

target printer, selecting, 35
tearing off palettes, 140
TechInfo Database, Internet
    access, 42
technical support, Help menu
    access, 42
telecommunications, 308
telephone numbers, BMUG, 203
templates. *See* stationery
text
  attributes, 65–66
  cutting/copying/pasting with
    Clipboard, 57–59
  Delete key techniques, 55–56
  deleting with Backspace
    key, 55
  formatting, 63–92
  hyphenations, 101
  insertion point cursor, 50
  page formatting, 84–92
  searching/replacing, 96–99
  selection techniques, 28, 53–55
  word processing entry, 50–51
  wrapping, 51
text alignment, 70–72
  spacebar avoidance, 59
  Tab key, 59
text blocks
  selecting/deleting, 55
  spell checking, 94
text boxes, frames, 176–177
text fields, described, 268
text formatting
  attributes, 65–66
  blocking, 73
  bold, 65
  date formats, 64
  default font setting, 65
  displaying invisible charac-
    ters, 64
  font color editing, 67
  font sizing, 66–67
  font style editing, 67
  fractional character widths, 64
  hanging indents, 77–78
  indents, 72–73
  italic text, 65
  line spacing, 79–80
  paragraph spacing, 80–81
  paragraph styles, 82–84
  paragraphs, 70–84

preference settings, 63–65
sentences, 70–84
showing/hiding invisible
    characters, 79
smart versus curly quotes, 64
styles, 68–70
underlined text, 65
when to apply, 66
text frames, linking, 191–193
text insertion cursor, 28
text rulers, 190–191
  alignment buttons, 71
  hiding/displaying, 70
  indent markers, 72
text styles, cell formatting, 220
text tool, 28
Text Wrap dialog box, 106
text wrapping
  around graphics, 104, 106–107
  cell formatting, 220–221
  draw document, 194
  versus Enter (Return) key, 60
text-based communications, 309
text-to-table conversion
    button, 311
Texture Editor dialog box, 144
textures, 141
  copying/pasting, 145
  editing, 144
Thesaurus dialog box, 100
time fields, 269, 271
time formats, spreadsheets, 219
time stamps, 84–85
times
  automatic database field
    entry, 271
  placeholders, 85
tint mode, 147
titles
  charts, 233
  locking/unlocking columns,
    228
Tool Panel, environment display
    differences, 26–27
Tool Panel button, toggling, 24
Tool Toggle button, hiding/
    displaying tools, 26
tools
  arc, 137, 152
  arrow pointer, 27, 104
  bezigon, 138, 165

brush, 148
dialog boxes, 136, 152–153
draw, 29
drawing, 165–166
eraser, 150
eyedropper, 141, 152
frame, 27–29
freehand, 165
lasso, 149
line, 137
magic wand, 149
modifier keys, 151–152
oval, 137
paint, 29
paint brush, 152–153
paint bucket, 146–147
pencil, 148
polygon, 137–138, 151–152, 165
rectangle, 137
regular polygon, 138, 152
regular shape, 165
round rectangle, 137, 152
selection, 149–152
selection (marquee)
    rectangle, 149
shape, 137–138
spray can, 148, 153
spreadsheet, 28
squiggle, 138, 176
text, 28
toggling, 26
ToolTips, button help, 26
topics
    outlines, 120
    rearranging, 121–122
transparent images, 323
transparent pattern mode, 147
Treitel, Mark, screenplay
    writing, 330
troubleshooting
    application links, 334
    Fractional Character
        Widths, 336
    invisible character hiding/
        displaying, 334
    mailing label field positions,
        336
    menu morphing, 333–334
    missing buttons, 334
    printer prints blank page, 335

spacebar used for text
    alignment, 335
spreadsheet print problems,
    336
undoing last action, 335
unexpected format
    change, 335

• *u* •

underlined text, 65
understrike fills, filled tabs,
    76–77
undoing last action, 31, 56, 335
URL (Uniform Resource
    Locator), Web publishing
    link, 314–317
user dictionary, spell checker
    additions, 95
user name, automatic database
    field entry, 271

• *v* •

value list fields, 273
version, displaying information
    about, 38, 41
view controls, interface, 23–24

• *w* •

Web browser. *See* browsers
Web help, 42
Web pages
    default home page, 299
    live links, 315
    URL links, 314–317
Web publishing
    backgrounds, 313–314
    book marking links, 316
    bookmark organization
        techniques, 316
    bulleted lists, 312
    Claris Home Page Lite
        creation, 319–326
    editing links, 318–319
    elements, 310–313
    file-naming conventions, 310
    font attributes, 311

HTML (Hypertext Markup
    Language), 310
HTML-translation preferences
    button, 313–314
images, 312
links, 314–319
Links palette, 317–318
live links, 315
Live Links button, 315
New Book Mark button, 316
New Document Link button,
    316–317
numbered lists, 312
overview, 309–310
Preview button, 314
QuickTime videos, 312
saving documents as HTML
    files, 310, 319
testing links, 318
URL link button, 314
URL links, 314–317
Web sites
    AMUG.org, 203
    Claris Emailer Lite, 302
    Claris Tech Support Home
        Page, 42
    database templates, 265
    LAMG's BBS, 203
    Netscape Navigator location
        field entry, 305
    URL access methods, 299–302
Weiss, Bob, magical products,
    329–330
whole word, find/replace
    search, 97
Window menu
    described, 31
    switching between open
        documents, 25
Windows Messaging, 302
Windows 95
    browser selections, 301
    cascading, 24
    Dial-Up Networking, 300
    HyperTerminal, 308
    Microsoft Exchange, 302
Windows PC
    ClarisWorks startup, 18
    document shortcuts, 20
    versus Mac keyboard, 50

(continued)

Windows PC *(continued)*
  My Documents folder, 32
  title bar application
    display, 19
windows
  splitting into panes, 24
  tiling, 24
word processing
  chart creation, 117–118
  described, 10–11
  Equation Editor, 60–62
  facing page formatting, 87–88
  finding/replacing text, 96–99
  image insertion, 103–108
  keyboard conventions, 50
  line spacing, 79–80
  mail merges, 289–294
  outlines, 119–126
  page formatting, 84–92
  paragraph spacing, 80–81
  paragraph styles, 82–84
  spacebar text alignment
    cautions, 59
  spell checker, 93–95
  Tab key text alignment, 59
  table formatting with
    spreadsheet environment,
    112–117
  text entry guidelines, 50–51
  text formatting, 63–92
  text navigation techniques,
    51–53
  text selection techniques,
    53–55
  text wrap versus Enter
    (Return) key, 60
  when to use, 19, 49–50
  wrapping text, 51
Word Services, utility, Mac, 64
words
  document count, 99
  hyphenations, 101
  match case find/replace, 97
  spell checker additions, 95
  synonyms, 99–100
  whole word find/replace, 97
World Wide Web, hypertext link
  underlines, 65
  save versus save as, 33
  saving, 32–34

wrapping text
  around graphics, 106–107
  around objects, 104
  draw document, 194
  versus Enter (Return) key, 60
  spreadsheet cell data, 220–221
  word processing, 51

• X •

X-Y line charts, 232

• Z •

zoom controls, 23–24

Discover Dummies Online!

The Dummies Web Site is your fun and friendly online resource for the latest information about ...*For Dummies*® books and your favorite topics. The Web site is the place to communicate with us, exchange ideas with other ...*For Dummies* readers, chat with authors, and have fun!

Ten Fun and Useful Things You Can Do at www.dummies.com

1. Win free ...*For Dummies* books and more!

2. Register your book and be entered in a prize drawing.

3. Meet your favorite authors through the IDG Books Author Chat Series.

4. Exchange helpful information with other ...*For Dummies* readers.

5. Discover other great ...*For Dummies* books you must have!

6. Purchase Dummieswear™ exclusively from our Web site.

7. Buy ...*For Dummies* books online.

8. Talk to us. Make comments, ask questions, get answers!

9. Download free software.

10. Find additional useful resources from authors.

Link directly to these ten fun and useful things at
http://www.dummies.com/10useful

For other technology titles from IDG Books Worldwide, go to
www.idgbooks.com

Not on the Web yet? It's easy to get started with *Dummies 101*®: *The Internet For Windows*®*95* or *The Internet For Dummies*®, 4th Edition, at local retailers everywhere.

Find other ...*For Dummies* books on these topics:

Business • Career • Databases • Food & Beverage • Games • Gardening • Graphics • Hardware
Health & Fitness • Internet and the World Wide Web • Networking • Office Suites
Operating Systems • Personal Finance • Pets • Programming • Recreation • Sports
Spreadsheets • Teacher Resources • Test Prep • Word Processing

IDG BOOKS WORLDWIDE BOOK REGISTRATION

Register This Book and Win!

We want to hear from you!

Visit **http://my2cents.dummies.com** to register this book and tell us how you liked it!

- Get entered in our monthly prize giveaway.

- Give us feedback about this book — tell us what you like best, what you like least, or maybe what you'd like to ask the author and us to change!

- Let us know any other ...*For Dummies*® topics that interest you.

Your feedback helps us determine what books to publish, tells us what coverage to add as we revise our books, and lets us know whether we're meeting your needs as a ...*For Dummies* reader. You're our most valuable resource, and what you have to say is important to us!

Not on the Web yet? It's easy to get started with *Dummies 101*®: *The Internet For Windows*® *95* or *The Internet For Dummies*®, 4th Edition, at local retailers everywhere.

Or let us know what you think by sending us a letter at the following address:

...*For Dummies* Book Registration
Dummies Press
7260 Shadeland Station, Suite 100
Indianapolis, IN 46256-3945
Fax 317-596-5498

BUSINESS AND
GENERAL
REFERENCE
BOOK SERIES
FROM IDG

COMPUTER
BOOK SERIES
FROM IDG